The
HIDDEN PLACES

of
EAST ANGLIA

NORFOLK, SUFFOLK, CAMBRIDGESHIRE & ESSEX

Edited by

Joanna Billing

Front Cover: Finchingfield, Essex
By Eleanor Tanner
One of a limited edition series available from
Crown Pictures, Lindsell. **See entry in this book.**

Acknowledgements

The Publishers would like to thank the following for their assistance in the production of this book: Elaine, Deborah , Kelly , and Jean for Administration. Graham,Timothy ,for Production. Colin, Paul, for Research . Joanna, Gerald and Graham for Writing. Sarah, Les, Graham and Timothy for Artwork., Simon at Scorpio for the maps.

OTHER TITLES IN THE HIDDEN PLACES SERIES

© **M & M Publishing Ltd. 118 Ashley Rd .Cheshire. U.K. WA14 2UN**

Foreword

The Hidden Places Series

This is an established collection of travel guides which covers the U.K and Ireland in 16 titles.

The aim of the books is to introduce readers to some of the less well known attractions of each area whilst not ignoring the more established ones.

We have included in this book a number of hotels, inns, restaurants, various types of accommodation, historic houses, museums, and general attractions which are to be found in this part of the country, together with historical background information.

There is a map at the beginning of each chapter with line drawings of the places featured, along with a description of the services offered.

We hope that the book prompts you to discover some of the fascinating "Hidden Places" which we found on our journey, and we are sure the places featured would be pleased if you mentioned that our book prompted your visit.

We wish you an enjoyable and safe journey.

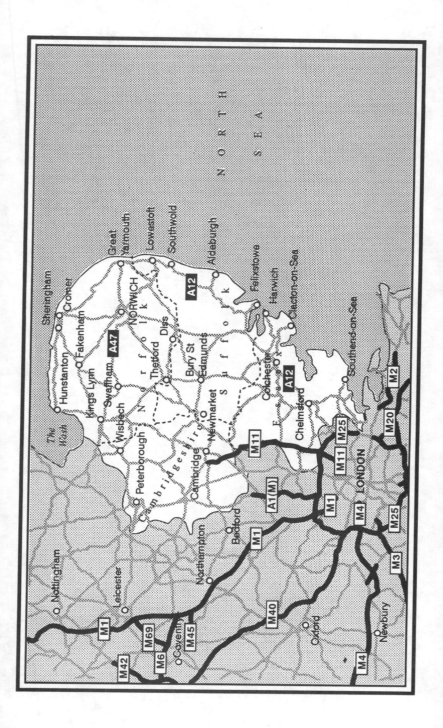

THE HIDDEN PLACES OF
EAST ANGLIA

CONTENTS

CHAPTER ONE

CAMBRIDGE AND SOUTH CAMBRIDGESHIRE

Kings College Chapel, Cambridge

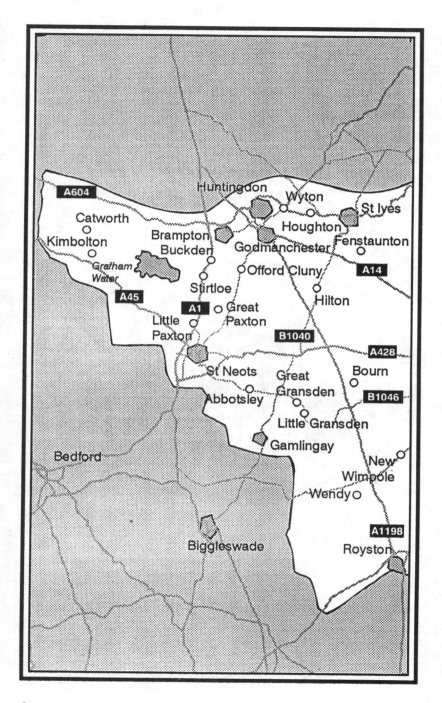

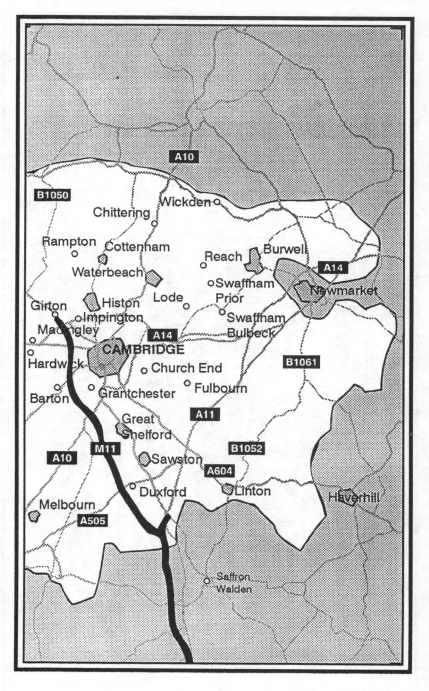

Christ's College, Cambridge

CHAPTER ONE

CAMBRIDGE AND SOUTH CAMBRIDGESHIRE

Cambridge and South East Cambridgeshire

CAMBRIDGE. The city of Cambridge really needs no introduction as it is, without doubt, one of the great centres of learning, with a unique history and reputation known throughout the world.

The growth of the City began in 1284 when the oldest college, Peterhouse, was founded by the Bishop of Ely. The 14th and 15th centuries saw rapid expansion with a cluster of buildings springing up along the River Cam. As much of the early learning was based on theological work the churches and chapels formed an integral part of the colleges and the jewel in this architectural crown is **King's College Chapel**. Best viewed from the River, this is a stunning building started in 1446 by Henry VI with an similarly spectacular interior. Of particular note is the fan vaulted ceiling, built 1512-15 and the stained glass windows added just after. More recently, the Rubens masterpiece 'The Adoration of the Magi' was donated and although well used by the world famous choir, the chapel is open to the public from 9 am to 3.45 pm during term time and until 5 pm in the vacations on Mondays to Saturdays. The times vary a little more on Sundays, but it is a must on your tour.

Among the many famous people who have studied at Cambridge, Trinity College boasts a host of poets including Byron, Dryden and Tennyson whilst Newton, Bacon and Rutherford, all with scientific leanings, also spent time there. John Harvard, the founder of the American university of that name, studied at Emmanuel.

The colleges themselves are also surprisingly visitor friendly and visitors can at least walk into most of the central courtyards and chapels. Please remember, however, that the colleges are closed to visitors during the exam period from May to mid June and that, being private property, there is no automatic right of way.

The **Bridge of Sighs**, over the River Cam at St John's College, resembles the bridge in Venice and was constructed in 1831, while the Mathematical Bridge at Queen's is built on physical principles and uses no bolts to maintain its construction.

There are also numerous opportunities for recreation and entertainment here which are not solely the preserve of the college community. The ubiquitous flat bottomed boats, or punts, can be hired while another way of avoiding the traffic congestion is to hire a bicycle (there are several firms in Cambridge offering this service).

5

A visit to the **Fitzwilliam Museum**, on Trumpington Street, conveniently placed in the centre near Peterhouse College, is well worthwhile. Dating back to 1816, the Fitzwilliam is one of the oldest museums in the country and its fine art treasures are particularly impressive with works from van Dyke to Monet and Matisse. Tel: (01223) 332900.

Still in this area, it will be of particular interest to American readers that the chapel to Peterhouse, originally called St Peter's and dating back to the 12th century, has a memorial tablet to Godfrey Washington showing the family crest of stars and stripes. Near to the bulk of the colleges but an antidote to the academic is the **Cambridge Folk Museum** which is full of artefacts showing how domestic life and local trades have developed over the centuries. There is also, on Lensfield Road, the **Scott Polar Research Institute** which displays memorabilia from Polar expeditions.

Cambridge is blessed with a large number of open spaces, most notably The Backs which stretch along the banks of the River Cam. Still very central and a short walk from the railway station is the **University Botanic Garden**. The gardens contain many rare species and are open to the public from 8.30 am to 6.30 pm with reduced hours on Sundays opening at 2.30 pm.

There are hundreds of pubs and restaurants here; it is advisable to book a table to avoid disappointment especially at weekends and during the summer when restaurants can fill up very quickly from 7 pm onwards. Entertainment is varied and ranges from street entertainers and musicians to mainstream theatre and concerts. The local press publish details as do the TIC; in fact, there is an excellent theatre, in the Corn Exchange, right by the tourist office on Wheeler Street. Box Office number is (01223) 463204.

AROUND CAMBRIDGE

Approximately 3 miles south east of the City, the oddly named **Gog Magog Hills** offer a good vantage point from which to observe the many towers and spires of the Cambridge colleges and chapels. There are also footpaths to Wandlebury Camp, the site of an Iron Age fort.

GRANTCHESTER. To the south of Cambridge and a pleasant stroll across the riverside meadows lies the most typical English village, Grantchester. A delightful area full of interesting thatched buildings, this was home to Rupert Brook the poet who wrote so eloquently about the futility of war.

MELBOURN. A charming village and somewhat smaller that its Australian namesake, Melbourn lies some nine miles south of Cambridge. With so many places to tour in the area, **SHEEN MILL COUNTRY HOTEL AND RESTAURANT** certainly has one of the most beautiful settings in the region and, with its elegant riverside restaurant and individually styled accommodation, it is truly an ideal venue for every occasion. Preserving many of its original features, this 17th

King's College, Cambridge

Punting on the Cam

century watermill has been beautifully restored. It is listed in the Domesday Book and was originally powered by the River Mel which still flows beneath the mill. The hotel is privately owned by Jenny and Carlo Cescutti who ensure that you always receive a very warm welcome and their personal attention. The bedrooms are very attractively presented and overlook both the gardens and river. All rooms have en-suite bathrooms and are equipped with every modern facility.

The restaurant has deservedly been awarded 2 AA Rosettes for its superb cuisine and its excellent standard of service. Renowned for the excellence of its food, Sheen Mill offers a superb selection of dishes on either the à la carte or table d'hôte menus where typically you could find; Ravioli of Chicken and Wild Mushrooms with a Basil Buerre Blanc, Timbale of Avocado and Fresh Crab lined with Smoked Salmon and Noisettes of Lamb with a Tagliatelle of Vegetables on a Redcurrant & Mint Jus. The excellent cuisine is prepared on the premises using only the very best fresh produce and is complemented by an outstanding wine list which should meet with even the most discerning of tastes.

Sheen Mill Country Hotel and Restaurant, Melbourn
Tel: 01763 261393 Fax: 01763 261376

DUXFORD. Close to the M11 motorway, and just 10 miles from Cambridge, lies the **Imperial War Museum** for aircraft. Dating back to beginning of the aviation age, Duxford was a military airfield during World War I and during the Battle of Britain it became a major base. It was from here that Douglas Bader's squadron flew. Home to the country's finest collection of both military and civil aircraft, Duxford has a Concorde, a number of military vehicles, and many special exhibitions. There is also an adventure playground and a restaurant as well as shops, all on a large but accessible site. Very easy to spend a few hours here. Open daily except Christmas and New Year's Day. Tel (01223) 835000.

LINTON. The long, narrow high street through this small town, itself boasting some fine buildings, is bisected by a branch of the River Cam. As well as the early 16th century black and white Trinity guildhall, also look out for the handsome pargetted Chaundlers. Just a short distance from the centre of Linton village, on the B1052, is **Linton Zoo**

and Gardens. Conservation is the keyword and there is always something new to discover as they take on board another endangered species. With large landscaped gardens to enjoy, it is an ideal spot for a picnic. A children's play area and souvenir shop are also on site and the zoo is open every day except Christmas Day. Phone (01223) 891308. Please note that dogs are not allowed in the park.

BARTON. In the heart of Barton village, just off the A603, is **THE HOOPS** inn. Mentioned in the Domesday Book, it is now a Grade II listed building and Green Kings oldest pub. A lot of important history is currently being verified and it has come to light that when the Fens flooded, the inn was used as a bolthole for smugglers; it has also seen the arrest and subsequent deportation of rustlers to Australia. The building has a cottage style appearance with red pantile roof and little dormer windows. To the side is a large garden where patrons may enjoy food and drink overlooking the duck pond. Now growing in popularity here, the French game of Petanque may be played at the pub. The bar has traditional appeal and a large log fire gives it a very cosy feel. There is a nicely presented restaurant area where wholesome traditional fayre is served but does include the more exotic such as 'Bobotie', a South African sweet and spicy lamb dish. Daily specials are also featured and afternoon teas are served in the summer period.

The Hoops, 1 School Lane, Barton Tel: 01223 262230

NEW WIMPOLE. A model village built in the 1840s along the Cambridge to Sandy road. The emparkment, by a series of landscape architects, at **Wimpole Hall** caused the population shift. The Hall, now in the hands of the National Trust, dates back over 300 years and has an imposing main house with a with a fine library and magnificent state rooms. For younger visitors, the estate has a well organised farm where they can meet the animals and see the workings of a farm first hand. The park is well landscaped and there are many different walks for you to enjoy. Open Tuesday to Saturday, Sunday and Bank Holiday Mondays. Admission charge payable; family tickets and group discounts available. Phone (01223) 207257.

GAMLINGAY. This was once a prosperous village and it retains many fine buildings, over sixty of which are listed despite a devastating fire in 1600.

BOURN is a peaceful, Cambridgeshire village noted as being home to Britain's oldest surviving postmill; the base and outer structure dating from 1636. The **GOLDEN LION** lies on the main street of Bourn. Dating back to the early 1700s, the pub has always been an ale house and is the village local. Many of the original features of this attractive old building remain, including much of the old bar area, though there have been additions over the years to the rear. Owned and personally run by Eileen Simmons, this is a very pleasant, relaxing place to stop for refreshment; there are two en-suite bedrooms available so you can always stay longer. Lovers of real ale are well catered for and there is a mouth-watering menu of delicious pub meals. Horse lovers too, will enjoy stopping here. Eileen's two daughters are keen horsewomen and their trophies are on display in the pub. Still competing regularly, their horses are stabled at the back of the building.

Golden Lion, High Street, Bourn Tel: 01954 719305

MADINGLEY. Lying four miles to the west of Cambridge is the **American Military Cemetery** at Madingley. Signposted from the A45, the cemetery has become a place of pilgrimage for the families of those American Servicemen who operated from the many bases in the area during the Second World War.

HARDWICK. **THE BLUE LION** at Hardwick is a well presented village inn with history from the 1800s. It serves as both village pub and busy restaurant with entry on three levels, one of which leads off to the conservatory. The character is rustic with a wealth of exposed beams and timbers and with low ceilings in all areas. To the far end of the bar, a wood and coal burning stove crackles in winter, whilst in the upper bar, also a waiting area for the restaurant, there is an open fire. A separate room is provided for families.

Many mouth-watering dishes are featured on the full à la carte menu, and additionally, freshly prepared barfood is available. The Prime Steak baked in a crust of fresh herbs and garlic breadcrumbs served with oyster, mushroom and red wine sauce, looked very tempting indeed. The wine list offers good variety especially at the budget end while Real ales such as IPA and Abbott are regularly available.

The Blue Lion, Hardwick Tel: 01954 210328

Just down the road from the Blue Lion pub on the southside of this small village is **WALLIS FARM**, a large arable farm. The large red brick farmhouse, owned by Linda and Peter Sadler, was rebuilt in 1836 and is very spacious and comfortable. Linda offers excellent farmhouse bed and breakfast accommodation in several rooms, one at the rear of the house with views over the large garden and farm beyond whilst the other rooms are situated in a converted cart shed. The conversion has provided well appointed guest rooms and many of the original features such as harness racks and roof beams remain. All the rooms are en-suite. The Wimpole Way dedicated footpath runs right through the farm and guests may also walk around the farm which, as well as growing wheat, barley and oil seed rape, also has some goats, sheep and donkeys around the place. ETB - 2 Crowns Highly Commended.

Wallis Farm, 98 Main Street, Hardwick Tel: 01954 210347

HISTON. As well as being close to the Chivers jam factory, the village is the home of Unwin's seeds but, despite the industry and new housing, the village has retained much of its old charm; a pretty village centre, ducks on the village green and a Norman church.

THE RED LION, on the main street, is very much a village pub. The building, originally a house, dates back to the 1700s and it became a pub following the Beer Act of 1830. The Red Lion is still very much in accord with the 1830 Act, which was designed to stimulate beer drinking and reduce brewery monopolies. This free house always has six cask conditioned ales from various regions on tap.

Traditionally decorated, the Red Lion has two separate bars, one appeals to the younger at heart drinker and the other to those who like to contemplate their pints and relax in a peaceful atmosphere. The beer garden is a pleasant place to sit in the summer and, as the evening wears on, it is lit up by old gas street lamps which add to the convivial atmosphere. There is also a good menu available at lunchtime with daily specials displayed on an ever changing blackboard.

The Red Lion, 27 High Street, Histon Tel: 01223 564437

WYNWYCH is a large chalet bungalow down a quiet private road just two minutes from the centre of the village. Owned by Jill and Henry Torrens, this charming and friendly couple offer wonderful bed and breakfast accommodation in four comfortable bedrooms.

Wynwych, 55 Narrow Lane, Histon Tel: 01223 232496

All the rooms, like the rest of the home, are exceedingly well decorated and furnished, have tea and coffee making facilities and colour televisions. This is a real home from home. Finally, Jill is a mine of information on the surrounding area and she has put plenty of tourist information in each of the guest bedrooms. Wynwych is a wonderful place where you will feel relaxed and one of the family.

IMPINGTON. Samuel Pepys was born here in 1633 and the village is also home to the **CHIVERS FARM SHOP**, which lies close to the main A14 road from Cambridge, just off the B1049 road to Histon, over a bridge and beside the BUPA hospital. A working arable farm, that began in the 1800s, the farm shop is set in an attractive early 1900s stable block. The world famous Chivers jam, from which the place gets its name, was first produced here in 1873 but the business was sold in 1989 when demand for the fine jams had outstripped the production capacity. Today the farm still grows strawberries and other soft fruits including raspberries, blackberries and gooseberries. In the season, June, July and August, the farm is a popular 'pick-your-own' shop. As well as selling the fruit, the farm shop has a lot more to offer. There are own label jams, marmalades, chutneys, fudges and apple juice, fresh vegetables and soups, smoked fish and meats and a whole host of other delicious items.

Chivers Farm Shop, New Road, Impington Tel: 01223 237799

If you have been hard at work picking your fruit out in the fields or just browsing round the shop, the tea rooms offer the perfect place to relax and regain your strength. With a wonderful smell of freshly ground coffee, steaming pots of freshly brewed tea, enjoy a delicious home-made cake or one of the mouth-watering cream teas.

RAMPTON. A charming village where graceful trees border the village green. **THE BLACK HORSE**, in the main street of Rampton, is very much the village pub. There has been an inn on this site since the 1600s, though the building you see today was constructed after the original inn burnt down in a great fire. More recently, the Black Horse also survived an attempt to close it down but public opposition swayed the brewery to change their minds.

Today the pub is owned and personally run by Helen Woodgate

with the help of her parents. The building is totally covered in a wonderful Virginia creeper that adds a real splash of green during the spring and summer, turning to the most magnificent reddy brown in autumn. Inside, the pub is cosy, with comfortable chairs and roaring fires in winter. A true meeting place for the locals, visitors are warmly welcomed, and there is some super real ale on tap to quench your thirst. Helen originally comes from Yorkshire and this is reflected in the delicious home-cooked menu here, where the specialities include Whitby Scampi, Grimsby fish, chips and mushy peas and Giant Yorkshire puddings. A wonderful pub with an atmosphere and the hospitality to match.

The Black Horse, 6 High Street, Rampton Tel: 01954 251296

CHITTERING. Just past the village of Chittering is the small site of **Denny Abbey** which was founded in the 12th century as a dependent priory of the large monastery at Ely. The remains include the church and the refectory and are well worth a visit. Admission charge payable; free to English Heritage members.

WICKDEN. This small village, from which the Octagon of Ely Cathedral can be seen, is famous for the fen which lies to the west. One of the most important wetland areas in Europe, **Wicken Fen** was a favourite Victorian insect hunting ground when, in 1899, it was declared the country's first nature reserve.

The reserve is host to thousands of birds and insects who thrive in this unspoilt habitat. Nowadays the water level is kept up whereas at one time vast areas of the fens were drained to provide farmland. Owned by the National Trust, there is a visitor centre which has lots of information, and there are raised walkways across the water which makes access to the centre of the fen quite easy.

BURWELL. This ancient and historic village is home to the **BURWELL MUSEUM**, which houses a unique record of Cambridgeshire village life on the 'Fen Edge', where the fertile chalk uplands met the marshy fens. Burwell village itself dates back to Saxon times and has a castle earthworks, the Devil's Dyke and wonderful Perpendicular church.

Anglesey Abbey

The museum has many fascinating exhibits and displays that recall the way of life in the village and how it was shaped by the seasons, landscape and passage of time. Many of the buildings here have been re-erected on the site and include a Forge and Wheelwright's Shop, a Nissen Hut and an 18th century timber-framed barn. From peat-cutting and fen-skating through to the days of World War II, there is plenty to interest everyone. The museum also holds a whole host of special events throughout the year that range from model railway displays to the days of Anglo-Saxon Britain.

Burwell Museum, Mill Close, Burwell Tel: 01638 741512

REACH. The village grew up where the Saxon earthwork the Devil's Dyke met Reach Lode. An extremely pretty place, with pink- and white-washed cottages overlooking the large village green. Reach Fair has been held on May Day since before 1201 and by the 14th century the village was a prosperous port, with timber, iron and agricultural produce passing through the port to King's Lynn.

SWAFFHAM PRIOR. A pretty fenland village, 1.5 miles from its neighbour Swaffham Bulbeck. Along with a delightful collection of elegant Georgian houses, the village also has a churchyard with two churches.

SWAFFHAM BULBECK. A picturesque and linear village of thatched cottages with Abbey House, a yellow and red 18th century building, on the site of an old nunnery.

LODE. A small village, once surrounded by low-lying fenland, Lode is well known for the Augustinian Priory established nearby. Now known as **Anglesey Abbey**, this is an outstanding building which was started in 1135 and the monks remained here for almost four centuries before the property underwent conversion to a Tudor manor house. Inside, however, there is a superb vaulted ceiling which is one of the clues to its earlier origins. Outside are large gardens in formal 18th century style with statues lining a walkway or providing a focal point for the wide variety of floral displays. There is much to see here and as a bonus do make a point of looking out for the **Lode Mill**. A mill has stood on the site since the time of the Domesday Book and once a month the mill grinds

The Cromwell Museum, Huntingdon

corn for sale to the public. The facilities at the Mill and Abbey include a shop and a licensed restaurant serving teas lunches and snacks. Free parking for cars and coaches. Admission charge and with the exception of guide dogs no dogs are allowed in the gardens. Phone (01223) 811200.

Huntingdon and Cromwell Country

HUNTINGDON. An ancient town, first settled by the Romans, the street plan, laid down sometime later by the Danes who sailed up the River Great Ouse, is still recognisable today. During the 13th century there were as many as 13 churches in the town though only two survive today. One of these, **All Saints'** in the market square, displays several architectural styles from medieval to Victorian times. A great wealth of Georgian building can also be found here including the fine, three-storey Town Hall.

Famous today for its local MP, John Major the Prime Minister, Huntingdon was also the birthplace of Oliver Cromwell in 1599. Rising to power as a Military Commander in the Civil War, Cromwell raised his troops from this area and the Falcon Inn was used as his headquarters. Appointed Lord Protector of England in 1653, Cromwell was never crowned King though he ruled until his death in 1658. Educated at Huntingdon Grammar School, which was also attended by the famous diarist, Samuel Pepys, who lived at nearby Brampton, the building is now a museum dedicated to the Civil War. **The Cromwell Museum** houses the only public collection which specifically relates to Oliver Cromwell and it is open throughout the year though closed on Mondays. Tel: (01480) 425830.

Though decimated by the plague in the 17th century, Huntington regained its prosperity in the 1700s as a major staging post on the Great North road.

There is a large market square in the centre and a short distance away is **Hinchingbrooke House** which today serves also as a school but has its origins in the Middle Ages when it was a nunnery. Formerly the home to both the Cromwell family and the Earls of Sandwich, Hinchingbrooke House is open to the public between May and August. Tel: (01480) 451121.

AROUND HUNTINGDON

GODMANCHESTER. An early 14th century bridge spans the Great Ouse to link the delightful, unspoilt village of Godmanchester with Huntingdon. With many charming buildings **Island Hall**, a mid 18th century mansion, is certainly the most architectural important. Open to the public during July, the house contains many interesting artefacts belonging to the owner's family who have lived here since 1804. Phone (01480) 459676.

Hitchingbrooke, Huntingdon

BUCKDEN. An historic village that has lost none 'of its charm, it was at **Buckden Towers**, the former Palace of the Bishops of Lincoln, that Henry VIII imprisoned his first wife, Catherine of Aragon in 1533. Henry visited Buckden again in 1541 with his fifth wife, Catherine Howard, and, in 1619, Buckden Towers entertained King James VI of Scotland. A splendid 15th century gatehouse and tower, the church and courtyard here are open to the public during daylight hours and there is also a visitor centre and bookshop. Tel: (01480) 811868.

THE GEORGE COACHING INN lies opposite Buckden Towers on the Great North Road. An impressive building which dates back to the 17th century, the coaching inn stood on the busy commercial route that linked York with London. The inn has two claims to fame. Firstly, its old corridor is said to have been that used by highwayman, Dick Turpin, to make good his escape from the law and, secondly, its commemorates an 18th century landlord and coachman, George Cartwright, who recorded the fastest time achieved by a mail coach and four on the Welwyn to Buckden stage of the London to York express.

The George Coaching Inn, Great North Road, Buckden Tel: 01480 810307

Today, travellers can expect a warm and friendly welcome when they visit the George Coaching Inn. None of the inn's great charm or character has been lost whilst guests have all the modern conveniences of the 20th century to ensure their stay is both relaxing and comfortable. During the summer drinks and meals can be enjoyed out on the garden terrace, whilst, as the evenings get colder, the roaring log fires make a welcoming sight. As with the rest of the establishment, the bar is tastefully decorated and comfortably furnished and provides the perfect place for a quick pre-dinner drink. There is also a comprehensive menu of bar meals and an excellent range of real ales, wines and spirits from which to choose. The attractive candlelit restaurant serves a range of excellent, well chosen dishes on its table d'hôte and à la carte menus and offers both quality and value for money. All the hotel's sixteen bedrooms are en-suite and family rooms are also available.

The Turpin Room is a delightful and pleasant suite that can be used for both conferences and private dinner parties and celebrations. Whether you are staying at the Inn on business or for pleasure you are sure to have a wonderful time.

BRAMPTON. The village of Brampton has the one time home of the famous diarist Samuel Pepys who so vividly described the major events of the 17th century, including The Great Fire of London. The Pepys' family home, 44 Huntingdon Road, is now known as Pepys House.

KIMBOLTON. The name Kimbolton comes from an Anglo-Saxon word meaning Cenebald's Tun or small estate. By 1200 the Lord of the Manor was Geoffrey Fitz-Piers, Chief Justicular to King John, who granted Geoffrey the right to hold a fair and a market.

Henry VIII's first wife, Catherine of Aragon, lived the last eighteen months of her life exiled at Kimbolton Castle. From the 17th to the 20th century the castle and estate was in the hands of the Montague family, subsequently the Dukes of Manchester. In 1950 the castle was sold to the grammar school.

ST NEOTS. A charming, small town that is well worth a little amble around on foot as there are some old pubs and other interesting buildings tucked away that are all too easy to miss. Founded in the 10th century by Benedictine monks, this old market town is named after St Neot, who was an adviser to King Alfred. Though his body was buried in Cornwall it is possible that the monks stole his bones and brought them to their new priory in this part of Cambridgeshire. The town has some fine buildings including the 15th century Church of St Mary.

Lying between St Neots and Kimbolton is **Grafham Water**. Though it is a huge reservoir don't be put off as it has good leisure facilities and the water company has done a good job in providing well signed walks as well as a host of water based activities.

ABBOTSLEY. It's interesting to record how name changes occur on inns and hostelries through the ages. Take for instance **THE EIGHT BELLS** at Abbotsley, a wonderful village pub, originally named The Six Bells, but due to an error by the signwriter of the day, who painted *eight*, it was thought cheaper to re-name the inn rather than repaint the sign!

The Eight Bells, Abbotsley Tel: 01767 677305

Owned and run by Kim and Sandra Geer, this public house has an exceptional selection of food available; choose from the comprehensive set menu where Rack of Lamb, Vermouth Salmon and Sunset Pork are some of the dishes on offer; or from the snack menu which includes five children's meals, Sunday Roast lunches and even fresh fish and chips on two days of the week. The wine list features wines from France, Spain, Portugal and Germany and for those preferring Real Ale, well, their tastes are catered for too, with IPA, Abbott and seasonal ales. The food is supplied locally and freshly prepared each day by Sandra. Situated in the centre of the village on the B1046.

RECTORY FARM HOUSE is just a short walk from The Eight Bells pub and is set back from the B1046 down its own drive. Built in 1840, the farmhouse is owned by David Hipwell who also farms the arable land around with wheat, winter barley and oil seed rape. Rectory Farm House has four comfortable bedrooms. A full English breakfast is served in the pleasant dining room. This farm house is in a peaceful and tranquil location and guests are free to walk the farm if they wish.

Rectory Farm House, Abbotsley Tel: 01767 677282

GREAT GRANSDEN. Like its twin, Little Gransden, the village is near the great Roman thoroughfare, Ermine Street. As well as having a 1674 post mill, there is also an ancient tract of woodland here cared for by the Cambridgeshire Wildlife Trust.

LITTLE GRANSDEN. Just outside Little Gransden, on the B1046 halfway to Longstowe, lies **GRANSDEN LODGE.** Originally built in 1895, this large farmhouse has been added to since 1951, when Mary and Peter Cox came to the farm. From this charming and friendly home, Mary and Peter offer excellent bed and breakfast accommodation in seven comfortable bedrooms. There is a comfortable lounge with a log burning fire and the full English breakfast, or something lighter, is served in an ornate dining room overlooking the garden. The large, pleasant garden is available to the guests and the arable farmland around the house provides many interesting walks.

Even if you do not see Mary's Bull Mastiffs, she has been breeding them for the past 25 years, you will not miss the pictures and statuettes around the house. A dog expert, Mary also judges at shows around the country, and further afield, including Crufts and your pet is welcome by arrangement. Gransden Lodge is Tourist Board Highly Commended and is also a no smoking establishment.

Gransden Lodge, Little Gransden Tel: 01767 677365 Fax: 01767 677647

HILTON. A charming and unspoilt village, Hilton has only one of eight turf mazes surviving in England. Though small, it is scheduled as an Ancient Monument and well worth a visit.

On the edge of the village green, opposite the church is **ST FRANCIS TOFT**, the home of Emily Davison. From her modern bungalow, Emily offers excellent farmhouse bed and breakfast accommodation in two comfortable bedrooms. A quiet and relaxing home from home, there is a choice of full English or a lighter continental breakfast to set you up for the day.

St Francis Toft, The Green, Hilton Tel: 01480 830426

This is a working livestock farm and riding stables and the farm has the largest showing herd of goats in the country. Guests may walk the farm, if accompanied by a member of staff, and it is well worth a stroll round as this is no ordinary farm. There are rare breeds of cattle and sheep out in the fields and Newfoundland dogs and native British ponies are also bred here. A comfortable and friendly place to stay that is also quiet unusual.

FENSTANTON. The famous architect and gardener, Capability Brown, lived here for some years and he is buried in the local church.

The **KING WILLIAM IV** is a charming pub and restaurant lying towards the western end of the main street in Fenstanton. Originally two cottages dating from the 16th and 17th centuries, the inn is warm and cosy, with plenty of interest and character. With low beamed ceilings throughout and horse brasses, tack and hunt pictures decorating the walls this is a super place to stop. A large brick log burning fire stands in the centre of the building, dividing the bars and the restaurant area, and also indicating the division between the original two buildings.

Owned and personally run by Jerry Schon Feldt, the King William IV is well known for its excellent ale and delicious cuisine. As well as offering an superb range of real ales, there is live blues and jazz music every Wednesday evenings. The restaurant features in the Egon Ronay good food guide and, as well as there being at least three vegetarian dishes and lots of fish, the King William IV is renowned for its steak and kidney pudding, though the breast of duck with apricot sauce sounds tempting.

King William IV, High Street, Fenstanton Tel: 01480 462467

ST IVES. An ancient town, St Ives once held a huge annual fair and sea-going barges once navigated up to the six arched bridge that was built across the Great Ouse here in the early 15th century. Particularly interesting is the very rare medieval chapel built, midstream, in 1426 and one of only three remaining chapel bridges in the country.

The town is named after St Ivo, said to have been a Persian bishop who came here in the Dark Ages to convert the heathen. In the Middle Ages, Kings of England bought cloth for their households at great wool fair and a market, particularly large at Bank Holidays, is still held here every Monday.

The **Norris Museum**, founded by a St Ivian Herbert Norris, opened in 1933 and is a museum of Huntingdonshire life. From the earliest times to present day, all that has influenced the life of the old county is here.

From the fossilized remains of Ammonites and Belemnites through to the displays of local lace-making and ice-skating on the Fens, there is plenty to see. Phone (01480) 465101.

THE AVIATOR public house lies next to the church on the main road into the town from the south. Dating back to the 1600s, the pub was probably a coaching inn. Obviously, at that time it had another name, it was renamed The Aviator after an accident in the early days of flying. Around the time of the First World War, an airman landed his biplane in a nearby meadow and came to the pub to ask for directions back to his airbase, now RAF Wyton. Having been given the correct bearings, he took off again only to hit the church steeple and be killed. The repairs to the steeple can still be seen and a painting by a local artist depicting the incident is displayed behind the pub's bar. Today, The Aviator is owned and personally run by Gerry and Paul Baldwin and they maintain the aviation theme with pictures of planes and other props adorning the walls. This free house serves an excellent selection of real ales and there is also some really good pub food. For the more adventurous why not try the wild boar or the fillet of kangaroo.

The Aviator, Ramsey Road, St Ives Tel: 01480 46441

CONNIE'S TRADITIONAL TEA ROOMS lies on The Quay at the heart of this old town's conservation area. Standing in a row dating back to the 1800s and originally an inn, the building was reconstructed in the 1920s following a fire. Since then it has been a solicitor's, accountant's and an antique shop before Connie Stevens opened the tea rooms just a few months ago.

Absolutely charming, it is a pleasure just to look inside. Many of the original features remain, including the fireplaces and their surrounds and the wonderful ornate skirting boards and picture rails. Furnished in a traditional style of round, clothed tables with spindle back chairs, four out of the five rooms have roaring log fires in winter to warm up even the most frozen of customers. All the food served at the tea rooms uses the freshest ingredients and everything is prepared on a daily basis, from the home-made soups to the traditional and lavish puddings. Described as traditional with a twist of innovative modern British, the cuisine is out of this world. As a light lunch the Welsh rarebit is very popular as are the home-made shortbread and fatless cakes. If Connie herself looks familiar, she might be as she has won the title of Masterchef of the East of England.

Finally, Connie's is the key holder for the Chapel on the Bridge, well worth a visit after your meal.

Connies Traditional Tea Rooms, 4 The Quay, St Ives Tel: 01480 498199

HOUGHTON. Now bypassed by the main road, Houghton is a charming, secluded village that has retained its traditional square, complete with pump and clock.

Situated here, on a small island in the River Ouse, is **Houghton Mill**, a National Trust property. A large timbered structure built in the 17th century that is believed to be the oldest remaining watermill on the River Ouse and there has probably been some form of mill here since the 11th century. With much of the milling machinery still in-tact, milling takes place on Sundays and Bank Holiday Mondays throughout the summer; the mill is open all weekend between April and October and all week except Thursdays and Fridays between July and September. Phone (01480) 301494.

WYTON. On the banks of the Great Ouse, Wyton is a pretty village, ideal for picnics and there is a boat slipway to allow watercraft on to the river and lakes. The **THREE JOLLY BUTCHERS** lies on the main road through the village of Wyton. The main bar part of the building dates back to the early 1500s and many of the original beams, themselves originally ships' timbers, are still in place. As might be expected from its name, the pub started life as a butcher's and, as was the practice in those days, an abattoir as well. In fact, behind one of the walls there is a mural painted in ox blood a photograph of which can be seen hanging in the main bar. What is now the restaurant was built in 1622, the date can be seen on the chimney, as a court house and an ale house.

Today, the Three Jolly Butchers is owned and personally run by Susan and Vanessa. A choice of five real ales is available from the bar and their restaurant serves traditional country dishes using only the freshest of local produce. Across the pub's extensive gardens and through a water meadow you will find the Great Ouse where the inn has its own moorings. If you are travelling by river, it is worth noting that the Three Jolly Butchers is the only pub on the river between Huntingdon and St Ives.

Three Jolly Butchers, Huntingdon Road, Wyton Tel: 01480 463228

CHAPTER TWO

NORTH CAMBRIDGESHIRE AND THE FENS

Ely Cathedral

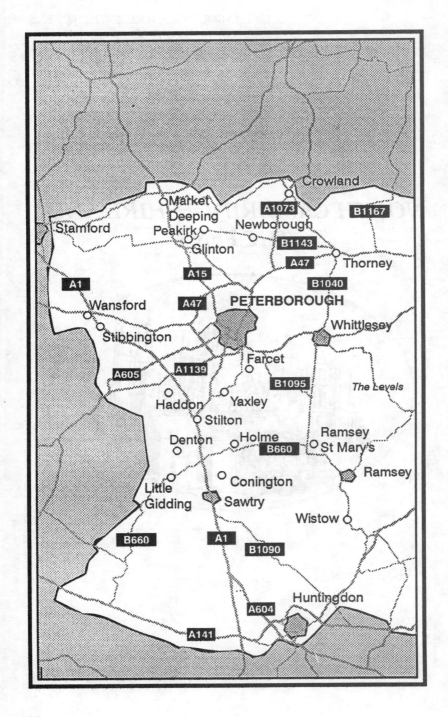

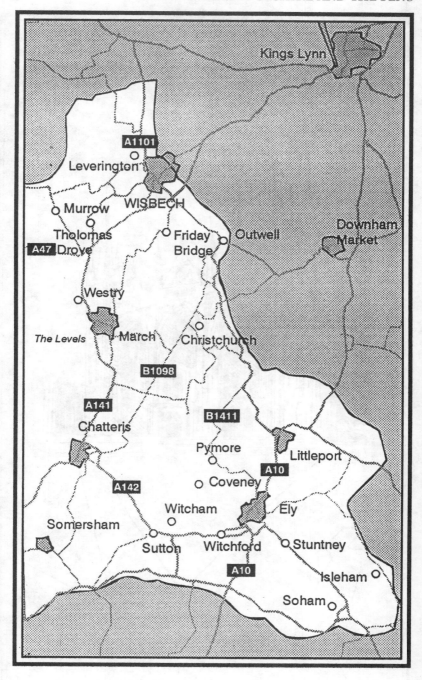

Peterborough Cathedral

CHAPTER TWO

NORTH CAMBRIDGESHIRE AND THE FENS

Peterborough and North Cambridgeshire

PETERBOROUGH. Dominating this part of the county, Peterborough is Cambridgeshire's second city. At its heart stands the great Norman Cathedral of St. Peter which gave the city its name. An important site of Christian worship since 655 AD, it retains two early Saxon sculptures. The present church, built from 1118 to 1238 as a Benedictine Abbey, was made a Cathedral by Henry VIII. His first Queen, Catherine of Aragon, is buried here, as was Mary Queen of Scots for a while after her execution at Fotheringhay.

Located in the centre, the **City Museum and Art Gallery** shows all aspects of the story of Peterborough with the first floor displays dealing with the natural environment and man's intervention. There are skeletons of the sea creatures which lived in Peterborough when dinosaurs roamed the earth and also displays of local archaeology. The second floor tells the more recent social history of the city and includes important displays of bone and straw work made by Napoleonic prisoners at nearby Norman Cross.

The **Queensgate Centre** at the heart of Peterborough provides everything you could possibly want from a shopping trip. With spacious marble halls, decorative fountains and high levels of natural lighting, the centre has maintained the standards of excellence that once earned it the title of Europe's best new covered shopping centre.

Just 2 miles east of the city centre, at Fourth Drove, **Fengate**, is **Flag Fen**. Described as one of the most exciting finds of the century, Flag Fen is one of the few ongoing excavations that are open to the public. From Easter to the end of October, guided tours of the excavation offer visitors the opportunity to watch archaeologists gradually uncovering a Bronze Age timber platform and 1,000 year old swords and spearheads.

Running from the centre of Peterborough, for 7 1/2 miles through Nene Park to Wansford, is the preserved **Nene Valley Steam Railway**. Services operate at weekends, from March to October and some mid-week days in the summer months. With the added highlight of occasional special events, like Thomas the Tank Engine days and Vintage weekends, this is an ideal outing for those who love steam and for younger members of the family. Phone (01780) 782854.

STAMFORD. This wonderful town stands in the southern part of Kesteven, Lincolnshire and just on the edge of the county border. Made up of a series of winding roads, lined with buildings of local stone mainly of the medieval and Georgian periods, Stamford was declared a conservation area in 1967 and proclaimed as 'the finest stone town in England'. The town was once held as an important religious centre which is apparent from the number of towers and spires that seem to appear round every corner.

The **Stamford Steam Brewery Museum** is a fascinating stop for those interested in drinking beer! Established in 1825, the Brewery was the longest surviving brewery in the town, eventually shutting down in 1974. Reopened as a museum, the original 19th century brewing equipment is displayed.

The facades of the town's shops remain ornate and decorative while offering modern services and facilities with good old fashioned hospitality. There is a pleasant walk along the River Welland which winds its way through Stamford and provides scenic views across the meadows and of the town centre itself, before flowing past the estate of Burghley House.

Burghley House is one of the largest and grandest houses of the Elizabethan age. Built by the 1st Lord Burghley, Lord High Treasurer to Queen Elizabeth I, it has been home to the Cecil family ever since. Situated on the edge of Stamford, Burghley House is set in a picturesque deer park designed by 'Capability' Brown and it is famous for hosting the Burghley Horse Trials each September. Guided tours take visitors through 18 magnificent rooms culminating in the state apartments with ceilings painted by Verrio. The rooms are also treasure troves of fine porcelain, paintings and furniture which will appeal to lovers of fine art.

PEAKIRK. A charming little village on the edge of the Fens and somewhat off the beaten track, Peakirk is only 7 miles north of Peterborough. The village church, of Norman origin, is the only one in the country to be dedicated to St Pega, whose cell became a hermitage and the remains of which can still be seen.

The Car Dyke, built by the Romans to gain access to the Fens, runs to the east of the village and in this wetland is the **Peakirk Waterfowl Gardens**. Opened in 1957 by the HRH The Duke of Gloucester, the Gardens are now home to 700 waterfowl of 108 different kinds, including geese, swans and flamingos. The large ponds and gardens make this an interesting and informative place to visit and the beautiful serenity of the park make it a mecca for artists and photographers.

THORNEY. The village was developed by the Dukes of Bedford as part of their estate and is a classic example of a 19th century model village with its own style of estate architecture. **The Heritage Centre** here tells the story of Thorney using objects, models, plans and photographs. The Abbey, founded here in the 7th century, dominates the history of the area and fragments of its remains can be found in St Mary and St Botolph's Church.

WHITTLESEY is a charming market town close to the western edge of the Fens. Whittlesey dates back to medieval times although there are few reminders left. More recent history has left its mark with a variety of well preserved buildings spanning several centuries. There are examples of timber framed dwellings with thatched roofs, occasional stone buildings and preponderance of mellow buff brick. Whittlesey is also noted for its rare thatched mud walls.

A local agricultural tradition of The Straw Bear is still celebrated in Whittlesey each year in early January. The Bear is a man dressed in straw who dances through the town on the Saturday before Plough Sunday (the first Sunday after 12th night). The original meaning of the tradition is obscure and it probably stems from pagan times when Corn Gods or other mythical symbols were to be placated or invoked in order to secure soil fertility for the coming season. Commencing on the Friday evening, dancing through the streets on Saturday lasts from 10.45 am to 3.30 pm and an evening barn dance follows. On the Sunday, the Straw Bear is burnt.

LITTLE GIDDING. A place of peace and contemplation, of community and prayer, in a fast and noisy world, the first community at Little Gidding was founded by Nicholas Ferrer. It comprised his own extended family and a number of single men and women. In addition to praying three times a day, they made and dispensed herbal medicines, they ran a school for their own and local children and practised various crafts. Before his death in 1637 Nicholas Ferrer handed over the leadership of the community to his brother, with the words "It is the right, good, old way you are in; keep in it." This remains the aspiration of the present community which was formed in the 1970s and has adopted the name **The Society of Christ the Sower.**

The centre piece of the community is, as in Nicholas Ferrer's day, the church. Restored by the Ferrers in the 1620s, the tiny church has some of the finest furnishings and brasswork of its period. Its powerful spiritual atmosphere has attracted countless pilgrims over the centuries. The original communion silver and brass font, the only one in England, are on display.

The present community welcomes visitors to its Parlour in the nearby farmhouse, open every day from 11 am to 5 pm. As well as an interesting exhibition on the community, there are excellent home-made refreshments and lunches. Cake and biscuits, as well as jam made with home-grown fruit, are also for sale, along with books, cards, plants and home-grown herbs produced by members of the society. Visitors may also walk around the small farm where traditional breeds of livestock and poultry are kept. Most of the work is done by hand though there is a venerable 1954 Ferguson tractor.

In one of the workshops furniture is made to order, including bookcases, cupboards, chairs, tables, and dressers. The Society also run

Ely Cathedral and Market Square

a building company that specialises in restoration of churches and older buildings, though they are happy to tackle any work, charging very fair rates.

Society of Christ the Sower, Manor Farm, Little Gidding
Tel: 01832 293383

WANSFORD. There is a splendid 12-arched bridge over the River Nene in this quiet Cambridgeshire village. The first arches date from 1577, the second from 1672-4, while the last were built in 1795.

The Haycock, a wonderful 17th century coaching inn, once had stabling for 150 horses, was one of the largest coaching inns ever built.

Wansford is a must for railway enthusiasts as it is the headquarters of the Nene Valley Railway.

STILTON's position, adjacent to the A1, made it a favourite stopping off point during the heyday of coaching when weary travellers could obtain refreshment and break their arduous journey. Such travel, at that time, was also dangerous for this too was the age of the highwayman and the most notorious of them all, Dick Turpin, is said to have hidden at The Bell in Stilton. This village is, of course, the home of the blue veined cheese which bears the same name.

Ely and the Fenland Towns

ELY. The city of Ely is the jewel in the Fen's crown. Not only a great place to pick up loads of information on what to see and where to go in this part of Cambridgeshire, but the Tourist Information Centre is a tourist attraction in its own right. The pretty black and white timbered building is the only remaining house, other than Hampton Court, where Oliver Cromwell and his family are known to have lived. The present east wing represents what is left of the original 13th century building. Some 750 years old, the house has a varied history. In the 1840s it was a public house aptly called 'The Cromwell Arms' and from 1905 to 1986 it was the vicarage for the adjoining St. Mary's Church. Inside, several rooms have been refurbished in Cromwellian style and an audio-visual presentation gives an insight into the domestic, military and political aspects of his life.

Both the Cathedral and the surrounding fens have played a major role in the history of Ely. The Fens' influence is even reflected in the city's name: Ely was once known as 'Elge' or 'Elig' because of the large number of eels which could be caught in the surrounding fenland (Elig meaning eel island).

Ely, however, owes its existence to St. Etheldreda who founded a religious community on the hill-top site in the 7th century but it was not until 1081 that building of the present **Cathedral** was begun by the Normans. Undoubtedly, the most outstanding feature of this fine example

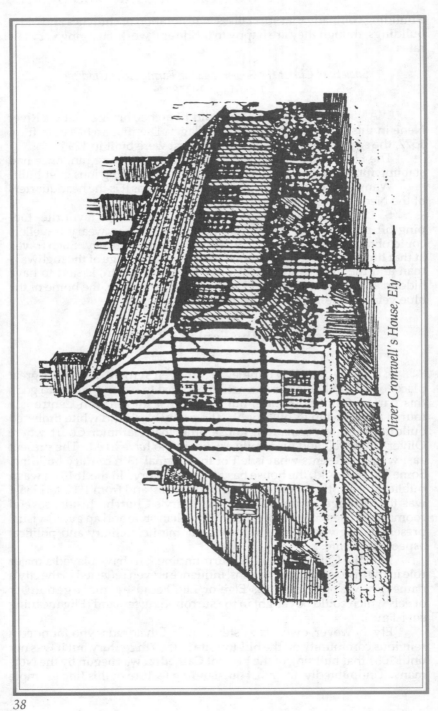

Oliver Cromwell's House, Ely

of Romanesque architecture is the Octagon and Lantern, built to replace the Norman tower which collapsed in 1322. They took 30 years and 8 huge oaks to build! Its framework is unique in the world, estimated to weigh 400 tons, and once included a set of bells. It is a medieval engineering feat still much admired by modern architects and builders. Also in the Cathedral are the **Brass Rubbing Centre** and **Stained Glass Museum**.

Near the river is **The Maltings**, a building which dates back to 1868 when it was constructed for malting barley (using high temperatures to cause the barley to sprout before it could be taken to the brewery). In 1971 it was converted into the delightful, attractive building seen today and is used as a public exhibition and conference centre, cinema and serves drinks, meals and snacks. The riverside walk in front of The Maltings is known as Quai D'Orsay, and was named shortly after the twinning of East Cambridgeshire District with the town of Orsay in France in the early 1980s.

AROUND ELY

WISBECH, one of the larger Fenland towns, lies in the northernmost corner of Cambridgeshire and it was not far from here that the luckless King John lost his baggage train together with a King's fortune in The Wash in 1216.

There was once a Norman castle in Wisbech, built in 1086, complete with moat and drawbridge. The castle is long gone but its impact is felt today. On the old fortress site now stands The Castle, a Regency villa, and the whole of the centre of town has a circular layout. Two crescents of fine Georgian houses run to the north and south of the Castle grounds. Also many houses built where the castle moat once was are now suffering from severe subsidence.

Wisbech has had a museum for over 150 years, and the present building was opened in 1847. There is a large collection of Continental and British pottery and porcelain, including a Sevres breakfast service once owned by Napoleon and a Burmese Buddha. The anti-slavery campaigner, Thomas Clarkson, came from Wisbech and the museum includes material gathered by him as evidence against the trade, as well as objects collected by a local man on the first European expedition up the Niger. A memorial to Clarkson stands beside the old bridge.

The Georgian theatre in Alexandra Road was built in 1793 and remained in use as a theatre for just over one hundred years. Since then it has had a chequered career as a school, a tent maker's and a church but, in recent years, live theatre has been re-introduced.

On the other side of the River Nene is the **Old Market**, now a neat garden laid out on the site of former shops which were demolished after the disastrous flood of 1978. The Old Market describes this triangular space surrounded by fine Georgian buildings which testify to the golden days of the river trade.

Wisbech Castle

THE FENS

Far removed from the hustle and bustle of modern life, the Fens are like a breath of fresh air. Extending over much of Cambridgeshire from the Wash, these flat, fenland fields contain some of the richest soil in England and the villages such as Soham and small towns like Ely rise out of the landscape on low hills.

Before the Fens were drained this was a world of mists, marshes and bogs; of small islands, inhabited by independent folk, their livelihood the fish and waterfowl of this eerie watery place. The region is full of legends of web-footed people, ghosts and witchcraft.

Today's landscape is a result of the ingenuity of man, his constant desire to tame the wilderness and create farmland. This fascinating story spans the centuries, from the earliest Roman and Anglo-Saxon times, when the first embankments and drains were constructed to lessen the frequent flooding.

Throughout the Middle Ages large areas of marsh and fen were reclaimed, with much of the work undertaken by the monasteries. By the early 17th century the attention turned to the remaining undrained fens. In 1630, the Dutch engineer Cornelius Vermuyden was commissioned by the Earl of Bedford to drain the remaining wetlands of Cambridgeshire. The significant influence of the Dutch lives on in the architecture and place names of the Fens.

Local opposition was considerable as the systematic drainage of the land threatened the traditional ways of life of the Fen dwellers and their fierce resistance, and destruction of the drainage works, earned them the name 'Fen Tigers'.

Today the Fens have a sophisticated network of drains, embankments and electric pumps which are capable of raising thousands of gallons of water a second to protect the land from the ever present threat of rain and tide.

The history of the drainage can be seen at **Stretham Beam Engine** and the **Prickwillow Land Drainage museum**, both near Ely, or at one of the many other small museums that seem to appear in each fenland town.

The pleasure of cruising in the Fens lies in the open, uncrowded waterways, recognised by seasoned boaters as probably the most atmospheric in England. The most popular waterways are the River Great Ouse which wends its way from Huntingdon through Ely and northwards to King's Lynn, and the Nene-Ouse navigation link, connecting Peterborough with the Great Ouse near Downham Market, passing through March and on to Outwell and Upwell.

North Brink, along the river from Old Market, is considered by many to be Wisbech's most outstanding feature and it was described by Pevsner as one of the finest Georgian brick streets in England. The buildings form a beautiful composition of Georgian designs which tend to be less grand as one gets further from the town. Among these buildings is the **North Brink Brewery**. Built in 1790, the frontage of this classical Georgian brewery has remained almost unchanged to the present day. The Brewery was purchased by its present owners, Elgoods, in 1878 and still supplies fifty public houses in the Wisbech area.

Further along the river bank, a little further away from the town centre, is **Peckover House**. This National Trust property, open to the public from April to October, has well furnished rooms, a fine staircase and an ornate garden containing an orangery and many rare specimens, for which it is justly famous. The house also contains an excellent collection of Cornwallis family portraits and an exhibition on the life and work of Wisbech-born Octavia Hill, a co-founder of the National Trust. Built in 1722, Peckover House is a Grade I listed building which makes it of outstanding national importance.

MARCH Once an island surrounded by marshes March grew and prospered as a trading and religious centre, a minor port and, in more recent times, as a market town, administrative and railway centre.

The influence of the railway has led to a large expansion north of the river where a huge marshalling yard was built in the 1930s.

The church, St. Wendreda's, named after the town's own Saint, is famous for its spectacular double hammer-beam roof which reflects the medieval prosperity of the town. There are some 120 carved angels decorating the beams. The roof represents the zenith of the carpenter's and carver's skill and is not merely decorative; it is a highly sophisticated piece of engineering. The roof was even mentioned by Dorothy Sayers in her novel 'The Nine Tailors'. St Wendreda's was described by Poet Laureate Sir John Betjeman as "worth cycling 40 miles in headwind to see"!

West End, an attractive path flanked on one side by cottages and on the other by the river and town park, is well worth a stroll along.

On the outskirts of March, and well signposted from the A141, is the **Stags Holt Farm Park and Stud**. Stags Holt offers a unique insight into an area not generally associated with tourism. The ancient parkland and Victorian farm buildings certainly provide an ideal backdrop for a day in the country. Among the many horses here are Suffolk Punches, a rare breed with a unique history spanning almost 300 years back to an ancestor known as Crisps Horse of Ufford, thought by some to be a Lincolnshire Trotting Stallion. Horses, however, only make up part of the story at Stags Holt, the collections of harness, carts, wagons, implements and hand tools are fascinating too.

CHATTERIS. A friendly little market town, Chatteris marks the centre of a nationally famous area of intensive arable farming based on the immensely fertile black fen soil. The Old and New Hundred Foot Rivers, to the south and east of the town, are two notable drainage

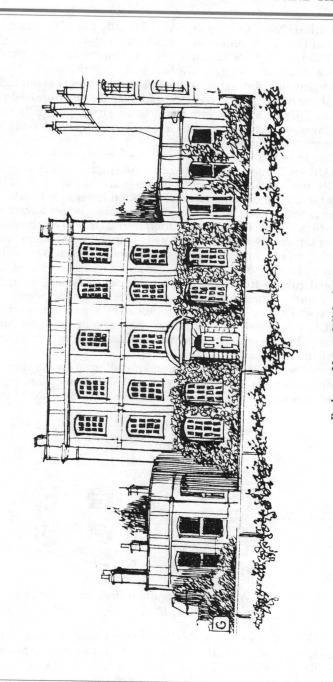

Peckover House, Wisbech

schemes.

Chatteris Museum has displays of locally found flint instruments through to Roman jewellery and medieval pottery. A splendid set of mobile stocks, used for holding petty criminals are preserved here, together with a wide range of material illustrating the town's past. There are also many old photographs, posters and handbills exhibited which help to show how Fenland has changed over the last hundred years.

RAMSEY. Once an important town surrounding its medieval abbey, Ramsey's main street, the Great Whyte, is exceptionally wide as a stream once ran down its length.

Now in its 18th year of business, the family run **BOW WINDOW RESTAURANT** goes from strength to strength. Occupying what is reputedly the oldest premises in Ramsey and dating from 1460, The Hartley family are certainly well established here, as is his chef Simon Harding who has been with them sixteen years. The restaurant can seat up to sixty people so in addition to their normal day to day business they also cater for small weddings and business meetings. Diners can choose from either an à la carte menu or a supper menu which is available from Tuesday to Friday. The a la carte menu features an excellent choice of traditional cuisine from which you could select for example: Sauté of Lambs Kidney Chasseur au Crouton or Cornets of Scotch smoked Salmon with Prawns 'Marie Rose', followed by a main course of Poached Fillet of Lemon Sole 'Bow Window', Noisette of English Lamb with Cranberry Tartlet and finish with a selection from the home-made dessert list.

A further selection of lighter meals is offered on the supper menu supplemented with blackboard specials. With such an established clientele, booking is recommended. Closed Sunday and Monday.

The Bow Window Restaurant, 6 High Street, Ramsey
Tel: 01487 812945

WISTOW. Conveniently situated for a holiday or a short break in this fascinating area is **POINTERS**, a large impressive farmhouse close to the village of Wistow. The property boasts a collection of ornamental

North Brink, Wisbech

ducks and pheasants, ponies, horses and sheep. There are three guest rooms available, one twin room with en-suite facilities and two doubles, all comfortably appointed. Breakfast is excellent, and an extensive evening menu is also available. Guests have the use of the luxurious lounge and may walk the 15 acres of landscaped gardens which have recently won a well deserved award for conservation work.

Pointers Bed and Breakfast, Wistow Tel: 01487 822366

CHAPTER THREE

KING'S LYNN & WEST NORFOLK

Custom House, King's Lynn

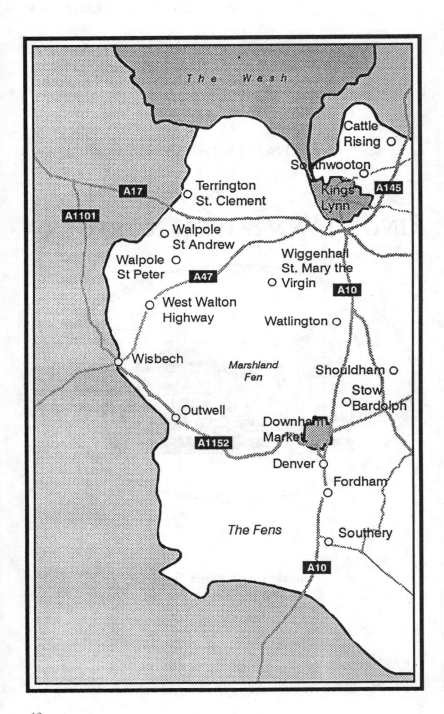

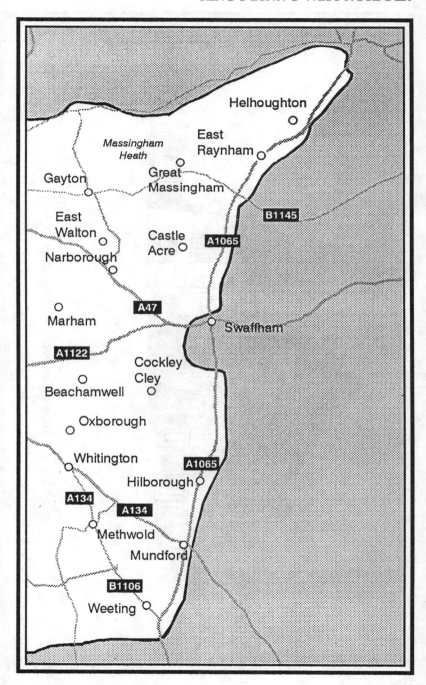

Ruins of Castle Acre, Nr Kings Lynn

CHAPTER THREE

KING'S LYNN & WEST NORFOLK

King's Lynn and The Great Ouse

KING'S LYNN. Situated on the eastern bank of the River Great Ouse at the southernmost end of The Wash, King's Lynn is Norfolk's third largest town.

For centuries this ancient sea-port was the gateway to the Midlands and an important trade-link with the Continent. First mentioned in the Domesday Book as the harbour of Lena (from the Celtic word 'lindo', meaning lake), it became known as Lynn Episcopi or 'Bishop's Lynn' during the Middle Ages when the town was officially founded by Herbert de Losinga, the first bishop of Norwich. In 1537, after the Dissolution of the Monasteries, Henry VIII firmly quashed this ecclesiastical association by granting it a charter and it took on its present name of Lynn Regis, or King's Lynn.

A previous charter had been granted by King John who visited the town in 1205 and it was on the occasion of his later visit in 1216, prior to his final trip to Newark, that he 'lost his jewels in the Wash'. When travelling between his estates King John tended to take many of his personal treasures with him and, after enjoying the local hospitality here in September of 1216, he decided to carry on to Swineshead. As his convoy traversed the estuary between Cross Keys and Long Sutton, the tide swept in unexpectedly quickly and the royal wagons became embroiled in the treacherous quicksands. An historical event that has caused much merriment in history lessons at school, sounding as it does like an unfortunate mishap in the launderette.

Over on the Lincolnshire border, the King must have lost much of his spirit as he witnessed his beloved treasure sinking below the waters. The Crown Jewels, his formal regalia, goblets and candelabra, his coronation robe and the Sword of Tristram given to him by his grandmother all disappeared within a matter of minutes. Presumably, these treasures still lie out at sea waiting for some lucky diver to recover them and, to add insult to injury, poor John contracted dysentery whilst in the town and later died at Newark. An alternative story claims that he fell ill at Swineshead after being given a dish of peaches and new ale and some believe he was poisoned by a monk who had heard that the King intended to raise the price of bread.

The heart of King's Lynn encapsulates the Georgian era with many charming houses from that period but it retains the feel of a much older harbour town. Architectural treasures such as the National Trust-owned **St George's Guildhall** can be seen in King Street; it is distinctively built of flint in a chequer-board design and is reputedly the oldest hall in England, built around 1406. Shakespeare is said to have performed here and this splendid building is still used for civic functions today.

The parish church of **St Margaret's** dates back to around 1100 and was founded by Bishop Herbert de Losinga. Particularly eye catching are the watermarks on the western towers. In 1953, a tremendous storm combined with an unusually high tide succeeded in rising the North Sea way beyond its normal level. Vast tracts of land from Yorkshire down to the Thames area and into Kent were affected and the entire east coast was flooded. King's Lynn itself was engulfed and the flood certainly left its mark on St Margaret's.

Other architectural highlights to look out for include the handsome **Custom House**, built in 1683 on the banks of the Purfleet, and the magnificent 15th century **South Gates** which stand proud at the entrance to the town. Buildings such as these, together with its many fascinating warehouses and narrow streets, all add to the charm of King's Lynn. Though it is by no means a pretty town, thanks to the efforts of the King's Lynn Preservation Trust, many of the town's more interesting buildings have been saved.

For those with a love of the sea **TRUE'S YARD** in North Street is a real treat to visit. The cottages with their lobster pots and fishing nets strewn abut outside really evoke the traditional feel of an old fishing village. Taking its name from Sir William True who owned the properties in 1789, this is the last remaining fisherman's yard in the town, and the North End Trust was specifically set up in 1987 to save it. Much restoration work was carried out, and today the Yard is often visited by school children and students as part of special educational projects, giving them a fascinating insight into the fishing trade of King's Lynn.

True's Yard, North Street, King's Lynn Tel: 01553 770479

Among the attractions here are a 19th century fishing smack, a museum, a gift shop and a tea-room. Nearby is the ancient Fisher Fleet from where a variety of fishing boats ply their daily trade. This would also be a wonderful place to spend an hour or two if you would like to trace your ancestry in the area, and plenty of help is on hand to assist you in this. Nearby stands the lovely mediaeval chapel of St Nicholas, the patron saint of fishermen, watching over the yard and its people. Here, chandlers, boat builders, rope and sail makers plied their trade at the turn of the century, before the decline of the fishing industry closed that particular chapter in the history of the town. It is good to know that there are still people out there who care enough about the past to dedicate their time and efforts to keeping this important part of it alive. A further expansion programme is in hand for 1997 which includes extending the facilities to include the shop, tea rooms and two extra galleries.

In one of the walls of a house on the northwest corner of the Tuesday Market there is a curious brick, shaped like a diamond with a heart carved in the centre. Legend has it that an unfortunate woman named Margaret Read was pronounced a witch and condemned to be burnt at the stake in the market place. As the fires consumed her, they say that her heart erupted from her body and hit the wall in this spot and was later seen heading off down the street before bounding into the Great Ouse!

The local arts scene can be discovered at the **King's Lynn Arts Centre**. The events and exhibitions change regularly and it is certainly worth turning up to see what musical or artistic show is being staged here that particular week. Workshops and courses on landscape painting are available throughout the year. Those interested should write to the King's Lynn Arts Centre, 27-29 King Street, King's Lynn, Norfolk PE30 1HA for details prior to visiting the area.

King's Lynn, along with the surrounding area of West Norfolk, has a rich and fascinating history, the story of which is told in two excellent museums, Lynn Museum and The Town House Museum of Lynn Life.

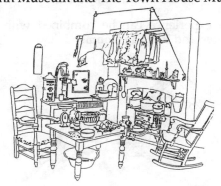

Lynn Museum, Market Street, King's Lynn Tel: 01553 775001

Lynn Museum is housed in a former non-conformist chapel, which was built in 1859 and is itself noteworthy for having a spire. The interior of the museum has been transformed to provide spacious and modern galleries which house exhibitions and displays of natural history, archaeology and local history. The museum has something to interest all age groups and is open from 10 am to 5 pm Tuesday to Saturday. There is wheelchair access throughout.

The **Town House Museum of Lynn Life** is situated in a handsome Victorian house which is set in the heart of the 'Old Town' district, next to the Guildhall. It tells the story of the merchants, tradesmen and families who, for nine hundred years, have made the town such a prosperous place. The key periods in the town's history, from the Middle Ages to present day, are all illustrated by means of room displays. These contain items and fittings which would have been in common usage at the time and provide a fascinating journey through history, one that really brings the past to life. Open from Monday to Saturday from 10 am to 5 pm and Sunday, 2 pm to 5 pm, in the Summertime; and Monday to Saturday, 10 am to 4 pm, in the Winter. Closed all Bank Holidays. There is wheelchair access available to the ground floor only.

The Edwardian Kitchen

The museum experience can be combined with a visit to the adjoining **Gaol House** and **Regalia Rooms**.

The Town House Museum of Lynn Life, 46 Queen Street, King's Lynn
Tel: 01553 773450

Caithness Crystal is based on the outskirts of the town at Oldmellow Road on the Hardwick Industrial Estate and is well worth a visit if you wish to purchase the beautiful crystal ware on offer there. A conducted tour will take you on a fascinating trip around the factory, allowing you a closer look at the intricate art of glass blowing, hand cutting and the skill of the polisher. After your tour and an opportunity to purchase some of the fine work on display (which you can have engraved while you wait) you may like to relax over a cream tea. The centre is open from March to December and no booking is required.

STUART HOUSE HOTEL AND RESTAURANT is situated down a leafy lane just a few minutes walk from the centre of King's Lynn. This charming, period house, standing in attractive, well established grounds, was purchased by David Armes in 1995. Following an extensive reno-vation programme the hotel now offers the very best in comfortable hospitality, with much of the original style and character of the old house remaining. The 19 guest bedrooms are individually decorated and furnished and most have en-suite bathrooms, tea and coffee making facilities, satellite television and telephone. The splendid honeymoon suite boasts a superb four-poster bed and Jacuzzi. The public rooms at Stuart House are equally well-appointed; the Victorian bar stocks three excellent real ales and an extensive range of malt whiskies and the Stuart Restaurant provides a full à la carte and table d'hôte menu. Stuart House Hotel, with its friendly and relaxed atmosphere and emphasis on quality and good value, is an ideal place to stay.

Stuart House Hotel, 35 Goodwins Road, King's Lynn
Tel: 01553 772169 Fax: 01553 774788

If you are looking for a quiet place to stay in this delightful area, then look no further than **THE BEECHES GUEST HOUSE**, which is situated in a secluded leafy road just off the town centre. This attractive Victorian townhouse dates back to 1880 and has only been owned by three persons in all that time. Its splendid condition stands as testimony to the standard of its construction. The current owner, Vivienne Shaw has recently had the original railings restored, and these, together with

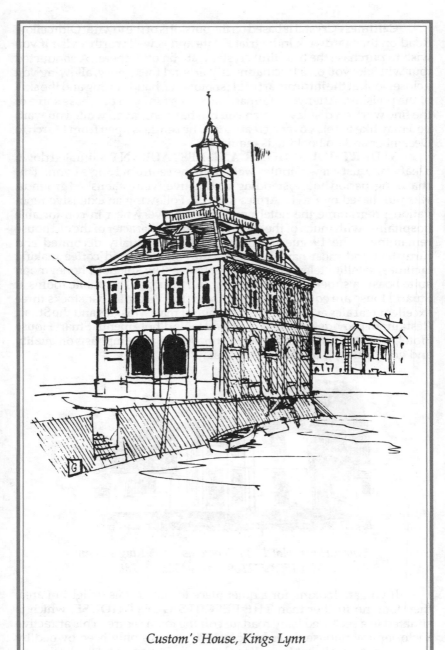

Custom's House, Kings Lynn

the beautiful garden create a fine setting for what is a deservedly popular place to stay. The guest house has eight bedrooms, four of which have en-suite facilities. Breakfast is excellent, Vivienne is renowned for her wonderful home cooking. It comes as no surprise to learn that The Beeches has an ETB 2 Crowns Commended Award.

The Beeches Guest House, 2 Guanock Terrace, King's Lynn
Tel: 01553 766577 Fax: 01553 776664

AROUND KING'S LYNN

CASTLE RISING. The impressive castle, with its huge earthworks, is a very popular local tourist attraction and the approach to the keep is via a brick bridge spanning a surprisingly high "ditch". The steep flights of stairs leading up to the interior of the keep and its splendid position on a lofty mound to the south of the romantically named village of Castle Rising, all give the impression of a virtually unassailable stronghold.

Built in the 12th century, the castle has enjoyed a distinguished history with many kings and queens having stayed there. Open daily except Mondays in winter; for those who enjoy the spectacle of knights on horseback take note that medieval tournaments are held here during the summer months.

Before the sea receded during the Middle Ages, it was possible to navigate the River Babingley from the Wash to Castle Rising and, indeed, the village was a busy port at that time. It remained an important town right up until the 17th century and one of the best buildings in the village, **Trinity Hospital**, dates from that era. A group of low, red brick almshouses, founded in 1614 by Henry Howard, the Earl of Northampton, to provide accommodation for poor spinsters, the hospital continues to operate as such today.

TERRINGTON ST CLEMENT is set right in the heart of the Terrington Marsh, a lush area of farmland. A sure sign of the village's prosperity is the splendid church of St Clement's. Sturdy and ornate, the internal fittings are superb, with a Georgian screen, various features from the Jacobean period and an impressive 17th century font cover with beautiful illustrations from both the Old and New Testaments.

With such fertile land around, it is not surprising to find **The African Violet Centre**, a nursery unique to Britain which specialises in African Violets, at Terrington St Clement. Founded in 1970 by author and broadcaster, the Reverend Tony Clements, some quarter of a million African violets are grown here annually, in a wide range of colour and type. The plant breeding programme ensures a constant stream of new varieties, and these may be seen and purchased both at the Centre itself and at the principal flower shows held throughout Britain each year.

WALPOLE ST PETER. One of the great delights of exploring this part of the county is discovering the wonderful churches scattered throughout the local villages. The church at Walpole St Peter is thought by many to be the most beautiful of all the churches in England and indeed its glorious interior makes it more deserving than most of the name 'Cathedral of the Fens'.

As well as its outstanding beauty, St Peter's also has a rather poor effigy of a local character known as 'Tom Hickathrift'. Said to have been a giant, the grave at Tilney where he is purported to be buried would put him at around 7ft tall. When still a young lad of 10 years of age, he had apparently already reached a height of 6ft and yet it seems that he was more renowned for his stupidity than any other distinguishing feature. He was born during the reign of William the Conqueror and there are various accounts of his great strength. One of his tasks was to deliver beer kegs to Wisbech from King's Lynn and he decided to take a short-cut across land belonging to a fearsome giant. Predictably enough, the giant emerged from his lair to challenge the intruder and, after a fight of epic proportions, Tom eventually defeated the creature. Discovering a hoard of treasure in the giant's cave, Tom came out of his adventure both victorious and rich and, from that day on, locals always referred to this 'great' hero as Mr Thomas Hickathrift!

WALPOLE ST ANDREW's church has an intriguing little chamber, most probably an anchorite's cell, set in the west wall and ,like so many places of worship in the region, the pure light from the Marsh streams through the windows and lights up the interior to great effect.

WATLINGTON. Those looking for exceptional bed and breakfast accommodation in beautiful West Norfolk should make a point of finding **ANDEL HOUSE**, the luxurious home of Anne and Derek Hurrell. This impressive establishment is housed in a refurbished 19th century public house which sits on the banks of the River Great Ouse between the villages of Watlington and Wiggenhall St Mary Magdalen, 6 miles south of King's Lynn. Now fully modernised, the house is open all year round and has easy access to miles of lovely riverside walks. The three beautifully-appointed guest bedrooms all look out onto the enclosed rear garden and are furnished to a very high standard. All have en suite bathrooms, and are equipped with remote-control colour TVs, tea/coffee making facilities and hair dryers. There is also a comfortable guest lounge and a spacious lounge bar, both ideal places to relax. Anne and

Derek provide the warmest of welcomes and the finest Norfolk hospitality. As well as serving an excellent English breakfast, they offer delicious home-cooked evening meals, if required. Andel House is English Tourist Board two crowns commended, and has been awarded 4Qs by the AA. Special off-season breaks available.

Andel House, Station Road, Watlington
Tel: 01553 811515 Fax: 01553 811429

SHOULDHAM. It is hard to believe that sleepy Shouldham was once a busy market town with two annual fairs and boasted a Gilbertine priory, a grammar school and the Silver Well, a famous natural spring. Today, it is a much quieter place with its collection of old dwellings, some thatched and some with red or blue pantiles, clustered round the village green. From the abundance of archaeological finds made in the immediate area, it would appear that Shouldham has been inhabited since Neolithic times.

STOW BARDOLPH. As well as having a splendid park, fine dwellings and lovingly restored Hall, Holy Trinity Church at Stow Bardolph has a most amusing and unusual effigy made of wax. Inside a large mahogany cupboard is a life-sized figure of Sarah Hare. A beauty she most certainly was not: she appears to be covered with boils. The daughter of Sir Thomas Hare, Sarah died in 1744 as a result, so the story goes, of pricking her finger while sewing on a Sunday. Apparently the figure is remarkably like its original, and the gown she wears was chosen by her sometime before her death.

DOWNHAM MARKET. Once the site for the great horse fairs, this striking market town stands on the very edge of the Fen and is built of the distinctive brick and Carr- (or iron-) stone. One of the finest examples of this can be seen at **Dial House** in Railway Road (now a guest house), which was built in the late 1600s.

High as the town is, the parish church is situated on even higher ground and is well worth a visit to admire the splendid glass chandelier which dates back to around 1730. Another feature of the town much loved by postcard manufacturers is the elegant if overly embellished cast-iron clock tower in the market place. This was built by William

Cunliffe in 1878 and its backdrop of attractive cottages makes the perfect setting for a holiday snap.

THE CROWN HOTEL, right in the market square of Downham Market, is a typical English inn. Dating back to the 17th century, this old coaching inn has the lot: low beams, flagstone floors, a welcoming landlord, good honest ales, excellent traditional food and lively conversation. Looking more or less the same as it did a hundred years ago, the oak-panelled bar, itself made from old sherry casks, is a cosy place for a quiet drink. Snacks are available in the less formal bar but, for something more formal, the Stables Restaurant or The Fox Room (a delightful, low beamed Dickensian parlour) offer a wonderful, traditional menu of roast joints, home-made pies and delicious puddings. With eleven comfortable guest bedrooms reached by taking one of the two fine Jacobean staircases and unique garden seating in the old alleyway where the coaches came through to the back of the inn, The Crown Hotel is a wonderful taste of old England with up to date facilities.

The Crown Hotel, Bridge Street, Downham Market Tel: 01366 382322

Viscount Horatio Nelson was born in the Norfolk village of Burnham Thorpe and came to Downham Market to be educated, while one of his school friends, Captain George William Manby, lived both in the town and at Denver Sluice. It was Manby who invented the life saving shore-to-ship rocket line. He served for some years as Barrack-master at the naval yards in Yarmouth and wrote extensively on methods of life saving, criminal law and other diverse subjects.

Close to the centre of Downham Market and situated on the main road towards Denver, **THE OLD SHOP** is a charming and homely bed and breakfast establishment owned and personally run by June and Eric Roberts. Originally three cottages dating back to 1815, the property was turned into shops some time later and, until the Roberts came here in 1988, it was still a general store. A delightful house, with sloping walls and crooked ceilings, there are lots of twists and turns as you move from one of the old cottages to another. As well as having three comfortable, en-suite letting bedrooms, there is also a guest lounge and an evening meal is available by prior arrangement. In such a short time, June and

Eric have gained an enviable reputation for the high standard of The Old Shop and it is an excellent place to stay where you will certainly feel relaxed and at home.

The Old Shop, 24 London Road, Downham Market Tel: 01366 382051

DENVER. Two miles west of Denver village, towards the Great Ouse, is the delightfully situated **Denver Sluice**, next to the Jenyns Arms pub and just upstream from the river's tidal limit. From this point, it's possible to reach over 200 miles of inland waterways from Cambridge in the south, to Bedford in the west.

As part of the scheme to drain around 20,000 acres of land owned by the Duke of Bedford, the Dutch engineer, Cornelius Vermuyden, built the first sluice at Denver in 1651. Various modifications were made to the system over the years but the basic principle remains the same, and the oldest surviving sluice, built in 1834, is still in use today. Opened in 1964, the new Great Denver Sluice runs parallel with this, and together they control the flow of a large complex of rivers and drainage channels and are able to divert floodwaters into the Flood Relief Channel that runs alongside the Great Ouse.

The two great drainage cuts constructed by Vermuyden are known as the Old and New Bedford Rivers, and the strip of land between them, no more than 1,000 yards wide at any one point, is called the Ouse Washes. This is deliberately allowed to flood during the winter months so that the fields on either side remain dry. The drains run side by side for 13 1/2 miles, from Denver to Earith in Cambridgeshire, and this has become a favourite route for walkers, with a rich variety of bird, animal and insect life for naturalists to enjoy.

DAYMOND BOAT HIRE is just upstream from the river's tidal limit and from here you can look out at the swans, and if you are very lucky, the occasional seal. From this point, it is also possible to reach over 200 miles of inland waterways from Cambridge in the south, to Bedford in the west.

Frank Daymond has greatly expanded his fleet since he established his boat hire operation here in 1986. Now able to cater for everything from an hour's trip in a rowing boat to a full week's hire of a four berth beaver canal boat, the most unique feature of Daymond Boat Hire is that the prices have remained the same, or gone down, since it was started. A small family firm, Frank prides himself on the standard of the craft and the quality of personal service.

Daymond Boat Hire, 4 Spruce Road, Clackclose Park, Downham Market
Tel: 01366 384404

North Breckland

INTRODUCTION TO BRECKLAND

The **Breckland** area of East Anglia covers some 300 square miles of sandy heathland which have been liberally planted with Scots and Corsican pine by the Forestry Commission to stabilise the thin soil. Densely populated in prehistoric times, the original deciduous woodland was converted to open heath. The region, in fact, takes its name from these small areas of cultivated land called 'brecks' or 'brakes'. However, by the Middle Ages, the poor quality of the soil led to a reduction in the number of settlers and the villages concentrated on the fringes of the heathland.

One of the strangest natural features of Breckland are the many meres or pools that appear regularly throughout the region. No matter what the mean rainfall has been, a mere will well up seemingly overnight and then later disappear, all subject to the level of the water table in the chalk below the heath. William the Conqueror set up camp in this wild country while ferreting out the native Saxons under the leadership of Hereward the Wake.

AROUND NORTH BRECKLAND

WEETING. Although Weeting village is undistinguished (apart from its 12th century moated castle which is maintained by English Heritage), the surrounding area is rich in archaeological sites; this is, after all, the earliest inhabited part of Norfolk. **Weeting Heath** is a marvellous spot for birdwatchers, although birds can only be observed from the many hides dotted around this lovely part of Breckland and permits may be obtained from the warden from April to August. The area is also well known for its plant and animal life as well as its great variety of birds .

Grimes Graves, 3 miles east of Weeting, are not graves at all but a series of Neolithic flint mines which are now managed by English Heritage. The massive site covers around 30 acres and contains over 300 pits and shafts dug by early man using deer antlers as picks some 4,000 years ago. It is probable that Breckland was at that time covered by an immense oak forest and flint tools would have been in great demand by

Stone Age farmers for clearing the land. Some of the shafts at Grimes Graves have been excavated and visitors can descend one of these to see the galleries 30ft below. There is also a museum which houses artifacts that have come to light during the excavations, and the surrounding area has been designated a Site of Special Scientific Interest due to the great variety of bird life to be found there.

MUNDFORD. This is a large Breckland village on the banks of the River Wissey. The flint-built cottages are clustered around the village green and, to the west of Mundford, a Saxon mass grave has been discovered.

THE CROWN HOTEL, an old and attractive building overlooking the village green at Mundford, is of considerable interest in the 'flat' lands of Norfolk because it is actually built into the side of a hill! That aside, the hotel, which dates back to 1652, has had a chequered history over the years. Starting life as a hunting inn, it has also played host to the local Magistrates court and its Old Court Restaurant, until recently, was a doctor's waiting room. Today, the Crown Hotel retains much of its original charm and character and, with the guidance of owner Barry Walker, offers good old fashioned hospitality. A lovely place to stay and to dine at where informality is the order of the day; there are two delightful restaurants, serving excellent cuisine, two bars and six comfortable en-suite bedrooms. A super place to bring the whole family where you will be guaranteed a relaxing and enjoyable stay.

The Crown Hotel, Crown Road, Mundford Tel: 01842 878233

OXBOROUGH. Before the Black Death in the 14th century, Oxborough village (the Hall has adopted the shorter spelling of the name) was situated a mile away on the River Wissey and was once an important port exporting grain and agricultural produce. Today, the large green at the centre of the village is the location for three interesting buildings: Oxburgh Hall itself; the 14th century parish church of St John the Evangelist which is famous for its 16th century early Renaissance terracotta monuments in the chantry chapel; and the historic Bedingfeld Arms inn which was probably once a coach house to the Hall.

A little bit tricky to find, but well worth the effort, is **Oxburgh Hall**, a National Trust property lying midway between Thetford and King's Lynn. To reach it, turn off the A134 at Stoke Ferry and drive a couple of miles north-east in the direction of Swaffham. Oxburgh Hall is a beautiful moated house, built around a courtyard by the Bedingfeld family in 1482 and remodelled many times since. The entrance is guarded by a massive Tudor gatehouse. From its roof, it is possible to see for miles across the surrounding Norfolk countryside.

In the courtyard, look out for the large sundial; the face was refigured in 1965. The internal rooms reflect the varied history of the house; the King's Room (so called because Henry VII stayed here in 1487) is cool and starkly furnished; the Saloon is a fine example of 18th century neo-classical opulence, and the library has a comfortable mid-Victorian feel. There is also a fine exhibition of needlework hangings some of which were worked by Mary Queen of Scots during her captivity in England. These hangings, formerly a family heirloom, are now lent back to the house by the Victoria and Albert Museum.

Outside, it's worth making a circuit of the moat before visiting the chapel, with its magnificent altarpiece, and the garden, with its orchard, beautiful herbaceous borders and immaculate French parterre.

Oxburgh Hall, Oxborough Tel: 01366 328258

HILBOROUGH. Lord Nelson's father was Rector and lived in the old Rectory for a while at Hilborough before moving to Burnham Thorpe where Lord Nelson was born. THE SWAN INN, an old coaching house, was built in 1718 and was originally part of the Hilborough estate. Today this is a traditional family pub offering the kind of atmosphere and welcome which is synonymous with this part of the country. The building also houses the local Post Office!

The Swan Inn, Hilborough Tel: 01760 756380

Geoff and Shirley are justly proud of the fine reputation which their pub justly enjoys. The warm, peaceful atmosphere of the interior is enhanced by the original oak beams, wood burning stove and open fires: this is the ideal spot to enjoy a quiet drink of one of the five real ales which are stocked or a tasty and filling home cooked pub meal in the characterful restaurant. Morning coffee and afternoon tea are also served.

The pub is open all day long in the summertime and has its own beer garden. If you are looking for somewhere to stay for a while, then look no further, for the Swan Inn has two guest rooms offering B&B of a high standard. The Swan Inn is situated on the main A1065, between Mundford and Swaffham.

COCKLEY CLEY. The charming hamlet of Cockley Cley (pronounced 'Cly') is home to a faithful reconstruction of an Iron Age village that was destroyed by the Romans around 60AD. The **Iceni Village** stands on the original site as was erected in 1971.

A diverted stream forms a defensive rectangular moat around the timber palisade which encloses the thatched huts and long houses. One of these houses a classroom where children can learn more of how the tribe lived.

The museum complex also features a cottage which illustrates what life was like in the 17th century for a wealthy farmer's family. The forge houses **The East Anglian Museum** where you can see a fine collection of agricultural engines and farm implements. Alongside the stream is a nature trail which is well worth exploring, it now boasts a birdwatching hide from which an incredibly wide variety of uncommon birds can be observed. Visitors can also enjoy a refreshing cup of tea and snack at the newly built tea room.

Iceni Village, Cockley Cley Estate, Cockley Cley Hall Tel: 01760 721339

BEACHAMWELL. St Mary's Church at Beachamwell is a delightful thatched church with a round Saxon tower to which an octagonal top was later added. During the 14th century, when the church was being rebuilt, the stonemasons scratched the figures of a demon and a woman on one of the columns - they can still be seen today. To the north of the village is part of the 'Devil's Dyke', an ancient earthwork which is generally thought to be a territorial boundary dating back to Saxon times.

THE GREAT DANE'S HEAD pub in Beachamwell is charmingly situated overlooking the village green and there is a large garden to the rear of the building. Jenny and Frank White, your hosts, came here from

Derbyshire some time ago and have created a typical English pub where good food, excellent ales and wines and friendly hospitality are guaranteed. The restaurant here is cosy and intimate and the menu, prepared by Jenny, features local produce and specialises in game and locally caught fish. An interesting and imaginative wine list, supplied by a wine merchant, has something to suit all tastes and there is always a range of excellent beers and ales on tap. The Great Dane's Head itself, has an interesting history; it was built around 1840 though the cellars are much older.

The Great Dane's Head, The Green, Beachamwell Tel: 01366 328443

NARBOROUGH. A charming village, enhanced by a picturesque bridge spanning the River Nar and by the old village mill which has been refurbished as a trout farm, Narborough also has the remains of an Iron Age settlement in the grounds of the Great Hall. Sir Henry Spelman who wrote the 'History of Sacrilege' lived at Narborough Hall and the parish church of All Saints has some splendid monuments to the Spelman family. Sir Henry was born in Congham and was High Sheriff of Norfolk in 1604. Along with several other ponderous tomes he also wrote the "Glossarium Archaiologicum" but more people may be familiar with his son Sir John Spelman's work on the life of King Alfred.

EAST WALTON. Strangely enough, the village of East Walton boasts an oven on its village green. However, this particular 'oven' is in fact an old wheelwright's oven, where the metal 'treads' or strips were heated and stretched before they were fitted on to the wooden waggon wheels, making them virtually indestructible. On the common to the west of the village (referred to as the Ramparts) there are some distinctive physical features attributable to the Ice Age. These 'pingos' were formed when great bubbles of ice expanded, pushing the earth aside and leaving hollows and mounds after the thaw. This created a boggy habitat where many rare species of plant now flourish.

CASTLE ACRE. Half way along the Peddars Way long-distance footpath stands the spectacular hillside village of Castle Acre, set around a green and standing within the outer Bailey of a ruined Norman Castle.

The original Castle, on a hill to the east of the village, was founded by William de Warenne, the Earl of Surrey, shortly after the Norman Conquest. Nothing more than a robust private dwelling, it was not seriously fortified until the middle of the 12th century.

Castle Acre is generally considered to be the 'jewel' of Norfolk's many picturesque villages. The approach from the south leads you through a narrow stone gateway (built in the 13th century to defend the northern entrance to the Castle) and on to the village green. Many of the attractive cottages are of local flint, much of it taken from the castle when it was abandoned, and modern building work is largely sympathetic.

In a grassy hollow to the west of the village is Castle Acre's other fascinating historic building, **Castle Acre Priory**, now in the care of English Heritage. Now in ruins, this superb 12th century priory still creates an imposing atmosphere. Many of the original priory buildings came through the Dissolution surprisingly intact, including large parts of the church, the Prior's Lodging, various agricultural buildings and the gatehouse.

It was at Castle Acre that the **Peddars Way** crossed the River Nar via a ford, taking travellers on to Holme-next-the-Sea. Unlikely as it may seem today, this little stream was, incidentally, once large enough for boats to navigate from the Wash.

Eating out in Castle Acre presents no problem thanks to the wonderful **CASTLEGATE RESTAURANT** in Stocks Green. Commanding one of the best positions in the village, this delightful eating place stands overlooking the green near the 18th century Ostrich Inn. It could be said that owners Rex and Alan have their fingers in a lot of pies, as they sell a tempting range of these, along with an impressive selection of more elaborate English and continental dishes. They are open seven days a week for breakfast, morning coffee, lunch and afternoon tea - a welcome relief for those seeking somewhere good to eat on a Sunday - with evening meals being served from Wednesday to Saturday.

Castlegate Restaurant, Stocks Green, Castle Acre
Tel: 01760 755340

GREAT MASSINGHAM. This is a peaceful little place where time seems to stand still. It is believed that the ponds on the village green, where ducks now harass passers-by for titbits, may be the pools once used to stock fish for the Augustinian priory that was founded at Great Massingham in the 13th century. Vestiges of this building (long since disappeared) can be seen at Abbey House and St Mary's Church is notable for its lovely 13th century south porch and 15th century hammerbeam roof.

EAST RAYNHAM. Raynham Hall in the village of East Raynham is home to an intriguing ghost story. The 'Brown Lady' is said to roam about the estate - a rather terrifying woman, elegantly dressed, but with no eyes! What is stranger is that she originally manifested herself at nearby Houghton Hall, but is thought to have moved to Raynham when the sister of Robert Walpole (who lived at Houghton) married Viscount Townshend. She has been sighted on several occasions, including once in 1926 when a member of the family saw her drifting down the stairs and 10 years later when she apparently posed for a photograph. However, it could be that she has since moved on, as a figure dressed in brown is reported to have been seen travelling the lanes between the villages of South and West Raynham.

Castle Rising

CHAPTER FOUR

NORTH NORFOLK - BABINGLEY TO WELLS-NEXT-THE-SEA

Norfolk Windmill

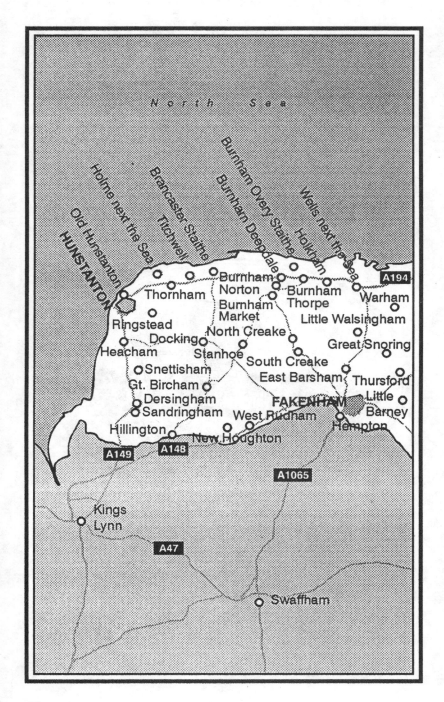

North Sea

HUNSTANTON
Old Hunstanton
Holme next the Sea
Brancaster Staithe
Titchwell
Burnham Deepdale
Burnham Overy Staithe
Holkham
Wells next the Sea

A194

Thornham
Burnham Norton
Burnham Thorpe
Warham

Ringstead
Burnham Market
Little Walsingham

Docking
North Creake
Great Snoring

Heacham
Stanhoe
South Creake

Snettisham
East Barsham
Thursford

Gt. Bircham
FAKENHAM
Little Barney

Dersingham
West Rudham
Hempton

Sandringham

Hillington
New Houghton

A149   A148

A1065

Kings Lynn

A47

Swaffham

CHAPTER FOUR

NORTH NORFOLK - BABINGLEY TO WELLS-NEXT-THE-SEA

Hunstanton and the Coastal Route

HUNSTANTON. Pronounced "Hunston", this is a charming Victorian seaside resort (the only one in East Anglia to face west, incidentally) with a fine sandy beach and rock pools and distinctive candy-striped cliffs. A layer of red chalk, then white and, finally, brown and yellow stone make these 60 ft high cliffs particularly interesting to geologists. At the northern end of the **Promenade**, next to the 1830 disused lighthouse, are the ruins of **St Edmund's Chapel** where Edmund, King of East Anglia, is reputed to have landed in 850AD.

The **Sea Life Centre** on the Promenade is a super place for children. The Ocean Tunnel gives visitors a unique opportunity to watch the varied and often weird forms of life that inhabit the British Isles without even getting wet!

Many of these creatures can be observed and handled in the 'Living Touch' rock pools and there is also an exciting audio-visual presentation which tells the story of man's involvement with the oceans. The Centre is open throughout the year and will appeal to young and old alike.

Elegant villas overlook Hunstanton's green and, even though past glories such as the pier, the railway and the impressive Sandringham Hotel have disappeared, visitors are still left with a very pleasing impression of this gracious town. For hundreds of years the local gentry were the Le Strange family who did much to develop the town. Their residence was the handsome moated Tudor Hall to the south of St Mary's church in Old Hunstanton. The family's hereditary title was Lord High Admirals of The Wash, giving them the rights to anything washed up on the shore or found out to sea as far as they could ride a horse at low tide and throw a spear. No doubt they kept their fingers crossed that King John's jewels might reappear at some time!

Entertainment at Hunstanton is plentiful and varied; catering for visitors of all ages. During the summer months you can take a boat trip out to the sandbank in The Wash known as **Seal Island**, where seals can sometimes be spotted sunbathing at low tide.

PINEWOOD HOUSE occupies a wonderful location and lies within 100 yards of the glorious sandy beaches of Hunstanton. Built in around 1870, this large Victorian townhouse, close to both the town centre and the seafront, is owned and personally run by Susan and Ivor. A

SANDRINGHAM (KING'S LYNN E IN NORFOLK.)

Sandringham House

charming, intimate house, you can be sure of a warm, friendly welcome and a relaxed and peaceful stay. There are eight comfortable bedrooms, with either en-suite or private bathroom facilities, that are also individually furnished and decorated to a high standard. Pinewood House is well renowned for its delicious breakfasts, complete with lashings of freshly brewed coffee and home-made marmalade. The cosy bar is just the place to relax in the evening over a drink and chat about the day. Once found, this is a place that you will want to return to again, many guests do just that!

Pinewood House, 26 Northgate, Hunstanton Tel: 01485 533068

AROUND HUNSTANTON

BABINGLEY. A delightful little village, right on the edge of the Sandringham estate, which has an intriguing village sign featuring a saint and a very special beaver.

In the fields to the west of Babingley stands the 14th century ruined church of St Felix, said to be the site of the first Christian church in East Anglia. Founded in 630AD by St Felix, legend has it that he crossed the sea from Burgundy in safety only to be shipwrecked in the Babingley River. The story goes that the saint was saved by beavers swimming in the river at the time and such was his gratitude that he made their leader a bishop! The village sign commemorates the legend most strikingly, showing St Felix and his ship with two beavers sitting above him, one of them sporting a crook and a mitre.

SANDRINGHAM. The Sandringham Estate, as one of the Royal family's favourite residences, is well worth a visit. Purchased for Edward VII in 1861 while he was still the Prince of Wales, the Estate covers 7,000 acres in all, encompassing seven villages and dominating the life and economy of the surrounding countryside. It takes its name from the sandy soils of the surrounding Country Park which was originally known as Sand Dersingham. The house is comparatively modern having been built between 1869-71 to replace the original Georgian building which burned down.

Sandringham became a firm favourite with the society set during the 49 years that Edward VII was in residence: he transformed it into a popular and lively place with a fine reputation for the excellence of its shooting. It has been the birthplace of several members of the Royal family: the Queen's father, her three uncles and aunt were all born at Sandringham, as was Diana, Princess of Wales when her father, the late Earl Spencer, held the position of equerry. One of the few people to remain singularly unimpressed was Edward VIII who apparently loathed the place and spent only one night there in his lifetime.

The grounds, entered through an oak door in the outer wall, are a profusion of colour during the spring and summer. The surprises include an unusual 'handkerchief' tree and a golden Buddha. The Norwich Gates, a wedding present to Edward VII from the people of Norfolk, span the driveway. The house itself has a cosy, friendly atmosphere about it and is open to the public except between 20th July and 8th August when the Royal Family is in residence.

There is also a museum here with a fascinating collection of Royal photographs and vintage motor cars. Tucked away in a corner of the park is the tiny, medieval church of St Mary Magdalene, home church of the Royal Family. It contains many private memorial brasses, and perhaps the most memorable of its treasures is the solid silver altar and reredos, presented in 1920 by the wealthy American, Rodman Wannamaker.

An impressive list of heads of state and members of foreign royal families have stayed at Sandringham over the years, including the Kaiser, the Tsar and many others. They would have arrived at the little railway station at Wolferton, two miles to the west of the house, where their hosts waited to receive them. Wolferton Station is now an intriguing museum filled with royal memorabilia, including (of all things!) Queen Victoria's travelling bed. It is all set out on one level, and although space is fairly confined with small steps in the doorways, access to wheelchair users is possible.

DERSINGHAM. The Church of St Nicholas has some impressive tombs and a remarkable carved chest of great antiquity, decorated with the symbols of the Evangelists. The ancient gabled tithe barn opposite the church dates back to 1671 and is now used by the county council as a storehouse for fragments from historic buildings.

THE GAMEKEEPER'S LODGE, in Chapel Road, is a truly charming establishment with plenty of character and a friendly, relaxed atmosphere. Refurbished in the last few years, the Lodge has a wonderful 'countrified' feel, making it a splendid place to stop off for a drink and a meal. Since coming here the Sutton family, who have experience in running pubs and hotels, have established an excellent reputation.

The restaurant here is very attractive indeed, with an excellent, international menu featuring a superb range of fish, meat, poultry and vegetarian dishes. Interesting and imaginative there is a always something to catch your eye and tickle the tastebuds. In addition to the restaurant fare, bar snacks and daily specials are also available, and even though all the food is distinctly upmarket, the prices are very reasonable. There is a fine selection of wines to accompany your meal, and if you are looking for somewhere special to eat out as the highlight of your holiday, you need look no further. To make things even better, accommodation is available in four, huge, en-suite bedrooms. There is no doubt that these facilities are of the same high standard as the rest of the Lodge.

The Gamekeeper's Lodge, Chapel Road, Dersingham Tel: 01485 543514

SNETTISHAM. The medieval stone spire of St Mary's Church which soars 175 ft high and overlooks the sprawling village of Snettisham. St Mary's was mentioned in LP Hartley's charming novel, 'The Shrimp and The Anemone', which was later made into a film. The exquisite tracery in the magnificent west window is truly beautiful and other interesting features of this lovely 14th century church include the circular seats set around the tall pillars of the nave and an oven that was once used to bake the communion wafers.

Right in the village centre, concealed by a wall and a fine procession of limes, is the gabled Old Hall, a handsome William and Mary residence which has been given a new lease of life as a Sue Ryder Home for the disabled. Several of the local businesses have the word 'Torc' in their names: this is a reference to the treasure trove of Iron Age torcs or 'collar' necklaces fashioned in gold which was discovered in the area.

Snettisham's charming water mill dates back to around 1800 and visitors may watch the mill in action at several daily corn grinding demonstrations. Further along is an RSPB nature reserve. Set out around a disused shingle pit overlooking The Wash, the reserve gives an opportunity to view many species of migratory birds.

Tucked away in the delightful village of Snettisham, **THE ROSE AND CROWN** is one of Norfolk's best loved pubs. This 14th Century freehouse is owned by Anthony Goodrich and expertly managed by Elaine Playford and offers excellent real ales, good food, friendly service and a very warm welcome. At the very heart of this traditional Inn are its three cosy and comfortable bars, each with its own individual character. With old oak beams and log fires in the depths of winter, the Rose and Crown has a fascinating collection of antique tools and prints of local interest with one of the bars being non-smoking. Each bar has an excellent selection of real ales including Bass and Abbot with all the wines supplied by Adnams, recent wine merchants of the year.

The menu offers some of the best food in the area, all being freshly prepared and cooked on the premises using hand selected local produce where possible. Meals may be eaten in any of the bars, the elegant restaurant or even in the relaxed and spacious surroundings of the Garden Room, where you can watch your food being cooked on the barbecue grill. If you are lucky enough to visit this haven of tranquillity in the summer then meals are served in the beautiful walled garden with its shady willow trees and herbaceous border. At The Rose and Crown children are very welcome, with a special children's menu and the garden has a large, well equipped play area complete with two forts, swinging walkway, playhouse and slide. Having recently won the Family Welcome Guide Gold Award, they also offer a menagerie of guinea pigs and budgerigars and large lawns, perfect for a good run around.

The Rose and Crown, Old Church Road, Snettisham
Tel: 01485 541382

HEACHAM. Caley Mill, at Heacham, is the home of **NORFOLK LAVENDER**. Established in 1932, this fascinating lavender farm is the oldest and largest of its kind in Britain. The information kiosk at the western entrance is a listed building and a renowned Norfolk landmark. On entering the site, visitors are struck by the strong and unmistakable fragrance which hangs in the air. Guided tours of the grounds run throughout the day between late-May and end-September, and during the harvest, visitors can tour the distillery and see how the wonderful fragrance is produced.

As well as being a working farm, this is also the home of the National Collection of Lavenders, a living dictionary which shows the many different colours, sizes and fragrances of this lovely plant. A further four acres devoted to aromatic plants opens in the spring of 1997. There is also a wonderful herb garden, a children's play area and a gift shop in the 19th century water mill which stocks the full range of Norfolk Lavender products. The recently-enlarged conservatory shop offers a wide variety of plants, as well all many attractive gifts for the gardener, and the Miller's Cottage Tearoom specialises in cream teas, home-made cakes and light lunches. Open all year, except Christmas; admission free.

Norfolk Lavender, Caley Mill, Heacham
Tel: 01485 570384 Fax: 01485 571176

RINGSTEAD. In a region which is well-stocked with excellent nature reserves, the one on **Ringstead Downs** is particularly attractive. The chalky soil of the valley is the perfect environment for the plants that thrive here and the beautiful butterflies they attract. The village itself is simply charming with wonderfully decorative Norfolk carrstone and pink and white-washed cottages, the early 14th century Church of St Andrew and ruinous churches.

OLD HUNSTANTON. Lying half a mile to the north of the town of Hunstanton, this is a lovely old and unspoilt fishing village with a quiet beach well protected by banks of sand dunes. Said to be one of the finest in the country, there are miles of golden sands and dunes, multi-coloured cliffs and many rock pools to discover.

Steeped in history, the village, with its lovely church and duck pond, has narrow streets and smuggler's lanes and a whole host of charming and pretty cottages. A select holiday location, there are also plenty of inns and restaurants and for golfers, a championship golf course.

Lying 200 yards from the beach in the heart of Old Hunstanton, **LE STRANGE OLD BARNS** is a fascinating antiques, arts and craft centre which offers hundreds of top quality items, mostly by local artists and craftspeople. There are also daily demonstrations. Proprietor Richard Weller and manager Carol Maloney have developed this unique complex into one of the most impressive of its kind in Norfolk. Highlights include an art gallery with around 200 original paintings, resident potter's studio, English crafts room; an antiques barn houses ten independent dealers offering thousands of items.

THE PEDDARS WAY

This long distance footpath starts at Knettishall in Suffolk and covers some 95 miles before arriving at the Norfolk coast at Holme next the Sea. The original road which the path follows was laid down in 61 AD and is a text book example of a straight-as-a-die Roman road. It is fitting then that its name is derived from the Latin word 'pedester' which means to travel on foot. The Roman thoroughfare has caused a great deal of head scratching among historians as it seems to end, rather abruptly, in The Wash.

A guide to the route can be obtained from the Countryside Commission and, although it is unlikely that anyone could lose their way on such a straightforward route, the guide does provide some interesting background details and also gives warnings of those places where the army might be training! Walkers of all ages and abilities can enjoy the Peddars Way as it crosses over gentle terrain and, if taken as a whole, provides a unique cross-section of the rural delights of Norfolk and Suffolk.

Starting on the banks of the Great Ouse, the footpath passes by most towns and villages on the way though it does call at Castle Acre. Here, travellers cross the River Nar via a ford and, unlikely as it may seem today, this little stream was once large enought for boats to navigate from The Wash.

The route is signposted using the regular acorn symbol of the National Trails. The Peddars Way Association (150 Armes Street, Norwich, NR2 4EG) provides a list of places to stay along the route, including campsites, and those wishing to travel the path are advised to be well prepared for variable weather conditions.

NORFOLK COAST PATH

At Holme, the Peddars Way joins the Norfolk Coast Path which carries along the coastline westwards to Cromer. This path appeals to ramblers who prefer the scents of the marshes and the nearness of the sea coupled with the isolation, wildlife and colours that only this remote territory can provide.

Richard Weller also has two cottages which make the ideal location for family holidays. Dolphin Cottage, sleeping six, is delightful and modern; well equipped and pleasingly furnished. The accommodation comprises three bedrooms, bathroom, lounge with dining area and a modern kitchen. The gardens to the front and rear are enclosed and there is a patio with garden furniture on the south facing front garden. Mermaid Cottage is similarly equipped and furnished to an equally high standard but is somewhat larger, sleeping up to eight. The cottages are adjacent to each other and can be hired together if a large family gathering is what you have in mind. Cots are provided for younger children.

Le Strange Old Barns, Golf Course Road,
Old Hunstanton Tel: 01485 533402 Fax: 01485 534743

Holiday Cottages, Golf Course Road, Old Hunstanton Tel: 01485 533402
Fax: 01485 534743

Standing within its own attractive grounds beside Hunstanton golf links, the **LINKSWAY COUNTRY HOUSE HOTEL** enjoys one of the finest views in north Norfolk. English Tourist Board three-crowns commended, it has fifteen beautifully-appointed bedrooms, each with en suite bath or shower, colour TV, hair dryer and tea/coffee making facilities. There is also an impressive heated indoor swimming pool, a relaxing guest lounge, and a fully-licensed bar. As well as magnificent views over the links, the restaurant offers first-class cuisine expertly prepared by the chef. The hotel stands adjacent to the coastal path and within two minutes walk of a beautiful sandy beach.

Linksway Country House Hotel, Golf Course Road, Old Hunstanton
Tel: 01485 532209/532653

HOLME NEXT THE SEA. Locals still talk about the day, in December 1626, when, with the wind blowing strong from the northwest, an unfortunate whale was washed up on the shore. Around 57 ft long, its carcass was to make £217 6s 7d profit for the village.

The path to the beach lies across the golf course at Hunstanton and, from the beach road, the track runs across the marshy shoreline to the **Holme Dunes Nature Reserve** and the **Holme Bird Observatory**. Permits for both are available from the wardens, and from here you can observe many rare species on their spring and autumn migrations.

White Horse Inn, Kirkgane Street, Holme next the Sea
Tel: 01485 525512

The delightful **WHITE HORSE INN** at Holme next the Sea has been in the Hayter family for over half-a-century. Paul and Sue are the third generation to be in charge of this first-rate pub and eating place which was originally constructed in the 1600s as a farm and stables. Recently upgraded, its three rooms retain their original character, with old oak beams and tasteful furnishings. The White Horse is renowned for its food, all freshly-prepared and ranging from ploughman's lunches and succulent Norfolk ham, to steaks and fresh local fish. There is also a special children's menu. The inn's attractive beer garden, one of the largest on this part of the coast, is a marvellous sun trap.

THORNHAM. A particularly charming village with cottages of flint and chalkstone, a tiny harbour and quiet beaches, Thornham is a wonderful place from which to explore the unspoilt coastline.

Thornham's buildings can boast a wide variety of architectural styles; from the Red House at the southern end of the village, a mainly 18th century house with much older parts at the back, to the striking Victorian school in glorious Gothic style at the western end. One of Thornham's best known residents was the acclaimed lady blacksmith, Mrs Ames Lyde, who died in 1914. This skilled craftswoman created many fine pieces of decorative ironwork in her forge including the garden gates at Sandringham.

This particular stretch of the Norfolk coast does not tend to suffer from great hordes of holiday makers and the beaches can be walked in virtual isolation. However, when the great flocks of migratory birds rally in spring and autumn, the birdwatchers suddenly appear in their hundreds armed with binoculars and note-books!

TITCHWELL. Perhaps befitting the village's name, the church of St Mary is quite tiny, and very pretty indeed. Its round (probably Norman) tower is topped by a little 'whisker' of a spire and inside is some fine late 19th century glass.

Just to the west of the village is a path leading to **Titchwell Marsh**, a nationally important RSPB reserve comprising some 420 acres of shingle beach, reed beds, freshwater and brackish marshes, and salt-marsh. These different habitats encourage a wide variety of birds to visit the area throughout the year and many of them breed on or around the reserve. Brent geese, ringed plovers, marsh harriers, terns, waders and shore larks may all be seen and two of the three hides available are accessible to wheelchair users.

BRANCASTER STAITHE. From here boats may be hired for trips out to **Scolt Head Island**, a remote sand and shingle bar of about 3 1/2 miles in length, separated from the mainland by a narrow tidal creek. The island is a haven for terns who flock there to breed and the nature trail leads past the ternery (closed during the breeding season of May, June and July) and on to a fascinating area where a rich variety of plant and wildlife abounds. During the summer the sea asters, sea lavender and sea pinks put on a colourful display and many different types of moths and butterflies may be observed.

BURNHAM DEEPDALE. The pride of this hamlet is undoubtedly the parish church of St Mary's, which contains what is widely held to be one of finest Norman fonts in Norfolk. Cut from a single block of stone, this square font is carved with 12 individual figures, each hard at work on a different task for each month of the year.

BURNHAM NORTON. This near-perfect little village, unravaged by time and modern development, stands on a hill with views across the fields and salt-marshes to the sea. St Margaret's Church, to the south of the village, has the most glorious 15th century wineglass pulpit. Appearing to balance precariously on its slender stem, its colourful panels depict the four Latin Doctors and, although it is no longer in use, it continues to grace the church as a beautiful object to be admired.

BURNHAM MARKET. The largest of the, in all, seven Burnhams situated along the Burn valley, Burnham Market, encompassing Westgate, Sutton and Ulph, has some elegant 18th century houses.

Fishes Restaurant, Market Place, Burnham Market
Tel: 01328 738588

The delightful **FISHES RESTAURANT** can be found in the Market Place, Burnham Market. This superb eating place specialises in fresh local seafood, including shellfish, shrimps from the Wash, lobster (when available), and fish landed on the beach at Holkham Bay. Starters include crab soup, smoked fish pate and oysters, as well as non-seafood dishes. There is also an impressive list of carefully-selected wines. In the 23 years that proprietor Gillian Cape has run Fishes she has built an enviable reputation for fine food and service. Her restaurant has a charming atmosphere, with comfortable cane furniture, attractive prints and paintings on the walls, and a fascinating collection of books.

BURNHAM OVERY STAITHE is a delightful place almost solely concerned with sailing: there is an annual regatta and facilities for windsurfing too. There is a restored tower mill, now a private residence, standing to the side of the main road just before entering the village. The attractive harbour, where boat trips to Scolt Head Island are available, lies in a creek some distance from the sea. Indeed, it could be said to have followed the sea northwards in a manner of speaking, as Overy Staithe was built after the sea receded from the original port of Burnham Overy. This lies a mile to the south on the B1155 and is now referred to as

Burnham Overy Town.

A good stopping place for walkers and bird watchers, the impressive **HERO INN** can be found on the main A149 at Burnham Overy Staithe, near the junction with East Harbour Way. This first-rate pub and eating place has a warm friendly atmosphere, with old-fashioned brasses and traditional hospitality. Owners Annie and Pat only purchased the Hero and the nearby caravan park after spending many years holidaying in the area. Since then, they have built up an enviable reputation for serving the finest real ales and pub food in the district. They also have a well-appointed standing caravan available to let which sleeps six.

The Hero Inn, Wells Road, Burnham Overy Staithe
Tel: 01328 738334

BURNHAM THORPE. The origins of 'The Hero' (Lord Nelson) himself can be found at Burnham Thorpe, for this is where Lord Nelson was born in 1758. His father, the Reverend Edmund Nelson, was rector of All Saint's church and, although the rectory itself was demolished in 1802, there are many mementoes of the great admiral in the church. This stands in a glorious setting on the banks of the River Burn and, among the various items of 'Nelsonia' inside, there is a cross and lectern which were both made from timbers taken from HMS Victory. Those with a fascination for maritime history will no doubt also enjoy visiting the Lord Nelson Inn where Burnham Thorpe's most famous son enjoyed a number of celebration dinners. Nelson was just 13 years old when he embarked upon his naval career in 1770 and he became a rear admiral at the age of 39. His success at the Battle of the Nile made him a national hero and he died at the age of 47 after his crushing defeat of the French fleet at the Battle of Trafalgar.

HOLKHAM. It was at this tiny hamlet that the Earl of Leicester built the splendid Palladian mansion, **Holkham Hall**, in the 1730s.

The Earl also successfully reclaimed much of his land from the sea but the topsoil was poor and crop yields were low. His great-nephew, Thomas Coke (pronounced Cook and later to be dubbed 'Coke of Norfolk') inherited the estate revitalised the soil by dragging up the lower clay level and planting turnips - a system pioneered by that other great Norfolk farmer, 'Turnip' Townsend. Rather like the rotation of crops, his scheme was to use sheep to clear the roots and to use their manure as fertilizer. The result was greatly improved soil with abundant yields: for the first time in Norfolk, corn and wheat crops flourished and with the advent of cattle herds he had successfully devised a good basis for mixed farming. Coke encouraged farmers from all over the country to come and see for themselves just how successful his methods had proved, and his prosperity was assured as a result of his brilliant vision.

The mansion itself has had its fair share of detractors (the somewhat austere yellow brick with which it was built is not to everyone's taste) but no one could fail to be impressed by the interior. Taking more than 30 years to complete, it boasts a magnificent hall with pink marble pillars. Furniture designed by William Kent (the principal architect of the house and much of the park) features throughout and the walls of the State rooms, which are hung with velvet and damask, make a wonderful backdrop to a superb collection of paintings by such masters as Van Dyck, Gainsborough and Rubens.

The exquisite library, richly decorated in shades of gold and white, houses hundreds of beautifully bound books, illuminated manuscripts, folios and other fascinating historic records. There is also an impressive collection of antique sculptures which Thomas Coke acquired in Italy and it is said that the large number of ilex trees which grace the estate are attributable to the fact that these sculptures arrived at Holkham packed in ilex seeds for protection.

As well as the magnificent house to explore, there are a number of ancillary attractions to make a visit even more rewarding. **Holkham Pottery**, founded by Elizabeth, Countess of Leicester in 1951, is open to visitors and the skilled team of potters can be watched at work and examples of their wares purchased. There is also a garden centre and craft centre and, in the 19th century stables, the **Holkham Bygones Museum**, a marvellous collection of Victorian and Edwardian agricultural tools and domestic equipment featuring everything from working steam engines and vintage tractors to craft tools and kitchenware.

A large deer park with around 600 head of fallow deer is another feature of the estate as is the **Holkham National Nature Reserve**, the largest coastal reserve in the country, which runs from Burnham Overy Staithe all the way along the coast to Blakeney. This 12-mile stretch of dunes, beaches and salt-marshes interrupted only by the harbour channel leading to Wells is reached via Holkham Gap, a vast, beautiful cove of grassy dunes where pine trees have been planted to stabilise the shifting sands.

WELLS-NEXT-THE-SEA. Very much a seaside town that has kept firmly to its origins, its working harbour gives it great character. The town's name, however, is something of a misnomer as the harbour now stands a mile from the sea beside a creek! The mile-long 'Embankment' was built in 1859 to prevent the harbour from silting up altogether and it provides a pleasant walk down to the sea. In addition to being the largest of North Norfolk's ports, Wells is also a popular resort.

Just to the east of the town the **Wells and Walsingham Steam Railway** takes passengers on a particularly lovely ride along the former Great Eastern Line with halts at Warham St Mary and Wighton. The Old Station for the Great Eastern Line at Wells has a charming restored signal box which now sells souvenirs and refreshments and the 1986 Garratt locomotive was built specifically for this railway.

One of the most interesting craft workshops in the area can be found in the Old Station at Wells-next-the-Sea, the home of the famous **BURNHAM POTTERY**.

Burnham Pottery, The Old Station, 2-4 Maryland, Wells-next-the-Sea Tel: 01328 710847 Fax: 01328 711566

Jan and Thom Borthwick started their pottery business in Burnham over a decade ago, but moved here as things expanded. They now produce a unique range of handmade domestic and decorative pottery, including vases, large terracotta pots for the patio or garden, and a delightful variety of animal figures including the immensely popular 'Burnham Colourful Cats'. These charming feline characters have names like Ambrose, Bertram, Claudia and Amelia, and are made in a variety of colours and poses. (Our favourite was Everard, captured with a cheeky expression that all cat lovers will recognise.) Another speciality of Burnham Pottery is their selection of hand-thrown items with a splash glaze; for collectors, they also produce a range of studio pottery with an attractive spongeware finish in limited edition. The Borthwicks have also managed to indulge their love of old and rare books, especially those with an emphasis on the eccentric and the humorous. Over the years they have accumulated a superb collection of secondhand titles which visitors are welcome to browse through and purchase.

THE NORMANS GUEST HOUSE, in Wells, is a superb listed building with a real atmosphere of genteel living about it. This grand house has an elegant façade and was once the home of the family of Ursula Bloom, authoress of 'The Rose of Norfolk'.

Today the house is owned by Carol Macdonald, who, with her partner Trevor Francis, has carried out a series of renovations and built up an excellent reputation for offering a very high standard of Bed & Breakfast accommodation in her lovely home. As you enter the three storey house, the lounge is on your left and the dining room is to the right, both rooms are beautifully decorated and feature period fireplaces. In between these two rooms is a superb Grade I listed spiral staircase. One bedroom is available with an en-suite bathroom, another 6 have an en-suite shower room, and all of the rooms are spacious, cosy and tastefully decorated, with colour television and tea and coffee making facilities. The top floor of the house has wonderful views over the salt marshes to the sea, and the quayside is only 100 yards away. Open all year round, The Normans would be a marvellous place to come for either a Winter break or a summer holiday and would be particularly suitable for those of you who enjoy birdwatching, walking or painting.

The Normans Guest House, Invaders Court, Standard Road, Wells-next-the-Sea Tel: 01328 710657 Fax: 01328 710468

On entering Wells-next-the-Sea, is the fine Edwardian house **WINGATE**, the home of Tim and Carolyn who cater for bed and breakfast guests throughout the year.

Wingate, Two Furlong Hill, Wells-next-the-Sea Tel: 01328 711814

The house is said to have been the wedding present for the famous local artist and wildfowler Frank Southgate from his father in law Mr. Winlove. Tim is no mean artist himself and he and Carolyn also run a successful Picture Framing, Gift shop and Gallery business in the town.

Although only a few minutes walk from the harbour and town centre, Wingate house offers a quiet location being set in nearly three quarters of an acre. Guests are welcome to use the large gardens. The bedrooms are light and airy, comfortably furnished and equipped with colour television, radio, and tea and coffee making facilities. Rooms are either en-suite or have private bathrooms. There is a spacious residents' lounge which has a selection of indoor games and the separate dining room overlooks the bird table which attracts many interesting visitors. An ideal place to stop and relax which also has an ETB 2 Crown Highly Commended rating.

The **EASTDENE GUEST HOUSE** is an ideal place to stay for those seeking first-rate accommodation within easy walking distance of the town centre. This attractive residence has its own private parking and is located in a quiet cul-de-sac off Northfield Lane, a couple of minutes walk from the harbour and coastal path. The bedrooms are well-appointed, with en suite bathrooms, colour televisions, and tea/coffee making facilities in all rooms. There is also a relaxing guest lounge. Proprietor Jean Court offers her guests a warm welcome. She also has an impressive knowledge of the surrounding area and keeps a bird record book for bird-watchers. Pets welcome.

Eastdene Guest House, Northfield Lane, Wells-next-the-Sea
Tel: 01328 710381

WARHAM is a fusion of two separate villages known as **Warham All Saints** and **Warham St Mary**. Now with almost no discernible border between the two communities, the village can be said to have two medieval churches, both with plenty to recommend them.

The **THREE HORSESHOES** provides a delightful step back in time for visitors to Warham All Saints. The main bar of this superb 18th century cottage inn is still gas-lit, and features stone floors and a beautiful inglenook fireplace. A pianola stands in the snug, and there is an exquisite 1940s fruit machine which now serves as a fund-raiser for charity. Real ale is served from the barrel and the restaurant area is decorated with a magnificent collection of historic implements. The inn's many amenities include a family room, a children's playroom, and an extensive beer garden.

Those interested in memorabilia, should remember to make an appointment to view the inn's wonderful collection of old gramophones. The Three Horseshoes is the assembly point for Warham All Saints' twice-yearly vintage car rally. Afterwards, many people choose to dine in the inn's impressive restaurant which offers an imaginative selection of daily specials in addition its regular menu of traditional Norfolk dishes. A range of mouthwatering desserts and fine wines is also served. The Three Horseshoes also offers extremely comfortable bed and breakfast accommodation in an adjoining building. The four guest bedrooms (one double, one twin, two single) are all tastefully refurbished and fitted with en suite facilities. One single room also boasts a luxurious four-poster bed.

Three Horseshoes, The Street, Warham All Saints
Tel: 01328 710547

Behind the Coast

FAKENHAM. Famous for its National Hunt **Racecourse**, Fakenham is a busy and distinctly well-to-do little market town as well as an important agricultural centre for the region. Straddling the River Wensum, this attractive country town has a number of fine late 18th and early 19th century brick buildings in and around the **Market Place** and it must surely be one of the few towns in England where the gasworks has been turned into a museum. The town's old corn mill, beside the mill race, is now a hotel with guest bedrooms overlooking the pond.

AROUND FAKENHAM

HEMPTON. Whilst touring the beautiful rolling hills of North Norfolk, the historic market town of Fakenham has many attractions and is well worth a visit. Being only 12 miles from the coast it is also a good touring base.

Tricia and Joe Beales provide bed and breakfast, with evening meals on request, in their modern home **YEW TREE HOUSE** at Hempton. It's a lovely location and Joe being a keen gardener ensures the lovely garden is kept in pristine order for guests to relax in. All rooms have wash basins, colour television and tea and coffee facilities. Good breakfasts - many visitors return for the food!

Yew Tree House, 2 East View, Hempton Tel: 01328 851450

LITTLE BARNEY. If you are here on a caravanning or camping holiday there is a marvellous establishment just one mile to the south east of Thursford. It is always a pleasure to come across a caravan and camping park which is not only attractive but has all the required amenities too, and **THE OLD BRICK KILNS** park at Little Barney is one such place. Owners Alan and Pam Greenhalgh have set their seven acre park on two levels, where the pleasant combination of wooded areas and open spaces creates a wonderfully peaceful atmosphere. The natural pond is a perfect habitat for many types of wildlife, and for the nature lovers among you, the wild bird reserves and beautiful beaches of the North Norfolk coast are only eight miles away.

There are 60 pitches in all, each has an electrical supply. The old brick drying shed has been converted to modern standards to provide all the main facilities of the park; and here you will find the reception area, a first aid room, and the shop, which operates a gas exchange and will supply all your basic food needs as well as home-made produce, crafts and gifts and a wide range of caravan accessories. There are luxury showers and toilets, including excellent facilities for the disabled, and other amenities include a vegetable preparation and washing-up room, a laundry room, a television room and a recreation room. Outdoor activities include fishing, a giant chess board and garden games (croquet etc). In addition there is a safe children's play area, and there are also cycles for hire if you want to take off for an hour or two along the country lanes.

Bearing in mind the pleasant aspect of the park and the high standard of all the facilities provided, it came as no surprise to discover that this fine park won the runner-up prize in the 1993 Calor Caravan Park Awards for the 'Best Caravan Park in England', such are its standards. This recognition is richly deserved, and if you would like to discover the pleasures of staying here for yourself, the park is open from the beginning of March to the end of October.

The Greenhalghs also offer superb bed and breakfast facilities throughout the year in their lovely family home, which has been converted from three brickworker's cottages. The accommodation comprises one twin, one double and one single room, all en-suite, well appointed and tastefully decorated.

The house is comfortable and spacious and you will be made to feel most welcome in the peaceful, relaxing atmosphere that pervades. The atmosphere is enhanced by the log fire in the winter, in the summer you will want to enjoy the sunny, sheltered garden. Guests also have access to all of the facilities in the park. The meals are excellent, all prepared by Pam using only the very best ingredients. The standards and attention to detail in both the park and the B&B accommodation are extremely high, this is one of the very best places from which to base your exploration of this rewarding area.

The Old Brick Kilns, Little Barney Tel: 01328 878305

THURSFORD. The tiny hamlet, just off the A148, is best known for the fascinating collection here. No one visiting East Anglia should miss the extraordinary exhibition, **THE THURSFORD COLLECTION.** Thursford might not seem the most likely place for a museum of fairgrounds and steam but in fact East Anglia has many connections with the history of festival and its trappings, and the real Norfolk traditional art is not water-colour painting but the practice of festival. There have been fairs all over Norfolk for over a thousand years.

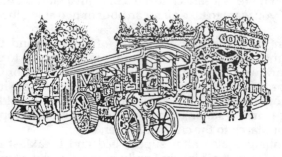

The Thursford Collection

Norfolk is full of folk history in which fairs were significant events for isolated communities. It is hard for us to imagine now the effect which the visit of a fair would have had on the isolated villages in Norfolk, in the late 19th and early 20th centuries. Out of the plain landscape came these exuberant vehicles and their mechanical mysteries with carved monsters and swinging chairs, all of them painted and polished in a style of power and colour. The cinema too had its beginnings in the fair, with the huge bioscopes which travelled between 1896 and 1914, some of them able to seat 1,000 people.

Above all else, the fairs brought electricity with them, at a time when most towns and villages themselves would have had only gas lighting! For many people, therefore, this would have been their first glimpse at electric light. Families would walk miles to see these things, because in a pre-television era this was the place where the truly spectacular could be experienced and, more importantly, shared. Among the scattered groups who went to the fair was one small boy, George Cushing, who instinctively understood these things, and has retained the image of it all his life to make The Thursford Collection a show for all of us to see and enjoy.

The Thursford Collection, Thursford, Fakenham Tel: 01328 878477

George Cushing was caring for and collecting steam engines when most men would not have given you £5 for one. Without his perceptive honesty the museum would not exist. All the exhibits have one thing in common, which is that they are beautiful objects made by craftsmen who knew their work. George Cushing's real love for these things has a countryman's sense of the intrinsic value of the objects: to bring together this collection, to see through the blindness or carelessness which allowed traction engines, for example, to go for scrap, and to re-make for all of us one of the best arrangements of steam engines and organs in the world. More than the skill, more than the money which it has taken to finance the museum, it has required his vision and enthusiasm.

Thursford: it's not just a museum but a total experience. Music: live music shows starring Robert Wolfe in the Wurlitzer show, plus music from nine mechanical organs. Shops: housed in renovated farm buildings, offering a wide and varied selection of goods, many locally made. Food: cream teas on the lawn, light snacks and delicious home-cooked lunches in the genuine Norfolk barn, home-made ice-cream from the parlour. And to top it all there are enough activities, including a Savage Venetian Gondola ride, to complete a wonderful visit.

THE HEATHERS, the lovely home of Sylvia and Derek Brangwyn, is a quiet house which offers a fine standard of B&B accommodation, ideally located as a base for a tour of this fascinating part of Norfolk.

The Heathers, Thursford Tel: 01328 878352

The house has recently been renovated to a very high standard, the bulk of the work having been carried out by Derek himself. You can be assured of enjoying your stay here, for the welcome that you will receive is genuinely warm, as is the peaceful and relaxing atmosphere that this fine home has. Take time to wander around the garden, for Derek has constructed a superb pond which contains his Koi carp. The rooms are all very well equipped and comfortable, they all have en-suite bathroom facilities and colour television. Smoking is permitted, but only in the lounge.

GREAT SNORING. The pair of villages Great and Little Snoring, whose names are a constant source of amusement and delight to visitors, owe their names to a Saxon family named Snear. Both have churches that are worth taking the time to visit.

To the west of St Mary's Church at Great Snoring is the superb Old Rectory, the original manor house built by Sir Ralph Shelton in 1525, opulently embellished with carved brickwork, octagonal turrets and ornamental Victorian chimneys.

THE OLD RECTORY at Great Snoring is an impressive former manor house which stands in a large and peaceful walled garden. The house was originally hexagonal in plan and is believed to date from 1500. At this time it was the seat of Sir Ralph Shelton. During the Victorian era the building was extended and restored to the configuration which exists today. The façades are interesting because they feature a frieze of terracotta tiles, the design of which includes male and female heads (thought to be representations of members of the Shelton family), the Shelton Rebus and heraldic shield.

Today this fine house offers an excellent standard of accommodation all year round for visitors to Norfolk. Situated with easy access to

Norwich and King's Lynn, and with the heritage coast just a short drive away, it would be difficult to find a better place to stay. The bedrooms are well appointed and each has its own private bathroom. Breakfast is of a high standard: mid-morning coffee, afternoon tea and dinner are also available.

This peaceful haven is a delightful place from which to base your exploration of Norfolk's 'Hidden Places'.

The Old Rectory, Great Snoring Tel 01328 820597 Fax: 01328 820048

LITTLE SNORING. St Andrew's Church at Little Snoring is particularly interesting with its mish-mash of architectural styles. The detached round tower with conical cap dates back to Saxon times and in fact belongs to a slightly earlier church from the same period.

EAST BARSHAM. The splendid early Tudor mansion, East Barsham Manor, was built by Sir Henry Fermor around 1520 and is testimony to the great skill of the 16th century brickmakers. The lavish ornamentation of moulded brick, the vertical buttresses and the embattled south front are all superb, but perhaps the most striking feature of the building is the group of 10 chimneys, all individually carved with an amazing variety of designs.

LITTLE WALSINGHAM. With a Shirehall, an Abbey and a Priory, there are plenty of attractions in this little town. Little Walsingham has also witnessed the arrival of thousands of pilgrims since the early part of the 12th century when the Lady of the Manor, Richelde of Fervaques, had a vision of the Virgin Mary. Transporting her in a dream to the Holy House at Nazareth where Mary had been told of the impending birth of Christ by the Archangel Gabriel, the Blessed Virgin instructed Richelde to build a replica of the house at Walsingham. An Augustinian priory was endowed around 1153 to look after the shrine, followed by a Franciscan friary in 1347, and before long a fully-fledged pilgrimage industry was underway.

Henry VIII was just one of several English monarchs to visit the shrine, barefoot and humble, although this devotion did not stop him from demolishing the priory in 1538. The largest surviving part of the priory is the splendid **Gatehouse** at the east side of the High Street,

Pump House, Little Walsingham

consisting of two slender towers supporting an arch, while just two cloisters and parts of the living quarters are all that remain of the friary, which stood just outside the village on the road to Houghton St Giles. The present **Shrine of Our Lady of Walsingham**, built between 1931-38 on what is purportedly the original site, can be found on the corner of Holt Road and has become a place of modern pilgrimage for believers of many denominations.

Quite apart from its main attraction, Walsingham has much more besides to keep its visitors entertained and enthralled. There are excellent shops, restaurants and inns, attractive timber-framed houses in the High Street, a market, and in Common Place, a 16th century octagonal pump house topped by a beacon brazier, a medieval well (several wells in the area were said to have curative powers) and the former Shirehall which is now a museum.

GREAT WALSINGHAM. Despite its name Great Walsingham is the smaller of the two Walsinghams and it couldn't be more different in atmosphere and appearance. A typical rural Norfolk village with attractive cottages set around a green, the 14th century St Peter's church has superb window tracery and 15th century benches are quite delightful.

SOUTH CREAKE. This is a pretty village of flint cottages with the River Burn flowing quietly alongside the main street. Some of the residents have to cross their own little wooden footbridges when entering and leaving their homes! Towering above the cottages in the centre of the village is one of South Creake's most interesting and incongruous sights: a truly hideous collection of dilapidated buildings that were originally built in the 1920s as a razor blade factory.

The factory owner was George Theophilus Money, a London-born entrepreneur, whose business sense failed to live up to the expectations of his name. Though the key to success in selling razor blades lies in their inherent disposability, George would have none of this and, instead, he offered to sharpen his customers' old ones! Needless to say, his factory was not in business for very long.

A delightful place to eat can be found overlooking the green in the heart of the conservation village of South Creake. **CARTWRIGHT'S TEAROOMS AND RESTAURANT** is an impressive 17th century structure which originally formed one side of a square set around a courtyard. The building incorporates a post office and general store, a beautiful walled garden and a renowned eating place serving delicious morning coffees, lunches, afternoon teas and evening meals. The interior is traditionally decorated, with low beamed ceilings, exposed timbers, and attractive framed pictures by local artists.

However, it is for the food that customers come from miles around, all home cooked by the manageress, Anita Woodget. The evening menu features steaks, seafood, and such specialities as pan fried rainbow trout and mushroom stroganoff, and there are equivalent delicacies on offer throughout the day. They also serve an excellent traditional Sunday lunch for which advance booking is advisable. The proprietors Jacqueline and Michael Seaman also have three very well-appointed holiday cottages to let, sleeping from two to six people. These are available throughout the year and are set amidst beautiful secluded gardens adjacent to the village green.

Cartwright's Tearoom and Restaurant, The Green, South Creake
Tel: 01328 823564 Fax: 01328 823335

NORTH CREAKE. A mile and a half up the road is the larger of the twin villages, North Creake. The little River Burn, more properly called a creek, from which both villages take their name, again flows through the village. To the north are the substantial ruins of **Creake Abbey**, a 12th century Augustinian monastery ravaged by fire and plague, now in the hands of English Heritage.

DOCKING. Just a short distance from the North Norfolk coast, this little village is home to the Seal Rescue Unit, run by the RSPCA, which was founded during the epidemic that killed hundreds of British seals.

STANHOE.

The Rickels, Bircham Road, Stanhoe Tel: 01485 518671

THE RICKELS caravan and camping site lies amid rolling fields just outside the village of Stanhoe, on the Bircham Road. A quiet and friendly family run site, Rickels has been awarded four ticks by the English Tourist Board. A not inconsiderable achievement since Heather Crown and her family only started the holiday park with a few vans.

Along with the glorious situation, Rickels has many excellent facilities to offer the visitor. As well as having electric hook-ups and a modern and convenient shower and toilet block, there are also laundry facilities and caravans for hire. With peaceful and relaxing atmosphere, this is a great holiday base for the whole family and quiet dogs are welcome. Children have their own safe play area and, just in case the weather is on the wet side, there is a play van for them equipped with a television.

GREAT BIRCHAM. Situated on the edge of the Sandringham Estate, while in the village it is certainly worth taking time out to visit **BIRCHAM WINDMILL**, which can be found on the B1155 about half a mile outside the village heading towards Snettisham. This is undoubtedly one of Norfolk's finest corn mills, and surrounded as it is by acres of unspoilt countryside, you could not wish for a more beautiful setting. The mill has been in use since the 1700s and if you are not afraid of heights, it is well worth climbing the five floors to see the milling machinery in action. It is certainly a long way to the top (and seems even further to the bottom!) but as you make the ascent you will find something interesting to look at on every level. On the ground floor, there are video displays and plenty of information on the history of the mill and the working of the machinery.

Another fascinating aspect of the mill is the small bakery where, on open days, you can buy bread and rolls which have been baked in the old fashioned way, except Saturdays when the Bakery is closed. The 200 year old coal-fired, brick oven was designed to bake over 100 loaves at a time, and still works today as good as new. You can also see many of the original baking utensils on display here.

After scaling the heights of the mill, it is good to come back to earth and enjoy a pot of tea with home-made cakes in the tea rooms. No ordinary tea rooms either, but Egon Ronay recommended; and as they are separate from the mill they can be enjoyed at any time. While you are here, you can also peruse the Gift shop and choose from a fascinating selection of items connected with milling and baking. We thought that this would be an ideal opportunity to pick up an unusual present for a friend or a relative.

In the old days, horse and cart was the mode of transport used by the miller and baker for their deliveries, and two ponies are still kept in the stables today. A marvellous way of enjoying this peaceful countryside is by bike, and cycle hire is available from the mill at hourly, daily or weekly rates. Day routes and traffic-free green lane routes are provided, together with a range of bikes to suit all ages and requirements.

Bircham Mill is open daily from Easter until the end of September. Free parking is available and coach parties are welcome by prior arrangement. There are numerous walks from the Mill itself with a guide that can be borrowed from the Bakery. If you require any further information on the mill or cycle hire, the number to call is 01485 578393.

Bircham Windmill, Great Bircham Tel: 01485 578393

The **KING'S HEAD HOTEL**, by the side of the B1153, is a fine hotel which, despite all its modern facilities, has a dignified and traditional atmosphere about it.

Owners Iris and Isidoro Verrando have put heart and soul into making the King's Head a truly welcoming establishment, and we think they have succeeded admirably. There is a rather charming air about the place and it has certainly found favour with 'Them up at the Big House', for several members of the Royal Family have popped in for lunch! We cannot guarantee that you will be keeping company with a prince or princess if you decide to do the same, but we can tell you that the food will be first class.

King's Head Hotel, Great Bircham Tel: 01485 578265

The Lodge Restaurant offers a superb à la carte Italian menu, and there are also many daily specials to choose from. Dishes such as Oak Smoked Scotch Salmon accompanied by a fine range of wines will find favour with the most discerning of guests; if the heavenly aroma emanating from the kitchen is anything to go by, you will certainly not be disappointed. If you are only passing through and a quick bite is all you have time for, then the extensive range of Bar Meals and Snacks with a distinctive English and Italian flavour might be your forte. Also, every last Friday of the month is the Italian evening which variously features chicken, lamb and fish main dishes on part of a five course set meal.

With six well appointed en-suite bedrooms, a residents' lounge, welcoming log fires, a large garden and two comfortable bars, this would make an excellent base from which to discover the huge range of holiday attractions in this unspoilt part of the county.

HILLINGTON. GATTON WATERS is a non-commercialised site that covers 24 acres of beautiful countryside and offers both camping, caravanning and bed & breakfast facilities. The name Gatton Waters comes from the medieval village that used to be on this site many years ago, but as no tax was paid the village was destroyed and has remained farmland ever since. Owned and very capably run by James and Carolyn Donaldson, the site has 40 electric hook-up points and the pitches are available from April 1st until October 7th. There are washing up facilities for all camping guests, with free showers and hot water in the four shower blocks and toilets. You will find a fully stocked bar on site that offers many real ales and bar food, opening everyday in high season and bank holidays with out of season times available on request. If camping is not your scene then maybe the relaxed atmosphere of the Bed & Breakfast option would appeal, each bedroom is individually decorated, right down to the handmade head boards and offers its guest a terrific view of the surrounding landscape. The dining room offers all sorts of culinary delights some of which are cooked and prepared by Carolyn's own fair hand and can be accompanied by a drink from the well stocked bar. Day fishing on the lake is from 8.00 am until dusk and tickets must be bought from the office before you start fishing.

Gatton Waters, Hillington, Nr Sandringham Tel: 01485 600643

WEST RUDHAM. If you are looking for somewhere ideally placed as a base for your holiday in this wonderful part of England, then you would do well to consider one of the excellent self-catering cottages which are available for holiday lettings all year round at **THE GRANGE**, situated at West Rudham, just two miles from East Rudham. Four delightful cottages are available: Sid's Cottage, North Cottage, South Cottage and Bertie's Cottage. Each has its own unique character, is immaculately maintained, well equipped and has everything that you are likely to require for a really good holiday, including a lovely heated swimming pool. Other local sporting facilities include golf, sailing, freshwater fishing, horse racing, tennis and roller skating. For wildlife enthusiasts, the area is a haven, having a number of reserves in close proximity. ETB Four Keys

Sid's Cottage, The Grange, West Rudham Tel: 01485 528229
NB. for North Cottage, South Cottage and Bertie's Cottage
Tel: 01282 445225

NEW HOUGHTON. Houghton Hall, built in the 1730s for Sir Robert Walpole, Britain's first Prime Minister, is perhaps the most magnificent house in the county. To improve the view from his splendid Palladian mansion, Walpole had Houghton village demolished and rebuilt on the edge of his estate as 'New Houghton'. He did, however, leave the church where it was presumably not wishing to disturb the resting place of his ancestors. The Hall is neo-Palladian architecture at its very best and the finely furnished staterooms are packed full of delights. It is one of the first houses where mahogany was used extensively throughout, and best of all is the enormous Stone Hall, undoubtedly one of the finest rooms in England.

CHAPTER FIVE

NORTH NORFOLK - STIFFKEY TO BACTON

Norfolk Broads

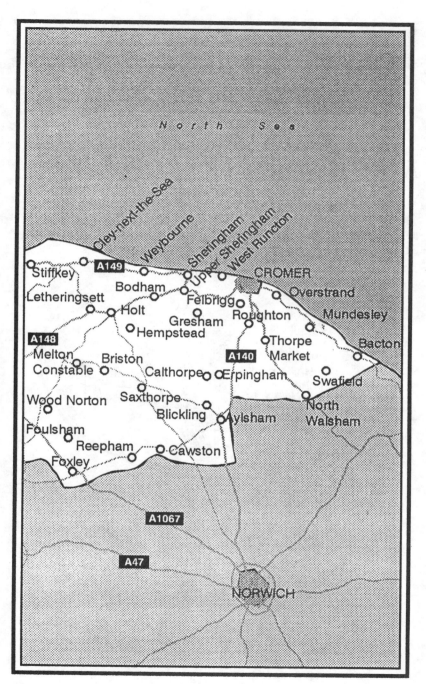

CHAPTER FIVE

NORTH NORFOLK - STIFFKEY TO FOULSHAM

Cromer and the Coast

CROMER. For many visitors Cromer certainly lives up to its self-styled reputation as the 'Gem of the North Norfolk Coast'. It is a charming seaside town as popular now as it was in the late 18th century when it first caught the eye of those seeking select bathing places in the summer. A port of no small significance, Cromer's importance as far back as medieval times can be found right in the centre of town where the magnificent tower of the 15th century church of St Peter and St Paul soars to a height of 160 ft, the tallest in the county. The main development of the town came towards the end of the 19th century and, although most of the superb Edwardian hotels that once graced the seafront have since been pulled down, the splendid **Hotel de Paris** and the **Pier** thankfully remain. Retaining many of its narrow streets in the older parts of the town, visitors soon come to appreciate that this is one of Norfolk's least spoilt seaside resorts.

Cromer Crabs, the local delicacy, are legendary and a dish of their succulent meat is well and truly fit for a king. Fishing may have declined somewhat over the years, yet a number of vessels still set out from here to bring back these delectable crustaceans; together with sole, plaice, mackerel and many other types of fish. The people of Cromer are also justly proud of their lifeboat and of the many brave men who have served in her over the years. The most famous of these was Henry Blogg, coxswain of the lifeboat from 1909 to 1947 and winner of many medals and honours, who is now commemorated by a bronze bust in North Lodge Park. The **Lifeboat Museum** stands at the foot of The Gangway, and features models and photographs illustrating the proud tradition and brave deeds of Cromer's lifeboatmen. The **Cromer Museum**, which is housed in a row of restored fishermen's cottages Brook Street, is also worth a visit to discover more about the geological, maritime and natural history of this area.

Cromer's Windmill, owned by English Heritage, is a unique 17th century mill situated right on the roadside. Open Sundays, Bank Holidays and 2nd and 4th Wednesdays between May and September; 2.30 to 5 pm.

Cromer really is the ideal place for a family holiday with its safe swimming on the sand and shingle beach, a small zoo, lovely walks, a boating lake, clubs offering family entertainment in the evenings, the summer season at the Pavilion Theatre and an excellent golf course.

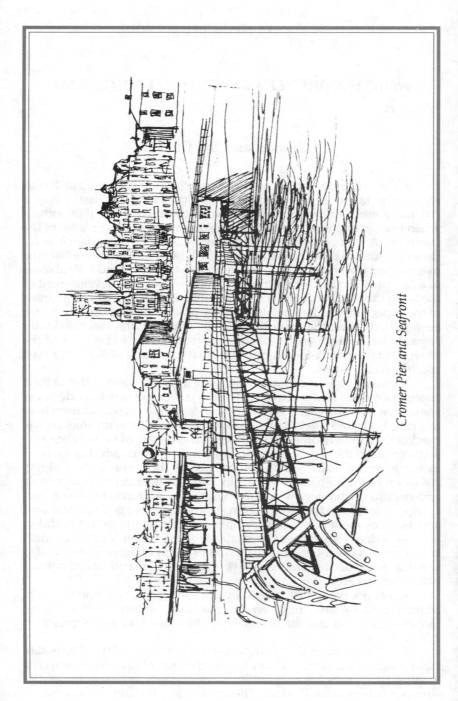

Cromer Pier and Seafront

As you arrive at the **BEACHCOMBER GUEST HOUSE** you will be struck by the bright yellow exterior and colourful sun blinds on this Victorian house. A splash of colour from the window boxes and plants at the entrance, creates an altogether most inviting appearance.

Beachcomber Guest House, 17 Macdonald Road, Cromer
Tel: 01263 513398

Anne and Brian Weinle are your very friendly hosts with a good sense of humour. All the rooms are light and airy and individually decorated in warm tones. Most of the bedrooms have en-suite facilities and all have colour television and hospitality trays. Anne caters with good English fayre and provides a three course dinner plus cheese and biscuits and a pot of coffee or tea. The breakfasts are substantial, though there is plenty of choice for those wanting to start the day on a lighter note. The location is approximately 300 yards from the beach. Awarded 2 Crown Highly Commended by ETB.

THE GROVE at Cromer was built in 1797 by Joseph Gurney of Norwich as a holiday home for his family. A delightful Country House of impressive proportions set in 3 acres of gardens.

The Grove and Cottages, 95, Overstrand Road, Cromer
Tel: 01263 512412 Fax: 01263 513416

The interior is beautifully decorated and furnished in classic style and has ten bedrooms for guests, most of which are en-suite. John and Ann Graveling also have Self-Catering Cottages which, with the help of the East Anglia Tourist Board, were converted from former barns at the Grove into three cottages. These proved so popular that an old coachman's cottage on the same site was also renovated together with the neighbouring barn. A small bungalow at the rear of the cottage makes a total of six holiday cottages all fully equipped and awarded 4 Keys Commended (Bungalow 3 Key Commended) The Grove is 2 Crown Commended. A beautiful setting near the cliffs and half a mile from town.

AROUND CROMER - WEST ALONG THE COAST

FELBRIGG. Just to the west of this pretty village, with its belt of ancient beech trees, is the National Trust property, **Felbrigg Hall**. This 17th century country mansion was built by the Windham family on the site of an earlier manor house. The mid 17th century saw a revolution in English architecture and the extraordinary contrast between the south and west wings of Felbrigg, separated by only 60 years, provides a clear illustration of this. The architect of the Jacobean south front was almost certainly the master mason Robert Lyminge, who, in the early 1620s, was also rebuilding Blickling for Sir Henry Hobart. The west wing was added in the 1680s; it was designed by William Samwell and still contains some sumptuous plasterwork of the period.

The interior of the house was extensively remodelled in the 18th century, and the internal decorations reflect this more consistent opulent style. Look out for the elegant library and the beautiful wallpaper in the Chinese bedroom which dates from the 1750s. In the grounds, be sure to visit the orangery, which was added in 1705, and the wonderful walled garden with its huge herbaceous borders, greenhouses and magnificent octagonal dovecote.

Felbrigg Hall & Sheringham Park, Felbrigg Tel: 01263 837444

AYLMERTON. There have been several sightings in the village of an unhappy ghost seen walking around The Shrieking Pits; a series of round depressions in the ground which are thought to be the sites of prehistoric dwellings or possibly flint mines. This unfortunate, unknown woman dressed in white seems doomed to perpetual misery as she clasps her hands in despair and shrieks into the pits.

EAST RUNCTON. The beach here is safe for swimming, with shingle leading to sand, and is approached through East Runton Gap. This peaceful village lies just inland within a designated Area of Outstanding Natural Beauty.

WEST RUNCTON. The 'Roman Camp' on **Beacon Hill**, near the village, is actually the site of an Anglo-Saxon iron-working settlement now in the care of the National Trust. From here there are memorable views across the Cromer Ridge and the North Sea and, at a height of 328 ft, it is the highest point in Norfolk.

West Runton is also home to the **North Norfolk Heavy Horse and Pony Centre**. The great Shires demonstrate their considerable strength, intelligence and charm twice daily and, after enjoying the display, there is plenty more to see and a pleasant picnic area to relax in and have lunch.

Fossilized sea urchins can often be found embedded in pieces of flint on the beach and, at one time, the Cromer area was a rich hunting ground for amber. Much scarcer today, it will most likely be found where the shingle meets the sand or in the rock pools. These rich deposits along the North Norfolk coast came from as far afield as the Rhine estuary and Scandinavia and the wide variety of rocks and minerals to be found here include quartz, calcite, serpentine and iron pyrites.

The **MIRABELLE RESTAURANT** in Station Road, is quite a find in this seaside village. Elegant and luxurious inside, the restaurant is named after the Mirabelle Palace in Salzberg. Proprietor Manfred Hollwoger serves an excellent variety of English and continental cuisine, including fresh locally-caught fish and Norfolk lamb. There is also an extensive list of carefully selected wines. The bar is a congenial meeting place for a pre-meal drink, and all major credit cards are accepted. The owner also has a well-appointed self-catering apartment to let which sleeps two, with lunch and dinner available in the restaurant, if required.

Mirabelle Restaurant, Station Road, West Runton Tel: 01263 837396

SHERINGHAM. A pleasant, bustling town, Sheringham has undergone the transition from quiet fishing village to small-scale resort quite gracefully. It is not a resort in the unattractive sense of the word but simply a place where everyone will find something to enjoy. The beach here is markedly different from the shingle beaches elsewhere on this part of the coast, consisting mainly of gently sloping sand; it is excellent for bathing and its adequate quota of lifeguards makes it ideal for families with children. Gorse flourishes along the cliff path and the tiny yellow flowers give out a perfume reminiscent of coconut.

A small fleet of fishing boats still operates from here and several original fishermen's cottages remain, some with lofts where the nets were mended, and baited pots for catching crabs are still set along the seafront as they would have been in bygone days.

Like so many other former fishing villages in England, Sheringham owes its transformation into a popular seaside resort to the coming of the railway which, in this instance, arrived in 1887. And you can still enjoy an authentic full-sized passenger steam railway ride on the **NORTH NORFOLK RAILWAY**. At one time, 64 trains a day used to steam into Sheringham station, but with the closure of the former Midland and Great Northern Joint Railway in 1967, the future of the line looked uncertain. With great efforts and enthusiasm from the M & GN Preservation Society, the full glory of the station has been maintained, and is now operated by the North Norfolk Railway Company. The Society had already bought the section of track beyond Weybourne as far as the Sheringham boundary when the Melton Constable to Sheringham line closed in 1964, and it took the opportunity of leasing the unused station in 1967. Prior to 1963, before the line had closed, the Society had formed a private company, the Norfolk Railway Company. They applied for a Light Railway Order which would grant them the status to carry fare paying passengers and by 1975 the first passengers enjoyed the rewards of all this labour.

North Norfolk Railway, Sheringham Station, Sheringham
Tel: 01263 822045

Today, the company runs steam locomotives between Sheringham, Weybourne and a new station at Holt, where there are plans to develop a museum and buildings on the site. Passengers are certainly well-catered for with a buffet provided on the trains, offering light refreshments or a full meal. Sheringham Station also has a gift shop where you can purchase all sorts of gifts and railway memorabilia souvenirs. Volunteers are always welcome to help restore and maintain the railways and stock, so do give them a ring on Sheringham 822045 if you feel you can offer your services. The railway opens between March - November and they have special events such as fun runs at Halloween and Santa Claus Specials.

Locals and visitors alike should give thanks to the National Trust for their policy of acquiring large parts of the heath and woodland that lie to the south of Sheringham, thereby halting the spread of suburbia so beloved by our town planners. The land here rises steeply to a sand and gravel ridge which runs parallel to the coastline from Cromer to Holt and reaches a height of more than 300 ft in places.

Situated just 2 minutes from Sheringham town centre and only 1 minute's walk from the local beach, you will find **CANTON HOUSE**. Built in 1900, this charming, weather-beaten, red bricked building used to be the staff quarters for landed gentry on their visits to the coast. Chris Rayment has run this very welcoming and friendly Bed & Breakfast for over 14 years, and you are guaranteed some of the warmest hospitality in the county. All the food is freshly home-cooked by Chris herself who is a trained chef, this is clearly reflected in her gorgeous breakfasts and especially the delicious homemade bread. There are three bedrooms available, all attractively decorated and furnished with all the usual home comforts. Canton House is ideally located for plenty of evening entertainment with its local pubs and for those summer days the beach will be the perfect spot for that afternoon picnic.

Canton House, 14 Cliff Road, Sheringham Tel: 01263 824861

Those looking for elegant accommodation with a delightful personal touch should make a point of finding **SOUTHLANDS HOTEL** in South Street. During the Second World War, this handsome Edwardian residence was commandeered as an officers' billet. Now an impressive family-run hotel, it is conveniently located within three minutes walk of the town centre and seafront. Proprietors Estelle and Anthony Preston assure their guests of the finest individual attention. Their sixteen well-appointed guest bedrooms all have private bathrooms and colour TV, and there is also a relaxing bar and a dining room serving the finest English dishes.

Southlands Hotel, South Street, Sheringham Tel/Fax: 01263 822679

UPPER SHERINGHAM. The 770 acres of National Trust parkland, **Sheringham Park**, was originally designed by Humphrey Repton in 1812. Visitors can follow waymarked trails through large areas of species rhododendrons and azaleas (at their best in late May and early June) and on towards the coastline. Magnificent views of the Norfolk coast and countryside can be obtained by climbing specially constructed viewing towers. The aptly-named **Pretty Corner**, just to the east of the A1082 at its junction with the A148, is a particularly beautiful area of woodland and it also offers superb views over the surrounding countryside.

Pretty Corner Tea Gardens, Upper Sheringham Tel: 01263 822766

Situated in the heart of the Sheringham woods in an area called Pretty Corner, you will find **PRETTY CORNER TEA GARDENS** in one of the best locations in Norfolk and is owned and run by Judy Padfield who moved here with her family a year ago and has already built up a great reputation. The tea rooms overlook 2 acres of landscape gardens, complete with ornamental fish pond and plenty of open air seating available when the weather allows. If the climate is a bit cold then nothing could be nicer than to warm yourself next to one of the open fires and sample some of Judy's wonderful cakes and a pot of freshly brewed coffee. Also available are sandwiches, snacks and freshly baked scones with lashings of jam and cream. Open from Easter to late October, Pretty Corner Tea Gardens is the perfect place to stop and rest awhile before roaming the many trails that can be found in the local Sheringham woods.

WEYBOURNE. Here, the shingle beach known as **Weybourne Hope** (or Hoop) slopes so steeply that it is said that an invading fleet could bring their ships practically to the shore. This gives rise to the local adage: 'He who would Old England Win, Must at Weybourne Hoop begin'. A map dated 1st May 1588 clearly shows 'Waborne Fort' opposite Weybourne Hope with an area of salt marsh dividing it from the sea. The Holt Parish Register for those times states: 'In this yeare was the town of Waborne fortified with a continuall garrison of men bothe of horse and foote with sconces (earthworks) ordinaunce and all manner of appoyntment to defend the Spannyards landing theare'. Firm evidence that Weybourne would have been considered a likely landing point for the Spanish Armada.

Heavily defended during both World Wars, the army camp that was established here was later to become the Anti-Aircraft Permanent Range and Radar Training Wing, providing training for national servicemen until the camp finally closed in March 1959. The site has since been returned to agricultural use but the original NAAFI building remains and now houses **The Muckleburgh Collection**, a fascinating museum of military equipment which has seen action in battlefields all around the world. Many of the tanks, armoured cars, amphibious vehicles and pieces of artillery on display have required complete restoration, and all can be touched and examined at close hand.

Despite Weybourne's long tradition of being ready to defend itself from invasion it was in fact only attacked once, by enemy aircraft on 11th July 1940. A stick of bombs landed in the main street and badly damaged two cottages.

CLEY NEXT THE SEA. Visitors a century ago would have seen ships moored alongside the church. Now the sea has receded dramatically and the village could be called Cley-a-mile-away-from-the-Sea!

Cley (which, like Cockley Cley, is pronounced 'Cly' and means 'clay') was at one time the largest port on the Glaven estuary but the inexorable forces of silt and land reclamation have left it high and dry and only accessible from the sea by small craft. Although the quayside remains, nothing is now left of the old harbour at the southern end of the village from which wool was once exported to the Netherlands. Norfolk is liberally dotted with windmills and the one situated on the old quayside at Cley is particularly fine.

The **Cley and Salthouse Marshes** lie between the coast road and the sea and around 650 acres of this land is a nature reserve run by the Norfolk Naturalists' Trust. A visitors' information centre has details of all the different species of bird that breed here. There is a car park at Cley Eye with access onto the beach but bathing is not advisable as the shingle shelves steeply under the sea.

An outstanding place to stay for those looking for accommodation with a difference can be found on the northern side of Cley next the Sea. One of the best-known landmarks on the north Norfolk coast, **CLEY MILL** is an early 18th century windmill which has been converted into a unique guesthouse with self-catering accommodation attached. This striking building stands in a secluded position overlooking Blakeney harbour, with breathtaking views of the salt marshes and the Cley bird sanctuary. It dates from the time when Cley next the Sea was an important wool and grain port, and remained as a working flour mill until 1919.

Renovated and converted to its present form by its current owners in 1983, Cley Mill is now managed by Chris Buisseret, a congenial host who combines the friendly atmosphere of a private home with the food and service of a fine hotel. As well as delicious breakfasts and excellent evening meals, picnic lunches can be provided on request. The mill's stables and boat sheds have been converted into two well-appointed self-catering apartments, each sleeping two people, which are available throughout the year. The mill is also open to the public between Whitsun and the end of September.

Cley Mill, Cley-next-the-Sea Tel/Fax: 01263 740209

THE HARNSER is a grand old former coaching inn dating back to the 18th century, built of traditional Norfolk flint and picturesquely situated on the edge of the marshes opposite Cley Windmill. In 1995 the Harnser changed ownership and Andrew Cooke, ably assisted by his sister Mandy, have transformed the Restaurant and the accommodation. Andrew trained as Chef at a well known hotel in Blakeney and has added many new customers to his client list. His particular menu speciality is fish which is guaranteed fresh from his father's fishing boat. The menu is extensive, running to some five pages and the food is superb. All the bedrooms have been completely refurbished, so for those wishing to spend a few days out on the marshes with camera or fishing rod, the comforts and very friendly atmosphere of The Harnser will ensure you have a most enjoyable stay.

The Harnser, Coast Road, Cley next the Sea Tel: 01263 740776.

WIVETON. At one time a thriving port on the River Glaven, Wiveton is now reduced to the status of quiet coastal village. Serving as reminders of its formal glory are the handsome church on the green with parts dating back to the 14th century, a medieval bridge and Wiveton Hall on the edge of Cley Marshes.

GLANDFORD. It is worth stopping off at Glandford to see the **Shell Museum**; a large collection housed in a fine old cottage designed in the Flemish style like several others in the village. The shells have been brought back to Norfolk from around the world and are beautifully presented in glass cases. Another interesting feature here is a striking embroidered panel created by John Craske, a Sheringham fisherman who was also renowned as an artist.

LETHERINGSETT. 'Larnsett' (as local dialect would have it) is a truly charming place in the most delightful setting. Among carefully landscaped trees, Letheringsett stands in the lovely Glaven valley on both banks of the river; the two halves of the village linked by an ornate iron bridge which was built in 1818 by local landowner William Hardy. The great watermill by St Andrew's Church still produces flour today and the gardens of the impressive 18th century Letheringsett Hall are open to visitors under the National Gardens Scheme.

THE KING'S HEAD at Letheringsett is a delightful place to stop on the A148 Fakenham to Cromer road. Mentioned in Sir John Betjeman's poem, 'Lord Cuzons Hardy', it has been a renowned pub and eating place for many decades. Its traditional atmosphere attracts visitors and locals alike, with a special welcome being given to families with children. As well as serving an excellent range of wines and ales, proprietors Pam and David Watts offer a wide selection of bar meals, including jacket potatoes, ploughman's lunches, steaks and vegetarian entrees. All items are home-cooked using fresh local ingredients where possible.

King's Head, Letheringsett Tel: 01263 712691

HOLT. An attractive market town whose more interesting houses are of the Georgian era; most of the town having been destroyed in a great fire in 1708.

Gresham's School was founded in 1555 as a grammar school by Sir John Gresham, then Lord Mayor of London. The original building was rebuilt Tudor-style in 1858 and still stands in the market place but the school itself was relocated to the eastern outskirts in 1900 and became a public school. One of Holt's most unusual buildings is **Home Place**. Designed and built in 1903-5 by ES Prior, an architect of the Arts and Crafts movement, the building's exterior is completely clad in local pebbles.

Holt's mixture of grand Georgian and Victorian houses, colour-washed buildings around the market place and traditional Norfolk flint cottages off the pretty main street makes for a very pleasant, often picturesque, combination of styles. Small wonder that the town has been designated a Conservation Area. Another interesting feature to look out for is the large obelisk-cum-milestone surmounted by a pineapple which can be found at the north end of town at the top of Letheringsett Hill. It was apparently a former gatepost from Melton Constable Park, and bearing in mind that Melton Constable lies some four miles to the south-west of Holt, it is obvious that the original inscriptions on the column showing distances to all the local villages are somewhat unreliable!

HEMPSTEAD. 'Quiet and secluded' - 'An oasis in the country' is how we saw **HEMPSTEAD HALL**, an attractive 19th century country house quietly set on a 300 acre arable farm, just two miles off the A148 and the Georgian town of Holt. Guests can walk in the gardens or on the farm and feed the ducks and donkeys; many like to stroll around the large kitchen garden and greenhouses. For the more adventurous there is a 5 mile circular walk to Holt Country Park. A lovely day can be enjoyed with a visit to the seal sanctuary at Blakeney Point by boat, or take a ride on the steam train from Holt. The house and its surroundings are very picturesque; wander down to the weeping willow by the pond or just amble around the grounds and soak up the peaceful atmosphere, visit the summerhouse and perhaps have a picnic. The bedrooms have either en-suite or private bathrooms and have television and tea/coffee making facilities. Of course, there is traditional farmhouse breakfast to set you up for the day. Book ahead for this treat. ETB. - 2 Crown Commended.

Hempstead Hall, Hempstead Tel: 01263 712224

BALE. An attractive farming hamlet with a little green where a cobbler once had his shop in the hollow of a giant oak tree. The ancient **Great Bale Oak** finally gave up the ghost and was felled in 1860 and the graceful grove of ilex trees, planted to replace it, now stands proud in front of All Saints' Church.

HINDRINGHAM. The landmark church of St Martin's stands high above the village on a hilltop. Along with the windmill at nearby **Lower Green**, they must make excellent navigational aids for the local birdlife!

BINHAM. The spectacular, ruined, Benedictine Priory, situated above the river and founded in 1091, must once have been a truly magnificent building. Evidence of superb workmanship still exists in the stone columns, and the monastic church, now used as the parish church, is a rare example of Early English architecture in Norfolk. Many of the houses in the village were built from stone from the Priory, the remains of which are now in the care of English Heritage.

LANGHAM. This lovely village was the home and final resting place of that well known English naval officer and novelist, Captain Frederick Marryat. After leading a fairly distinguished naval career, he went on to write a series of novels concerning life at sea, the most famous of which was 'Mr Midshipman Easy'. Although he did extremely well in his new career his extravagant lifestyle inevitably led him into financial embarrassment. In 1843 he settled on a small farm at Langham and spent the rest of his days as a gentleman farmer and writing children's stories.

BLAKENEY. This charming village was a commercial port until the beginning of the 20th century when the silting up of the estuary prevented anything but pleasure craft from gaining access at high tide.

The old Guildhall stands on Blakeney's attractive High Street, which runs down to the harbour. By the side of the main road is the beautifully restored Church of St Nicholas, its magnificent west tower stands over 100 ft high and acts as a landmark for miles around. A light in the smaller turret at the east end of the chancel was once used as a beacon for guiding ships safely into Blakeney harbour.

MORSTON. From the little quay visitors are ferried over to the huge spit of sand and shingle known as **Blakeney Point**, where Norfolk's very first nature reserve was established. As this is the northernmost part of the county it is visited by a wide variety of migrating birds and, in winter, local boatmen will take you out to see the large colony of common seals which basks on the sandbanks off the Point.

Morston village itself lies about a mile south of the tidal creek which flows through the marshes between the Point and the mainland and all but dries up completely at low tide. It is a particularly pleasant little place with quiet lanes and clusters of cottages built from local cobbles. Watch out for the patched-up tower of All Saints' Church which was struck by lightning in 1743.

STIFFKEY. The straggling brick and flint village of Stiffkey stands on the coast road above the river of the same name. Pronounced 'Stewkey', the name means 'island of stumps' and is most likely a reference to the marshy river valley of reed beds and fallen trees which indeed gives the village the appearance of an island. At the east end of the village is the church of St John the Baptist and from the churchyard there are fine views of the river and of **Stiffkey Hall** to the south. All that now remains of this impressive building, built by the Bacon family in 1578, are the towers, one wing of the house and the 17th century gatehouse. The stately ruins of the Great Hall have been transformed into a rose terrace and sunken garden and open to the public.

The former rectory is a grand Georgian building, famous as the residence of the Reverend Harold Davidson, rector of Stiffkey during the 1920s and 1930s. The Reverend Davidson's personal crusade for saving the 'fallen women' of London's West End caused much gossip and scandal at the time, not unlike the central character in Michael Palin's film, 'The Missionary'. Despite the fact that his notoriety regularly filled the church to capacity, he constantly fell foul of the ecclesiastical authorities and eventually lost his living. There is a bizarre ending to his story: after handing over the keys of Stiffkey Rectory he joined a travelling show and was later killed by the lion whose cage he shared!

To the north of the village are the **Stiffkey Salt Marshes**, a National Trust nature reserve which turns a delicate shade of purple in July when the sea lavender is in bloom. Here on the sandflats the famous 'Stewkey blues' can be found: a cockle by any other name, and considered to be a delicacy at markets all over England where they are sold.

AROUND CROMER - EAST ALONG THE COAST

OVERSTRAND. This stretch of coast was a favourite place for the upper-classes to come and build their summer houses and Overstrand, in particular, boasts some outstanding examples of that period. Overstrand Hall was built by Edwin Lutyens in 1899 for Lord Hillingdon, while The Pleasaunce, built for Lady Battersea two years earlier, boasts gardens designed by Gertrude Jekyll, who is enjoying something of a revival.

A quaint little crab fishing village which has gradually developed into a popular holiday resort with a safe, sandy beach, Overstrand is built near cliffs which are fast eroding. The Church of St Martin was built to replace a much earlier church which fell into the sea in the 14th century and east of here there is no access to the sea at all until you reach Mundesley, five miles further along the coast.

NORTHREPPS. A tranquil village, its buildings are centred around the 15th century St Mary's Church. Verily Anderson's book, 'The Northrepps Grandchildren', vividly describes the life at Northrepps Hall and makes excellent background reading for all visitors to the northern part of the county.

TRUNCH. Here the grave of Horatio, son of Lord Nelson by his mistress Lady Hamilton, can be found in the beautiful church of St Mary's. The roof is very fine indeed, but by far the best feature of the church is the font with its splendid overhead canopy, a gloriously embellished piece of carving standing on six tall legs. It must be quite a struggle for the vicar to negotiate the platform with a wriggling baby without bashing its head against one of the supports!

MUNDESLEY. After the hazards of the coastline immediately to the north, where cliffs, fields and houses have all been eroded away by the relentless sea, it is a pleasure to arrive at the quiet holiday resort of Mundesley with its superb sandy beach. Mundesley (pronounced 'Munsley') is totally unspoilt, yet it has all the facilities needed for a relaxing family holiday. Golf, bowling and fishing can all be enjoyed and, perhaps best of all, there is safe swimming in the sea while children can splash about in the many shallow pools or 'lowies' left behind by the ebbing tide.

PASTON. This little hamlet has an enormous thatched barn to the west of the church. Superbly restored, the barn dates back to 1581 and is all that is left of the original home of the Paston family. Their fortune was made in the wool trade and they are best remembered for the famous 'Paston Letters': written by several members of the family in the mid-15th century, they provide a vivid insight into how the Pastons' many estates were run during those unsettled times of the Wars of the Roses.

BACTON ON SEA. To the south of the village is the ruined gateway of **Bromholm Priory**, which enjoyed great acclaim during the Middle Ages for its proud possession of a piece of the 'True Cross'. This relic from Calvary was purported to cure various ailments, from leprosy to death, and even gets a mention in Chaucer's 'Reeve's Tale'. Bromholm was referred to many times in the 'Paston Letters' and also commanded the attention of that famous witch and prophetess, Mother Shipton, who foretold that the priory would become a farm. As it happened, she was quite correct, for that is just what it is today!

Originally built for an Indian Princess, **THE POACHER'S POCKET MOTEL** is positioned on the very edge of the beach with absolutely fantastic sea views. This wonderful property has been managed by Gary, Suzanna and Martin for the past 18 months and really does the family credit as a party atmosphere is always in the air. There are 5 chalets available for the traveller. Each chalet is en-suite with television, tea and coffee making facilities and full central heating and double glazing; each can be hired on a daily Bed and Breakfast basis. The pub serves up to 12 real ales on draught and offers a games room and family room with Eurosport on Sky Satellite if the local pool team doesn't keep you entranced. The restaurant is seasonally open all day and offers a fine choice of food at an excellent price. Fresh local fish is the specialty of the house, with fresh prawns and scampi, scallops and crab being top of the menu. Griddled steaks are also available, each being plump and succulent and served with chips, onion rings, mushrooms and salad, delicious! A large Private Function Room is available for weddings, parties and seminars; with a Disco and live music played every weekend the party atmosphere goes on and on.

Poachers Pocket Motel, Walcott Road, Bacton on Sea Tel: 01692 650467

North Walsham and Behind the Coast

NORTH WALSHAM is a prosperous little market town which has held a weekly market for over 700 years. Much of this prosperity came from selling the woven goods made at the nearby village of Worstead, from which the famous woollen cloth takes its name.

The fine timber Market Cross with its lead-covered domed roof and lantern was rebuilt after a fire in 1602 destroyed many of the town buildings. St Nicholas' Church, in Market Street, dates back to the 15th century; the stump of its fallen tower (which once stood 147 ft high) formed the perfect accompaniment to the tower of the earlier Saxon church just to the north. Across the square is the Paston Grammar School, founded in 1606, where Lord Nelson spent part of his schooldays.

Also in the heart of North Walsham, and appropriately situated opposite the Black Cat Garage, is the fascinating **CAT POTTERY**. Jenny Winstanley has been making her unique earthenware cats and dogs here for over three decades. Each one is individually modelled, painted and glazed, then after hard-firing, is fitted with specially-made cathedral-glass eyes. Jenny's animals are highly collectible and are sold all over the world. Her studio is a centuries-old tinsmith's workshop which she shares with her glass-sculptor husband Ken Allen and their son Nick.

Over the years, the building has also become home to Nick's unique collection of railway memorabilia and transport curiosities. Open 9am to 5pm Mondays to Fridays, and 11am to 1pm Saturdays (11 am to 3 pm on Saturdays during the school holidays).

Cat Pottery, 1 Grammar School Road, North Walsham
Tel: 01692 402962

The **BEECHWOOD HOTEL** in North Walsham provides a friendly and comfortable base for touring the beautiful countryside and coastline of north Norfolk. This handsome Georgian redbrick residence was built in 1800 and for many decades was the home of the local doctor. It is only three minutes walk from the marketplace and yet is surrounded by an extensive lawned garden which is noted for its beautiful rose walk, fish pond and charming sunken garden.

Converted to a hotel in 1972, it now offers some of the most elegant and comfortable accommodation in the area. The ten spacious guest bedrooms are individually furnished with fine antiques, and each has its own en suite bath or shower-room, remote-control television and direct-dial telephone. Resident proprietor Lindsay Spalding and his staff offer their guests the finest individual attention. The restaurant is renowned for its traditional English cuisine and impressive wine list, and after their meal, guests can relax with one of the many books in the drawing room, whose elegant French windows open onto the garden. The hotel offers a variety of attractive off-peak concessions, and the recent introduction of Murder Mystery evenings has been a great success.

Beechwood Hotel, Cromer Road, North Walsham
Tel: 01692 403231 Fax: 01692 407284

The delightful **HILL HOUSE COUNTRY HOTEL** is set within eight acres of secluded grounds on the southern edge of North Walsham. With parts dating back to the late 18th-century, this handsome old building stands in an elevated position surrounded by beautiful rolling lawns and mature woodland. Recently refurbished, it now offers first-class accommodation in an atmosphere which is relaxed and welcoming. All the bedrooms have private bathrooms and colour TV, and there is also an excellent restaurant, a fully-licensed bar, and a charming guest lounge with French windows leading out into the garden.

Hill House Country Hotel, Old Yarmouth Road, North Walsham
Tel/Fax: 01692 402151

AROUND NORTH WALSHAM

THORPE MARKET. To the east of the picturesque village green, a fine avenue of trees leads to St Margaret's Church. Dating back to 1796, this is Norfolk's only example of a Gothick (or Gothic Revival) church. Featuring turrets with little spires on each corner of the building and two open-work screens dividing the church into three separate parts, there are also two individual porches; one for the priest and the other for the congregation.

POPPYLAND COTTAGE, CRAFT AND COFFEE SHOPPE overlooks the village green and the owners, Patricia and Philip, provide a warm welcome, whether you are stopping for morning coffee and pastries or a light lunch and a glass of wine, or maybe afternoon tea with scones and cream. All round you are surrounded by flowers, craftwork and paintings and it is difficult to concentrate on the menu but do so, because ingredients are fresh and home-cooked. All the baking is done on the premises each day, those with a sweet tooth watch out! As you are made to feel so welcome, it is tempting to linger so it is worth remembering that accommodation is available in Puddleduck Holiday Cottage and their peaceful Caravan club site.

Poppyland Cottage, The Green, Thorpe Market Tel: 01263 833219

The name 'Poppyland' was coined by Clement Scott in a newspaper article at the end of the 19th century, when this became quite a fashionable area up to the first World War - so much so that the village of Overstrand became known as the 'village of the millionaires'.

A mile or two to the south-west is the lovely little church of St Andrew in Gunton Park. Built by Robert Adam in 1769, it features a Doric portico of great Tuscan columns at the west entrance and resembles a temple rather than a church. **Gunton Hall** has been largely restored though parts of the house, which was badly damaged by fire in 1882, stand in ruins in a lovely formal garden.

The **SUFFIELD ARMS** in Church Road, opposite Gunton Station, is a lively free house which is renowned for its good food and friendly atmosphere. The interior is warmed by a wood-burning stove in winter, and in summer customers can sit outside on the patio or on the lawn. As well as an impressive selection of real ales, proprietors Paul and Mary Mason serve a range of excellent value pub meals, including a separate children's menu. According to legend, the local landowner closed the pub in Suffield after finding his workers drunk one afternoon; in its place built the Suffield Arms in its present location, too far from the estate to be reached at lunchtime.

Suffield Arms, Church Road, Thorpe Market Tel: 01263 833461

Only 4 miles from the coast at Cromer and set in the heart of the beautiful, unspoilt North Norfolk countryside overlooking Gunton Deer Park, the **ELDERTON LODGE HOTEL AND RESTAURANT** dates back to earlier, perhaps more graceful, times. Once the Shooting Lodge and Dower House to the adjacent Gunton Hall Estate, the lodge was a favoured retreat for Lillie Langtry, the noted Edwardian beauty. According to local lore it was here that she entertained Edward V11, then Prince of Wales, who frequently visited Gunton Hall, family home of the Earls of Suffield.

Elderton Lodge Hotel, Thorpe Market Tel: 01263 833547
Fax: 01263 834673

Today, Elderton Lodge remains a sanctuary from the madding

crowd, set well back from the road standing in six acres of mature gardens and enjoying spectacular views of the herds of deer and sunsets across the thousand-plus acres of Gunton Park. Built in the latter half of the eighteenth century, Elderton Lodge (Grade II listed) still retains many original features. The eight en-suite, individually decorated bedrooms are traditional in style and tastefully appointed with all modern amenities. The elegant Georgian candlelit restaurant is noted for its fine food and imaginative dishes. The emphasis is on fresh local produce with seafood from the coast and game, in season, from the adjacent estates, always featured. Elderton Lodge is open throughout the year and its owners Martin and Christine Worby will ensure your stay is both relaxing and memorable. ETB - 3 Crown Commended.

ROUGHTON. St Mary's Church with its Saxon round tower stands at one end of the long village street.

To the south of Roughton, on the A140, is a fascinating working crafts complex housed in a well-restored group of brick and flint farm buildings. **Alby Gardens** with its comprehensive range of wild and wetland plants, together with the **Alby Lace Museum**. As well as having a stunning collection of lace, some of it over 300 years old, visitors can the intricate art of bobbin lace making. Handmade lace, lacemakers' requisites and books on the subject can all be purchased at the shop. Here too is the Charles Matts Furniture Showroom, where you can buy or commission beautifully crafted furniture made from locally grown hardwoods in a great variety of original designs.

ERPINGHAM. The name of the village is spelt out around the parapet of the tall 15th century tower of St Mary's Church which stands on Gallows Hill overlooking Erpingham.

BLICKLING. **Blickling Hall** is a magnificent redbrick mansion built on the site of a late-medieval moated house purchased in 1616 by Sir Henry Hobart.

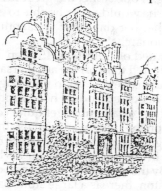

Blickling Hall, Blicking Tel: 01263 733471

Hobart commissioned the architect of Hatfield House, Robert Lyminge, to design his new country residence and in 1628 Blickling was completed. Inside, is the Great Hall with its carved Jacobean double-flight staircase, the splendid library in the Long Gallery and the Peter the Great Room which is dominated by a massive tapestry of the Battle of Poltawa. This was given by the Empress Catherine the Great to John Hobart, the Second Earl of Buckinghamshire, whilst ambassador to the Russian court.

In the grounds is an 18th century orangery, an extensive parterre, a delightful secret garden and huge yew hedges originally planted in the 17th century. In late spring, the garden is ablaze with rhododendrons and azaleas; in high summer, the large exotic herbaceous borders dominate. The parks and woods contain several miles of footpaths, a mile long crescent-shaped lake and the unusual pyramidal mausoleum of the Second Earl of Buckinghamshire. Look out for special events and guided walks throughout the year. Adjacent to Blickling, and within the National Trust estate, stands the famous Buckinghamshire Arms public house, itself a Grade II listed building and an ideal stopping place for those wanting good food and drink in genuinely historc surroundings.

Standing 45 ft high, the pyramid at Blickling is undoubtedly the finest of its kind in England. It is strikingly different to its Egyptian relatives in that it has a large portico at the main entrance to the mausoleum, which is surmounted by the Earl of Buckinghamshire's arms. Its builder was Ignatius Bonomi, an architect with a definite penchant for the Egyptian style, and he is also renowned as the builder of a particularly splendid mill in Yorkshire, where his 'Egypt-mania' was given full rein.

One resident of the original house at Blickling was Sir John Fastolf and it only required a minor change of his name to give Shakespeare one of his most endearing characters. Sir John sold the house to Geoffrey Boleyn, the great-grandfather of Anne Boleyn and it is possible that she was in fact born here. Poor Anne, the great love of Henry VIII until it became evident that she would never be able to give him an heir. If only Henry had known that her daughter Elizabeth would become one of England's greatest monarchs!

Anne was executed on 19th May 1536 on a charge of treason and adultery and it is reported that, on the anniversary of her death, a coach drawn by headless horses drives up to Blickling Hall with the unfortunate Anne clutching her disembodied head inside. The phantom traffic on the roads around the estate must get quite congested at this time of year, as it is said that on the same evening her father, Thomas Boleyn, can also be spotted charging along the lanes in his coach - his task to cross over 40 of Norfolk's bridges as penance for his betrayal of the King.

CAWSTON. By the side of the B1149, and close to its junction with the B1145 near Cawston, there is a large stone ball on a plinth called the Duelling Stone. It commemorates a duel fought between Sir Henry Hobart and Oliver La Neve in 1698 and the National Trust plaque states that their quarrel arose from words spoken in anger during an election campaign. Sir Henry was mortally wounded and died at Blickling the following day, while La Neve fled to Holland then later returned to stand

Blicking Hall, Blicking

trial and was acquitted. La Neve came from nearby Great Witchingham Hall, better known today perhaps as the original HQ of one of Norfolk's more famous sons, Bernard Matthews CBE - he of 'bootiful' turkey-roll fame!

The most memorable thing about Cawston itself is the impressive Church of St Agnes with its stunning hammerbeam roof and 120 ft high tower that soars above the houses of this little town.

THE WALNUTS is a large and comfortable detached country house which offers a high standard of bed and breakfast accommodation, ideally situated for a holiday or short break exploring all of the 'Hidden Places' which are described in this chapter. The house is set in well kept gardens and has a private swimming pool and changing rooms, which are available for guests to use. The bedrooms are beautifully decorated and furnished and have en-suite facilities, colour television, radio / alarm clock and tea & coffee making facilities. Full English Breakfast is served in the dining room. There are many good pubs and restaurants nearby Smoking is permitted only in the garden. Kennels are available nearby.

The Walnuts is situated on the B1145, convenient for Norwich City Centre, Norwich Airport and the Coast. ETB Highly Commended.

The Walnuts, 8/12 New Street, Cawston Tel: 01603 871357

If you are fascinated by horses, then base your holiday at **ALBION RIDES** which is situated in an unspoilt and sparsely populated area of Norfolk countryside near the village of Cawston. During your stay, you will tavel on horseback along grassy bridleways flanked by high hedges, through ancient woodlands and modern plantations. You might gallop over wild heathlands, or pass quietly through sleepy villages, enjoying an idyllic view of a beautiful landscape. The horses are Irish Draught, cob and hunter crosses, they will reliably carry you all day and give a good ride at a variety of paces. It is expected that you can ride competently and be sensitive to the needs of the horse and the conditions. If you are not experienced, then Albion Rides will be pleased to offer tuition using qualified BHS instructors. If you just wish to have one day riding whilst you are in the area, then that too can be accommodated. This is an excellent way to see Norfolk, and very good value for money. Be sure to ring for full details of all of the holidays and breaks which are available.

Albion Rides, Duck Row, Cawston Tel: 01603 871725

SALLE. The little village of Salle (pronounced 'Saul') has three great local families - the Briggs, the Fountaines and the Boleyns - to thank for providing the magnificent and massive 15th century Church of St Peter and St Paul. There are treasures inside: from the Seven Sacrament font complete with original beam and pulley to lift the cover, to the three-decker pulpit, medieval stained glass and abundance of wonderful carvings and brasses. This is also thought, by some, to be Anne Boleyn's final resting place.

REEPHAM. The spacious square in the centre of this small market town is surrounded by mellow Georgian buildings. The churchyard here once held three churches though now only two remain. All Saints Church, the old parish church of Hackford, was destroyed by fire in 1543 and only a part of the tower wall remains. The surviving churches, St Mary's and St Michael's, are linked by a common choir vestry. This was the place where the parish boundaries of Reepham, Hackford and Whitwell met and each village insisted on having its own church and all three were built on the same site. Later, the three villages merged into Reepham.

Quite apart from its churches, Reepham has a number of fine old buildings that will catch your eye as you explore the town. One of the best of these is known locally as the Dial House due to a sun-dial above its portico, which is inscribed with the words: 'I do not count the hours unless they are sunny/happy'.

SAXTHORPE. At St Andrew's church a delightful story concerns the 17th century altar rails, which have unusually large knobs on the posts. It appears that the knobs are in fact so large that they have actually been confirmed on several occasions by short-sighted bishops!

LITTLE BARNINGHAM. The tiny church of St Mary's has a particularly fine example of the type of off-beat humour sometimes to be found in English churches. On the corner post of a box pew stands the wooden carving of a skeleton decked out Grim Reaper-style, complete with shroud, hour-glass and scythe. The pew was dedicated by one

Stephen Crosbie in 1640 and the inscription reads: 'As you are now, even so was I, Remember death for ye must dye'. This otherwise conventional message is given a somewhat macabre twist by an additional inscription on the back of the pew, which states: 'For couples joined in wedlock this seat did I intend'.

Just to the south of the village are **Mannington Hall Gardens**, which are well worth a visit. The Rose Gardens, created in an old walled kitchen garden, feature roses in small gardens reflecting their period of origin. Lord and Lady Walpole have provided 20 miles of way-marked footpaths, including nature, local history and farm trails. These are open every day with just a small parking fee. There is access for wheelchair users, over a boardwalk, across a traditional wet meadow and light refreshments are available when the gardens are open.

About a mile to the east, Lord and Lady Walpole are also busily restoring their home, **Wolterton Hall**, to its former splendour. The Old Brew House is being opened as a Visitor Centre and Wolterton is the centre for the Hawk and Owl Trust. A number of musical events and lectures are held in the saloon of the handsome red-brick house, which was built by Horatio Walpole (with Thomas Ripley as architect) in 1741. Information on both of these estates can be obtained from Mannington Hall (Telephone: 01263 874175).

Two 'castles' lie a few miles to the north of here; not really castles at all in the accepted sense, but fortified moated manor houses built by two other important local families. The first is Baconsthorpe Castle, built by the Heydons in the 15th century and pulled down in 1654; some of its stone to be used at Felbrigg Hall further east. Its remains are now in the hands of English Heritage. The other is Gresham Castle, one of the Paston family's many properties, the ruins of which can be seen in the fields to the south of Gresham village.

MELTON CONSTABLE. **Melton Constable Hall** stands in a beautiful park with a lake and was the home of the Astley family for over 700 years (1236 to 1956). The present late 17th century building, has been used as a set in various films, including 'The Go-Between' with Julie Christie and Alan Bates. Although neglected for many years, the Hall's current owners have embarked upon a long campaign of restoration to bring the house back to its former glory. The tall tower surmounted by a glass observatory that was built by the Astleys in 1588 can be seen from the B1110 to the north-west of the village. It was used then as a look-out post to warn of the approach of the Armada and for similar purposes during the Napoleonic Wars and both World Wars.

BRISTON. This was once the centre of the Midland & Great Northern Joint Railway, its lines linking Norfolk to the Midlands, but no trace of the lines or the station remain today.

John Pole and his wife Liz are recent owners of **THE GREEN MAN**, a well-established old public house with origins back in the 18th century situated on the outskirts of Briston. Its 'olde Worlde' style is reflected in low-beamed ceilings and huge roaring fire under an original inglenook fireplace. A special attraction for pool fans is the exceptional pool room positioned at one end of the inn. This room and its table is reminiscent of a gentleman's snooker room, and is one of the best we have ever seen. On Sunday lunchtimes, the room is transformed into a superb dining area where traditional Sunday roasts are served. Bar meals are available every lunchtime and evening, except Sundays. There is a set menu comprising a good range of starters, main meals, snacks and deserts, and additional daily specials board tempting you with mouthwatering dishes such as homemade beef casserole, barbecued spare ribs, honey roast ham and rump steak. Delicious! John and Liz have an ambitious refurbishing programme which when complete will include a new restaurant specialising in Italian and Mediterranean food. Open all day, every day, except Sunday when normal licensing hours apply. All in all, it's a very classy inn.

The Green Man, Hall Street, Briston Tel: 01263 861449

FOULSHAM. The attractive market place was rebuilt after a devastating fire in 1771 and the village's imposing Georgian houses are dominated by the 15th century tower of Holy Innocents' Church.

THE QUEEN'S HEAD in Foulsham dates back in parts to the 17th century and is full of character, both inside and out. Colin Rowe and his partner Dorothy Deadman have been here for 15 years and have worked hard to produce a truly outstanding establishment. The interior is charming, with low beams, feature fireplaces and a pleasant clutter of antiques and knick-knacks giving it a cosy and intriguing atmosphere. All meals are prepared using fresh local produce and the menu offers an excellent range. You can choose from sandwiches with great fillings, to juicy steaks and some interesting vegetarian dishes such as the tasty cauliflower cheese with a dash of white wine. A children's menu is available too, and all prices are extremely reasonable.

Children can let off steam in the large garden, which boasts a pets' corner, complete with turkeys, chickens, small sheep and goats. This is a super place to sit out and relax when the weather permits. There is a bowling green for the grown ups, and every May Day, the pub plays host to an annual *Fun Run* - not to be missed! One of Colin and Dorothy's latest improvements has been to refurbish an old stable block to a very high standard; and this now provides a comfortable function room for meetings and parties of all kinds. A wide range of buffet menus are available here to suit different occasions, and a television is provided. The Queens Head is also a great place to visit over the festive season, for what could be better than enjoying traditional Christmas Fayre next to a roaring log fire in the friendly atmosphere of a lively village pub?

The Queens Head, High Street, Foulsham Tel: 01362 84339

WOOD NORTON. MANOR FARM is a 16th century farmhouse which is situated in the midst of quality farmland near Fakenham. Just 20 miles from Norwich City, 16 miles from the coast and within reach of all of the other 'hidden places' featured in this book, it is the ideal place to base a stay in this fascinating area. The building is listed because of its fine Dutch gable feature and offers a high standard of accommodation and a very warm and friendly welcome. An excellent home cooked full English breakfast is included in the very reasonable tariff, evening meals are available by arrangement. Non-smokers and children over the age of ten are welcome, but pets are sadly not permitted

Manor Farm B & B, Hall Lane, Wood Norton Tel: 01362 683231

CHAPTER SIX

CENTRAL NORFOLK

Norwich Castle Keep

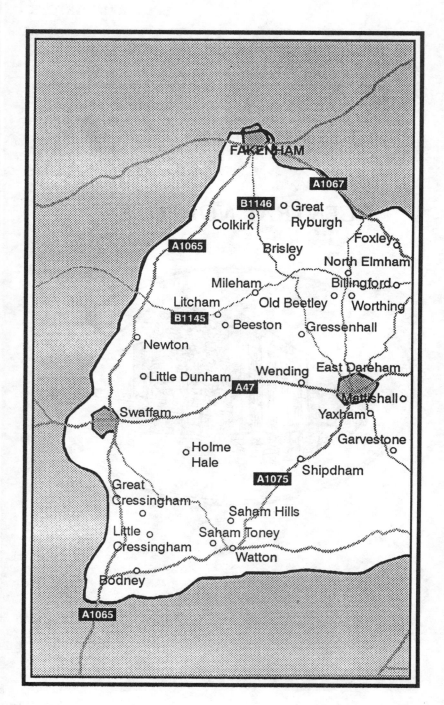

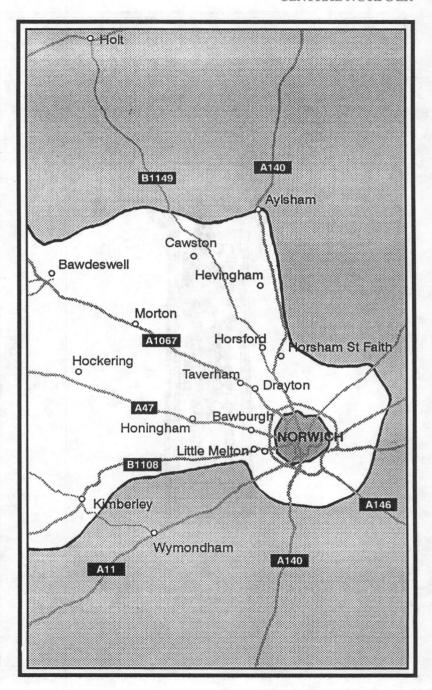

The Pedler on Swaffham's Town Sign

CHAPTER SIX

CENTRAL NORFOLK

Swaffham and the Wissey Valley

SWAFFHAM. A charming, but increasingly busy, market town, Swaffham's centre piece is the large wedge-shaped market place, surrounded by many fine Georgian houses. The main gathering place, and the heart of the town's social life in the early 19th century, was the Assembly Room at the northern end of the market place, which dates back to 1817. Nearby is the former Headmaster's House (now the Sixth Form Centre), Oakley House, the Corn Exchange and Plowright Place, a collection of old workshops now transformed into a delightful shopping precinct.

The main focus of the market place is the so-called Butter Cross (from the fact that beneath it, butter-sellers once displayed their wares), which was presented to the town by the Earl of Orford in 1783. It is not a cross at all but a classical lead-covered dome standing on eight pillars, surmounted by a life-sized statue of Ceres, the Roman goddess of agriculture. An appropriate symbol for a market town that has long relied upon the rewards which a good harvest would bring!

In contrast to Ceres and her pagan associations, the quite magnificent 15th century church of St Peter and St Paul lies to the east of the market place. Its tower dates back to the early 1500s and features a fine lead and timber Georgian spire crowned by a copper ball. Inside is one of the very best double hammerbeam roofs in the county, strikingly embellished with many angels. Here too are some carved bench-ends representing a little man and a dog on a chain, a figure that has also been incorporated into the town's coat of arms. This is a reference to John Chapman, the legendary 'Pedlar of Swaffham', whose change in fortune was to prove so beneficial to the church.

The story goes that Chapman, an impoverished tinker who lived in Swaffham some time during the 15th century, had a dream which foretold that if he made his way to London Bridge he would meet a man who would make him rich. So, he set off with his faithful dog and tramped all the way to London to find his fortune. There, on London Bridge, he met a shopkeeper who told him that he too had had a strange dream - in which a pedlar from Swaffham discovered gold buried in his garden! Returning back home post-haste, Chapman was amply rewarded for his long journey when he unearthed two large pots of gold coins beneath a tree in his garden. In thanks, Chapman donated a generous part of his fortune to the church and the north aisle was built as a consequence.

John Chapman and his dog are further commemorated in the town sign which stands just beyond the market place. The sign here was carved by the same talented craftsman, who carved the 'Bishop Beaver' featured in the village sign at Babingley, a schoolmaster called Harry Carter who was a Swaffham man. Harry rose to prominence during the 1950s when the villages of Norfolk felt the need to commemorate the Queen's Coronation in a way that would be both visually striking and permanent. Today, beautifully carved and brightly painted signs can be found all over the county; many of them created by Harry himself and others by the craftsmen of the Queen's Carving School at Sandringham who carried on his good work. As well as the name of the village or town in which it stands, each sign depicts the history of the place by reference to a local personality or legend.

Saturday is market day in Swaffham and the famous open-air market and public auction held here each week has attracted thousands of visitors over the years. Nearby is the **Swaffham Museum**, at the Town Hall in London Street, which offers a fascinating insight into the life and history of the town.

Swaffham's one-time title of 'the Montpelier of England' has been justly earned and, indeed, one of the most graceful buildings in the market place is Montpelier House. It is said that this is where Lady Nelson stayed whenever she visited the town. Lord Nelson was also a regular visitor, as was Lady Hamilton.

BRECKLAND MEADOWS TOURING PARK is a delightful caravan and camping park with 25 well-spaced pitches lying on the outskirts of the historic market town of Swaffham. Since taking over in 1988, proprietor Betty Martin has built up an enviable reputation for providing a warm welcome and first-rate facilities, including electric hook-ups, hot showers, chemical disposal point, and children's play area. The Swaffeas Way passes close by and offers a six-mile circular walk which connects with the Peddars Way long-distance footpath. The park is also ideally situated for reaching King's Lynn, Sandringham, Norwich and the beautiful beaches of north Norfolk.

Breckland Meadows Touring Park, Lynn Road, Swaffham Tel: 01760 721246

AROUND SWAFFHAM

LITTLE DUNHAM. This is an attractive Georgian village and home to Dunham Museum, with its imaginative displays of working tools and machinery.

GREAT CRESSINGHAM lies in the lovely valley of the River Wissey. About a quarter of a mile to the north of St Michael's Church stand the remains of Great Cressingham Priory, a fine brick house that dates back to around 1545 and is now merged into the fabric of the farmhouse that occupies the site. The original south front survives, with its terracotta panelling and elaborate moulded brickwork.

If you feel in need of a good meal or just a refreshing drink, call in at **THE WINDMILL INN** which is situated on the edge of Great Cressingham, just off the main road. This first class country inn with its real oak beams and roaring log fires has all the charm of years gone by. There are three bars which hold a good selection of real ales including Adnams, Broadside, Sam Smiths, Bass Charrington and a guest variety.

The Windmill Inn, Waterend, Great Cressingham
Tel: 01760 756232

There is also a good selection of bar meals, snacks for those wanting a light lunch and dinners for those needing something a little more filling. Children are welcome and are very well catered for, having access to a play area with a pony, three family rooms, games room and conservatory. If the sun is shining you may want to eat and drink in the Windmill's large beer garden while watching the children play. Run by the Halls family who are celebrating their 40th year in the Windmill!

THE VINES is a charming house that is, as its name suggests, covered in vines, which lies just two hundred yards from The Windmill in Great Cressingham. Dating back to the 1500s, the house is owned by Mollie and John Wymer who offer excellent bed and breakfast accommodation from their charming and interesting home.

Many of the original features of this old house can still be seen; exposed beams hold up the ceilings in many of the rooms and the reception rooms have wonderful open fireplaces. This is a warm and friendly establishment and Mollie and John certainly make you feel at home. There are fresh eggs from the couple's own hens for breakfast and deer roam in the meadow behind the house. John is an archaeologist by profession.

The Vines, The Street, Great Cressingham Tel: 01760 756303

LITTLE CRESSINGHAM. The pretty village of Little Cressingham, standing on a tributary of the River Wissey, retains its old windmill and miller's house which have now been faithfully restored by the Norfolk Windmill Trust. Across the fields is **Clermont Hall**, a handsome 18th century country house built in 1812 by William Pilkington and once owned by the Second Duke of Wellington.

Visitors to St Andrew's Church enter dramatically through the massive, ruined west tower and arcade. A great storm which raged across the region in the 18th century is thought to have toppled the tower and the part of the nave on which it fell still remains without a roof today.

The White Horse, Little Cressingham Tel: 01953 883434

THE WHITE HORSE is a delightful white-painted inn which stands in a secluded position in the heart of Little Cressingham, just north of the B1108. With its traditional furnishings, beamed ceilings and open fires, this charming free house has a genuinely welcoming atmosphere. Proprietors Paul and Lynne stock an excellent selection of guest beers and offer one of the most imaginative pub menus in Norfolk. Paul specialises in authentic Balti recipes, and also prepares such mouthwatering dishes as Japanese king prawns, as well as a full range of traditional pub fare. There are also three well-appointed guest bedrooms for those wanting accommodation.

SAHAM TONEY. North-east of the Cressinghams on the B1077 is the oddly-named Saham Toney, a village built around a large mere surrounded by trees. Peat was once extracted here in large quantities and the resulting hole filled with water to become a much needed natural reservoir, as well as one of the prettiest meres in the Breckland area.

BROOM HALL is a delightful Victorian residence standing in fifteen acres of parkland in the quiet village of Saham Toney. A charming country house, Broom Hall is owned and personally run by Angela and Nigel Rowling who make every effort to ensure that your stay is as enjoyable and comfortable as possible.

There are eight beautiful, individually decorated and furnished en-suite bedrooms all with colour television and tea and coffee making facilities. The large lounge with its cheery open fire is a lovely room in which to sit and relax, meet the other guests and talk about your day. Tea, coffee and home-made cakes are served each day in a charming panelled room that was originally the library. A delicious three course, home-cooked evening meal is served in the restaurant which overlooks the well tended garden and is opened to non-residents on Thursday, Friday and Saturday evenings. Fresh vegetables are always served, when ever possible coming from the Hall's own garden, and there is also a comprehensive wine list. For the more energetic there is also a large indoor swimming pool.

Broom Hall, Richmond Road, Saham Toney Tel: 01953 882125

SAHAM HILLS. **LOWE CARAVAN PARK/HIRE** lies in the centre of the village of Saham Hills, near Watton, down a quiet road and close to Richmond Park Golf Club. Owned and personally run by May and Chris Lowe, who have many years experience in the business, this is a ten caravan park surrounded by mature trees. The flat, one acre park, with electricity hook-ups, makes for easy and convenient pitching of your van and there is also a toilet and shower block on the site. The grassy field is alive with rabbits and plenty of bird life and, in such quiet and tranquil surroundings, you will be sure to see them at play. They also offer superb modern touring caravans for hire, all fully equipped with crockery, cutlery, cooking utensil and a shower, and the couple hire out awnings to give even more space to the four/five berth vans.

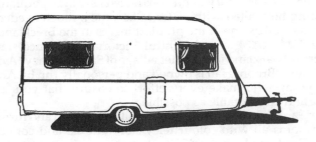

Lowe Caravan Hire, Ashdale, Hills Road, Saham Hills
Tel: 01953 881051

EAST DEREHAM. Geographically, East Dereham is at the centre of the county and, although there is a West Dereham village near Downham Market, it is usually called Dereham. The town's origins go way back to 654 AD, when St Withburga, a daughter of Anna, King of the East Angles, founded a convent here. Local legend has it that the nuns were kept alive during a famine by the milk of two deer, who providently appeared in response to Withburga's prayers.

It is thought that Dereham derives its name from this miraculous event and the legend was quickly seized upon by Harry Carter as the theme of the town sign; spanning the High Street, it is the largest and perhaps most ambitious of his works. Withburga was buried in the churchyard of **St Nicholas' Church** and her shrine was said to have been the scene of a number of miracles. Unscrupulous monks removed her bones several hundred years later to lay them next to those of her sister, Etheldreda, who had founded their own community at Ely. The intention was, of course, to divert the steady stream of pilgrims from Dereham to Ely, but the monks' plan backfired: the desecrated grave filled with water which was discovered to have miraculous properties. It was promptly dubbed 'St Withburga's Well' and Dereham became even more popular than before despite its recently vacated resident!

Another resident of the churchyard is the poet, William Cowper. Known for his deeply melancholic nature, he attempted suicide at one stage before eventually dying here of natural causes in 1800. He left a legacy of several much-loved hymns, poems such as the brilliant 'Castaway' and 'The Task' which looks at the everyday life of rural folk, and a number of translations of Milton and the works of Homer.

Another local writer was George Borrow, who was born in the nearby hamlet of Dumpling Green in 1803. His great love of travelling led to such works as 'The Zencali, or an account of the Gypsies in Spain', 'The Romany Rye' and 'The Word-book of the English-Gypsy Language'.

To the east of St Nicholas' Church is an exquisite row of thatched cottages called Bishop Bonner's Cottages, named after the 16th century rector who resided there and later became Bishop of London. The cottages now house a museum, and the delightful pargetry work which forms a frieze of flower and fruit designs below the eaves is extremely rare in Norfolk. Such beauty is in fact completely at odds with Bishop Bonner's character: 'Bloody Bonner', they called him, as he was responsible for sending many unfortunate Protestants to the stake during Mary Tudor's reign.

AROUND EAST DEREHAM - TO THE SOUTH

MATTISHALL. The pretty little market town of Mattishall was once an important wool trading centre and the local lanes around here were used for the old sheep droves. It is thanks to the wealth from this trade that the handsome church of All Saints received its fine hammerbeam roof.

YAXHAM. The little village of Yaxham, just to the south of Dereham, boasts a simple and gracious church dedicated to St Peter and features a round Saxon tower and a fine 14th century font. In the chancel is a memorial to the Reverend Dr John Johnson, who looked after his cousin William Cowper in the poet's declining years. Cowper referred to him fondly as 'Johnny of Norfolk'.

SHIPDHAM. The handsome parish church of All Saints' in this interesting village is quite a landmark in the area. As well has having a church tower with a unique wooden cupola, the church also features a superb wooden lectern carved with Tudor roses. This dates back to around 1500 and is one of the best examples of its kind in the country.

In the churchyard is a plaque commemorating the American airmen of the 44th Bomber group, who came to Shipdham in 1942 and flew their final mission from here on 25th April 1945. 'The Flying Eightballs', as they were known, flew numerous sorties over Europe and fought some of the bloodiest air battles of the war, losing 153 aircraft in their 343 missions.

Some of the veterans of the group returned to Shipdham with their families in September 1983 to dedicate the plaque in honour of their fallen comrades. 'The Flying Eightballs' certainly left their mark on the life of the village and both the living and the dead are remembered by the locals with a touching combination of pride and affection.

BILLINGFORD. St Peter's Church, in this pleasant village, is notable for its octagonal tower and a most impressive eagle lectern which dates back to the 15th century. There is also a fine five-storey windmill, with its bright white sails, that is open to the public at weekends.

WORTHING. This lovely village stands in the valley of the River Wensum, a couple of miles downstream from the remains of a Saxon cathedral. The tiny Saxon church of St Margaret's, with its round tower and Norman door, stands in lonely isolation by the river.

TANNERY HOUSE also lies in this lovely village. Owned and personally run by Belinda and George Eve, Tannery House is the place to come if you are looking for exceptional bed and breakfast accommodation in this beautiful part of central Norfolk. Used as a tannery until the 1970s, it was also the last remaining wool loft in Norfolk, the house stands in glorious grounds surround by the River Wensum. The charming and unique accommodation is located in a tastefully converted first-floor winery, and has en-suite shower/WC, television and tea and coffee making facilities. Guests are free to stroll around the lovely three acre grounds which contain an outdoor swimming pool (heated in summer) and 250 yards of superb river frontage where guests can fish free of charge.

Tannery House, Worthing Tel: 01362 668202

OLD BEETLEY. **SHILLINGSTONE** is a charming house, belonging to Jeanne Partridge, in the quiet village of Old Beetley, which lies between Norwich and Kings Lynn. Next door to the village church, Shillingstone is a modern country house set in its own extensive grounds and with a Victorian Conservatory. From this delightful home Jeanne offers excellent bed and breakfast accommodation in three comfortable bedrooms. There is also a lounge with colour television for guests which opens out directly into the garden. A real home from home with a warm and friendly atmosphere, Jeanne also offers an evening meal and all the meals are home cooked with produce from the garden when available.

A delightful place to stay and an ideal base from which to explore East Anglia, Norwich and the Broads.

Shillingstone, Church Road, Old Beetley
Tel: 01362 861099 Mobile: 0421 306190

NORTH ELMHAM. This sprawling village straggles along for nearly half a mile on both sides of the B1110; some of its larger houses hidden from passers-by behind the tall flint and brick walls that line the main street. Opposite the park entrance of Elmham House are the dramatic ruins of a Saxon cathedral. The grounds at Elmham House are now open to the public under the National Gardens Scheme and together with the large park they also feature vineyards and a wild garden which are well worth seeing. Lovers of the grape will also find a rather fine winery and vineyard in the village.

The cathedral ruins to the north of St Mary's Church are, together with those at South Elmham in Suffolk, the only visible Saxon cathedral remains in England. In the 7th century, North Elmham was the centre of the diocese of the North Folk, while South Elmham served that of the South Folk. The North Folk see moved to Thetford in 1072 after the Danish invasions, then the two dioceses were combined in 1093 and transferred to Norwich. Over 120 ft long and with twin towers, the cathedral here was a very impressive building indeed for those times; but today the remains, though extensive, stand only 10 ft high. The reason that the building has survived at all is that the Bishop of Norwich, Henry le Despenser, converted the abandoned cathedral into a hunting lodge in the late 14th century. From the number of jugs and drinking vessels excavated at the site, it would appear that Henry was certainly a 'dispenser' of merriment and good cheer.

Sightseers with a taste for more modern buildings will enjoy a visit to the County School Station, where the former railway station has been converted to a Visitor Centre surrounded by pleasant country walks and a picnic area. The station, half a mile north of the village, was built in 1873 specifically to provide a service for the County School and was in use up until 1953. There is plenty to see, with maps and photographs recalling those bygone days and the line now operates a diesel train and brake van run by the Fakenham and Dereham Railway Society.

There is some excellent literature at the centre on the many Wensum Valley walks available in the area; one walk in particular (which is conveniently circular) takes a track alongside a section of the old railway line through a glorious mixture of grassland and woodland. The ruins of the old Bishop's Chapel are en-route as is the lovely 14th century St Mary's Church with its painted rood screen and beautiful stained glass.

Straddling the River Wensum and standing proudly in seven acres of beautiful grounds, **ELMHAM MILL** dates back to the Middle Ages and remained in use as a water mill until the 1960s. It has now been sympathetically converted to provide comfortable and spacious residences, each catering for two to six persons. All enjoy delightful views of the river and the surrounding beautiful open countryside. The apartments are available for short breaks and include; luxurious living room (with colour TV), a fully equipped modern kitchen (with fridge, microwave and dishwasher), a modern bathroom, all bed linen and towels, and central heating. Access for persons with limited mobility is excellent, a lift serves all floors of the building. There is also a central, fully equipped laundry room on the ground floor, a superb indoor heated swimming pool, spa pool and sauna, and an indoor games room, with pool, table tennis and darts.

This is the ideal base from which to explore all of the 'hidden places' featured in this book. In addition there are no less than six golf courses within easy reach. The narrow, but clear River Wensum offers enjoyable coarse fishing; specimen Chub, Bream, Roach, Perch, Dace and Pike are commonly caught.

Elmham Water Mill, Billingford Road, North Elmham
Tel: 01362 668928 Fax: 01362 668019

BRISLEY. The moated Tudor manor house, with barns, and houses in the village cluster around the handsome 14th century church of St Bartholomew and large green. A sweeping, semi-circled stone driveway leads up to **THE BRISLEY BELL**, which stands proud on The Green, surrounded by open countryside. The building dates back to 1511 and it has been an alehouse for over 200 years. This lovely old inn exudes charm and character both inside and out, from its gabled end which was made from clay lumps from local ponds to the beamed interior, stone walls and feature fireplace. Les Philp, John Baeur and Jo Slattery own the inn and they have a wealth of experience in hotels and catering. It shows, for not only is the service excellent, but the atmosphere is very friendly and relaxed.

The Brisley Bell Inn and Restaurant

A wide range of cask condition real ales are stocked and there is a good range of pub meals available which offer excellent value for money. The pride and joy is the wonderful restaurant, which is beautifully decorated and has a truly welcoming atmosphere. To say that the menu is extensive would be an understatement indeed: with a minimum of 18 starters and 20 main meals to choose from, no one could possibly leave here feeling hungry or dissatisfied. Seafood is the particular speciality of this fine restaurant. All of the fish and seafood ingredients on the menu are purchased from Lowestoft Fish Market *the same day,* indeed all the food is brought daily, so you are guaranteed that everything you eat is freshly prepared as well as being attractively presented and cooked to perfection. Unsurprisingly the restaurant has, for the past three years, achieved a coveted Egon Ronay Award (a Gold Award in 1995).

Did You Know...

There is a full

Town and Village Index

at the back of the book?

The Brisley Bell Inn & Restaurant, The Green, Brisley
Tel: 01362 668686

This is the ideal place for the whole family. In the summertime Les often organizes barbecues or 'hog roasts' and these take place in the lovely garden. Why not ring for details of the next event, you will not be disappointed.

The restaurant is open Tuesday to Saturday from 7.00 pm - 10.00 pm, with traditional Sunday lunches served from 12.00 am - 3.00 pm.

To the rear of the inn is a cottage which has been completely refurbished. It was here that Richard Taverner translated the Bible from Latin into English in 1570. And on a lighter note, The Brisley Bell has also been used as a location by the BBC when some of the sketches in the comedy series 'You Rang, M'Lord?' were filmed here. This is a 5-Star inn with 5-Star hosts, do make the effort to pay it a visit, you will probably want to return again and again.

GODWICK is one of a staggering 200 'lost' villages in Norfolk and the only one open to the public. Head along the B1146 northwards from Brisely, after about a mile, take the left-hand turning to Whissonsett. From here, head south-west towards Tittleshall and a turning to the left leads to the parking area at Godwick Hall Farm.

This is a fascinating site, undisturbed for many years that owes its preservation to the fact that this has always been grazing land and has remained untouched by the plough over the centuries. The Saxons were the first to settle here and the village continued to be lived in right up until the 17th century. It was eventually absorbed into the parish of **Tittleshall** in the 19th century. The decline of the village was not marked by a sudden exodus brought about by plague, famine or war; it was just an inevitable fact of nature where poor harvests and an unyielding clay soil meant that the villagers simply could not eke out a living from the land.

A leaflet is available to show how the village was once laid out with church, streets, 'tofts' (individual homesteads) and even a watermill and millpond. The great house here was Godwick Manor, a handsome brick manor house built in 1585 for Sir Edward Coke, and, though its ruins were demolished in 1962, its outline can still be made out. The great Barn has stood the test of time; it is a fine building in its own right, with surprisingly ornate features such as the elaborate windows which were never in fact designed for anyone to look out of! The 13th century church was pulled down some time during the 17th century and the ruined tower was then used as the base of a folly which was built in its place. Sir Edward and his wife now lie in the mausoleum in Tittleshall church, where there are also many monuments to other members of the Coke family including Thomas 'Coke of Norfolk', the renowned agriculturalist.

The Godwick site is now managed and preserved by English Heritage and the landowner has kindly consented to allow visitors to park their cars in the farmyard. Please remember to keep dogs on a lead as this is a working environment.

GREAT RYBURGH. **THE BOAR INN** is the only pub in the village of Great Ryburgh so it is hard to miss. Known to have been standing here since 1777, the Boar Inn, due to its proximity to the village church of

St Andrew's, could easily date back as far as the 14th century.

The Boar Inn, Great Ryburgh Tel: 01328 829212

Built around a central courtyard, the inn is real picture and over the years the owners, father and son Jim and Michael Corson, have established an excellent reputation for a warm welcome and outstanding hospitality. Backed by the Egon Ronay award for its food, the Boar Inn's restaurant is something rather special. All home-cooked, the interesting and imaginative range of tasty and delicious dishes is well worth trying. Add to this the superb range of real ales on tap in the bar and you have the perfect inn. Egon Ronay also recommends the accommodation in 'cottagey' bedrooms.

COLKIRK. From its unostentatious though well kept exterior, you might ordinarily pass by **THE COLKIRK CROWN** in the village of Colkirk - but what a mistake that would be!

The Colkirk Crown, Colkirk Tel: 01328 862172

This local village pub is definitely not one to be missed. On this spot has stood a pub for over 300 years and Licensees Pat and Rosemary Whitmore have been resident here for seventeen of them, all the while building business and attracting custom to the Crown for their delicious food, expertise and knowledge of wine and most pleasant and convivial atmosphere. Pat, who makes regular buying trips to French vineyards says "I always make a point of selling wine by the glass, which means it's easier to try more wines than would be possible buying a bottle every time". Rosemary's strength lies behind the scenes creating interesting traditional menus which offer a wide choice for everyone's taste, including Vegetarian dishes, Salads, fish, chicken and grills, not to mention the fateful hot puddings and desserts. The food is cooked to perfection and the portions generous. Find it at all costs! (Between the B1146 and A1065.)

MILEHAM. The straggling village of Mileham, which, although still very much alive in contrast to Godwick, shares a similar sense of history. Its main features of interest are the remains of the motte-and-bailey Mileham Castle, the 14th century church of St John the Baptist with its outstanding stained glass and nearby Burghwood Hall which occupies the site of Burghwood Manor, the birthplace of Sir Edward Coke. A precious relic in the form of a 10th century Viking sword was discovered here and is now on display in the museum at Norwich.

LITCHAM. More than a village and yet not quite a town, Litcham is a pleasant enough place. The attractive Georgian houses that line the main street and the 17th century tower of All Saints' Church are of red brick and the 18th century farmhouse, that includes the remains of the former priory at the southern end of the village, was once the home of Matthew Hulcott, who financed the building of the church. The common land surrounding Litcham has been turned into a 60 acre nature reserve and provides a superb natural habitat for wetland creatures and plants.

BEESTON. St Mary's Church, standing rather forlorn in the fields, has several notable features including a superb hammerbeam roof, a painted rood screen and two elaborate parclose screens. In contrast to the peace and tranquility of the church, there is a memorial in the churchyard to Jem Mace, a one-time bare-fisted boxing world champion who was apparently born in the village!

GRESSENHALL. The **Norfolk Rural Life Museum** is housed in a former 'house of industry', ie, a workhouse, which was built in 1777 to house up to 700 people. When workhouses were abolished in 1930, Norfolk County Council took over the building and used it as an old people's home until 1975. A year later the museum was founded which, over the years, has grown to its present size. The purpose of the museum is to preserve a sense of the past 150 years of rural Norfolk life. Agriculture has always formed an important part of the county's economy and farm machinery and utensils form the central exhibits. These are displayed according to the months of the year, starting in October when farm tenancies changed hands and the winter work began. In 1990, Union Farm was incorporated in the museum. This 50 acre working farm was originally cultivated by the inmates of the workhouse. It now operates the traditional 'Norfolk four course' system of crop rotation and makes use of two Suffolk heavy horses. Also to be seen on the farm are examples of local rare breeds. Cherry Tree Cottage and its adjacent Edwardian cottage garden show how a farm cottage would have looked around 1910. There is also a wildlife garden, a network of nature trails leading through beautiful riverside meadows, a gift shop selling locally made products, and a cafeteria serving light lunches and local home-made specialities. The Museum is open from Easter until the end of October.

Norfolk Rural Life Museum, Beech House, Gressenhall Tel: 01362 860563

The Capital of East Anglia

NORWICH. The capital of East Anglia and the county town of Norfolk, Norwich is a lively and exciting city, whose unique character has, in the main, been sensitively preserved.

The earliest known reference to Norwich is on coins struck during the reign of King Athelstan, as far back as 930 AD, and by the time of the Norman Conquest it was one of the largest towns in England. The arrival of the Normans heralded a period of continued expansion which would see an increase in overseas trade and a steady influx of immigrants, many of them craftsmen who would leave their mark on the architecture of the town. The building of the castle and the transfer of the Seat of the Bishops of East Anglia from Thetford to Norwich obviously did much to sustain this growth. By the end of the 14th century the population had grown to around 6,000 and the town's prosperity was firmly bound up in the wool trade; the Rivers Wensum and Yare providing a convenient link with the coast from which the raw material was then exported to the Low Countries.

The only way to even begin to appreciate the many sights and attractions of Norwich is on foot. The city is a maze of narrow streets and passages and the enthusiastic newcomer could quite easily lose his or her bearings so a map is essential!

A good place to start is at the colourful **Market Place**, which has been trading now for over 500 years and is one of the largest permanent markets in England. It has an almost Continental feel to it with its many

Norwich Cathedral

stalls set out under bright canvas awnings known locally as 'tilts'.

The Market Place is surrounded by noteworthy buildings, both old and modern. At one end is the impressive **City Hall** with its soaring 202 ft high clock tower opened by George VI in 1938; whilst, to the right, is the **Guildhall**, built of flint at the beginning of the 15th century in a striking chequerboard design, once the seat of local government and now housing the Tourist Information Centre.

And on the south side of the Market Place is **St Peter Mancroft**, one of England's largest and finest medieval parish churches. It was built between 1430 and 1455 and is a superb example of the Perpendicular style; its ornate stone tower crowned with turrets and a graceful but slightly incongruous Gothick spirelet. The many delights of the interior include an impressive 15th century font canopy (albeit largely rebuilt in 1887), the boss-studded hammerbeam roof, and the beautiful east window with its superb collection of 15th century glass illustrating the lives of the saints.

This is just one of over 30 medieval churches that still survive in Norwich today, yet it is of course the **Cathedral** that really draws the crowds. The main entrances to the Cathedral Close are the Erpingham and St Ethelbert Gates which lie at either end of Tombland, a cobbled thoroughfare lined with delightful old houses and trees, and the site of the original Saxon market place. It takes its name from the table tops from which the merchants sold their wares. The magnificent Erpingham Gate was presented to the city in 1420 by that famous hero of the Battle of Agincourt, Sir Thomas Erpingham (his kneeling figure can be seen in a recess at the top of its tall arch).

On entering the old monastic precinct of the Cathedral Close, the noise and bustle of the city itself seems far away; it is almost like stepping back in time into the heart of a medieval village. The Close is divided into the Upper Close, where a statue of Horatio Nelson now watches over the old 14th century Grammar School he attended as a boy; and the Lower Close, which leads down to Pull's Ferry on the River Wensum. The grey flint gateway here, with its picturesque arch, has guarded the river approach to the Cathedral since the 15th century and it was from this spot that a little canal was dug to ship building materials direct to the Cathedral site. This would have included the beautiful white Caen stone of the Cathedral's exterior, which was off-loaded at Pull's Ferry after its journey from Normandy via Great Yarmouth and the Wensum. Today, it is a pleasant stroll down to the river, along the quiet lane which follows the course of the old canal, where there is a memorable view of the Cathedral.

Norwich Cathedral, or to give it its full and proper title, the Cathedral Church of the Holy and Undivided Trinity, was begun in 1096 by Bishop Herbert de Losinga, two years after he transferred the see from Thetford. Its turbulent history is a catalogue of fires, riots and natural disasters which all inflicted various degrees of damage; yet each succeeding period of rebuilding and restoration has improved upon the original, making this, the mother church of all East Anglia, one of England's finest cathedrals.

The wonderful nave roof, added in the 15th and 16th centuries after the original had been destroyed by fire, is undoubtedly its crowning glory. Supported by the soaring trunks of the flying buttresses, its coloured and gilded bosses (now beautifully restored) are carved with a series of biblical scenes illustrating the story of man from the Creation to the Last Judgement. There are 2,000 in all and those in the cloister, which is among the largest of any cathedral in the country, have a variety of themes and can be studied closely with ease. Another addition at the end of the 15th century was Norwich's famous cathedral spire; at 315 ft it is the tallest in England apart from Salisbury.

Around the apse are a number of small chapels which were desecrated at the time of the Dissolution, but faithfully restored during the 1930s. They are quite delightfully furnished and offer the visitor an opportunity to sit peacefully and enjoy a moment or two of quiet contemplation whilst studying the impressive display of rare medieval painted panels. Best of these is the reredos in St Luke's Chapel, which was commissioned by Bishop Henry le Despenser in 1381 and is said to be the finest work of the Norwich School of painters.

Two special women who are commemorated at the Cathedral. The first is Edith Louisa Cavell, whose simple grave can be found outside the east end of the great south transept. This English nurse, a daughter of the rector of Swardeston to the south of Norwich, was one of the great heroines of the First World War. Working at a Red Cross hospital in occupied Brussels, she helped around 200 Allied prisoners to escape to neutral Holland. For this selfless act of bravery she was court-martialled and executed by the Germans in 1915.

The other woman of note, who is commemorated here on 8th May each year, is Julian (or Juliana) of Norwich, an anchoress who lived in a cell attached to the chancel. Born around 1342, this English mystic had a series of visions on 8th May 1373 and her written account of these, including her interpretations of their significance (published as 'Revelations of Divine Love') constitutes the first book to be written in the English language by a woman.

The other great Norman building here is the **Castle**, which dates from the beginning of the 12th century (replacing an earlier wooden fort) and is Norwich's second most significant landmark. The huge stone keep, one of the largest in England, dominates the skyline from the castle mound and no visit would be complete without climbing the stairs to take a walk around the battlements and enjoy the superb views of the city below. The Castle was used as the county gaol for over 600 years of its life and, to get some idea of what it was like to be incarcerated in such a place, the dungeons houses a display of the instruments of torture and the death masks of some of the prisoners who were executed here. One of the most famous characters in Norfolk's history, Robert Kett, was hanged from the walls of the Castle in 1549.

The keep now houses one of the best provincial museums in the country and its varied attractions include a superb, though rather sad, array of stuffed birds, a fine collection of Lowestoft porcelain, and an art gallery featuring many works by members of the Norwich School of painters. A brand new attraction is the **Castle Mall**. This will consist of a vast shopping complex with car parks under the Castle Bailey, and a large park and conservatory above.

Art lovers should also make a point of visiting the **Sainsbury Centre for Visual Arts**, which is based in the grounds of the somewhat utilitarian University of East Anglia, three miles to the west of the city centre. This modern, purpose-built gallery opened in 1978 and, although Norman Foster's building may resemble an aircraft hangar from the outside, the interior is extremely restful and must surely be one of the best laid out galleries around. It makes an excellent setting for the intriguingly diverse range of styles on display, which includes everything from ethnic and modernist works of art to the substantial creations of Henry Moore. Thanks must go to Sir Robert and Lady Sainsbury for donating such a unique collection for all to enjoy.

Norwich is of course the main shopping centre for the region and all the familiar national stores can be found in the city centre. However, there are plenty of interesting alternatives. Antique shops and craft shops abound, and there is one particular shop that is quite unique.

The Mustard Shop, 3 Bridewell Alley, Norwich Tel: 01603 627889

On February 15th 1823, Jeremiah Colman took his nephew James into partnership, and created the famous firm of J & J Colman. To mark the anniversary of this event, **Colmans** opened a **MUSTARD SHOP**, the only one of its kind in Britain, in 1973. The shop can be found in 18th century quarters in Bridewell Alley, one of the attractive little alleyways in the old centre of Norwich which are wonderful to explore. The shop has now become a major tourist attraction for both overseas and British tourists visiting East Anglia. Its fame and popularity has become worldwide. The premises have been extensively restored and decorated in the late 19th century style. The shop houses a mustard museum, which takes the form of a series of displays illustrating the history of Colman's

Norwich Castle Keep

mustard from the early years to the present day. Many of the articles offered for sale are based on old designs taken from the company's archives, and are unique to the shop. There is an extensive range of powdered and prepared mustards ranging from Tarragon and Thyme to the ultimate 'Genuine Double Superfine'. When buying any of the powdered mustards a 'Hot Tips' leaflet with recipe ideas for using mustard in cooking is given free of charge.

Further along Bridewell Alley is another museum, the **Bridewell Museum**, with exhibits on local crafts and industries throughout the city's history, such as fishing, weaving and brewing. The latter, incidentally, is something that Norwich knows a lot about: it is said that at one time the city had enough pubs for you to drink in a different one every day of the year!

This may or may not still be the case, but the Dutch-gabled Adam and Eve in Bishopsgate, which dates back in parts some 700 years, is certainly worth visiting.

Another hostelry with plenty of history is the Maid's Head Hotel, the oldest inn in East Anglia and referred to as early as 1287. Among its more famous guests were Queen Elizabeth I and the Black Prince and it was from here that 'The Norwich Machine', the city's first stage coach, left for London in 1762.

From here it is just a short distance to the bottom of Elm Hill, a charming, narrow cobbled street of timber-framed and colour-washed Tudor and Georgian buildings, which was thankfully saved from the threat of demolition through the determined efforts of a local conservation group, the Norwich Society. It is very atmospheric at any time, but particularly at night when the magical effects of the award-winning street lighting can be enjoyed.

The thatched Briton's Arms at the top of the street was the only house to survive the fire of 1507 which destroyed all its neighbours; but alas, the nearby elm tree from which the street takes its name fell victim to Dutch elm disease and is no more.

Among the many other buildings worth seeing, the following are of the 'not-to-be-missed' variety. There is the Music House in Rouen Road, the Assembly House, Carnery College to the right of the western front of the Cathedral, the Bishop's Palace at Palace Plain, the Great Hospital, the Regency houses of Quayside, the Roman Catholic Cathedral of St John on the way to the University, and over at Whitefriars Bridge, the imposing 19th century Yarn Mill hidden under its thickets of creeper.

With so much to do and see at Norwich it is also worth making an overnight stop. For evening entertainment, the **Theatre Royal**, next door to the Assembly House, makes a pleasant change. Its two predecessors were both destroyed by fire, and the present building, erected in 1936, was extensively altered in 1970. Today it is one of the leading theatres in the provinces, with a constantly changing programme of first-class productions.

For sheer diversity, the **Maddermarket Theatre** is hard to beat. This building was converted into an Elizabethan-style theatre in 1926 and the Norwich Players, mostly amateur but with a professional producer and designer, give enthusiastic and lively performances of plays ranging from Restoration comedies to modern works from around the world. Next door is the fascinating **Stranger's Hall Museum**, a rambling medieval house with exhibits of domestic life and furniture from Tudor to Victorian times.

Finally, a boat trip around the city provides an excellent opportunity to see a good selection of Norwich's historic buildings and, with a running commentary from your professional guide on both the past and the future of this great city, there is no better way of experiencing something of its character.

The **GEORGIAN HOUSE HOTEL** is a charming family run hotel conveniently located just off Norwich's inner ring road and directly adjacent to the Roman Catholic Cathedral. Originally two Victorian houses, they have been tastefully linked together to form the hotel which sits in fine, established gardens. Retaining many of the original Victorian features, the Georgian House Hotel also offers guests a warm, friendly welcome and the latest in modern comforts.

All the 27 en-suite bedrooms are decorated and furnished to a high standard and create a relax atmosphere. Renowned for its excellent cuisine and fine selection of wines, dining at the Georgian House Hotel is an experience. The menu's are prepared from carefully selected local produce and served in the intimate surroundings of the charming dining room. The pleasant ambience of the cosy bar makes it the place to enjoy a pre-dinner drink or to relax after your meal.

Georgian House Hotel, 32-34 Unthank Road, Norwich Tel: 01603 615655

THE COPPER KETTLE restaurant and cafe lies just up the road from the Tourist Information Centre in the heart of Norwich. Opening its doors early, at 8 am, to serve a hearty and tasty breakfast, this is a popular place with local businessmen and shoppers alike. The breakfasts are served all day so you don't have to get up too early to try this delicious concoction. In fact, the Copper Kettle serves a whole range of tasty snacks and dishes, from light lunches right through to wonderful three course meals. Everything is home-cooked on the premises and the home-made pies are a real treat with melt-in-the-mouth pastry. A busy, bustling place, ideal to drop into when in the centre of the city, the Copper Kettle is part of a training project run by a local charity for young people with learning difficulties.

The Copper Kettle, 4 Lower Goat Lane, Norwich Tel: 01603 626870

AROUND NORWICH

BAWBURGH. This pretty village enjoys a picturesque setting on the River Yare, on one side of which is a former 19th century water mill (now a private house). The mill, which previously stood on the same site, was once owned by a local miller called Jeremiah Colman; he who later went on to found the mustard dynasty of Norwich.

Unlikely as it may seem today, this quiet spot was one of England's most popular pilgrimage centres during the Middle Ages. The individual responsible was a humble farmhand named Walstan, who died here in 1016. When he was buried one of those familiar 'miraculous' springs erupted from his grave and soon pilgrims from around the world were flocking to Bawburgh to catch a glimpse of St Walstan's Well and the shrine that was built alongside. Parts of the well can still be seen today in a farmyard near the little village church; which is, incidentally, dedicated to St Mary and St Walstan.

LITTLE MELTON. **THE OLD RECTORY** is easy to find, just five miles west of the centre of Norwich on the B1108 main road to Watton, it is just one mile west of the Norwich southern by-pass between Little Melton and Bawburgh. A charming and attractive early Victorian country house built 1840 it has been fully restored to a high standard to provide the elegance that is offered to today's guests. Owned and personally run by Carol Key and Malcolm Turner, the couple offer superior bed and breakfast accommodation in three tastefully decorated and furnished bedrooms, all of which have either en-suite or private bathrooms. Breakfast is served in the elegant dining room which overlooks the extensive gardens and grounds. A pleasant, friendly and relaxing place to stay, guests have the opportunity to explore the gardens, play croquet on the lawns or simply relax on the terraces.

The Old Rectory, Watton Road, Little Melton Tel: 01603 812121

TAVERHAM. A smiling St Walstan is depicted in Harry Carter's village sign here, complete with scythe to commemorate his years of toil in the fields. Apparently this was once a quiet little hamlet but, due to its close proximity to Norwich, Taverham has suffered from a bad case of 'galloping development'.

HORSHAM ST FAITH. At Abbey Farm, next to the 15th century church of St Mary and St Andrew, are the ruins of the Priory of St Faith, a Benedictine priory founded in 1105. Parts of the cloister and chapter house are still in evidence, together with the Norman door of the refectory which is now part of the farmhouse. While this building was being restored in recent years, a series of 13th century wall paintings was discovered. They illustrate scenes from the life of Robert Fitzwilliam who, so legend has it, was returning with his wife from a pilgrimage to Rome when they were imprisoned. Prayers to St Faith secured their release and they showed their gratitude by founding the monastery when they arrived safely back home.

CHAPTER SEVEN

NORTH-EAST NORFOLK

Beeston Hall, Nr Neatishead

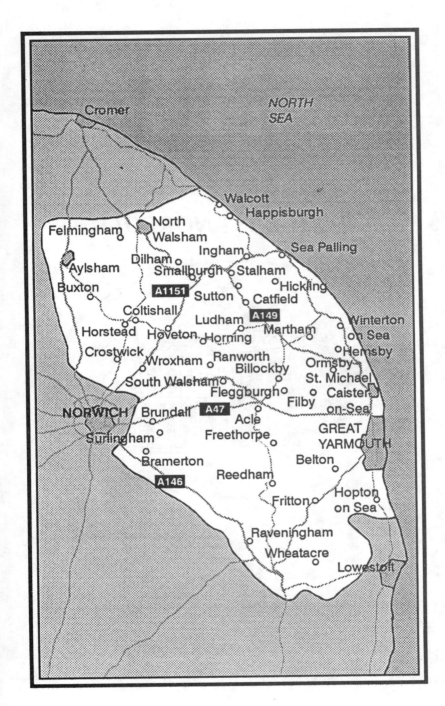

CHAPTER SEVEN

NORTH-EAST NORFOLK

Aylsham and the Bure Valley

AYLSHAM. This lovely market town was recorded in the Domesday Book as 'Elesham' and the town's origins go back to before the Norman Conquest. In 1372 its long-term prosperity was assured when, along with several other Norfolk manors and estates, Edward III presented the town to his son, John of Gaunt. This enthusiastic landowner was determined to put Aylsham firmly on the map and its steady development into one of Norfolk's most flourishing markets dates from this time.

It is a stalwart place of red brick and flint, with some of its most handsome buildings grouped around the town's centrepiece, its splendid **Market Place**. In Red Lion Street the majority of buildings still retain their original shop fronts.

Aylsham's affluence first came about through the manufacture of linen, then of wool and worsted in the 16th century. The prosperity of any town can normally be gauged by the appearance of its church. **St Michael's Church** provides ample evidence that the town has channelled a significant part of its wealth this imposing edifice. This 14th and 15th century flint-faced parish church, with its tall west tower, was much restored in 1824 and has a fine pulpit dating back to 1637. Humphry Repton, the great landscape gardener who was responsible for designing many of our best late 18th century country parks, was buried here in 1818. It was his love of the informal, the picturesque, that heralded the final demise of the old concept of gardens as formal layouts.

From 1792 until the beginning of this century, the River Bure was navigable from Coltishall to Aylsham and the area known as Millgate was a bustling place with shallow-bottomed wherries making their way to the harbour from Norwich and Yarmouth. But the coming of the railway and a devastating flood in 1912, which caused the channel to silt up, put pay to Millgate's future as a working harbour. Now it is a quiet residential area; with just its handsome 18th century houses and large mill as a reminder of busier days.

Perfect for any trainspotter is **THE BURE VALLEY RAILWAY**, built on the abandoned trackbed of the historic East Norfolk Railway's Wroxham to Aylsham line. Fast becoming one of Norfolk's most popular tourist attractions Bure Valley Railway is a nine mile long line that runs through some of the county's most beautiful and unspoilt countryside, from the lively market town of Aylsham to the 'Capital of the Broads' at Wroxham. Housing a unique collection of narrow gauge steam and diesel locomotives, Bure Valley is the proud owner of 2 half-scale locomotives that were introduced in 1994 and have become firm favourites with all the visitors. The coaches have been built to a very high standard and have large windows that offer an uninterrupted view of the stunning scenery that passes before your eyes on this fascinating trip.

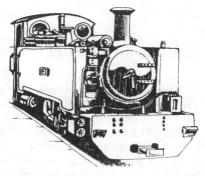

Bure Valley Railway, Alysham Station, Norwich Road, Aylsham
Tel: 01263 733858

Complete with all workshops and locomotive sheds, the Aylsham station is the headquarters of the BVR and offers the tourist a well-stocked shop which sells all sorts of souvenirs and train memorabilia. Also available is a picnic area where you can relax and enjoy your sandwiches, but for something more formal then the Whistle Top Restaurant is the perfect place for a hot meal.

There are many special events organised for year round entertainment, on the 20th and 21st of July there are 'Friends of Thomas the Tank Engine' days. The Fat Controller will be in command and Toby the Tram will be giving rides at the Aylsham Station with side shows and model railway keep you occupied. Santa Specials have become an integral part of the Bure Valley Railway pre-Christmas celebrations and specially heated coaches keep out all the winter chills. Every child who attends this wonderful ride will receive a special present from Santa himself and all the family are invited to partake in the seasonal refreshment in the festively decorated restaurant.

Maybe you would like to learn to drive a steam train, the Bure Valley Railway is the place to go. Join one of their Steam Driving Courses, either one day or two, and experience for yourself the exhilarating feeling that only driving a real Steam Train can bring. Making the perfect Birthday or Christmas present, the course fees include everything from tuition to lunch and you can guarantee that this will make one of the most unusual gifts anyone could receive.

Just a hundred yards or so from the town square of Alysham, one can step through a small private gateway, rather like Alice in wonderland, and discover the most delightful Queen Anne house in a totally private and secluded garden of around three quarters of an acre. This is surely the house style so popularly used for the classic Dolls House. The lawns stretch out before it with established trees and a small private wooded area providing the cover and privacy which the visiting squirrels and many guests enjoy so much.

The Old Bank House, 3 Norwich Road, Alysham Tel: 01263 733843

Enid Parry is the fortunate owner of **THE OLD BANK HOUSE** and is happy to share her home and extensive local knowledge with her guests who return time and time again to enjoy her hospitality and accommodation. The back part of the house which dates from 1613 was originally the Old Angel Inn and later became the Alysham Private Bank. Nowadays, the cellar of the house provides fun and entertainment for all the family with its games room, sauna and Victorian shower. Enid is a wonderful host and you will leave this lovely house with regret and the intention to return. Private parking in the rear courtyard.

10 Church Terrace, Aylsham Tel: 01263 734319

Exceptional bed and breakfast accommodation in the heart of Aylsham is offered by Jill Hunter Rowe at her home in **CHURCH TERRACE**. Standing in the shadow of the church tower, this elegant Georgian residence offers a choice of well-appointed bedrooms, all with private bath or shower-room. There is also a guest sitting room with colour TV and a delightful relaxed atmosphere. Mrs Hunter Rowe is renowned for her excellent hospitality and outstanding home cooking. As well as delicious breakfasts, she prepares three-course evening meals for her guests by arrangement. Unsuitable for smokers.

THE OLD PUMP HOUSE is a comfortable Georgian family home in which David and Hazel cater for guests with bed and breakfast. It is situated beside the thatched pump, one minute's walk from the historic Aylsham's Church and Market Square. The original small 18th century farmhouse has grown over the years to a seven bedroom home, and now, sympathetically restored and traditionally decorated, it provides five double or twin bedded guest rooms, all with central heating, colour television, hair dryer and beverage facilities. David is the cook and serves up an incredibly good breakfast which is taken in the pine-shuttered Red Sitting Room overlooking the peaceful garden. Pre-booked evening meals are available outside high season. The house is non-smoking throughout. Pets can usually be accommodated. Lovely location for taking a restful holiday or visiting Norwich, the Broads, and the Norfolk Coast. ETB 2 Crown Highly Commended.

The Old Pump House, Holman Road, Aylsham Tel: 01263 733789

AROUND AYLSHAM

FELMINGHAM. This picturesque village is dominated by the 16th century tower of St Andrew's Church, although the rest of the building was rebuilt in 1742 after a fire.

MARSHAM. A pleasant village where Marsham Hall and Bolwick Hall stand on either side of the Mermaid Stream. St Andrew's Church has a moving monument to a little girl called Mary Ann Kent, who died in 1773 at the age of four, following a small pox vaccination. A plaque on the chancel wall relates that '...her fond Parents, deluded by prevalent Custom, suffered the rough officious hand of Art to wound the flourishing root of Nature, and rob the little innocent of the gracious Gift of Life'. It is also worth paying a quick visit to pretty All Saints' Church to see its fine 15th century hammerbeam roof and Seven-Sacrament font.

The Bure Valley Steam Railway runs through the village and trains stop here en route from Aylsham to the Broads Centre at Wroxham. There is also excellent fishing nearby and many miles of country walks including Dudwick Park with its resident herd of deer.

HORSTEAD. An attractive and unpretentious village with some fine 19th century houses flanking the street like soldiers on parade!

COLTISHALL. Beside the River Bure, Coltishall is a pretty village of elegant Dutch-gabled houses and grassy watermeadows. This makes an excellent place to watch the activity on and around the Bure; anglers line the banks and a whole host of craft plying up and down the water. The village also has several pubs whose patrons spill out on to the common during fine weather.

John the Baptist was another individual who spent a lot of his time in rivers, so perhaps it is appropriate that the village church, a thatched building with a 15th century tower and porch, is dedicated to him.

THE RED LION INN, an exceptional pub and restaurant, stands opposite the church, 400 metres up the hill from the Staithe. The original inn building was built in the early 1700s as an alehouse with three separate adjoining alms houses. Over the years, these cottages have been incorporated into the pub and they now form the kitchens and lower bar area. The restaurant, with 45 covers, was added in the early 1980s but was carefully designed to blend in with the original architecture. The Red Lion now operates on two levels - there is an upper bar and restaurant and a short flight of stairs leads down to the lower bar area. Inside there are beams, wood-panelled walls and feature fireplaces; the walls are decorated with Norfolk memorabilia including a collection of sepia and black and white photographs and prints, many of which are for sale. There is also an interesting collection of pewter tankards in the lower bar.

The Red Lion Inn, Church Street, Coltishall Tel: 01603 737402

The Red Lion has been run for the last seven years by Monica and Andrew Burrell-Saward. We found them friendly and welcoming, and the food and drink they serve is excellent. They offer an exceptional choice of top quality bar meals (examples from the menu include swordfish steak, wild Greenland salmon and home-cured Norfolk ham) and their

Bure Valley Railway

cask conditioned ales are excellent. On the day we visited, there were six beers available including the famous 'Couteshall Weasel' brewed exclusively for the Red Lion by the award-winning brewers, Woodfordes of Woodbastwick; the inn has also featured in the Good Beer Guide for an amazing 17 consecutive years. Outside in the garden is a children's play area which includes a large play fort and adjoining the pub is a suntrap patio area, which overlooks the large car park.

During the late 18th and 19th centuries, lime was used in great quantities as a fertiliser to improve farmland, as an ingredient of mortar to meet the increased demands of the building trade, and for whitewash. Lime is obtained by heating chalk in a lime kiln. A particularly high quality of chalk is to be found in the underlying stratum of the area around Coltishall and Horstead. To reach the chalk, the quarrymen merely had to cut through layers of clay, which were themselves suitable for brick making. This area was thus heavily quarried and many lime kilns and brick kilns were operated, most of which have since disappeared without trace. One excellently maintained example of a lime kiln does still exist, however, and it can be found at **THE RAILWAY TAVERN** in Coltishall.

The Ancient Limekiln, The Railway Tavern, Station Road, Coltishall. Tel: 01603 738316

This **ANCIENT LIME KILN**, one of the few surviving in the country, is a listed building of finely finished brickwork, a style unique to Norfolk. It consists of a circular tapered kiln 'pot', the top of which is level with the ground. This pot leads to an underground 'stem', around which is a vaulted walkway. In the stem are openings guarded by iron bars through which the lime was raked out. A passage leads underground to the walkway. Working conditions here were harsh, for when fresh lime makes contact with damp surfaces (including skin, mouth, nose and hands) it becomes burning hot. Lime which was to be used for fertiliser, mortar or whitewash had to first be slaked by adding water. Lime produced here was taken by horse drawn wagon to the nearby railway station, or by coastal barges to London.

Today the lime kiln is no longer in use and is often inhabited by a colony of hibernating bats. Bats are an endangered species and are protected by law. Their roost must not be disturbed during the months from October to March, so if you wish to visit this fascinating example of industrial architecture, then ring the Railway Tavern first to check that the kiln is open.

Whether or not you can access the kiln, the Railway Tavern is well worth visiting in its own right. It was constructed in 1687 and, until 1703, was called the White Swan. Today it is a friendly pub, owned by Clem and Ann, where you can be sure of a warm welcome and a good quality pint of beer to slake your thirst. A small selection of bar snacks is also available. The pub sits in over two acres of land and has a popular beer garden with swings, a slide and a climbing frame to keep the children occupied.

Also in the grounds, Clem and Ann run a rescue home for unwanted animals including donkeys, rabbits and guinea pigs. In addition, injured seagulls, ducks and swans are often taken in and cared for.

This is a fascinating 'Hidden Place' to visit, with something to interest and delight all of the family. Be sure to call in for a visit whilst you are on your travels.

THE KING'S HEAD public house, next to the River Bure, is a fine establishment and well worth a visit. Owned by Kevin and Sue, this traditional freehouse has a vibrant and welcoming atmosphere, and offers a super selection of real ales, with different guest ales every week. The interior of the pub is full of character and features oak beams and exposed brickwork which add to its charm and warmth. During the warm summer months, the pub stages events such as barbecues and hog roasts in the courtyard. A good selection of dishes is available in the restaurant, excellent fresh fish dishes are featured weekly. All offer good value for money.

The Kings Head also has a number of letting rooms available at very reasonable prices, they are ideal as a base for exploring the area, or simply as a stop over point for one night.

The King's Head, Coltishall Common, Wroxham Road, Coltishall
Tel: 01603 737426

RISINGS lies close to the Red Lion Inn on Church Street. This charming house dates back to 1690 and retains the original gables at the front which give it a Dutch feel. Owned by Dorothy and Brian Hobson, Risings is a wonderful bed and breakfast establishment with a craft shop and self-catering holiday cottage as well. The house has three comfortable bedrooms and a great farmhouse style breakfast is served. With an attractive garden and sun patio to enjoy, all guests receive a warm and friendly welcome. The holiday cottage, with two bedrooms, is fully-equipped and the accommodation here matches the same high standards of those of the main house.

Coltishall Crafts, adjacent to the Risings, is an exciting showroom displaying a wide range of handcrafted products made by Norfolk's finest crafts people. Whether you just drop in to browse, are buying or commissioning, there is plenty to attract your attention. With picture frames, miniatures, chess sets, cushions, preserves, confectionery gift packs, glassware, dried flowers, pottery, soft and educational toys, paintings, wood carvings and turned items, patchwork, knitwear and much, much more there is sure to be something for everyone.

Risings, Church Street, Coltishall Tel: 01603 737549

To the north of Coltishall is the famous RAF station where Spitfires and Hurricanes of Fighter Command were based during the Second World War. That great war hero, Sir Douglas Bader, spent part of the war years here during the Battle of Britain and the story of the brave fighter pilot, who was determined to fly again and serve his country despite losing both his legs in a flying accident, was a great inspiration to many. His tireless endeavours after the war to improve the quality of life for the disabled earned him a CBE in 1956 and he was knighted 20 years later.

CROSTWICK. Located in the pretty village of Crostwick you will find 'The best pub in Crostwick', **THE WHITE HORSE**. This spacious Inn is owned and run by Sharleen and Wayne with their daughter Lucy and offers a warm and very friendly welcome to all guests. The bar offers 5 real ales as well as plenty of guest ales throughout the year. In the heat of the summer you can sit outside on the spacious patio which is covered with potted plants and flowers giving off a glorious aroma on those warm summer evenings. Open all day, every day, The White Horse serves food in the non-smoking conservatory and all food is freshly home-cooked to order. The food is varied and delicious with such specialities as Fresh dressed Crabs and Lobsters, Home-made pies and various rice dishes and curries. They offer 2 double bedrooms which are both en-suite and supply all home comforts including a colour television with tea and coffee making facilities. The White Horse offers a very comfortable and relaxed environment where the weary traveller can rest up and catch their breath for a while before continuing to explore this gorgeous part of England.

White Horse, Crostwick Tel: 01603 737560

WROXHAM. This riverside village, linked to its twin Hoveton by a hump-backed bridge over the River Bure, is the self-styled 'capital' of the Norfolk Broads. As such, it gets extremely busy here during the summer, with visitors jostling for elbow room in the pubs by the river and those who have come for a boating holiday quickly becoming acquainted with the workings of their hired craft. The banks of the river are chock-a-block with boatyards full of cruisers of all shapes and sizes. As an alternative to hiring a boat for a few days or weeks, there are also piloted river trips of an hour or two.

Despite the crowds, Wroxham enjoys an extremely pleasant setting and is the logical place from which to set off on your exploration of the Broads. It is also the main shopping centre for holidaymakers in the area and it is worth remembering Roy's, with its proud boast of being 'the largest village store in the world'.

Sanctuary from the hustle and bustle can be found at 15th century St Mary's Church with its splendid south doorway, a Norman showpiece of quite magnificent ornamental carvings.

RACKHEATH. An attractive village, unusual in that it used to stand approximately one mile from its present location. All that remains of the original village is the church, the rest having been lost in the great plague.

ASHMANHAUGH. A tiny village with, reputedly, the smallest church tower in England and certainly the smallest in Norfolk. The other point of interest at St Swithin's is the tomb of Honor Bacon, a young bride who died in 1591 on the eve of her wedding.

WORSTEAD. Hard to imagine now, but this was a busy industrial town during the Middle Ages. Today it has dwindled in size to become little more than a quiet and picturesque village with some fine Jacobean houses grouped around its square. Worstead lent its name to the tough woollen cloth produced in the region and many of the original weavers' cottages can still be seen in the narrow side streets. Worsted cloth, woven from tightly twisted yarn, was introduced by Flemish weavers and became popular throughout England from the 13th century onwards. These immigrants settled happily into the East Anglian way of life and seem to have influenced its architecture almost as strongly as its weaving industry.

The lovely 14th century church of St Mary provides ample evidence of Worstead's former prosperity. Its many treasures include a fine hammerbeam roof, the chancel screen with its remarkable painted dado, and a magnificent traceried font complete with cover. The village has an annual weekend of events to raise money for the continuing restoration of the church and the 'glory days' are kept very much alive by the presence of a still-functioning Guild of Weavers. Looms stand in the north aisle of St Mary's and visitors can watch the weavers demonstrating their skills at certain times.

Great Yarmouth and the Coast

GREAT YARMOUTH. The River Yare, from which the town takes its name, is the largest in Broadland and sea-going cargo ships sail from here to Norwich along with pleasure boats, yachts, dinghies and the rest. After meeting the River Bure and widening out into Breydon Water, the river then takes a sharp turn to the south, forming a 3 mile long peninsula between its eastern bank and the sea. It was here that the old town of Yarmouth was built, later spreading along the west bank of the Yare. When Henry III granted Yarmouth its charter in 1272, the 'Great' was proudly added to its name, and the town became known as a harbour and shipbuilding centre. The herring industry also brought great prosperity to the town for many centuries and, when overfishing led to its decline after the two World Wars, Yarmouth was given a new lease of life by the discovery of North Sea oil.

Visitors soon discover that much of Yarmouth's special character comes from its unique blend of the old with the new. Certainly it is a most popular seaside resort, with 5 miles of sandy beach, two piers and an impressive range of holiday amenities and entertainments; yet, at the same time, it has one of the most complete medieval town walls in the country and many outstanding historic buildings going right back to the Middle Ages. The 13th century **Tolhouse** in Tolhouse Street is one example: once the town's courthouse and gaol, it is said to be the oldest civic building in Britain. Its dungeons are now open to the public and it also houses a fascinating museum of local history.

The broad **Market Place** is one of the largest in England (Yarmouth claims many places in the record books!) and is crammed with stalls on Wednesdays and Saturdays and on Fridays during the summer. At its northern end is the splendidly restored 12th century **Church of St Nicholas**. Badly damaged by fire during the Second World War, it was rebuilt between 1957-60; its original medieval form being perfectly preserved. It also claims (naturally enough!) to be the largest parish church in England. To the south is a delightful group of handsome Georgian houses and, among them, the half-timbered town house where Anna Sewell, the author of 'Black Beauty', was born. St George's Church, at the opposite end of the Market Place to St Nicholas', now serves as a theatre and arts centre; while on the north-east corner is the delightfully-named Hospital for Decayed Fishermen, now dedicated to retired sea-farers.

Some of Yarmouth's best buildings can be found in **The Rows**, a network of narrow alleys and courts whose alignment has not been changed since medieval times. Many of these were destroyed when the town was bombed during the war, but some survived and a number of the more historic buildings have been restored. Other places of interest that come well recommended include: The **Marina Centre**; the exciting new **Sealife Centre**; and The **Maritime Museum** on Marine Parade was once a home for shipwrecked sailors, but today houses a superb collection of model vessels.

South Quay, with its elegant mixture of Tudor, Georgian and Victorian merchants' houses, must be seen. In particular Number 4, which is now the **Elizabethan House Museum**, a museum of domestic life containing a number of oak-panelled Elizabethan rooms with superb plasterwork ceilings. In total opposition to such elegance and charm, these houses look across to the port itself, a tough, noisy, working environment, stretching for nearly 2 miles along the River Yare.

Finally, the **Norfolk Pillar** can be found, surrounded by factories, a mile of the south of Old Yarmouth and behind South Beach. This landmark monument to Lord Nelson was erected in 1819 to commemorate the Admiral's landings at Yarmouth following his victories at the Battles of the Nile and Copenhagen. Standing at the top of the 144 ft column is not Nelson himself (his figure was reserved for the more famous column in Trafalgar Square 10 years later), but Britannia. To climb the 217 steps to the viewing platform is an awesome experience and, in fact, only allowed during July and August. The view from the top, however, is well worth the climb!

ALONG THE COAST

WALCOTT. A pleasant seaside village on the scenic B1159 coast road. Here, there are long stretches of fine sandy beaches that are ideal for swimming and coastal walks.

All Saints' Church is yet another place with Nelson connections. It was heavily restored in Victorian times and much of the finance for this was attributable to the Reverend Horatio Nelson William Comyn, a godson of Lord Nelson and who was actually baptised on board the 'Victory'. It seems that Reverend Comyn would do just about anything to raise money for his beloved church, even trotting around the countryside hawking wares from his pony and trap!

THE LIGHTHOUSE INN, Walcott's first free house, is a comfortable, friendly pub that has been owned and personally run by Shirley and Steve Bullimore since 1989. Previously a farmhouse, this has been a pub for over 150 years and, overlooking the North Sea, the lighthouse after which the inn is named lies some 2 miles away. A busy inn, frequented by holidaymakers and locals alike, this is a great place for an excellent pint and some delicious home-cooked food. Meals are served every day and only the freshest local produce is used. Fresh fish is a speciality and the home-made steak and kidney pie is certainly a dish to savour. With separate dining room and a family room, this is an inn the whole family can enjoy. Featured in both the Good Food Guide and the Good Beer Guide, it comes as no surprise that the bar serves a super range of real ales including its own Lighthouse Bitter. Throughout the season The Lighthouse Inn organises barbeques, children's entertainers and outside discos and the pub can cater for weddings, parties and other special occasions.

The Lighthouse Inn, Coast Road, Walcott Tel: 01692 650371

HAPPISBURGH. The coastal waters off Happisburgh (or 'Hazeborough' to give it its unlikely but correct pronunciation) have been the setting of many shipwrecks over the centuries and the unfortunate victims of these lie buried in the churchyard. The large grassy mound which lies to the north side of St Mary's Church contains the bodies of the ill-fated crew of HMS Invincible, which was wrecked on the treacherous sandbanks in 1801. The ship was on its way to join up with Nelson's fleet at Copenhagen when tragedy struck and resulted in the death of 119 crew members. Happisburgh's distinctive lighthouse, built in 1791 and striped like a barber's pole, certainly proved ineffectual in this instance; as did the soaring 110 ft tower of the church itself, which could normally be relied upon to act as a 'back-up' warning to mariners.

Inside the Church is a splendid 15th century octagonal font carved with the figures of lions, satyrs and musicians as well as the Evangelists. Embedded in pillars along the aisle, the marks left by shrapnel from German bombs which were dropped on the village in 1940 can still be seen.

Happisburgh is also the stomping ground of a particularly gruesome smuggler who is said to haunt the area. Legless, with his head dangling down his back on a strip of skin, he must present a pretty unprepossessing sight as he emerges from the sea, 'heading off' (as it were) towards Well Corner with a large sack in his arms! Local farmers first spotted him sometime around 1800 and, in order to find out what he was up to, they arranged a nightly vigil. For several nights they watched him drop his bundle down a well which then stood on the site, then jump in himself. When they investigated the well, they discovered the mutilated torso of a man with his legs and head stuffed into a sack nearby. It seems likely that he was murdered by his fellow smugglers, probably following an argument over how to split their ill-gotten gains.

The Hill House, Happisburgh Tel: 01692 650004

Located in the centre of the pretty village of Happisburgh is the favourite retreat of Sir Arthur Conan Doyle, **THE HILL HOUSE**. Built in the 16th Century this Freehouse is owned and run by Sue and Clive Stockton and offers a very homely and easy going atmosphere with a warm and friendly welcome. The Hill House offers en-suite accommodation in the converted 1900 Old Railway Signal Box, you will be treated to splendid sea views and comfortable furnishings. Great for the family, you will find a large children's room complete with toys, books and games situated in the old stable block and in the bar area a pool table and dart board. Open for breakfast every morning from 8.30 am until 10.00 am, Hill House also caters for the individual or group throughout the day and late into the evening. The daily selection of home-made food and speciality dishes is a wide and varied one, from Salmon Steak in Brandy Sauce to a delicious T-Bone Steak with a delicious Alexandra sauce,

174

comprising of Stilton, Chives and Fresh Cream. Complete with spacious beer garden and original open fires, The Hill House Inn is the perfect choice for any traveller passing through this beautiful part of the country.

LESSINGHAM. From the village a lane winds down to the southern end of **Eccles Beach**. The dunes here look spectacular, the tough marram grass creating a firm anchor for the sand which would otherwise be blown inland. A little further north is **Cart Gap**, which provides the only official parking place on this stretch of coast before you reach Sea Palling. The beach at Cart Gap is particularly well suited to families as the sands slope gradually down to the sea, while Eccles on Sea is a rather odd little place hidden behind the dunes, with its rows of beach huts and houses creating a rather dispirited atmosphere when the season is over.

INGHAM. This is the epitome of a traditional North Norfolk village with its beautiful church acting as a landmark for miles around; its cricket ground enclosed by trees and its village inn. **THE SWAN INN** is owned and managed by Ray and Teresa Howe and forms a focal point to the village for quality food, refreshment and accommodation. This lovely inn was built in the 14th century and was originally part of Ingham Priory, until its destruction under Henry VIII, in the 16th century. Its neatly thatched roof atop a clean white exterior presents an inviting prospect and guests will find a warm welcome in this traditional inn, known locally for its home-cooked food and real ale. The interesting accommodation is in a tastefully renovated stable which has to be seen to be believed! All five rooms feature a charming hand-crafted four poster bed, en-suite facilities, remote control television, shaver points tea/coffee tray and other luxuries. Breakfast and any other meals are taken in the main Inn. Open all day 11 am to 11 pm except Sunday.

The Swan Inn, Ingham, Nr. Stalham Tel: 01692 581099

SEA PALLING is another excellent place to bathe, but the dunes have been declared off-limits to the public to allow the marram grass to flourish. Some eight miles of sea defences from Happisburgh to Winterton were prompted by the floods of January 1953 and the natural sea wall of marram grass seems to provide a pretty effective barrier against the ravages of the North Sea.

This little village has a 17th century pub, **THE HALL INN**, which originally was the village manor house. It was converted some years ago into this very charming pub complete with oak beams. There are two marvellous inglenooks, and super open fires which burn those large logs that throw out warmth, and lend an atmosphere to the inn. There is something very welcoming and homely about the whole place. The restaurant is personally run by Carole whose specialities include home-made Stilton soup and special Scotch steak. Locally caught fish and fresh crab (in season) is available, otherwise there's a wide range of dishes at very realistic prices. Book in for Sunday lunch or try a summer barbecue. Should you wish to stay in this quiet and peaceful place, the inn has six letting rooms, some with en suite facilities. The beer garden is a pleasure to sit in, and you need have no fear of difficulty parking; the car park is large. The Hall Inn is privately owned by Bob Gard, Mym and Georgio and guests will find this free house comfortable, warm and friendly. There is reputedly a ghost here known as the Grey Lady who is thought to have been a resident many years ago. Since the Hall Inn is such a nice place to be, perhaps she prefers to remain in its comfortable surroundings.

The Hall Inn, Waxham Road, Sea Palling Tel: 01692 598323

WAXHAM. Just outside Sea Palling lies the tiny village of Waxham where, surprisingly enough, there are impressively tall trees firmly rooted in the dunes. By the derelict church of St John are the remains of a Tudor wall with corner turrets and a splendid 15th century gatehouse. This was once part of Waxham Hall, now a farmhouse, which is reputedly haunted by several members of the Brograve family - each of whom died a violent death during some of the most famous wars and battles in English history.

HORSEY. The little hamlet of Horsey lies on the marshes about a mile from the sea. Standing little more than three feet above sea level, the village has survived against great odds since Roman times and still fights its constant battle with the sea. This was almost lost in 1938 when Horsey was flooded and became completely cut off for over four months; the villagers having to be evacuated until the waters receded. In the village, the delightful thatched church of All Saints' is hidden away beneath the trees surrounding its overgrown churchyard.

To the west of Horsey is **Horsey Mere**, one of the outermost and least spoiled of the Norfolk Broads. Now owned by the National Trust, it covers around 120 acres and many visitors to the Broads manage to find their way here to moor their boats at Horsey staithe. Overlooking the staithe is an impressive four-storey brick-built windmill, built in 1912 to pump water from drainage ditches into the mere. The National Trust has done a splendid restoration job on the building and from the high viewing gallery there are unrivalled view across the mere and the surrounding marshland.

At the mere, a number of different species of wildfowl bob up and down on the water competing for space with a veritable flotilla of sailing boats. A strange but moving local legend relates that the Romans would place the bodies of their dead children into the mere and, on one particular night of the year, it is transformed into a garden where all the children ever laid to rest there can be seen at play.

WEST SOMERTON is a pleasant little village with access to Martham Broad and the River Thurne. It is popular with sailors as the flat, open countryside it traverses offers little resistance to the sea breezes that fill their sails.

The village was the birthplace of the 'Norfolk Giant', Robert Hales, who stood 7 ft 8 in tall in his stockinged feet and weighed in at 32 stone. He used his great size to good advantage, faring pretty well from touring both England and America and later became a publican in London where he was presented to Queen Victoria. Hales died in Great Yarmouth in 1863 at the age of 43 and his grave and memorial can be seen in the churchyard of St Mary the Virgin here in the village. Unfortunately nobody knows where his sister Mary, the 'Norfolk Giantess', ended up. She grew to a very respectable 7 ft herself!

WINTERTON-ON-SEA. The landmark church tower at Winterton-on-Sea is hard to miss for it soars to a height of 132 ft! Inside Holy Trinity Church is the so-called 'Fisherman's Corner', a striking tribute to all those who have lost their lives in these waters, with ropes, nets, a ship's lantern and an anchor - even the cross is fashioned from the timbers of a ship. This memorial was conceived and set up by the Reverend Clarence Porter, who, ironically enough, was himself drowned whilst rescuing a young choirboy from the sea.

Indeed, many of the houses in the village in the early part of the 18th century were said to be built from timbers washed ashore from the wrecks. Closer to the beach are some even stranger looking dwellings; round thatched buildings which evoke an impression of the African plains. The Hotel Humanus has very bravely modelled its guest accommodation on the mud huts of South Africa and it must be great fun to stay in one.

The beach at Winterton is wide and sandy and, at low tide, youngsters will delight in the numerous rock pools that form there with their little underwater worlds. However, do be wary of the very real dangers of drowning; markers are set out to warn bathers of the area to be avoided and notices insist that children should be accompanied by an adult at all times.

MARTHAM. A lovely village with attractive Georgian houses and cottages surrounding the village green and the massive west tower of St Mary's Church dominating the northern end. The village is also home to the **Countryside Collection**, a working museum of rural life and bygones where craftsmen such as a wheelwright and a blacksmith demonstrate their skills and, during the summer months, heavy horses can be seen hard at work in the fields.

ORMESBY ST MICHAEL. The **Norfolk Rare Breeds Centre** is a farm dedicated to breeding unusual animals and, in particular, rare breeds of pigs, cattle and fowl.

The area between Ormesby and Rollesby broads is an interesting area from an archaeological point of view, as metal pots found in nearby barrows would suggest that a community of Beaker Folk inhabited the vicinity around 2000 BC.

ROLLESBY. A pleasant village with the Norman church of St George which has a round tower and dates back mainly to the 14th century. A mile to the south-east of the village is the 200 acre Rollesby Broad which, together with Ormesby, is one of the largest of the Broads.

FILBY. A pretty Broadland village close to Filby Broad, an easily accessible and beautiful stretch of water.

The King's Head, Main Road, Filby Tel: 01493 730992

Located in the picturesque area of Filby you will find **THE KING'S HEAD**, a large and very attractive local Inn. This lovely pub is newly owned and run by Mandi and Daniel Drew, who offer a very hospitable and friendly welcome from the moment that you step through the door. The bar itself serves a wide selection of well kept real ales, with guest ales being introduced on a regular basis. The King's Head caters for children and pets by way of a large family room which offers Sky Cartoons for the youngsters all day long. Also for the family group is the colourful Beer garden, the perfect place for your kids to play in safety. Climbing frames, a round-a-bout, a large play area, swings and a see saw are all there for your convenience. For those animal lovers amongst you, Pets Corner is the place to find all your furry friends, but if the feathered variety is more to your liking then the Bird Avery should keep you entertained. The Kings Head also has a Restaurant that offers home-made specials such as Rabbit in Cider Casserole and Pheasant in Red Wine, to a full range of bar snacks and a special children's menu for the younger ones. If you are lucky enough to be passing through this beautiful area then why not stop for a while and relax at the Kings Head Inn, a place where families are so superbly catered for.

THRINGBY. Around the village can be spotted the large, sprawling flower, known as the Alexander, growing along the verges. It looks rather like a yellow-hued cow-parsley and can also be seen growing around the lanes near the old Roman fort at Reculver on the Kent coast. The Alexander is, in fact, a descendant of a plant which the Romans brought over from Macedonia; they used it in salads and it is said that it tastes rather like celery.

The present **Thrigby Hall** was built in 1876 on the remains of a previous mansion. This country building stands in old landscaped grounds amid an interesting collection of Asian wildlife. The gardens are one of the top attractions in Norfolk, set between Norwich and the Great Yarmouth coast, they are the ideal place to visit and an exciting outing for all the family. Other features include a tree house overlooking the willow pattern garden, children's adventure playground and ample picnic spots. The fine gift shop and cafe are open from Easter until late October.

FLEGGBURGH. Also known as **Burgh St Margaret**, the village is home to wonderful and different attraction that will suit all the family.

The Village, Burgh St Margaret, Fleggburgh Tel: 01493 369770

THE VILLAGE is a leisure park with a difference. Set within 35 acres of picturesque and tranquil parkland and woodland, the Village has something for everyone, whatever their age. Whenever you come to the Village, there will always be plenty going on and there is an ever changing programme of special events throughout the year including summer concerts, apple pressing and visits by well known celebrities. Laid out around the grounds, with plenty of places for picnics, the various buildings are linked together by paths and a railway runs round the grounds. Working steam engines, live entertainment, a unique collection of models, a traditional fairground, old style shops such as a bakery and sweet shop, and a range of working crafts some that visitors can try their hand at, there really is so much to do here. Finally, the newly renovated Regent Concert Hall, which houses an extremely rare 5 manual Compton-Christie cinema organ, takes you back to the good old days of the 1920s and there are plenty of places to stop and enjoy a thirst quenching drink and some delicious home-cooked food.

CAISTER-ON-SEA. The Romans settled here in the 2nd century (the name derives from the Latin 'castra' meaning a 'camp' or 'fortress') and excavations have verified the town's importance as a Roman port. Before then, however, Caister was an important town of the Iceni tribe.

A mile to the west of the town is the splendid ruin of **Caister Castle**, which was the first castle to be built of brick in England and, indeed, one of the earliest brick buildings of any kind in this country. The 90 ft tower survives, together with much of the moated wall and gatehouse, now lapped by still waters and with ivy relentlessly encroaching. It may look like the sort of place where only bats and owls should dwell, but it is in fact open to the public during the summer. As an additional attraction to visitors, the castle grounds house an impressive collection of motor vehicles, including a car used in the film of Ian Fleming's 'Chitty-Chitty-Bang-Bang'.

Caister Castle was built between 1432-5 by Sir John Fastolf. Though there is the possibility of Sir John being the prototype of Shakespeare's boisterous character, Falstaff, purists believe otherwise. Whether Fastolf deserves this distinction or not, he was certainly a hero not just at Agincourt, but also during the so-called 'Battle of the Herrings' in 1429. An unusual name, it refers to a clever tactic employed by Sir John during the Siege of Orleans when his convoy of ships taking supplies to the English army formed a laager of herring barrels and beat off the French.

The Kings Arms, West Road, Caister-on-Sea Tel: 01493 720648

THE KINGS ARMS, situated on West Road in Caister-on-Sea is a 16th century coach house which was rebuilt in the 1930s. This impressive public house is arguably the best in the area, it is certainly one of the most popular. It has two bars, a large games room with two pool tables and a dart board. The atmosphere is lively every evening of the week. For some bizarre reason, a Christmas tree and decorations are kept up all year! Be sure to give this vibrant pub a visit, you will not be disappointed.

The Broads

ACLE. An attractive village that is now, thankfully, by-passed by the busy A47 Norwich to Great Yarmouth road. The River Bure and its large marina at Acle Bridge are only a mile away to the north-east, so Acle gets its fair share of summer holidaymakers stocking up on essentials. The bridge that once stood here was apparently the scene of numerous executions, with victims hung on the parapet and left to dangle over the Bure and rot!

The **EAST NORWICH INN**, near the centre of the village of Acle, offers comfortable accommodation and first rate food. Formerly municipal offices, this grand and stylish building was converted to an inn in 1979. Locally called 'The Cabin, it is now owned and personally run by Liz and Robin Graves-Morris. There are nine spacious en-suite bedrooms available and the inn offers a good selection of excellently-priced dishes including a choice for vegetarians. The Inn is also a freehouse and there is a wide variety of bitters, lagers and ales on tap. There is a warm and friendly family atmosphere here and this is very much the village pub. The East Norwich Inn has been awarded ETB 3 crowns and pets are welcome.

East Norwich Hotel, Acle Old Road, Acle Tel: 01493 751112

Heading down the A47 to Great Yarmouth the road passes the Stracey Arms Windpump, which was built of brick in 1883 and stands close to the pub of the same name. Its function was to draw off surplus water from the surrounding marshland and pump it into the Bure. It has

Beeston Hall

Caister Castle

now been fully restored by the Norfolk Windmills Trust and visitors can also see an educational exhibition of photographs outlining the history of windpumps in the region.

For a more unusual dining experience, **ST MARGARET'S MILL RESTAURANT**, located one mile out of Acle on the Caister Road near Acle Bridge, in an old windmill circa 1747, offers an interesting venue for candlelit dinners, receptions and dinner parties. The ruined windmill was bought by actor John Glynn-Jones in 1960 for £50. In 1970 it was sold, became a restaurant, and eventually, in 1984, it came into the hands of the present owners - Brian and Maxine Kennard. They have travelled extensively, living in Argentina and West Africa for some years and diners will find the flavour of these countries reflected in some of the inventive dishes created by chef, Brian. Specialities of the restaurant include a superb Seafood Grill, Paella, Lobster Thermidor, Dover Sole with Prawns, Crab Claws or King Prawns in garlic butter, Scampi Provencal and Mussels Mariniere. Beef Wellington and Steak Diane are popular among the extensive range of meat and poultry dishes available and of course Norfolk Duckling in Brandy and Orange sauce. Vegetarian and special diet meals are catered for. Talk to Brian about flying as he is also a glider pilot and instructor at the Norfolk Gliding Club in his spare time and you could be taking to the skies above Norfolk, hence the need to book in advance for lunch! Open 7 pm to 10 pm (last food orders) daily in summer and Tuesday to Saturday in Winter. Readers of Hidden Places are invited to a complimentary glass of wine.

St. Margaret's Mill, Caister Road, Acle Tel: 01493 750182

THE VILLAGES OF THE NORFOLK BROADS

THURNE. A quiet village which stands on the river of the same name and just upstream from where it joins the Bure at Thurne Mouth.

About a mile to the south-west of Thurne, and only approachable by boat or on foot, stands the decidedly odd-looking ruin of **St Benet's Abbey** by the River Bure. The original abbey that stood on this site was destroyed by the Danes in the 9th century and its replacement was founded by King Canute in 1020. It fell into ruin after the Dissolution, when the abbot became the Bishop of Norwich and surrendered the episcopal estates to the Crown. The Bishop's present-day successor still holds both titles and conducts a special annual service at the abbey ruins on the first Sunday in August - arriving, of course, by boat.

LUDHAM. A beautiful and unspoilt Broadland village that is very popular with the boating fraternity. Rows of picturesque thatched cottages, handsome 18th century houses around the market place, and the 14th and 15th century church dedicated to St Catherine make up the heart of Ludham. At **How Hill** there is an unusual open-framed timber-built windpump known as Boardman's Mill, which is open every day to visitors.

In part of a Grade II listed thatched cottage, in the centre of this picturesque village, you will find **THE ALFRESCO EATING HOUSE**. You can be assured of a friendly greeting in a relaxed atmosphere, children are very welcome and dogs and their owners can be accommodated in their walled garden. Over the last 3 to 4 years Alfresco has consolidated its reputation for excellent afternoon teas but has developed into a bona fide lunch venue, where there is a standard choice of 7 items on the lunch menu, plus daily specials. The eating house itself is furnished with pine furniture, lace tablecloths, plants and beautiful displays of dried flowers and pictures by local artists. All the lunches are prepared to order on the premises, this gives the food its proper flavour and nutritional value. Whether your choice is pasta, crepe, chicken or fish you can guarantee excellent service and quality. Alfresco will also be of special interest to Vegetarians where they will find a wide choice of meals. Whether it's morning coffee, late breakfast, lunch, afternoon tea or dinner, Alfresco is the place to go to taste the difference.

Alfresco Eating House, Norwich Road, Ludham Tel: 01692 678384

POTTER HEIGHAM. The notorious medieval hump-backed bridge spanning the River Thurne in the village has a headroom of only seven feet and puts the fear of God into all novice sailors who attempt to negotiate it without the recommended professional pilot to guide them safely through.

Essentially, Potter Heigham is an entirely new village that has sprung up around the old bridge, the hub of it being the Broads Haven Marina which caters for all the needs of the tourist afloat. The village proper lies a good mile further north and its name is said to derive from the fact that a Roman pottery once stood here. A visit to St Nicholas' Church in the old village is very worthwhile. Mainly 14th century, it has a thatched nave, a circular tower supporting a 15th century octagonal belfry and, inside, a unique brick-built font.

However, far and away the most intriguing of Potter Heigham's architectural features is the peculiar building on the riverbank a few hundred yards downstream from the bridge. At first glance it resembles a somewhat stunted windmill upon which someone has draped an old sou'wester to shield it from the elements, but on closer inspection it is revealed to be the top section of a helter-skelter! Lopped off and transplanted here as a holiday cottage, it originally stood on the Britannia Pier at Great Yarmouth and must have been an even more impressive sight in its working days.

CATFIELD. Purpose built in a traditional old barn style in October 1992, **GROVE FARM STUDIO AND GALLERY** features tall windows front and side that create a light and airy atmosphere. This Gallery displays the artist's own works of art, but it is also his home and farm which he works himself. The property is family run by the artist (Sid to his friends) and his wife Jean, they have farmed and lived here since 1971.

Grove Farm Studio and Gallery, Sharp Street, Catfield Tel: 01692 670679

Over recent years SF Clarke has had many successful exhibitions which has now resulted in an ever-increasing demand for his paintings. Examples of his work are bought by discerning collectors and hang in Canada, USA, Uruguay, New Zealand, Australia and Europe as well as many parts of the United Kingdom. The adequate floor and wall space gives excellent viewing to browse at your leisure, not only the paintings but also the fine collection of limited edition figure study sculptures in cold cast bronze by Sue Riley, and the display of occasional antique furniture by A Bates and Sons. The Gallery is set in 1.5 acres of water garden recently reclaimed from an overgrown bogland by the artist and

THE NORFOLK BROADS

This is a fascinating and varied area, with a rich and interesting past, a unique landscape and a wide variety of wildlife. Whether exploring the area on foot, by car or by boat, the Broadlands offer remoteness and tranquility as well as restored windmills, medieval churches and beautiful gardens.

The landscape enjoyed by so many has developed over the years and is a delicate balance between man's use of the land and changing natural conditions. In medieval East Anglia, the thriving peat-digging industry left huge pits in the land. Then, as the sea level rose, these pits flooded and created the shallow lakes, known today as the Broads.

It is worth remembering that the Broads and surrounding wetlands are a fragile environment, having been under threat from the increasing amount of water traffic over the years. The wash from motor-boats has eroded the banks of rivers and broads at an alarming rate, the mud settling on the bottom and gradually filling in the waterways. However, this is not the only cause for concern.

Much has been written on the problem of pollution here, with nitrates from fertilisers and phosphates from sewage and detergents causing the spread of algae, and the subsequent choking of the indigenous plant life as its light is blocked out and its oxygen stolen. Once familiar sights such as the massive wild water-lily meadows have virtually disappeared, and the death of aquatic plants has affected the entire food chain - insects, fish and birds have all suffered the consequences. There are 46 Broads altogether in the region, and today, only four of these have perfectly clear water and only half a dozen or so have any plant life at all. The rest are sterile wastes.

Many of the Broads may now be beyond help, but the future of the region is not totally one of doom. Whether or not the conservationists have their way and motor-boats become a thing of the past, the Broads Authority and the various conservation bodies are implementing other measures to ensure the survival of this unique place. Broadland has finally been designated a National Park and over 20 Sites of Special Scientific Interest have been declared. Mud is gradually being pumped out of the barren waterways, the plants are being replaced by more resistant species, and hopefully it is not too late to turn the tide.

Two thirds of Norfolk and a large part of North Suffolk are drained by the main Broads rivers: north of Acle are the Ant, Thurne and Bure rivers and to the south the Yare, Chet and Waveney. With over 120 miles of waterways, boats have always been an important form of transport. Each village having a 'staithe' or quay for moorings and the area even had its own special 'style' of boat: the single-sailed wherries. These shallow-draught boasts, specially built for the shallow waters of the area delivered their cargoes of corn, coal, reed and sedge to the villagers. As rail and road transport developed and the holiday industry took over, many have been adapted and restored to provide the most pleasureable of holiday homes.

The towns and villages of the area have their own special character. Many have beautiful churches, sometimes with thatched roods, and many of the old staithes remain where boats can still be moored. The 'Cathedral of the Broads', St Helen's at Ranworth, is particularly impressive and, dating back to 1370, its tower is a landmark for miles around. From Roman ruins to wonderful Victorian mansions with magnificent gardens there are plenty of places to visit.

The whole of **Hickling Broad** has been a nature reserve since 1945 and there is a great variety of wild flowers and animals as well as many rare birds including the graceful avocet. The reserve is open all year, daily except Tuesdays.

The **Carlton Marshes Nature Reserve**, at Carlton Colville, borders on land drained for crops and its situation provides a clear contrast between a traditional grazed landscape and a more intesively farmed one. Owned by the Suffolk Wildlife Trust, the reserve is home to many marsh birds, dragonflies, butterflies and grass snakes.

The **Otter Trust** at Earsham near Bungay is the place to see these interesting creatures. Kept in walled enclosures, so visitors can observe them easily, the best time to visit is feeding time (between noon and 4 pm).

The large stretch of **Breydon Water** lies to the west of Great Yarmouth and the main channel is a busy route for small shipping, especially holiday craft, during the summer. In the winter months, it is a wild and desolate place with a charm of its own. The whole area became a local nature reserve in 1968 and it is a unique attraction for bird life. There are geese, ducks and waders in plenty and, during the spring and autumn, it is a favourite with migrating birds. Many interesting plants also grow on the edge of the marshland, including the samphire, a local delicacy sometimes seen in the fishmongers.

Strumpshaw Fen, close to the River Yare, has over 5 miles of footpaths through woodland, grazing marshes, reedbeds and along the river bank. Managed by the RSPB, the reserve is open all year and, in one relatively small area, provides a huge variety of plant, bird and animal life.

the grounds and gardens are landscaped in a Broadlands theme. When you visit Grove Farm Studio and Gallery you can be assured of a warm welcome in this most relaxed and unhurried atmosphere.

HICKLING. Despite the remoteness, which can be approached by road or river, Hickling was bombed during both world wars. To the east lies **Hickling Broad**, the largest and least spoilt of all the Norfolk Broads. It now forms part of a 1,400 acre national nature reserve (one of the first to be established in England) managed by the Norfolk Naturalists Trust and those exploring it by boat must keep strictly within the markers.

Although the marsh harriers and bitterns which could once be spotted frequently on Hickling Broad are now rare, careful controls have enabled it to remain a rich habitat for many other types of bird. Reed bunting, willow, sedge and grasshopper warblers, redshank and snipe are just some of the species which have held their own and the magnificent swallowtail butterfly (Britain's largest) still breeds here. It is also possible to visit the reed beds (Norfolk reed has been used for thatching for centuries) by making an appointment with the Warden.

There is a rather touching local legend associated with Hickling Broad. A young lass from Potter Heigham fell in love with a drummer boy who was shortly due to leave for the Battle of Waterloo. As the girl's father did not approve of the attachment, they were forced to meet in secret at a place called Swim Coots on the Heigham side of the Broad; the young soldier skating across the winter ice to join his sweetheart. One evening the ice gave way and the boy was drowned, but they say that his ghost can sometimes still be seen on winter evenings, scudding across the ice and beating his drum as he faithfully maintains his tryst.

The Greyhound Inn, The Green, Hickling Tel: 01692 598306

THE GREYHOUND INN can be found in the charming village of Hickling, you won't be able to miss this hidden gem as it is the only pub in the village! The Inn is circa 1735 and is covered by a local by law that states that if there is a fire in Hickling the pub must open to supply liquid refreshment to the Firemen! This village Inn offers an excellent and very extensive menu including bar snacks, children's menu, Sunday roast and a vegetarian menu. All the food is prepared and cooked to order and offers many speciality dishes including Home Cooked Beef and Onion Pie with Gravy, or you may even be up to trying the He-man Grill which is based around 20 oz of meat with egg, fried bread, mushrooms, tomato and onion rings, definitely not for the faint hearted! There is a large beer garden with play areas at the rear of the pub, a great place for the whole family to entertain themselves, although children are welcome so long as they are bolted down! The Greyhound Inn serves a terrific range of real ales, draught beers and lagers, and wines and spirits, Port and Brandy is also available. The Inn is situated on Weavers Way, a famous foot path from Cromer to Great Yarmouth and is also only 25 to 30 minutes stroll from over 1,200 acres of nature reserves.

THE PLEASURE BOAT INN is on the edge of Hickling Broad at Pleasureboat Staithe. Surrounded by a most attractive group of buildings, this is a popular meeting place for the sailing fraternity. The Inn is over 150 years old and used to be the rendezvous point of the wherries, which would drop their cargoes and collect local produce to transport to Great Yarmouth. Today, The Pleasure Boat is run by Andrew and Jenny Haylett, who have been providing an excellent service for their many customers over their last six years in residence. The Inn is very tastefully decorated and has a dining area that boasts magnificent views over the Broads. A comprehensive set menu contains many varied dishes, including vegetarian and a good selection of children's meals. Daily specials include roast dinners, and for those who like a drink with their meal, a good wine list is available. On a warm day you can sit outside with your drink, watching the numerous breeds of bird and taking in the scenery, and perhaps enjoy a delicious salad from the amply stocked salad bar, or maybe a walk down to the village. Families are made to feel very welcome and with live music at weekends and free mooring outside, The Pleasure Boat Inn will suit almost any type of traveller.

The Pleasure Boat Inn, State Road, Hickling Tel: 01603 270241

SUTTON. The village is home to **Sutton Windmill**, the tallest in Britain, and the **Broadlands Museum**. The historic windmill was constructed in the 18th century and remained in use until 1940. In recent years, a lengthy programme of restoration work has been carried out by

Helter-Skelter House, Potter Heigham

the present owners, the Nunn family, using authentic materials wherever possible. Their ultimate aim is to restore the sails of this nine-storey windmill to working order. Visitors are welcome to view the historic corn-milling machinery with its four sets of millstones and to experience the superb views from the top. Over the past 30 years, the Nunn family have also built up a fascinating private collection of artifacts which reflect the social history of England since World War I. These are on show in the family's privately-owned Broadlands Museum and include many interesting examples of domestic and kitchen appliances, banknotes, cigarette packets, razors and leather- and barrel-making tools.

The Broads Museum & Sutton Windmill, Sutton Tel: 01692 581195

STALHAM. The ancient market town of Stalham, lying three miles inland just off the A149, provides an excellent base for exploring the northern reaches of the Norfolk Broads. From Stalham Staithe, boats can be hired for day trips along the River Ant and beyond, or water tours can be taken to the beautiful gardens at How Hill. Hickling Broad with its nature reserve is only two miles away and is popular with bird watchers. For those more interested in walking, the famous Weavers Way passes through Stalham on its route from Great Yarmouth to Cromer.

Strawberries are the very essence of summer and picking your own from a farm means you can select the very best for your table, we have found the perfect place to do just that, **HALL FARM**. Owned and run by David and Della King and their children Daniel, Tanita and Rupert, this farm has been in the family for over 3 generations and was purchased back in the 1930s by David's grandfather. Set in the glorious countryside of Stalham, Hill Farm has 30 acres of fruit, from Strawberries, Raspberries, Gooseberries, Loganberries and Blackberries to the more obscure, such as Sunberries and Josterberries. Also available are Black, Red and White Currants, Sweetcorn and free range eggs from the farms own chickens. Open every day 9 am - 5 pm from the third week in June until first week in September, this superb property has a children's play area called The Fort where the kids can be entertained and Gemma the Dartmoor pony is available for some attention at any time! Over 75 acres of prime land is dedicated to growing Blackcurrants which are used in

Ribena and you will find plenty of staff on hand who will be pleased to help you in any way that they can. Hall Farm really is a super place to spend a summers afternoon, phone them on 01692 580229 and pay the family a visit soon.

Hall Farm, Old Yarmouth Road, Stalham Tel: 01692 580229

DILHAM. Located between Walsham Rocks and Stalham is **THE CROSS KEYS INN**, a traditional pub in beautiful surroundings. Built in 1780 and owned and run by John and Brenda Greengrass, this pub is a hidden gem, with open fires and original oak beams you will feel at home from the moment that you enter. The Cross Keys has a super bowling green that was originally laid in 1927 and in the summer afternoons many a match is played between the locals and visiting teams. The atmosphere in this pub is very friendly and warm with a large beer garden and real wood furnishings that complement the overall feel of this lovely Inn. John is an avid collector of ashtrays and you will find hundreds dotted around the walls and tables adding a distinct air of eccentricity. The food is good and plentiful with Chicken, Cod, Plaice and Scampi all for under five pounds and the beer is good and very reasonably priced.

Cross Keys, The Street, Dilham Tel: 01692 536398

NEATISHEAD. A charming village, Limekiln Dyke runs down from here to the western side of Barton Broad and, although its cottages and farms are fairly spread out, the heart of the village is centred around the main street with its late Georgian houses. **Beeston Hall** is normally open in the afternoons during the summer. Standing just half a mile to the north-west of Neatishead, it is a charming building of the 18th century with flint facade and laudable Gothic pretensions. Much of the charm of a house of this calibre comes from the fact that it is still very much a family home, and the Prestons have lived here for centuries.

WOODBASTWICK. The open waters and skies of the Broads have inspired many artists since the area was first discovered as a holiday destination at the end of the last century. The Broads is similar to a national park area, a place protected for its special landscape and wildlife and a place for everyone to enjoy. Imagine a typical well-kept English village of thatched cottages around a village green and you have imagined Woodbastwick. Unfortunately it is an Estate village so you can't easily explore much of the surrounding countryside. However there is a tiny car park at **Woodbastwick Staithe** where you can watch the antics of other boat users as they moor at The Ferry Inn on the opposite bank. This is also the starting point for a boarded walkway (suitable for wheelchair users) to Cockshoot Broad. Do go if you have the chance as here you will see a clean broad with thriving plant and animal life. Why not visit **Toad Hole Cottage Museum**, near How Hill on the River Ant. This tiny eel-catcher's cottage takes you back into the country life of the Victorian age. For an unforgettable experience of hidden creeks, marshes and wildlife, you can take a trip on the 'Electric Eel' which leaves from the Cottage on the hour. Also if you in the Ranworth area then don't forget to take a trip on Maurice at the Ranworth Ferry which will take you across the water from Ranworth to the Conservation Centre.

Broads Authority, 18 Colegate, Norwich Tel: 01603 610734

HORNING. Although it is now a popular boating centre, Horning does not yet suffer from the same degree of commercialisation as nearby Wroxham. With its pretty reed-thatched cottages, the main street of this ancient village runs parallel to the River Bure for almost a mile and the trim lawns of half-timbered Edwardian houses sweep down to thatched boathouses on the water's edge.

Many of the pubs and hotels along the river offer mooring space, one of them being the 15th century Old Ferry Inn. This historic inn stands at the point of the river where the old chain ferry once transported its passengers from one bank to the other and was, at one time, used as a mead storehouse for St Benet's Abbey. It seems that more than one kind of spirit can be found at the inn, for it is said to be haunted by the ghost of a young woman dressed in a flowing green cloak, sometimes seen walking through the bar before sinking into the river. The story goes that she was raped and murdered by monks from the abbey who went on a drunken rampage then tried to hide the corpse in the river.

St Benedict's Church, which stands on a hill outside the village, is well worth a visit. Its soaring 14th century tower has the Four Evangelists on its pinnacles and, inside, there are some unusual medieval bench-ends - one of a particularly horrific nature depicting the Devil pushing a man into the fiery mouth of a dragon.

RANWORTH. The beautiful Broadland village of Ranworth is famous for its church and its position on the Ranworth Marshes. From the top of St Helen's church tower it is possible to see five Norfolk Broads, Horsey Mill and the sea at Great Yarmouth. Inside, is a 15th century service book and one of the finest rood-screens in the country. The church is open daily and visitors are welcome.

The Norfolk Naturalist's Trust chose to locate the **Broadland Conservation Centre** at the nearby nature reserve. An exhibition on the Broads, past and present, can be found here, as well as a quarter-mile nature trail which starts in the village. For those approaching by boat, there are 24 hour public moorings at the entrance to Ranworth Broad, although no land access to the village is possible from here. Alternatively, it is possible to anchor in Malthouse Broad where landings can be made at the village staithe. The staithe was once a thriving mooring for the old Norfolk trading wherries. These would sail into Ranworth to unload their cargoes of coal and barley for the maltings and reload with locally produced wool and woven cloth. (The famous woollen town of Worstead is only a few miles away to the north). The wherries ceased trading in 1950 and little has changed here since. There are still magnificent views across Ranworth Marshes and a solitary disused wherry resting by the quay.

Built in 1762, **THE MALTSTERS** is a pub with a very much traditional flavour. Owned and run for the past 14 years by Keith and Jessie Pawsey, the atmosphere is very relaxed and friendly with Keith using the bar area as his own personal front room!. The Inn retains many of its original features and offers a family room complete with piano for any would be pianists. The Bow of a ship is used to separate the bar area from the games room, it was built in 1948 by H. T. Percival who used to own a boat yard in Horning and was previously used as the bar itself. There is a separate dining area which is non-smoking and offers a host of home cooked daily specials and bar snacks including some wonderful fresh home baked fruit pies, delicious. For the family you will find a roomy beer garden complete with children's play area and a beautiful patio where you can sit and enjoy a cool glass of wine on a hot summers day. In season The Maltsters will stay open all day with normal opening hours in the winter, although if there is a demand the pub will remain open until late.

Did You Know...

The Hidden Places Series

Covers most of Britain?

For our full list see back of book

The Maltsters, The Hill, Ranworth Tel: 01603 270241

SOUTH WALSHAM. An ancient village that remains an idyllic escape from the hustle and bustle of daily life. There are several places of interest around South Walsham.

Be prepared to spend many happy hours at the **FAIRHAVEN GARDEN TRUST**. The village was first recorded in history during the reign of King Harold. After the battle of Hastings, William the Conqueror took over the land and gave the manor of South Walsham to the Earl of Norfolk, later to become the Duke of Norfolk. There is much of interest to see and we should have drawn your attention in the beginning to the 15th century rood screen and carved poppy heads on the pews in St Mary's church. The fine 18th century organ in the church was originally built for the assembly House, Norwich, but was donated to St Mary's by the late Lord Fairhaven. About a mile to the north lies Malthouse Broad, leading to Ranworth Broad and its Nature Reserve.

To the north east there is road access to the public South Walsham Outer Broad; this leads through a narrow channel called 'The Weirs' into the private Inner Broad, which forms part of the Fairhaven Garden Trust. Lord Fairhaven was not only a gardener, but also a naturalist. He purchased the South Walsham Estate in 1947, and the whole garden was a wilderness. The dykes of the present garden existed, but the whole area presented an impenetrable jungle of fallen trees, brambles and nettles. Also new for 1996 is the 42 seater Tea Room which serves Light Lunches and snacks throughout the day. Inspired by his friend, Sir Eric Savill, creator of one of the first woodland garden in Norfolk. The Jungle was slowly cleared, and as each new area was conquered, shade and water-loving plants were introduced, primulas by the thousand, Lysichitum

Americanum, which now grows in almost wild profusion, camellias and rhododendrons were just a few of the plants chosen. What you can see today took 15 years to create, and Lord Fairhaven achieved it with the help of a single woodsman, Jack Debbage. Since then there has always been a Debbage at Fairhaven. The head gardener and resident warden is now George Debbage. The Fairhaven Garden Trust property covers about 170 acres including the Inner Broad, and a further 60 acres comprising of the bird sanctuary to the west of Ranworth Road. To complement your visit to Fairhaven Gardens there are unique vintage style river launch cruises that show you the real beauty of The Norfolk Broads. There have been 92 varieties of birds in the woods around South Walsham, and the bird sanctuary may be visited by prior arrangement with the warden. So much more could be written about Fairhaven Garden Trust, but seeing is better than reading, so do go and experience this enchantment for yourself.

Fairhaven Garden Trust, 2 The Woodlands, Wymers Lane, South Walsham
Tel: 01603 270449

Leading on from the Fairhaven Garden Trust, and the South Walsham Estate, it should be noted that South Walsham Hall, on the northern edge of this lovely Broadland village was originally the Manor House of the Estate and the present Lord Fairhaven 111 was born at the Hall, then the family home.

SOUTH WALSHAM HALL is now an exceptional hotel, restaurant and country club which has been run for the last 12 years by Swiss-born Alex Suss and his staff. The present house dates from the Elizabethan era and was added to in Georgian, Victorian and Edwardian times. It is set in 30 acres of private grounds with sloping lawns, beautiful lakes and many specimen trees and shrubs. Inside, a magnificent carved staircase leads to the ten luxurious bedrooms; all have en-suite bath/shower and every modern facility. To the rear, a further seven rooms are located in the tastefully-converted gun room, carriage house and blacksmith's workshop. The 'Fairhaven' restaurant is open to non-residents and offers a wide-ranging menu with a large choice of specialities including fish, pheasant and partridge (when in season) for which the region is renowned. Guests will find a wine list to suit all palates. South Walsham Sports and Leisure Centre is integrated into the grounds of the Hall and offers many activities which include the Hotel's heated outdoor swimming pool. South Walsham Hall offers travellers and visitors a rare opportunity to experience country house luxury living at a very reasonable price. Featured in Access Guide for Disabled and awarded ETB 4 Crowns.

South Walsham Hall, South Walsham Tel: 01603 270378

BRAMERTON. **ROLLING ACRE** lies up a long country lane, 200 yards from the riverside Woods End Tavern off the Bramerton to Norwich road. This delightful house is in a beautiful location and 10 minutes from Norwich and it was built in 1860. A warm, friendly home, Jill and John Barton offer excellent bed and breakfast accommodation in a choice of two bedrooms. The hearty, home-cooked breakfast is served overlooking the magnificent countryside of river and rolling hills. The large garden is a lovely place to saunter round on a quiet summer's evening and with the pub just 5 minutes walk away this is an ideal spot for an overnight stop, a weekend break or a holiday. Guests are advised to phone in advance as Jill and John appreciate a couple of hours notice (24 hours during the winter).

Rolling Acre, Woods End, Bramerton Tel: 01508 538529

SURLINGHAM. THE HERMITAGE, a house owned by Anne Pinder offering wonderful bed and breakfast accommodation, lies in the quiet village of Surlingham yet it is just 6 miles from Norwich city centre. Surrounded by peaceful and tranquil gardens, this charming cottage was originally two worker's cottages until, in the 1750s, they were converted into one dwelling. Still known as 'the house with two staircases' in the village, The Hermitage is one of the oldest buildings in Surlingham. Accommodation is offered in a choice of three individually decorated bedrooms, with en-suite or private facilities, and guests have their own lounge, complete with roaring log fire in the winter. Well known for its breakfasts, you can be sure of a delicious, hearty meal that will keep you going until teatime. A charming and delightful house, it is a pleasure to stay here.

The Hermitage, Chapel Loke, Surlingham Tel: 01508 538431

BRUNDALL. Hidden away in the pretty town of Brundall, only 100 yards from Brundall Church you will find **THE RAM INN**, the oldest building in the local area. This 300 year old Pub is owned and run by Ros Long and her daughter Dianne, offering real family hospitality and a warm and friendly greeting.

The Ram Inn, 108 High Street, Brundall Tel: 01603 716926

The Ram Inn started off its life as a single room pub and has been gradually added to over the years and is even now due to be refurbished again in October 1996. Real Ales are served in the spacious bar which is locally known for its Darts and Crib team. In the summer the large beer garden is the perfect place to sit, enjoy a drink and let the kids have fun on the numerous play equipment that makes the Ram Inn a perfect family retreat. All the bar food is home-made by Ros herself, all the food is displayed on black boards and is changed frequently with steak and kidney pie and a delicious treacle tart being the pub speciality.

FREETHORPE. **THE RAMPANT HORSE** in Freethorpe is a super pub and country restaurant that you really should make a point of going to visit whilst you are in the area. Situated just half a mile from the Norman church on the Reedham road, this traditional village pub has a wonderful atmosphere and serves only the very best real ales. The restaurant is one of the most popular in the area and is renowned for its steak and seafood dishes. If you visit on a Sunday, then make a point of trying the carvery, it is delicious and excellent value for money besides. The interior of the building is full of character, replete with original oak beams and real fires. There is also a courtyard which has a small aviary. This is a charming pub, and a fine restaurant, a 'hidden place' which is well worth visiting.

The Rampant Horse, 2 Chapelfields, Freethorpe Tel: 01493 700545

WICKHAMPTON. East Wickhampton is a maze of fields and dykes where many of the old windpumps have been restored (though not necessarily to working order) and are now open to visitors. **Berney Arms Mill**, standing 70 ft high and in working order, was built in the 1860s to grind cement and was later converted to a pumping mill. It is now owned and run by English Heritage.

Close by, the Berney Arms public house must be one of the most isolated pubs in the country, with no access by road at all. To reach it you must come by footpath, by train from Yarmouth or Reedham (the halt is half a mile away over the fields), or by boat. Holidaymakers who start their boating holiday in Beccles and chug up the River Waveney to visit Yarmouth often take advantage of the safe mooring place here before venturing onto the tidal waters of Breydon Water.

There are two rather strange effigies in the chancel of St Andrew's Church. The figures have been badly defaced over the centuries, but they represent Sir William Gerbygge and his wife, who originally both clasped a small stone heart to their chests - presumably signifying their devotion to God or perhaps their love for one another. However, local folklore gives a quite different identity to the figures and a far more disturbing reason for their presence. Parents of fractious children would tell them that this couple were actually two brothers named Hampton, who argued fiercely following a dispute over local parish boundaries and tore each other's hearts out! They were then turned to stone by the wrath of God and left in the church as a warning to all those who are in the habit of losing their temper!

REEDHAM is an essential stop for exploring the countryside to the south of the River Yare, as its chain ferry provides the sole crossing for vehicles over the river between Great Yarmouth and Norwich.

St John the Baptist's Church in the village was almost totally destroyed by fire in 1981, but a programme of restoration was begun at once. Rather like the tiny plants that shoot up from the ashes of a forest fire, something good can be said to have come from the disaster as the ruined plaster was being chiselled off the wall of the nave, a glorious pattern of alternating herringbone and horizontal tiles was revealed.

Reedham is also the home of the enterprising 'Hales Snails' which is the place to go for edible snails. These gastronomic delights are even exported to France! Unfortunately, the snail centre is not open to visitors, but visitors are welcome to 'Pettitts', the local taxidermy firm! Besides seeing the experts at work on new commissions (they number many film and theatre companies amongst their clients), there is also a display of previous works in the form of various stuffed animals and birds. The company is also involved with breeding the delightful Falabella miniature horses.

The Lord Nelson, Riverside, Reedham Tel: 01493701239

Ideally placed for the boating community **THE LORD NELSON** is situated right next to the river bank and any boat can moor up alongside this beautiful pub. Owned and run by Jon and Sheena Collorick, The Lord Nelson was converted into a pub between 1918 and 1928 and still retains many of its original features including real wooden beams that lend a traditional feel to the property. Jon's original trade was as a singer and live music can be heard bringing down the rafters on most nights of the week, adding to the already lively atmosphere that this character pub possesses. This Freehouse prides itself on its large selection of real ales and regularly makes room for a range of guest ales which you can sit and savour in front of the open fires that roar away in the winter time. The candle lit restaurant serves some very interesting home-made specialties and boasts that they will cook up absolutely anything if enough notice is given! They also offer a take away menu which is very useful if you are on a boat and in the summer huge barbecues are held in the gardens, perfect for those long balmy evenings. If you feel that you would like to stay a bit longer in this glorious part of Norfolk, and who can blame you, then Jon can even fix you up with some accommodation in the local village, he really is a very nice man.

THE RAILWAY TAVERN at Reedham is a charming Grade II Listed building, constructed in 1844, which retains many of its original features - as well as offering excellent, warm and friendly hospitality to all. Owned and personally run by Kathy and Ivor this award-winning freehouse has been listed in CAMRA's Good Beer Guide for three years running. Beer Festivals are held biennially, in spring and autumn; the excellence of their beers has been recognised by their visitors from near and far, as well as in awards received. In the charming, friendly atmosphere you can enjoy a good selection of wines supplied by 'Wine Merchants of the Year', Adnams, and choose from a selection of about 70 malt whiskies.

The Railway Tavern, 17 The Havaker, Reedham Tel: 01493 700340

The cosy Pullman Dining Room, with only 14 covers, provides an intimate setting for wonderful meals provided by chef - the extensive menu includes a selection for vegetarians too. With the newly-refurbished en-suite rooms in the Old Stables, the standard of bed and breakfast accommodation here is second to none. For guests, should they be railway enthusiasts, walkers, cyclists or anglers, The Railway Tavern has much to offer.

RAVENINGHAM. The beautiful Elizabethan Castell Farm and its adjoining stable block is the perfect backdrop for the family run businesses, **COUNTRY PINE** and **EAST INDIA TRADING DEPOT**. Attracting large numbers of visitors from all over the Eastern Counties, these two young and dynamic companies offer a huge range of goods at very competitive prices together with a friendly and efficient service. Formed in the recession, Country Pine realised that antique furniture was no longer affordable to the average customer and that another form of cost effective furniture should be provided. The flexibility and quality of pine appeals to almost everyone and Country Pine customers come from country homes, cottages, flats and modern homes alike, infact from all over the UK as well as France and Germany. The East India Trading Depot has built up an astonishing stock of rugs and carpets over the last three years. A steady flow of customers from all over England ensure that the display is always varied and interesting, with spacious, well laid out showrooms and constantly changing ranges of furniture.

Country Pine, The Raveningham Centre, Beccles Road, Raveningham
Tel: 01508 548441

You will find the showrooms full of Eastern delights, the rugs, kilims and furniture collected from all over the mystical East, then move on to the enchanting pine furniture forests, full of dressers, beds and chests. Rows and rows of beautiful ethnic clothes appear in front of you, with pottery, candles, jewellery and gifts. Search through the many different pieces in this terrific collection and you will find such treasures as Tribal artifacts and old traditional agricultural pieces, English and Eastern antiques and other collectable oddities. There is Free Delivery offered to all in the Norfolk and Suffolk area and if you purchase a rug from the incredible selection you can try it in your own home and if it doesn't suit the intended position just bring it back and a full refund will be yours. Laura and friends can often be found playing musical instruments in the beautiful gardens that surround this haven and instrument demonstrations are given in the busy coffee bar. Picnickers are welcome to stretch out in the gardens and watch the ducks and carp that swim about in the large pond and relax in the tranquil atmosphere that prevails this wonderful hidden place.

WHEATACRE. Built in the 18th Century by a Lowestoft Wherryman, **THE WHITE LION** is a very traditional and established Inn. You can discover this hidden place in the pretty village of Wheatacre, many years ago this quite community was once a Viking settlement and is steeped in generations of history, perfect for any would be time travellers. The White Lion Inn is owned and run by Peter and Jackie Daines, who will be celebrating their 20th anniversary of residency in 1997, so a warm and very proficient welcome is assured. This Freehouse serves a host of real ales which you can sit and enjoy in front of the large woodburning stove on those wintry cold evenings. But if you are visiting the area in the summer then why not sit out in the colourful beer garden, which offers climbing frames and swings for the kids and somewhere for the dog to relax too. Although the pub does not serve food, Peter and Jackie are happy for you to bring along your own picnic, just make sure you don't miss out on the local beer! The atmosphere is friendly and can sometimes be literally buzzing, with all the locals and travellers alike gathering in this lovely watering hole which can stay open all day if there is a demand for it.

The White Lion, Wheatacre Tel: 01502 677388

HADDISCOE. St Mary's Church boasts a fine Saxon round tower and two splendid Norman doorways.

ST OLAVES. A remote hamlet with the ruins of the Augustinian St Olaves' Priory and a lovely little boarded trestle mill called Priory Mill.

FRITTON. The oak trees lining the village common are famous for their cuckoos. Passing through the village of Fritton we came across the **DECOY TAVERN**, which takes its name from a nearby expanse of water. Built 150 years ago as two cottages, the Decoy has a very neat appearance with tables, chairs and benches at the front where a huge colourful Toby Jug watching over the comings and goings of the inn. Eric and Mo have been owners here for the past eight years and provide for all the needs of the local and visiting trade. The interior light-coloured walls display all manner of interesting bits and pieces and the brick fireplaces where real fires burn give this pub a really nice atmosphere. All food is home-cooked and a vast selection of about 30 starters and 40 main dishes and sweets are available at very reasonable prices. Well kept ales include five Bitters and two real ales. There is also a secluded beer garden which seats about 60 people. A few yards up the road is a children's play area and Fritton Woods which one can amble through down to the Norfolk Broads.

Decoy Tavern, Beccles Road, Fritton

BELTON. Whether you are an experienced gardener or a complete novice, you will be sure to enjoy a visit to **BELTON NURSERIES**.

Belton Nurseries, 35 Station Road South, Belton Tel: 01493 78049

The nurseries cover two acres and stock many kinds of plants and shrubs, all grown on site. Of particular note are their delightful hanging baskets and potted patio plants, displays which are sold complete and would grace any garden. In addition, no less than 65 specialist varieties of clematis are grown. Helpful, expert staff are always on hand to help you to select the right plant to suit the conditions and design of your garden. No matter how deep or shallow your interest in gardening, you will be inspired by the wonderful selection of plants and will probably want to set about tending your own garden with renewed vigour. Open from March to July 9.00 am to 5.00 pm every day.

BURGH CASTLE. The village itself has little to offer apart from its caravan sites, but just to the south are the impressive ruins of the old Roman fortress of Gariannonum, three of its flint and brick walls still standing today to a height of 15 ft. One of a chain of forts on the south-east coast, it was built during the 3rd century as a defence against Saxon marauders who would sail across the North Sea on their frequent raids. Although this site now lies over 3 miles from the sea on flat marshland at the southern end of Breydon Water, things were very different in Roman times. The fort would then have stood on one bank of a huge estuary, looking across to Caister on the opposite shore and commanding a vital position at the head of a vast river which would take enemies deep into the heart of East Anglia.

The river has now dwindled to become Breydon Water - although those of a nervous disposition who come here on a boating holiday for the first time would claim that it is quite large enough as it is, as they gingerly steer their craft between the 'telegraph poles' marking the route to take if you wish to avoid the mudflats! Excavations at Burgh Castle also point to the fact that a monastery was established here around 635 AD by the Irish missionary, St Fursa, and it is likely that the Normans built a timber fort on the site. So much history, combined with the varied wildlife of Breydon Water and the haunting peace of the surrounding marshes make a lasting impression on most visitors.

Sailing on the Broads

CHAPTER EIGHT

SOUTH NORFOLK

Village of Eye

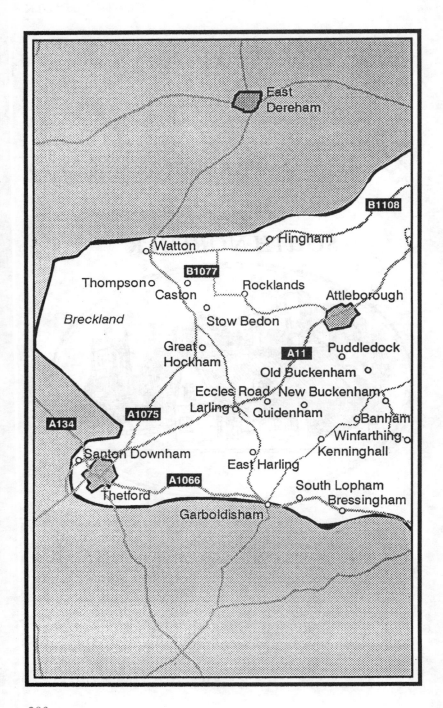

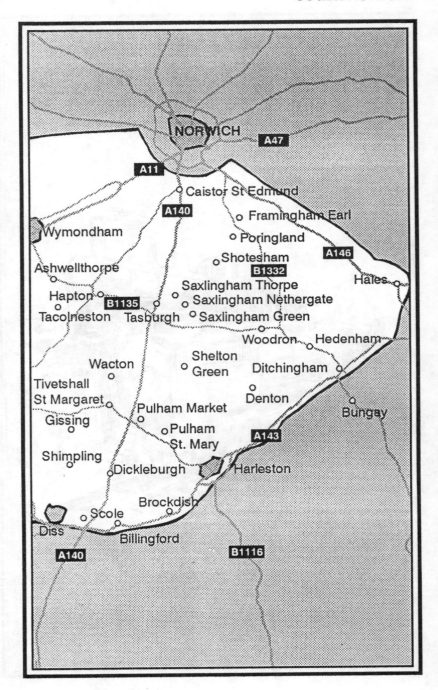

Bressingham Steam Museum

CHAPTER EIGHT

SOUTH NORFOLK

South of Norwich

One of the most famous episodes in Norfolk's history was Kett's Rebellion, an event which shattered the peace of the countryside around Wymondham in the mid 16th century. At that time peasants all over England were rising in protest against unscrupulous landowners who were fencing off large areas of common land for their own use and profit. In July 1549, an angry mob at Wymondham voiced their grievances by tearing down the offending fences put up by the local squire. They were confronted by Robert Kett, who, although a landowner himself, had been born the son of a humble tanner and listened sympathetically to the peasants. Deciding that their cause was just, Kett and his brother William marched on Norwich; the size of their rebel army swelling to over 16,000 by the time they established their camp outside the city on Mousehold Heath.

The King offered a free pardon for all if the rebels would agree to surrender before any blood was spilt, but Kett's army responded by launching a full-scale attack and capturing the city. After an unsuccessful attempt to drive them out, the Earl of Warwick arrived on the scene with 12,000 soldiers and recaptured Norwich, forcing the rebels back to Mousehold. Kett then made the fatal mistake of quitting this relatively safe position in favour of lower ground closer to the city and, when Warwick attacked the new camp, the peasant army was promptly defeated. Those who fled for their lives were mercilessly hunted down and executed and the Kett brothers were both hanged for their part in the revolt - Robert from the walls of Norwich Castle and William from one of the towers of Wymondham Abbey.

The two towers at **Wymondham Abbey** (where the nave has been preserved as the parish church) were the subject of fierce local dispute for many years. It was intended right from the start that both the Benedictine monks and the people of Wymondham should share the building between them, but, predictably enough, there was much argument over who should make use of what space inside! Eventually, an interior wall was built to divide the church in two and the parishioners, not to be outdone by the monks' octagonal tower (which now stands at the east end of the church), erected their own 142 ft tower at the west end sometime around 1450. Though now ruined, the monastic tower has been carefully restored and both towers offer an impressive sight. Inside the Norman nave there is a splendid hammerbeam roof; a superb font with wonderful carvings; and, perhaps best of all, the beautiful reredos and tester were provided by Sir Ninian Comper as a memorial to local men who lost their lives in the First World War.

Wymondham (pronounced 'Wyndham') boasts a number of other attractive historic buildings: medieval buildings sit comfortably with elegant Georgian and Victorian residences, with only a slight jarring note from modern housing. An ancient Bridewell or gaol can be seen in Bridewell Street, with some of its windows still barred, and the handsome 14th century chapel dedicated to Thomas a Becket stands next to one of the oldest pubs in England, the half-timbered Green Dragon Inn. The chapel now houses the county library and, although rumours of a tunnel connecting this building to the Abbey have persisted for many years, it is probably nothing more exciting than part of the disused Victorian sewage system!

Many of Wymondham's oldest buildings were lost in 1615 when a fire raged through the town destroying more than 300 houses. Most of the townsfolk were at church when the fire occurred, so loss of life was not so dreadful as it might have been. The picturesque octagonal **Market Cross** that stands in the town centre was rebuilt two years after the fire. Crowned by a pyramid roof, this attractive timber-framed building is open on all sides on the ground floor, with an outside stairway leading up to the room on the first floor.

THE WHITE HART, in town centre, dates back to the 1700s when the present building was rebuilt after a great fire. Many of the original features of this old coaching inn remain, including the ceiling beams and open fireplaces. Comfortable and spacious inside the interior is undergoing refurbishment due to be completed by the summer of 1996. Maintaining the feel of the golden days of coach travel, the White Hart, owned and personally run by Alison and Tony Mann, also offers excellent real ales, with guest beers and seasonal ales, to locals and visitors alike. With a games room and a weekly Karaoke night, this lively pub is a super place to drop into and relax in a warm and friendly atmosphere. With a beer garden to the rear, this is a great place for a pint or two of good ale.

The White Hart, 29 Market Street, Wymondham

Built at the same time as the historic Market Cross in 1617, **THE CROSS KEYS INN** is just across the road from this landmark. Its black and white exterior has a striking appearance and with soft lights glowing through the leaded windows, looks inviting. Inside, you'll find old wood beams, exposed brickwork and open fires.

Cross Keys Inn, Market Place, Wymondham Tel: 01953 602152

Eddie and Anne are the owners with twenty one years of establishment and whose motto is "in this bar there are no strangers, just friends we have not met yet", which gives an indication of the friendly welcome. This is a popular venue for good food with local people where home-cooked daily specials are well known. Open all day Friday and Saturday and from 7.30 am for breakfast. There are seven guest rooms all equipped with showers. Children are welcome. The less able will find Eddie and Anne very considerate and helpful. Try out the food and the welcome!

THE WYMONDHAM CONSORT HOTEL, an elegant family run town house Hotel, situated in centre of the town, is an ideal base from which to explore Historic Norwich, the Broads, National Trust properties and the unspoilt beaches of the Norfolk coast.

Wymondham Consort Hotel, 28 Market Street, Wymondham
Tel: 01953 606721 Fax: 01953 601361

This fine town house hotel has its own private car park and grounds to the rear, including a walled garden with an original Pump Well and an informal lawn area where guests can relax. The hotel is tastefully decorated and furnished with two lounges (one non-smoking) and a comfortable and welcoming bar. Noted for its cuisine, the owners pride themselves on their home style Cordon Bleu cooking with imaginative dishes prepared to please the most discerning palate. The twenty guest rooms offer a variety of styles and sizes, all very nicely presented and with full en-suite facilities. The usual luxury appointments are to be found with tea/coffee facilities, television, telephone etc. Complimentary use of the local Leisure Centre and all its facilities is offered to guests. Being a family run hotel, every effort is made to ensure guests feel 'at home' and welcome. ETB - 3 Crowns Commended.

AROUND WYMONDHAM

ASHWELLTHORPE. All Saints Church, is unusual in that there is a step down into the chancel rather than a step up! Inside is the striking alabaster tomb and effigies of Sir Edmund de Thorpe and his wife; he dressed in full armour and his Lady wearing a fine example of the great 'horned' headdress that is associated with noble-women of the Middle Ages.

FUNDENHALL NURSERY, on the B1113 near this sleepy village, is a wonderful, friendly garden centre where the staff always find the time to talk to the customers. Owned and personally run by Lynn and Carl, who have a great deal of expertise in gardening and landscaping, the centre specialises in outdoor plants and shrubs but also sells a whole host of seeds, terracotta and ornaments. With sweets and ice-creams on hand to keep the children quiet and happy, this is just the place to come to if you have run out of ideas for your own garden. You will certainly pick up some excellent tips here. And, for that extra splash of summer colour, ready planted hanging baskets are available containing many colourful plants or have your own baskets filled by them. What could be easier!

Fundenhall Nursery, Norwich Road, Ashwellthorpe Tel: 01508 488399

THE KING'S HEAD, on the edge of Ashwellthorpe, is over four hundred years old and was once a coaching inn when the village lay on the main Norwich Turnpike. Now in a sleepy village, the pub maintains its olde worlde charm and character and is a busy, bustling meeting place for the locals. Owned and personally run by Brian, Pat, Elaine and Ian Robinson, this is the place to come to for good pub food, a pint or two of fine beer and a friendly atmosphere. Henry, the fifty year old parrot, adds to the attractions of the place as does the climbing frame and swings out in the garden that will amuse the children for hours.

The King's Head, Norwich Road, Ashwellthorpe Tel: 01508 489419

TACOLNESTON. This charming village, with a medieval church, lies on the B1113 road which used to be a main coaching route through Talcolneston to Bury St Edmunds and London. Consequently **THE PELICAN**, which years before boasted its own 'Smithy', would have been a useful halt en-route. Thought to have been built around the 1600s, the inn has a beamed interior and large open fireplace. To the rear is a conservatory where the Pelican's owners Eddie and Judith have provided a very large and safe play area, known as 'Pelican Park', with swings and climbing frame. There are also aviaries and a lot of rabbits and chickens in the garden, so this is a great place for a day out with the family. The Pelican, with its growing reputation for the quality of its food, is open all day at weekends and provides a no smoking room for dining.

The Pelican, Norwich Road, Tacolneston Tel: 01508 489521

TASBURGH. The gardens at Rainthorpe Hall are exquisite and, as well as having a magnificent Elizabethan garden, Rainthorpe is noted for its range of bamboo plants. The Hall itself dates back to the 16th century, is timber-framed and features an impressive collection of medieval stained glass in its windows. The gardens are open to the public on Sundays throughout the summer months.

Tasburgh village is especially appealing as it nestles at the base of a hill which was used as an encampment during the Iron Age. Today, the Church of St Mary sits up on the hillside enjoying the view; a charming little building with an early Saxon tower. The River Tas winds through the village and nearby Rainthorpe Hall gardens.

BARN LODGE, at Tasburgh just nine miles south of Norwich on the main A140, is a charming old barn, built in the 1840s, that has recently been beautifully converted. Owned by Chris and Ron Coley, the extensive renovation work that was carried out has created an interesting and unusual home from which the couple offer excellent bed and breakfast accommodation. All the accommodation is on the ground floor and, with only room for six guests, you can be assured of the best of personal attention. All the rooms have telephone, tea and coffee making facilities and a television as well as either an en-suite or a private bathroom. Barn Lodge is fully licensed and guests can enjoy a drink at the bar or in the gardens. With a warm, family atmosphere, this is a lovely, relaxing place to stay that you will find very hard to beat.

Barn Lodge, Church Road, Tasburgh Tel: 01508 470755

SAXLINGHAM THORPE, SAXLINGHAM NETHERGATE and **SAXLINGHAM GREEN**. Further evidence of Saxon settlement in the area can be deduced from these village names. Each has its own particular charm: Thorpe with its church a virtual ruin, situated in a lonely pasture; Green with its quaint reed-thatched cottages; and Nethergate, whose Church of St Mary boasts a fine collection of Norwich stained glass from the 13th to 15th centuries.

SHOTESHAM. This part of the county is particularly rich in churches and this rural village alone has four within its parish boundaries. Admittedly, St Martin's and St Botolph's are now both ruins, but All Saints' Church still stands proud high up on a hill above the delightful village. The tower of the church has an unusual exterior staircase made of iron, and the views from the churchyard are quite superb. Down below, a tributary of the Tas winds its way north-westwards, flanked by charming thatched cottages and willow trees and crossed at intervals by a series of little white bridges.

PORINGLAND. **THE ROYAL OAK** is a traditional Norfolk pub which offers a warm welcome and a vibrant atmosphere. Situated in the centre of the village of Poringland, just 250 yards from All Saints' Church and next door to an excellent fish and chip shop, this fine establishment features strongly as the hub of village life.

The pub is a popular one, but quiet corners can easily be found. The interior is comfortable and intimate, with open fires and original oak beams. A wide range of real ales are stocked and all are kept in tip top condition. The best time to sample them is during 'happy hour', from 5.00 - 7.00 pm, when the price of a pint is reduced by 30p. OAPs are also given a discount of 30p at lunchtimes. A good selection of delicious bar meals are also available and offer excellent value for money. The Royal Oak is open throughout the week, all day on Friday, Saturday and Sunday. Make sure that you find time to pop in, for this is an establishment that you will want to return to again and again.

The Royal Oak, 44 The Street, Poringland Tel: 01508 493734

CAISTOR ST EDMUND. This is an ancient village and it is thought to have been the headquarters of Queen Bodicea when she fought the Romans. The rugged outline of sturdy Roman walls can still be made out with a little Saxon church huddled against them.

CAISTOR HALL is set in the attractive countryside of the Tas valley and is conveniently situated just three miles south of Norwich near Stoke Holy Cross, the site of the 1st century Roman town of Venta Icenorum. There has been a dwelling on the present site of the Hall for over 900 years and it was mentioned in the Domesday Book of 1086. A beautiful house, stepped in history, Caistor Hall is a super holiday whether you are on business, touring East Anglia or just seeking a peaceful holiday.

Beautifully decorated and furnished throughout, Caistor Hall has the air of a grand country house with a warm and friendly atmosphere. All the bedrooms have private bathrooms and many have period furnishings including four poster and half tester beds. The cuisine here is well known in the local area and the various menus provide a wide variety of dishes with the emphasis on fresh seasonal food and good wines. Whether you eat in the mirrored, formal dining room or in the cosy and intimate bistro bar you will certainly be in for a treat. With several splendid public rooms to relax in and enjoy a quiet drink or read,

Caistor Hall also caters for business meetings, conferences and celebration events.

Caistor Hall, Caistor St Edmund, Norwich Tel: 01603 624406

FRAMINGHAM EARL. Along with its twin, Framingham Pigot, the village lies in peaceful farmland dotted with woods. **THE RAILWAY TAVERN**, a freehouse, was built in the 1870s to accommodate the railway workers involved in the building of the line from Trowse to Bungay, unfortunately the line was never built. Today this fine building, with its cobbled stone walls and oak beams is a popular pub, with a welcoming atmosphere and a selection of real ales second to none. You will find here no gimmicks, no cheapies, just good quality standards and service. A wide selection of delicious home made food is always on the menu, in addition to the daily specials listed on the blackboard. Lunches are served daily from 12.00 to 2.00 pm and on Sundays until 4.30 pm. Evening meals are served from 7.00 pm and a traditional roast is available every Sunday. The Railway Tavern is popular and is apt to get busy, so if you decide to enjoy a meal here, then be sure to book in advance.

The Railway Tavern, Norwich Road, Framingham Earl
Tel: 01508 494811

Along the Border with Suffolk

DISS. Many visitors find Diss to be one of the most attractive country towns in this part of the county. The fascination of the place lies in its pleasing mixture of Tudor, Georgian and Victorian houses, grouped around the 6 acre mere from which the name of the town is derived (from the Anglo-Saxon word for 'standing water'). Up a narrow street leading from the public park by the side of the mere is the small Market Place.

This former poultry market is dominated by the somewhat over-restored St Mary's Church. The church was built over 700 years ago, though the windows in the nave date from the 19th century. The St Nicholas Chapel is particularly enjoyable, with its wonderful corbels, angels in the roof and gargoyles. Also close by the Market Place is the delightful Victorian Shambles with its cast-iron veranda and small museum inside. Most visitors to the town agree with John Betjeman when he voted Diss his favourite Norfolk town!

THE PARK HOTEL is an attractive East Anglian home on the outskirts of Diss and close to the famous mere, said to be the deepest lake in England. After becoming a popular and successful restaurant in the 1960s, whose reputation was well known throughout East Anglia, it was bought by Rhonda and Robin Twigge. Today, the Park Hotel is a charming, friendly, family run hotel and it is a real treat to stay here.

The Park Hotel, 29 Denmark Street, Diss Tel: 01379 642244

There are seventeen beautifully decorated and furnished en-suite bedrooms split between two site: the hotel itself and the Limes, a separate house set in the lovely landscaped gardens. The Curtis Restaurant offers a variety of different cuisines on its extensive à la carte menu; there is a quick businessmen's lunchtime menu and a special choice for children. If you prefer something lighter and less formal, but equally delicious, Twigge's Bar offers a fine selection of real ales as well as a tasty bar snack. Morning coffee and afternoon tea can also be taken here.

Park Hotel also has a number of function rooms that vary in size to accommodate every conceivable event requirement. In such delightful surroundings and with a team of professional and helpful staff your day will certainly go well.

AROUND DISS

HEDENHAM. The **MERMAID INN**, which dates back to the 15th century, is situated in centre of the village of Hedenham, opposite Hedenham Hall, which was once a Convent. The inn has a long and interesting history, originally having been a trading post, and then a 'safe house' during the Civil War, a tunnel is reputed to link the pub with the Hall over the road through which pursued Royalists could effect an escape. Rather bizarrely the Inn has not always been called The Mermaid Inn, during the Second World War it was nicknamed 'The Swinging Tit'!

Today the inn has lost none of its character or sense of history. It retains its original tiled floors, oak beams and open fireplaces. The atmosphere is happy and welcoming, attracting a mixed clientele of locals and visitors from far afield. Jackie and Jo, the owners serve a good selection of real ales and bar food, which offer excellent value for money.

This is a great place to have a tasty meal and a refreshing drink during your exploration of the area. The Mermaid Inn is painted bright yellow, so there is no way that you could drive past without noticing. Be sure to pay it a visit, you will not be disappointed.

The Mermaid Inn, Norwich Road, Hedenham Tel: 01508 482480

DITCHINGHAM. Ditchingham Hall dates from the early Georgian period and it stands next to a lake in a park that was designed by Capability Brown. The Victorian writer, Sir (Henry) Rider Haggard, lived at the Hall for many years and, in the north aisle of St Mary's Church, is a memorial window commemorating his life. Two of his wonderful adventure stories, 'King Solomon's Mines' and the hauntingly romantic 'She', are the stuff of 'Boy's Own' fantasies and have both been made into films.

PULHAM ST MARY. This attractive village is the smaller of the two Pulhams. An avenue of lime trees leads down to the splendid 15th century church of St Mary the Virgin, which was exceptionally well restored in 1886. Carvings on the parapets depict the story of St Edmund, the local king and saint who took refuge in one of the local churches before he was captured and killed by the Danes. He is also remembered in the name of the village pub, the Kings Head, which was originally called the King Edmund.

THE KING'S HEAD is situated in the centre of this lovely village, and is owned and run by Graham Scott. Offering character oak beamed non-smoking accommodation, this Inn was built in the late 1600s with some parts of the property dating back to the Saxon times. On entering the main bar you are greeted by the cheerful glow of a large open fire, this coupled with the wooden beams and real slate floors gives the King's Head a warm and welcoming atmosphere. Guests at the Freehouse will find very comfortable en-suite guest rooms, with the family rooms sleeping up to four people. On waking they will be pleased to know that a full English breakfast is available and, of course, not forgetting the morning paper which is all included in the very reasonable bed and breakfast rate. The restaurant is fully air-conditioned and non-smoking, offering a great value menu with such treats as roasted local duck served in a black cherry sauce and Liqueur Ice Cream Sundaes which are apparently big enough for two to share! The Inn also offers off road overnight parking and beer garden with separated children's play area so you can easily enjoy a meal and a drink with the whole family.

The King's Head, Pulham St Mary Tel: 01379 676318

PULHAM MARKET. In the 16th and 17th centuries this was a thriving place, famous for its cottage industries, manufacturing linen cloth for hangings, carpets and vestments. The old houses remaining in the village are far more numerous than in any surrounding parish.

Pulham Market (from the Saxon meaning 'village of pools') and neighbouring Pulham St Mary once gained fame as the home of the Airships. During the First World War airships played an important role in the defence of the British coast. In 1912, the surveyors and land agents Thomas Gaze and Son acquired land at Pulham St Mary and Rushall, on behalf of the Admiralty, and Pulham Air Station was established here as part of a chain of such stations along the east coast. Because of the low-lying landscape and relative lack of trees in the area, coupled with the fact that the site was well inland and out of range of the German guns, Pulham made an ideal base.

The airships were used, in the main, to detect submarines and mines and to aid shipping. These 'Pulham Pigs', so-called because of their bloated appearance and buff-coloured skin, became a familiar sight over the Norfolk coast. The first operational vessels were powered by a 'car' made up of two aeroplane fuselages mounted back to back, providing an engine at both ends of the ship. They patrolled an area from Margate to Dunkirk in the south and from Mablethorpe to Holland in the north and proved to be an effective way of keeping an eye on enemy activities.

The Pulham Market Society has produced an excellent booklet, entitled 'The Story of Pulham and its Airships', which covers, in some detail, the early prototypes, life on the station at Pulham, the coming of the 'rigid' airships, and their adventures and accomplishments during and after the war until their eventual decline. The Society has also produced another booklet, called 'A Village Walk', which provides a good insight into the history of Pulham Market and as well as a special 'guided' tour of the village and its many fascinating houses and buildings.

TIVETSHALL ST MARGARET. St Margaret's Church is outstanding and well worth a visit to see its impressive and huge royal arms of Elizabeth I. **THE RAILWAY HOTEL,** situated next to the railway line in Tivetshall, was built in 1890 and is today a popular and vibrant establishment. The bar serves a selection of cask condition real ales and a wide range of excellent value for money meals. This traditional pub has a happy atmosphere and sports a number of successful teams for such diverse events as ferret racing, crib, darts, pool and crown green bowls (the Railway Inn has its own bowling green). There is live Country Music every Tuesday and Saturday, and an organ in the bar should you wish to entertain everyone with a rendition of your favourite tune. Open all day, seven days a week.

The Railway Hotel, Station Road, Tivetshall St Margaret
Tel: 01379 677253

HARLESTON. This pretty market town is notable for its attractive Georgian houses (particularly Candlers House at the northern end of town; a favourite of that renowned authority on English architecture, Nikolaus Pevsner) and the original shop fronts on either side of the town's main streets.

BILLINGFORD. The fine, five storey windmill, with its splendid white sails, is open at weekends during the summer months. This pretty village also has some early 14th century wall-paintings in its Church of St Leonard.

SCOLE. The superb Scole Inn is more like a mansion than an public house with its Dutch gables, giant pilasters and towering chimney stacks. Built in 1655 of red brick, this was the most important of the old coaching inns on the main road between Ipswich and Norwich and is, without doubt, one of the finest examples surviving in England today.

DICKLEBURGH. This is the birthplace of the 19th century painter George Cattermole, who is perhaps best known for his illustrations in Sir Walter Scott's 'Waverley Novels'.

SHIMPLING. Here, St George's Church commands an idyllic position looking across to the woods, and over the fields is Shimpling Place, a handsome moated Tudor manor house which was once the home of the Shardelow family.

GISSING. St Mary's Church with its Saxon round tower and two Norman doorways is well worth seeing; the double hammerbeam roof to the nave is quite exquisite.

WINFARTHING. The abundance of majestic trees here points to the fact that this area was once part of an ancient forest. In the church of St Mary there is a window depicting a sword. The 'Winfarthing Sword', or 'Sword of the Good Thief' as it later came to be known, has since been lost, but it was said to have been left here when a thief sought sanctuary in the church. The whereabouts of sword and other details of the story are lost in the mists of time but local folklore relates that village women who had had enough of their husbands held the sword in great esteem. Whether this was simply with a view to using it as a cold instrument of dispatch or perhaps the sword had some other more subtle properties which would grant them what they desired - nobody knows.

BRESSINGHAM. The village is the home of the famous **Bressingham Steam Museum.** From those with a casual interest to serious steam enthusiasts, people of all ages will find a day out spent here a fascinating and rewarding experience. Bressingham has one of the world's finest collections of British and Continental locomotives, perhaps the most famous being the 'Royal Scot'. A number of locomotives on display here are on loan from the National Railway Museum at York. All are housed under cover in the museum's extensive locomotive sheds, which also contain a large collection of steam-driven industrial engines, traction engines, and a recently opened exhibition entitled 'A Journey Back to Steam'. Visitors can view the interior of the Royal Coach and admire the many fine examples of these mighty machines from the

golden age of steam.

The Fire Museum has a collection of fire engines and fire fighting equipment which could form a complete museum in its own right. Exhibits range from hand-pumped and horse-drawn machines to the one used on the royal estate at Sandringham until the 1960s. There are four different gauges of railway within the grounds and visitors can ride along 5 miles of track through the woods and gardens. Bressingham has 6 acres of internationally famous landscaped grounds. Beautiful trees, shrubs and flowers can be enjoyed in the superb Dell Garden which was created by Alan Bloom, Bressingham's founder. A 2 acre plant centre adjoins the gardens where thousands of plant specimens, many of them rare, are available for visitors to purchase.

Bressingham Steam Museum, Bressingham Tel: 01379 58382

Bressingham is renowned for its 'special days' when engines can be seen in full steam on the three narrow gauge lines, and talks and footplate rides are given on the standard gauge locomotives. There are also demonstrations of traction and industrial engines, and rides on the magnificent steam-driven 'Gallopers' roundabout with musical accompaniment from the Chiappa organ. 'Special days' are every Sunday, Thursday and Bank Holiday, plus every Wednesday in July and August.

Refreshments can be found in the 'Gallopers' restaurant, on the terrace, or in the picnic area. There is also the 'Garden Seat' coffee shop and a complete set of souvenirs available in the museum's 'Goods Depot'. Alan Bloom now also welcomes guests for short bed and breakfast breaks at Bressingham Hall. The museum is open daily from 10.00 am to 5.30 pm.

SOUTH LOPHAM. The village, along with its neighbour and twin North Lopham, shares a Fen that is home to the rare great raft spider and the 'Lopham wonders' - a stile-shaped tree. THE WHITE HORSE lies on the main A1066 at South Lopham near Diss and only three miles from the Steam Museum. Dating back to the 1600s, the interior reflects the age of the original building although there have been some alterations over the years. Surrounded by open countryside, there is a large garden at the

back of the White Horse with safe children's play area and plenty of tables and chairs. Owned and personally run by Wendy and Gerald Turner, this pub has a lot to offer. Cosy and comfortable inside, with wooden floors and open fires, the bar serves excellent real ales with special guest ales available during the summer. There is also a delicious range of tasty pub food available that is sure to satisfy even the hungriest. This is a charming place to stop, with a warm and friendly atmosphere, where you are sure to feel at home.

The White Horse, The Street, South Lopham Tel: 01379 687252

Less than half a mile off the main A1066 down Blo'Norton Road, South Lopham, can be found **MALTING FARM**, situated on the Norfolk/Suffolk border amid open countryside. Brecklands, the Norfolk Broads and the coast can be easily reached from here. There are many local attractions too, such as Nature Reserves, an Otter Trust, Blooms Gardens and Steam Museum, Wildlife Parks and National Trust properties. The historic city of Norwich is within easy driving distance and well worth a visit. South Lopham village with its church, Pub and shops are a short walk away.

Maltings Farm, Blo'Norton Road, South Lopham Tel: 01379 687201

Maltings Farm is a working Dairy Farm and guests and especially children can enjoy watching 'milking time', gathering the hens' eggs and making friends with the farmyard pets. The Farmhouse is a rendered Elizabethan timber framed building with inglenook fireplaces and central heating offering warm and comfortable accommodation and there is always a very friendly welcome from the owner Cynthia Huggins, whose guests return again and again. All the bedrooms have hand wash basins, some have four-poster beds and one has en-suite facilities, tea and coffee making facilities are available on the landing area. There is a private guest lounge with colour TV. Cynthia is a keen craftswoman and is active in the local societies of Embroiderers, Quilters, Spinners and Weavers; she is also a fine cook so you can look forward to a very good breakfast. Children are very welcome and swings and games are provided for them. Non-smokers are preferred. ETB - 2 Crowns Commended.

GARBOLDISHAM. Pronounced 'Garblesham', there is some fine pre-Raphaelite glass in the church of St Mary the Virgin. Just west of the village lies part of the Devil's Dyke, an ancient earthwork whose origins are still the subject of debate amongst archaeologists. Some argue that it was erected by the Romans as a defence against Anglo-Saxon invaders, while others insist that the Saxons themselves built the dyke to mark out the boundary of their newly conquered territory. Both arguments were thrown into doubt by the excavations of 1924, which indicated that the dyke was in fact more likely to have been built by the East Anglian people in the 8th century as a defence against the neighbouring kingdom of Mercia.

EAST HARLING. This attractive village boasts a beautiful 15th century church which, unusually for a Norfolk church, has a spire. Inside can be found the marble tomb of Robert Harling, one of Henry V's knights who died at the siege of Paris in 1435. Refrigeration being a technique long in the future, his body was stewed and brought back to East Harling for burial.

Why travel abroad to experience a vineyard and sample fine wines when you can come and visit **HARLING VINEYARD**, one of Norfolk's premier vineyards. Situated in the picturesque village of East Harling, next to the imposing and historic village church, the vineyard is set in the beautiful grounds of a listed Victorian Gothic mansion, Eastfield House which was built circa 1870. Since 1992 this has been home to David Issitt and his family, who offer a warm and friendly welcome to all, though Sam, their yellow Labrador, often does this first. The visit begins with a guided tour through the easily accessible, level, grassed vineyards, where vine-growing is explained informally yet informatively. Experimental vineyards were established here in 1969 and the existing Muller-Thurgau vines were planted soon afterwards on two sites. Now comprising nearly seven acres, the grape varieties now grown include Bacchus, Siegerrebe, Chardonnay and Pinot Noir.

After the outside tour, visitors move inside or onto an adjacent patio for the wine-tasting. The 'Herling' wines, discussed in an unpretentious and knowledgeable fashion, are white, fruity and very refreshing; the style ranging from dry to medium. After three years, the drier wines become full and rich, developing a fine bouquet and sometimes a faint, pleasing spritz. Unusually, there are several vintages available. The vineyard shop sells wine and gifts all year round and tours, with several wine tastings, run from Good Friday to October, 10.30 am to 6 pm. Arrangements can be made for other times and groups are welcome. Accompanied children free of charge.

Harling Vineyard, Eastfield House, East Harling Tel: 01953 717341

KENNINGHALL. The houses here are full of interest, with plenty of timber and plasterwork giving the village real character.

It is easy to imagine how it must have looked in the days when Mary Tudor came here to stay at **Kenninghall Place**, still owned today by the Duke of Norfolk. Mary hastened on to Framlingham Castle in Suffolk where she was proclaimed Queen, little knowing that her reign would last a mere five years. She died in 1558, childless, ravaged by sickness and grief at the cruelty of her husband, Phillip II of Spain; and, although it is dubious whether she was directly responsible for all the persecutions carried out in her name, she would be forever remembered in history as 'Bloody Mary'. On her death, her younger half-sister, Elizabeth I, took the throne and, in St Mary's Church, there is a rare and quite superb example of Elizabeth's coat of arms.

Next to the church is a chapel which has remained virtually unchanged since it was first built in 1807. Outside the Chapel, there is a listed, early 19th century walled garden that is open to visitors. There are a number of old tombstones in the garden and, as a classic example of bizarre coincidence at work, the inscriptions on a couple of these reveal that the deceased parties were named 'Potter'!

BANHAM. A lovely old village built around a rectangular village green, the brick kilns that once stood at neighbouring Hunt's Green supplied the brick and tile for a number of interesting local houses. These include the 19th century Norfolk House, the timber-framed Guildhall, and a handsome Georgian house with Dutch gables called the Priory. Banham has also been a cider-making centre for hundreds of years.

Just outside the village, along the B1113 in the direction of Kenninghall is both the **Banham Motor Museum** and **Banham Zoo**. Quite apart from the zoo's fine collection of rare and endangered species from around the world (including otters, exotic monkeys, seals and snow leopards), many other attractions for the whole family to enjoy can be found in the adjoining 'Appleyard' Craft Courtyard.

Just half a mile from the Zoo, **LA TAVERNA** is a superb Italian restaurant and bar which is well worth seeking out. Situated on Crown street in Banham, in a listed building which is estimated to date from 1730, this small, but popular restaurant has a typically vibrant Latin atmosphere and serves authentic Italian cuisine of the finest quality, using only the very best fresh ingredients. All of the dishes are prepared in the spotlessly clean kitchen. The atmosphere in the restaurant is enhanced by the welcoming open fire and careful choice of background music (Pavarotti is a favourite). The owners Antonio and Cheryl are from an Italian background, which explains the authentic feel of the whole establishment. The ice cream is home-made, delicious and particularly worthy of note, be sure to sample some. It is recommended that you book a reservation in advance as the restaurant is apt to get rather busy, particularly in the evenings and at weekends. A large car park is conveniently situated close by.

La Taverna, Crown Street, Banham Tel: 01953 887265

OLD BUCKENHAM. Boasting one of the largest village greens in England it is surrounded by the scattered hamlets that make up this village. The village also wins the prize for some of the oddest street names to be found in this part of the world. 'Hog's Snout' and 'Loos Wroo' are two favourites, and there are plenty more!

NEW BUCKENHAM. Despite its name, the castle here was founded in 1146, only a few years after the castle at Old Buckenham. It was then that the son of William d'Albini abandoned his father's castle at the original village (no trace of that building now remains) and built a new round keep on this site, the earliest example of its kind in the country. The orderly system of streets, the market place (now the village green) and St Mary's Chapel (New Buckenham's first church and now part of a barn) all survive to this day and together they form a superb 'living' example of Norman town planning. Thatched and timber-framed cottages line the streets, and on the green stands the Court House, a fine 16th century building with Tuscan columns.

ECCLES ROAD. The village name is derived from the word 'ecclesiastical' and this is an area which has proved to be of great interest to archaeologists. Many weapons of the Romans and Early Britons have been discovered here and the story goes that a hoard of treasure is buried somewhere in the vicinity. A peaceful place today, but during the Middle Ages, it is said that soldiers marched here from Norwich, sacked the village and hanged the vicar!

ATTLEBOROUGH. The impressive church of St Mary dominates the centre of town, and in the churchyard there is a strange memorial pyramid. More modest in size and less imposing than that at Blickling Hall, this one stands about 6 ft high. It was erected in 1929 to mark the grave of a local solicitor with the rather splendid name of Melancthon William Henry Brooke, or 'Lawyer' Brooke as he was more familiarly known. Apparently, Brooke was most particular about the precise measurements of the pyramid and left detailed instructions regarding its construction in his will - possibly an attempt to preserve his bones by replicating the supposed magical properties of those fabled Egyptian pyramids!

The interior of the church is also worth a visit as it contains one of Norfolk's most outstanding chancel screens. Stretching the width of the church, this huge 15th century screen is beautifully embellished and is one of the few to survive the Reformation intact.

What wouldn't you give to own such a beautiful and charming house as **SHERBOURNE COUNTRY HOUSE HOTEL**? Built in 1700 it has recently been refurbished to a high standard of excellence. It stands in an acre of newly landscaped gardens with its neatly trimmed lawn and gravel footpaths running along neat flower borders.

Sherbourne Country House Hotel, Norwich Road, Attleborough
Tel: 01953 454363 Fax: 01953 453509

This is a family owned hotel, and the proprietors, John and Felicia

Sharples have created just the right atmosphere; the rooms are furnished with thought and taste. In the lounge bar, games are provided, and on some evenings John plays the grand piano after dinner. The bedrooms all have their individual character and are well equipped with luxury features; some have spa baths. Dining in the new Restaurant is a wonderful experience. The new menu draws its origins from the Provence Region of the South of France. All dishes are cooked to order; nothing is pre-prepared, not even the sauces! Certainly, the extensive à la carte menu offers considerable choice and the wine list will be found to be truly international, moderately priced and supplied by Adnams (wine merchant of the year). Children are welcome. ETB 3 Crown Highly Commended.

North Breckland

WATTON. A small market town from where, along with the neighbouring village of **Griston**, a local legend arose which would later inspire that famous nursery story, 'Babes in the Wood'.

The legend, which dates from the 16th century, relates how, as poor Arthur Truelove lay dying, he decided that the only hope for his two children was to leave them in the care of their uncle. Unfortunately, the uncle decided to help himself to their inheritance and paid two men to take the children into nearby Wayland Wood and kill them. In a moment of compassion, one of the men decided that he couldn't do the dreadful deed, so he disposed of his accomplice instead and abandoned the children in the wood to suffer whatever fate befell them. Sadly, unlike the nursery tale where the children find their way back home and live happily ever after, this unfortunate brother and sister perished and their ghosts are said to wander lonely through the woods to this day.

Outside the 17th century Clock Tower in Watton, the striking bronze town sign depicts the story of the 'Babes', and their sad tale is further remembered in the name of the wood itself - Wayland being a corruption of 'wailing'. The wood is now owned by the Norfolk Naturalist Trust and is said to be one of the oldest in England. **Griston Hall**, a Grade II listed ancient manor house which stands half a mile south of Wayland Wood and one mile from Watton on the A1075, was reputedly the home of the 'Wicked Uncle'. Today, it is part of Hall Farm.

The **CROWN HOTEL**, in the centre of Watton, is a traditional town pub. Dating back to the 1760, it was the town's stage coach inn and horse sales were held here right up to 1900. There are three different bars, named Toby, Brass and Plate, each of which offers the same excellent range of real ales and beers. With log fires and uneven floors, the atmosphere is from a bygone age. The busiest pub in Watton, it is cheerful, friendly and comfortable. Owned and personally run by Greet and Roger Edwards, there is the usual selection of tasty bar snacks available and they are very popular at lunchtime and on Saturday nights there is live music.

The separate restaurant, with 29 covers, also does a roaring trade. In the tradition of coaching inns, as this once was, The Crown Hotel also offers reasonably priced accommodation in nine attractive and comfortable bedrooms.

Crown Hotel, 25 High Street, Watton Tel: 01953 882375

Situated on the busy High Street of the village of Watton, **THE BULL** is a 'Hidden Place' that should not be missed at any cost. This one hundred year old traditional English public house has everything that you could expect; a warm welcome and a vibrant atmosphere of the type that has become synonymous with this fascinating part of the country. The pub has a pool table, the prices are reasonable and there is live music and a disco as a regular event on Fridays and Saturdays. Don't miss it!

The Bull, High Street, Watton Tel: 01953 881245

RICHMOND PARK GOLF CLUB is just one mile from the centre of Watton and enjoys a quiet and tranquil position in typical Norfolk rural countryside. A warm and friendly club that is open to non-members, it has excellent amenities as well as a very playable 18-hole parkland course. The attractive colonial wooden club house has many picture windows which offer great views of the course and beyond in all directions. There is also a terrace where you can relax and quench your thirst whilst discussing the finer points of your game. The Wood's and Pavilion Restaurants serve a whole range of delicious dishes and can be hired for private functions whilst, in the bar, tasty hot snacks or something more substantial are available all day.

Richmond Park Golf Course, Saham Road, Watton Tel: 01953 881803

AROUND WATTON

HINGHAM. This charming Norfolk town conjures up the gentility of 18th century England at its very best; the large Market Place flanked by elegant Georgian houses. The town also boasts a very influential (if not exactly famous) son, a weaver called Samuel Lincoln who was baptised in the church in 1622.

During the first half of the 17th century, many local people followed the rector Robert Peck and emigrated to America founding a colony in Massachusetts called Bare Cove. Samuel set out to make a new life for himself there in 1637 and though he didn't know it at the time, his great-great-great-great-grandson would turn out to be the 16th American President, Abraham Lincoln! Bare Cove was later renamed Hingham, and the two towns retain strong links to this day. A bronze bust of Abraham Lincoln can be seen in St Andrew's Church, which also features a superb 15th century monument to Lord Morley.

Situated on Fairlands Green in this picturesque town, in what was the old fire station, opposite St Andrews church, is **NEW LINCOLN'S TEA AND COFFEE SHOPPE**, a hidden gem that really is worth a visit. The restaurant is family run serving a wide variety of food, Full English Breakfasts, freshly filled rolls and sandwiches, jacket potatoes and freshly made baguettes. Especially noteworthy are the *Lincoln's All Rounders*, large granary baps with lots of tasty salad fillings. All of the snacks are exceptional value for money either eaten in or take away.

Homecooked specials and lunches are served daily. Lincoln's is famous for its Sunday Roast giving a choice of two or more succulent joints freshly cooked, all served with Chef's seasonal vegetables, followed by a wide choice of hot or cold home-made desserts which are simply delicious!

Booking for Sunday lunch is advisable as the old world charm country Tea Shoppe gets very busy at peak times. Enjoy yourself with surroundings and service as they used to be! Open Tuesday-Sunday 10 to 4 in the Winter, 9 to 5 in the Summer and every Bank Holiday.

New Lincoln's Tea and Coffee Shoppe, 7/8 Fairland Court, Hingham
Tel: 01953 851357

Prominently situated in the centre of Hingham, on the market square, is the **WHITE HART HOTEL** pub and restaurant. This impressive Georgian building is approximately 250 years old and is largely original throughout. It is also reputed to have a ghost!

The White Hart Hotel, 3 Market Place, Hingham Tel: 01953 850214

The White Hart Hotel is a traditional coaching house which is popular with locals and visitors alike. It consequently has the type of warm and welcoming atmosphere that this area is famous for. The ambience of the interior is enhanced by its original oak beams and open fires: refreshingly there is no juke box or loud music, so this is an ideal place to enjoy a conversation and savour the delights of the well kept real ales which are always stocked. The pub occasionally has a 'singalong' evening or live Country and Western band; be sure to ring in advance to check the details of future events, they are not to be missed.

The White Hart hotel incorporates a very good restaurant. The wide variety of food on offer here is of excellent quality and represents unusually good value for money. Be sure to sample the speciality dish *Chicken White Hart*, breast of chicken filled with honeyroast ham and served in a rich sherry, cream and french mustard sauce, it is delicious.

If you are looking for somewhere to stay in this delightful area, then look no further, for the White Hart Hotel also has three double guest rooms, all well appointed and with en-suite bathrooms.

This 'Hidden Place' is well worth seeking out, be it for a short stay, a meal, or just a quiet drink. Establishments of this standard are few and far between.

GREAT HOCKHAM. There is a marvellous country walk along the disused railway line between Stow Bedon and Great Hockham, which is known as the Pingo Trail. The 8 mile circular walk is renowned for the many species of birds that can be seen en route. To the north-west of Great Hockham is Cranberry Rough, a reserve owned by the Norfolk Naturalists Trust, where the rare White Admiral butterflies breed.

PUDDLEDOCK FARM lies just off the A1075 near the village of Great Hockham. This delightful touring caravan park is in a beautiful and tranquil setting and its five acres back directly on to Thetford Forest. This is an idyllic spot for a family holiday, where the children can play safely, the family dog can join in the fun and everyone has a chance to get away from it all. Run by the Rands family, Puddledock Farm is a member of both the Caravan and the Camping Club and also offers such amenities as a modern shower and toilet block and children's play area.

But that is not all, Puddledock Farm has much more to offer. Open all year round, there is a bowling green where you can enjoy a gentle game or two to while away the lazy afternoons, Thetford Forest has many paths and walks running through it that can be reached straight from the farm and there is a wonderful nursery and dried flower shop. The flowers are grown here as well as dried and they make a very colourful and long-lasting display.

Puddledock Farm, Great Hockham Tel: 01953 498455

ROCKLANDS. For those interested in plants take the B1077 road from Attleborough to Watton and look out for **Ridgeons** at Rocklands. Take the second turning on the right after Ridgeons into Scoulton Road and look out for the sign directing you to **WALNUT TREE FARM NURSERY**. This popular Nursery is one of the very best garden centres in the area. Its stock ranges from roses, heathers, fuschias and geraniums through to alpines, perennials, trees, shrubs, conifers and seasonal bedding plants. Many of the pubs and restaurants that have been featured in this book have had their appearances enhanced with hanging baskets supplied by this helpful Garden Centre. Be sure to pay it a visit.

Walnut Tree Farm Nursery, Flymoor Lane, Rocklands Tel: 01953 488163

CASTON. Offering far more than a traditional pub, **THE RED LION** next to the village green at Caston is a 'Hidden Place' that is worth seeking out.

The Red Lion, The Green, Caston Tel: 01953 488236

Once you have visited this fine establishment, you will likely want to return again and again. More of a dining room with bars than a pub, the Red Lion offers good old fashioned hospitality combined with fine English cuisine, an excellent place for an enjoyable lunch or dinner, especially when coupled with the outstandingly large array of high

Wymondham Market Cross

quality wines which are always stocked. All of the dishes are cooked to order, using only the very finest of fresh ingredients. The menu offers a selection of hot sandwiches, daily specials and a la carte menus, all available daily, except for Sunday Lunch when a selection of traditional roasts are available to tempt your palate.

The building is a handsome one, and typical of the architectural style of the area, with knapped flint walls and a pantile roof, enhanced by beautiful handing baskets. The interior of the Red Lion is different to other restaurants and pubs, walking into it for the first time, you could almost be forgiven for thinking you were in the front room of a lovely house, so homely is the atmosphere. The restaurant area has a piano, an open fire and is air conditioned throughout.

The Red Lion can also cater for corporate or private functions such as dinner parties and marquee weddings; additionally, contract catering, toastmaster and staff hire services can also be arranged.

THOMPSON. This is a quiet village with a marshy, man-made lake, Thompson Water, and a wild common. One of the loveliest country inns in Norfolk can be found hidden in the lanes to the west of the A1075 in Thompson. The **CHEQUERS INN** is a charming low thatched building which nestles between tall hedges at the end of a secluded drive, with only a solitary pub sign to denote it is there at all. A tile in the cellar at the rear of the inn bears the date 1661, although the building is almost certainly older, perhaps dating back to the 15th century. Owned by the Merton Hall estate until the early 1900s, for centuries it consisted only of a single parlour (now the central bar), the buildings on either side having been occupied by estate workers' families. Since taking over in 1987, proprietors Wendy and Bob Rourke have built up a well-deserved reputation for their excellent hospitality, and superb food and drink. They serve a choice of local ales and a wonderful selection of home-cooked meals, ranging from ploughman's and jacket potatoes, to succulent steaks, fish and vegetarian dishes. Daily specials include unusual recipes such as beef and oyster pie, and there is also a mouthwatering selection of starters and desserts.

The Chequers Inn, Christen Road, Thompson Tel: 01953 483360

The Heart of Breckland

THETFORD. The Little Ouse meets the River Thet here, at what has been an important settlement for well over 1,000 years. When the Normans arrived here they found a prosperous community with its own mint and an extremely successful pottery industry. It remained the seat of the Bishop of East Anglia until 1094 when the see was transferred to Norwich and there is no doubt that until this event, Thetford was the most important town in the region and among the top six in England. Thetford's first castle was probably built sometime around the 8th century and the Norman motte that replaced it was demolished in 1173. Built to defend the place where the Icknield Way crosses the rivers Little Ouse and Thet, energetic visitors can enjoy fine views of the town and surrounding countryside by climbing up the steep banks of the huge mound that dominates the site; this is all that remains of the castle today.

The decline of the town began in the mid 16th century after the Dissolution of the Monasteries; Thetford once boasted 24 medieval churches, but only three of these still survive. Of particular interest are the remains of the 12th century Cluniac priory which was founded by the Norman knight John Bigod. He was a poor warrior who acquired the earldom of Norfolk from King Stephen in 1136; an earldom which would become extinct less than 200 years later. The priory ruins can be found near the railway station and are maintained by English Heritage.

Thetford made a number of unsuccessful attempts to ward off its steady decline. In 1700 it became a port, with an eye to regaining the lucrative wool trade from the towns and villages on the east coast. The plan was doomed from the start and its failure was compounded with the coming of the railways in the mid 19th century. More surprisingly, Thetford also had aspirations to become a flourishing spa town after a medicinal spring was discovered here in 1746. Its attempts to lure the fashionable elite of London society were, however, largely unsuccessful, although the Pump Room that was built in 1819 can still be seen in Spring Walk.

Thetford remained a quiet market town with a steadily dwindling population up until the 1960s, when its status was altered dramatically by its becoming an overspill town for London. Housing and industrial estates became to spring up on the edges of town and it was during excavations for one such estate in the 1980s that an extensive Iron Age enclosure was discovered - so extensive, in fact, that they have led many experts to believe that Thetford may well have been the capital of the redoubtable Iceni tribe.

Anyone with an interest in local history and artifacts should not miss out on the chance to visit the **Ancient House Museum** in White Hart Street, particularly for the many items relating to Breckland's ancient flint-knapping 'industry'. The building itself is quite magnificent: a half-timbered, early Tudor house with superb carved oak ceilings. It has been admirably restored throughout and it also acts as the local Tourist

Information Centre.

Thetford's most famous son was that great champion of human rights, Thomas Paine, who emigrated to America in 1774 where he edited the 'Pennsylvania Gazette'. He was an ardent supporter of both the American and French Revolutions and called for the overthrow of the British monarchy and, on his return to England in 1787, he published his most famous work, 'The Rights of Man'. A statue of this brave and outspoken man, who died ostracized and penniless on his farm in New York State, stands in front of King's House in King Street.

The **Childhood Treasures Museum** in Raymond Street is a must for old and young alike. A precious collection of old toys, dolls and their private residences, much loved and much coveted by younger visitors; this is a very pleasant place to spend an hour or so. The **Charles Burrell Steam Museum** in Minstergate is one of Thetford's newest attractions and well worth a visit for all those who are fascinated by the age of steam. The impressive collection of steam engines and recreated workshops are housed in the former paint finishing shop of Charles Burrell and Sons, a company that was at one time famous throughout the world for its construction of steam traction and threshing engines.

Notwithstanding the spread of modern housing and factories which the overspill agreement brought to the town the ancient heart of Thetford still survives and medieval and Georgian buildings can be found at nearly every turn. The town also seems to have more than its fair share of legends too: an ancient palace with a glorious treasure is said to lie deep beneath the castle mound. Others believe that the mound is the hiding place for six silver bells from the Priory, secreted there at the time of the Dissolution to prevent Henry VIII from getting his hands on them. Castle Hill has also been associated with sun worship and one of the more fanciful legends claims that the hill is in fact no more than the scrapings of mud from Old Nick's boots, left there in a pile after he had finished digging the Devil's Pits at Weeting!

Thetford Forest, covering an area of some 83 square miles, is the largest lowland forest in Britain. The Forestry Commission began planting in 1922 and, although it is largely given over to conifers with Scots and Corsican Pine and Douglas Fir predominating; oak, sycamore and beech can also be seen throughout. There is a particularly varied trail which leads from the Forestry Commission Information Centre at **Santon Downham**. Creatures to look out for are roe deer, squirrels, grass snakes and lizards, as well as a wide variety of birds and butterflies. To see things from a different perspective it is possible to explore parts of the forest on horse-back and permits can also be obtained for carriage driving.

Two miles north-west of Thetford are the ruins of the 14th century **Thetford Warren Lodge**, where the Prior's gamekeeper once kept a wary eye open for poachers who dared to take liberties in the Priory's hunting grounds. Exploring the forest at different times of the year can also prove very rewarding, as its atmosphere and appearance alters dramatically with the changing of the seasons. The heart of Thetford Forest is bisected by the county boundary, and whether your visit here gives you your final glimpse of Norfolk or your first sight of Suffolk, its quiet beauty is sure to make a lasting impression on you.

AROUND THETFORD

SANTON DOWNHAM. In 1668 the village was swamped by sand that blew in from the wastes of Breckland in a 10 mile wide band, temporarily choking the Little Ouse river as well. This catastrophe was the direct result of centuries of cultivation followed by over-grazing. After visiting the area several years later, the diarist John Evelyn (famous for his treatise on air pollution in 17th century London) said of the disaster that it reminded him of 'the sands in the deserts of Libya'. The planting of trees to hold down the light sandy soil of Breckland and prevent further disasters of this type began as far back as 1805.

CHAPTER NINE

WEST SUFFOLK

Friary Gate

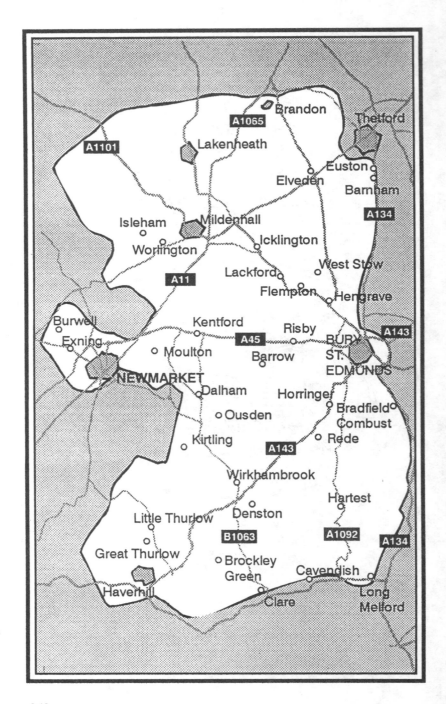

CHAPTER NINE

WEST SUFFOLK

Mildenhall and the Border with Cambridgeshire and Norfolk

MILDENHALL. The ancient Suffolk town of Mildenhall has proved to be an important centre of archaeological discovery over the years. Nearby excavations in 1988 revealed what is believed to be the earliest site of human occupation in this country, and over 2,000 flint tools and other artifacts have been discovered on the site of an ancient lake that existed some 500,000 years ago. The remains of extinct species of elephant, horse and rhinoceros were also found - the tooth of the latter being around 400,000 years old. A previous exciting discovery came in 1946, when a ploughman uncovered what was to become known as the Mildenhall Treasure. This was a remarkable collection of silver dishes, goblets and baptismal spoons, over 30 pieces in all, left behind by the Romans when they pulled out of Britain at the end of the 4th century. The collection can now be viewed in the British Museum, while the **Mildenhall and District Museum** in King Street has many other local artifacts on display.

The parish of Mildenhall is the largest in Suffolk and one of the largest in England, covering some 14,000 acres. The hammerbeam ceiling of St Mary and St Andrew's Church is, rather unusually, decorated with carved dragons.

The Bunburys were lords of the manor here from 1747 to 1933 and, were it not for an unlucky gamble, their name would now be immortalised in one of our most famous horse races. This occurred in 1780, when Sir Thomas Bunbury and Lord Derby flipped a coin to decide who should lend their name to a new annual race at Epsom. Lord Derby won the toss, but ironically, it was Sir Thomas' horse Diomed who came first past the post on that premiere of Derby Day.

Both Mildenhall and Lakenheath are situated on the edge of massive US Air Force bases and at **RAF Lakenheath** guided tours for 12 to 50 visitors can be arranged. For more details contact the base's public affairs office on (01638) 522151. During the Second World War, airfields were put up in quick succession all over East Anglia, 19 of them being established in Suffolk alone and 1992 was the 50th anniversary of the US Air Force arriving in Britain. Films such as 'Yanks' and 'Memphis Belle' have documented the initial reservations felt by the locals on meeting these glamorous American heroes, who seemed determined to lure away every young woman they encountered. However, the truth is that, romantic conquests aside, great friendships sprang up from this coming together of the Old and New Worlds; friendships that have endured to this day, with American veterans coming back to relive their experiences in Suffolk and to be reunited with the acquaintances they made here.

The **RIVERSIDE HOTEL** stands on the banks of the River Lark in an idyllic setting in the heart of the town. Resident owners John and Carolyn Child and Keith and Alison Lardner have a wealth of experience between them in the hotel profession - the family having, in fact, owned and managed The Bell Hotel in Mildenhall for over 60 years before moving to this most impressive establishment by the river. This elegant, early Georgian residence is perfectly set off by mature trees and spacious lawns which sweep down to the riverbank; a setting which can be especially enjoyed whilst having a meal in the restored hotel restaurant, with its fine views over the gardens. Largely due to the imagination and skills of the resident Chef, David Revill, the restaurant has established an excellent local and regional reputation for the superb quality of the food it serves. Local game, fowl and fish are a regular feature of the menu and venison offers a truly royal alternative to roast beef.

Christmas time and New Year's Eve are probably the busiest times in the Hotel. The atmosphere and meals are truly festive; the Riverside Hotel is an ideal place to book for your Christmas party or, indeed any special occasion.

The hotel has twenty one bedrooms, all with en-suite facilities and excellent equipment. The luxury rooms are especially popular with honeymooners and those seeking a romantic break.

Additionally, the Riverside Hotel is renowned for providing special Bridge weekends, which can be enjoyed by enthusiasts and beginners alike, and keen anglers can also fish in the hotel's own private stretch of river.

The Riverside Hotel and Restaurant, Mill Street, Mildenhall
Tel: 01638 717274 Fax 01638 715997

The **QUEEN'S ARMS** at Mildenhall is a delightful inn which is especially rewarding for anyone with an interest in horse-racing. Owned
244

by former jockey Paul Goodge and his wife Diane, the interior is filled with a fascinating collection of memorabilia which was accumulated during Paul's career in the saddle. The bar has a friendly sporting atmosphere, with traditional pub games and a gathering of eager punters studying form at the bar. There is also a large secluded garden and four well-appointed guest bedrooms which are particularly popular with visitors to the nearby US air base. On race days, Paul and Diane organise special packages which include transport and admission to Newmarket racecourse.

Queen's Arms, 42 Queensway, Mildenhall Tel: 01638 713657

AROUND MILDENHALL

EUSTON. Euston Hall, which is open to the public on Thursdays during the summer months, has been the seat of the Dukes of Grafton for around 300 years. Originally built in 1666, the Hall was rebuilt in 1902 after a fire and features a fine collection of family portraits by such artists as Van Dyck and Stubbs. It stands in a great park with gardens landscaped by William Kent and Capability Brown, and the garden created by the present Duke is renowned for its creative use of colour.

Euston village itself has only been in its present position since the 17th century, when it was moved outside the gates of the park because it 'spoilt the view' from the Hall - a fate which has befallen several other villages around the British Isles. Only St Genevieve's Church was left undisturbed and throughout are some delicate wood carvings which are attributed to Grinling Gibbons. There is also an attractive ice-house disguised as an Italianate temple within the grounds.

ELVEDEN **Elveden Hall** is remembered as the one-time home of Prince Duleep Singh of the Punjab, the man who was 'persuaded' to hand over the famous Koh-i-Noor diamond to Queen Victoria. Deposed from his kingdom and exiled to England for his part in the Sikh wars, the young prince was nevertheless granted a handsome pension and bought the Georgian house at Elveden in 1813.

His enormous wealth enabled him to later transform it into a stunning replica of an oriental palace, to remind him of those he had left behind at Delhi and Lahore. So extravagant was this rebuilding and refurbishment (which included a copper dome and literally tons of Italian marble) that the prince died a bankrupt. The Hall was then bought by Lord Iveagh, of the Guinness family, who added even more lavish adornments to the place including a replica Taj Mahal, and also rebuilt the village and the church in 1904-6. The present Earl of Iveagh sold off the contents of the house in 1984 and it now stands empty.

During the First World War the quiet countryside hereabouts resounded to the sounds of the first training exercises of the then most secret tanks. The area is also particularly rich in Neolithic sites: in 1888, Sir Arthur Evans, who excavated the ancient Cretan city of Knossos, was brought in to throw light on the discovery of an Iron Age burial site at Elveden. All in all, this proved to be quite a diverse place to visit!

BRANDON. Once a thriving port on the Little Ouse, this town is probably better known for its flint. The **Brandon Heritage Centre** in George Street has excellent exhibits relating to the Stone Age, the story of the early flint-knappers, and much information ranging from the Neolithic period to modern times. The town is largely built of flint and Brandon flints were renowned throughout the world for their use in the old flintlock guns. The industry guaranteed steady employment in the area for centuries and still survives in a small way to this day.

With the close proximity of the warrens and their incumbent rabbit population, another important industry here was the production of felt for hats from rabbit pelts. In the warrens near Thetford, a local legend relates how a White Rabbit with blazing eyes haunted the area and was said to be a harbinger of death. The hunting of rabbits and game up on the warrens may well have encouraged Prince Duleep to settle at Elveden, as he was a most enthusiastic sportsman. As well as being close to Thetford Forest, **Brandon Country Park**, near the town, offers 30 acres of woodland and beautifully laid out gardens in which to enjoy the countryside.

BRIDGE HOUSE HOTEL lies next to the bridge over the River Little Ouse in the heart of the town. Like many of the buildings here it is built of the local flint and dates back to 1876 when it was originally constructed as the bridge toll house. Owned and run by Linda Gordon and Roy Kalies, the hotel, with its charming Conservatory Restaurant, has gained a well earned reputation in the area and is particularly popular with canal boaters. Linda is the chef of the partnership and she has undoubted skill in creating interesting and unusual menus using the very best of local produce. The delicious home-cooked food is beautifully complemented by an extensive wine list.

All the guest bedrooms are comfortable and fully-equipped with all the modern conveniences including en-suite bathroom, colour television and tea and coffee making facilities. From summer 1996 Linda and Roy will also be offering accommodation in a six berth narrow boat permanently moored on the river bank. Moorings at the hotel are also available for boaters and rowing boats are available for hire. This is a delightful hotel and restaurant in a peaceful and tranquil situation.

Bridge House Hotel, High Street, Brandon Tel: 01842 813137

The **GREAT EASTERN HOTEL** on the outskirts of Brandon is an attractive, privately run hotel and freehouse under the management of Chris and Don Arnold. With a bar, restaurant, comfortable accommodation and a friendly and efficient staff, the Great Eastern has a lot to offer all its visitors. The Tavern Bar is a great place to meet and eat; there is a fine selection of cask ales, lagers, wines and spirits and a menu of tasty and reasonably priced bar meals. The restaurant is a popular venue for business lunches as well as intimate candlelit dinners where you can enjoy a delicious à la carte meal using the very best of local fresh ingredients.

The Hotel offers accommodation in a range of single, double and family rooms all of which have their own shower, telephone and satellite television. Finally, the Great Eastern Hotel is open all day for coffee and teas and serves full English or continental breakfast to passing travellers until mid-morning. There is ample parking at the rear of the hotel.

Great Eastern Hotel, Bridge Street, Brandon Tel: 01842 810229

LAKENHEATH. St Mary's Church, in this sprawling village which straddles the border between Breckland and fenland countryside, is renowned for its fine wall paintings and 13th century font.

Lakenheath was the setting for Charles Wesley's first Methodist sermon in the region in 1754, and the ancestors of Lord Kitchener are buried in the churchyard.

The 15th century bench-ends here are exquisite; they are carved with imaginative scenes portraying acrobats and fishes, together with the unusual image of a tiger gazing vainly into a mirror. The humour and eccentricity of these designs is quite captivating, and it is thought that the carvers here were also responsible for those at the church of St Mary and St Andrew at Mildenhall. Indeed, the great dragons that peer down from the hammerbeam roof of Mildenhall's beautiful church seemed to be a distinctly pagan image to find in a Christian place of worship.

WORLINGTON. Close to the River Lark, this small village is home to the 16th century mansion, Wamil Hall, that is reputedly haunted by a woman called Lady Rainbow.

THE OLD FORGE lies just off the A11 opposite the Walnut Tree public house in this picturesque village. Built in 1704, this charming black and white cottage was originally a forge, hence its name, and it is now owned by Lesley Wilson who offers first class bed and breakfast accommodation from her home. From the outside, standing in a pretty, mature garden, the cottage is a real picture. Inside, the cottage is warm and cosy, with tasteful decorations and a real cottage feel. There are two bedrooms both with comfortable pine beds, plenty of hanging space and no television which makes a pleasant change. Children and pets are welcome and Lesley serves a wonderful traditional English breakfast to set you up for the day. The pub across the road is ideal for evening meals.

The Old Forge, Newmarket Road, Worlington Tel: 01638 718014

ISLEHAM. Just over the border into Cambridgeshire and approximately half way between Ely and Newmarket, this delightful village has a lovely 12th century priory maintained by English Heritage. Complete with its village green where cricket is played every Sunday during the summer months, this is a super English village.

Bury St Edmunds and South of Breckland

BURY ST EDMUNDS. Widely held to be the jewel of Suffolk's towns, Bury St Edmunds is rich in archaeological treasures and places of great historical interest. It has long been known as one of the least spoilt towns in England; a reputation that has been greatly enhanced by the building of the A45 by-pass.

The town takes its name from St Edmund, who was born in Nuremberg in 841 AD and arrived on these shores 14 years later to become King of East Anglia. He was a renowned soldier and a fervent Christian. The latter was to prove his undoing, for when he was captured by the Danes in 870 AD he refused to deny his Christianity and was brutally murdered by being tied to a tree, shot full of arrows and beheaded.

At this point, legend mingles with fact, for it is said that although his body was recovered, his head could not be found. His men searched desperately for it for 40 days, then heard his voice directing them to it from the depths of a wood, where they discovered it lying protected between the paws of a wolf. When the head was taken back to his body they were miraculously joined, with no apparent signs of damage. To commemorate the wolf's benign influence, the crest of the town's armorial bearings depicts a wolf with a man's head.

Edmund was buried first at Hoxne, the site of his martyrdom, but when he was canonised some 30 years later his remains were transferred to the monastery at what was then called Beodricksworth. The town changed its name to St Edmundsbury and a shrine was built here in his honour, later to be incorporated into the Normans' Abbey Church after the monastery was granted abbey status by King Canute in 1032. It became a place of international pilgrimage and the monks were quick to realise its potential by stocking the abbey with an imaginative array of relics. Edmund was the patron saint of England for many years, later to be 'deposed' by St George - this seems a bit hard, considering that the 'historical' George is little more than a myth.

Further history was made here on 20th November 1214, when on St Edmund's Feast Day, the Archbishop of Canterbury, Simon Langton, met with a gathering of barons and swore on Edmund's shrine to uphold the Magna Carta and to make certain that King John would honour its proposals. With Edmund's burial here and the ratification of this important historical document, Bury well deserves its motto: 'Shrine of a King; Cradle of the Law'.

All that remains of the abbey and its church today are the romantic ruins which stand within the beautiful municipal park known as the **Abbey Gardens**. These can be reached from the broad thoroughfare (or medieval 'square') called **Angel Hill** by going through the superb Abbey Gate. This was originally built for defensive purposes and once led into the monastery courtyard.

Angel Hill itself is full of interest. Firstly, there is the impressive

Abbeygate, Bury St Edmunds

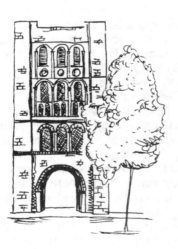

Norman Tower, Bury St Edmunds

Norman Tower, the original gateway to the Abbey Church which was built by Abbot Anselm in the 12th century. It now serves as a belfry for the cathedral church of St James which stands alongside. St James's was rebuilt in the 16th century and was elevated to the status of cathedral when the diocese of St Edmundsbury and Ipswich was created in 1914. To the south on Crown Street is the 15th century St Mary's Church, renowned for its wonderful oak roof and famous as the burial place of Henry VIII's sister, Mary Tudor. To the west is the **Athenaeum**, the centre of Bury's social life in Regency times, and the place where Charles Dickens gave two of his stirring public readings. He also stayed at the adjacent Angel Hotel, which was to be immortalised as the place where Mr Pickwick learns of the intended lawsuit against him by the 'spurned' Mrs Bardell.

The lovely Abbey Gardens were created in 1831, their central feature being a one acre circle filled with flower beds, set out along the lines of the Royal Botanic Gardens in Brussels. This had been transferred to its new site from Nathaniel Hodson's original garden to the east of the Abbey Churchyard, and it is estimated that some 2,000 plants were used. This botanic garden was conceived strictly as a scientific establishment, with native flowers and herbs laid out in their botanical orders; but ornamental plants were later introduced so that the fee-paying public could take over the financing of the project.

Today, some of those original ornamental trees can still be seen, including the Tree of Heaven, Turkish Hazel, False Acacia and Fern Leaved Beech; and many other features that were introduced at a later date can be enjoyed. These include a garden for the blind (combining a range of particularly fragrant plants), the Water Garden and the John Appleby Rose Garden; while splendid shows of shrub roses, ferns, heather banks and hostas (now making a big comeback) all add to the stunning picture.

The pretty River Lark flows through the Abbey grounds and converges with the smaller River Linnet at the place where Bury's first monastery was built - these are surely two of the most charmingly named rivers in the country. The Gardens also have a most unusual tribute to our American allies in the form of a park bench made entirely from the metal framework of a 'Flying Fortress' bomber.

There is so much to see and do in Bury that it is quite difficult to condense it down into just a few paragraphs. In addition to those places 'not to be missed' the following are well worth discovering.

No visitor should miss the opportunity of taking a leisurely stroll along **Abbeygate Street**, which leads up from Angel Hill and features a fascinating and diverse variety of old shop fronts. Past the Victorian **Corn Exchange** on The Traverse is the charming **Nutshell** - which claims to be the smallest pub in England and belies its name by offering large-scale hospitality. Further along is the handsome **Cupola House**, a fine old inn that was built in 1693 and reputedly numbered Daniel Defoe amongst its guests. At the end of The Traverse and facing Cornhill is the

Market Cross, originally built as a market hall and theatre combined (note the tell-tale masks of tragedy and comedy), later to become the town hall, and now housing an art gallery on its upper storey.

Moyses Hall Museum in the Butter Market is said to be the oldest stone domestic building in England. Although its precise origins are unclear, it is thought to have been built sometime around 1180; of flint and limestone in a town whose secular buildings were strictly made of wood. The fact that these materials would have been transported from quarries more than 70 miles away implies that whoever it was built for must have been a person of no small distinction. The Hall has served various functions over the centuries; it has been a prison and a workhouse, a police station and a railway office, and in 1899 it became the Borough museum - which it remains to this day. With around 10,000 objects on display, this unique building makes a wonderful setting for such diverse exhibits as Anglo-Saxon grave jewellery, Roman pottery and a 19th century doll's house. It seems particularly ironic that one of the town's most recent developments, the **Cornhill Shopping Centre** in Brentgovel Street, stands alongside Bury's oldest house. A curious juxtaposition of the old and new indeed!

For horologists, the **Manor House Museum** on Honey Hill is devoted to timepieces of all shapes and sizes; from clocks and watches to sundials and a replica of a 15th century planetarium. Around 200 exhibits from the Gershom Parkington Collection are displayed, formerly housed at the Clock Museum on Angel Hill, and, in addition, there are some fine works of art by such painters as James Tissot and Joshua Reynolds.

Not far from here, at the junction of Crown Street and Westgate Street, evidence of Regency patronage can be seen in the handsome architecture of the **Theatre Royal**, now in the care of the National Trust, though still a working theatre. It was built in 1819 by William Wilkins (also the architect of the National Gallery) and can claim the distinction of being the first theatre in the world to premiere 'Charley's Aunt', apparently before an audience of five!

A visit to Bury St Edmunds is definitely one of the highlights of a tour of Suffolk. It is a charming town of great character, and yet unlike other historic towns, it is still very much alive with plenty of modern entertainments and facilities. High on this particular list would be 'Rollerbury', the National Rollerskating Rink; the superb Sports & Leisure Centre on Beetons Way; and the annual Bury St Edmunds Festival in May, when the town plays host to both national and international artists from the world of the performing arts.

With so much to enjoy it is almost impossible to 'do' Bury in a day, and an overnight stay will enhance any visit to this area and there is a wide choice of accommodation.

Another local attraction not to be missed is **ICKWORTH HOUSE**, owned by the National Trust and easily found in Horringer Village, three miles south-west of Bury St Edmunds on the A143. Ickworth's spectacular elliptical rotunda makes this one of the most extraordinary mansions in England. The design was inspired by Belle Isle, a house built on an island in Lake Windermere in the mid 18th century. Construction of Ickworth got underway in 1795, but because of technical problems and the death of Frederick, 4th Earl of Bristol and Bishop of Derry in 1803, it wasn't completed until 1829.

The Earl-Bishop's son even considered demolishing his father's highly impractical house before deciding that the state rooms in the rotunda would make an excellent setting for the family's extensive art collection. Works now on view include those by Titian, Velasquez, Gainsborough, Hogarth and Reynolds. Inside, the state rooms are spectacular. The hall, dining room, library and drawing room follow the same grandiose style and are furnished with late-Regency and 18th century French furniture. Be sure not to miss the collection of Georgian silver, one of the finest private collections ever assembled.

Outside, the grounds are arranged as a semi-formal Italian garden. Here we suggest a visit to the orangery and a walk along the terrace which overlooks the park beyond. In the park, there are several miles of way marked trails, including a seven mile Grand Tour which includes some fabulous views of the rotunda.

Ickworth House, Horringer, Bury St Edmunds Tel: 01284 88270

Adjacent to the park is the Community Centre, where Horringer Crafts 'open their door' to the public every Sunday and Bank Holiday Monday from 2.00 - 6.00 pm. There is a small admission charge although accompanied children are free, and you can spend a pleasant hour or so watching the local artists and craftsmen at work before making your selection from the wide range of high quality, individually made items available for sale. The group emphasises that they are more than happy to demonstrate their skills and discuss their work in detail with you, so do feel free to ask questions! To round off a pleasant and interesting afternoon in their company, they can also provide you with afternoon tea. Any local craftspeople who would like to join the group should phone (01284) 766326 for details.

The **SCANDINAVIA COFFEE HOUSE**, opposite Abbeygate, on

Angel Hill, is a wonderful coffee house and tea rooms owned and run by Derek and Monica Dawkins. Hard to miss as the building is painted a pastel pink and situated on a street corner, there are plenty of window seats from which to watch the world go by. The appetising smell of fresh, hot home-made scones mingles with the rich aroma of freshly ground coffee each morning. All the cakes and pastries are baked on the premises but the Scandinavia Coffee House really specialises in delicious sandwiches. The smoked mackerel and lemon mayonnaise filling makes a heavenly combination and the club sandwiches really are a meal in themselves.

Scandinavia Coffee House, 5 Angel Hill, Bury St Edmunds
Tel: 01284 700853

TALISMAN 2 on Out Westgate, just out of the centre of Bury St Edmunds, is a real treasure trove. Owned and run by Shirley McNaught, the premises has been in her family for some five generations, evolving from a butchers shop to the antiques and curios shop it is now. Stocked full of eclectic clutter, Shirley has a weakness for the peculiar, this is a wonderful place to shop and look around. You never know what you might find!

Talisman 2 Antiques and Collectables, 18 Out Westgate, Bury St Edmunds
Tel: 01284 725712

The 16th century **ASH COTTAGE**, situated in Bury St Edmund's' conservation area is within walking distance of the Theatre Royal, restaurants, churches, Abbey Gardens and all of the other places of interest in the town. This lovely medieval house is surrounded by a beautiful garden and offers a high standard of B & B accommodation throughout the year.

Ash Cottage is the home of Elizabeth Barber-Lomax who extends a warm welcome to all of her guests. The house is full of character and has oak beamed ceilings and comfortable rooms, each with its own private shower or en-suite. Breakfast is excellent and the atmosphere is informal and friendly. This is the ideal base for a break spent exploring this historic town and all of the other 'hidden places' described in this book. A no-smoking establishment.

Ash Cottage, 59 Whiting Street, Bury St Edmunds Tel: 01284 755098

HILLTOP, the home of Mavis and Peter Hanson, lies in a quiet residential cul-de-sac on the western edge of Bury St Edmunds. Ideal for exploring the delights of the town itself and the surrounding villages and countryside, Hilltop provides bed and breakfast accommodation in a warm and friendly environment. Well recommended by several guides, there is a choice of three bedrooms, all with television and tea and coffee making facilities; the family room on the ground floor has its own shower and toilet. Mavis is a wonderful cook and provides a hearty breakfast, along with an evening meal for those that prefer not to dine out. A real home from home where you will certainly be made to feel like a long lost friend.

Hilltop, 22 Bronyon Close, Bury St Edmunds Tel: 01284 767066

SOUTH HILL HOUSE, on the way into Bury St Edmunds from the main A134 road, is owned by Sarah Green and offers bed and breakfast accommodation in pleasant and relaxing surroundings. In the mid 1800s, the building became an Academy for Young Ladies and is reputed to be the school mentioned in Chapter XVI of Pickwick Papers. The connection with Charles Dickens is further enhanced by visits he made here to read to the pupils. Later it became a Boy's Boarding School and the unique bell tower is a reminder of that time. The two guest rooms, both large, have either an en suite shower or bathroom, television and tea and coffee making facilities. Children can easily be accommodated. This is an ideal place to stay while visiting this historic town and the surrounding area.

South Hill House, 43 Southgate Street, Bury St Edmunds
Tel: 01284 755650

AROUND BURY ST EDMUNDS

ICKLINGHAM. St James's is now the parish church, but the now redundant thatched church of All Saints is more interesting. Note the medieval tiles on the chancel floor and the beautiful east windows in the south aisle.

LACKFORD. Former gravel pits have been restored to provide a habitat for wildfowl and waders. There is access to two hides, one being suitable for wheelchair users, and groups of 10 or more should contact the warden or ring the Suffolk Wildlife Trust for details on Saxmundham 3765.

HENGRAVE. This is a charming, old-world village of thatched and flint cottages. Archaeological excavations show that there has been a settlement here since Neolithic times and the Bronze Age. However, Hengrave's best known feature is Hengrave Hall, now a religious retreat centre and open to the public by appointment only. It was built during the period 1535-38 and was visited in 1578 by Elizabeth I and her court. The tiny church of St John Lateran which stands adjacent to the Hall completes the idyllic setting within this beautiful parkland.

WEST STOW. It was the discovery of an Anglo-Saxon cemetery in 1849 that first put West Stow on the map. In 1940 Roman kilns were also found here, and in 1947, the actual layout of the original Anglo-Saxon village was revealed. A Trust was set up to discover more about the Anglo-Saxon way of life and the building and craft techniques employed by this ancient farming community, which is known to have existed here from 420-650 AD. Using the tools and techniques of those times, a group of thatched wooden houses and a communal hall were reconstructed on the site, each one testing different ideas. This unique attraction is open daily from 10.00 am - 5.00 pm, and a choice of cassette-tape guides are available.

The village lies within the **West Stow Country Park**, which encompasses 125 acres of woodland, marshes and heath, as well as a large lake and a beautiful stretch of the River Lark. All are linked by paths and a 5 mile nature trail, which gives plenty of opportunity to study the abundance of plants, birds and wildlife that thrive in this particular part of Breckland. There is an excellent Visitor Centre with plenty of written information and audio-visual displays, as well as an adventure playground for the children, picnic tables, toilet facilities and a large car park.

RISBY. The medieval tithe barn in the village is home to the Risby Barn Antiques Centre and the 15th century manor house is a Grade II listed building.

REDE. **REDE HALL FARM PARK**, on the A143 between Bury St Edmunds and Haverhill, is a working farm based on the agricultural life of the 1930s to the 1950s. Open daily between April and September, visitors can see the working Suffolk horses pulling agricultural implements from a bygone age, hauling waggons and helping in woodland management. Young English oxen are also trained for farm work and forestry.

Rede Hall Farm Park, Rede Hall, Rede Tel: 01284 850695

The poultry, including game fowl, guinea fowl and pea fowl, roam freely around the farm. From marked farm walks taking in a small lake, conservation area and new woodland, traditional East Anglian breeds of livestock can be seen in the meadows. Other attractions include a working farrier shop, children's play and picnic area and cart rides. There is a well stocked gift shop and a cafeteria serving a wide variety of homebaked cakes. Throughout the year a range of activities, demonstrations and displays are organised and, from April 1996, a museum of agricultural life will be open which will include a washhouse and dairy.

On land adjacent to the farm is a registered Caravan Club of Great Britain site with room for five caravans.

BRADFIELD COMBUST. The curious name of this attractive village is apparently derived from the fact that the local hall was burnt to the ground in the 14th century, during riots against the Abbot of St Edmundsbury.

Newmarket and the Famous Heath

NEWMARKET. This is, of course, the headquarters of British horse racing and bloodstock breeding, with two of the most famous racecourses in the world. On either side of the town are 4 square miles of land used to train the horses who have such vast amounts of cash hanging on their performances. There are something like 60 training stables and 50 stud farms within the area, and Newmarket is without doubt the premier place to purchase pure bred racehorses in Britain.

It is said that Bodicea herself enjoyed the spirit of horse racing, although the shaggy ponies that pulled the ancient Iceni chariots are a far cry from the long-legged equine beauties that grace the paddocks of Newmarket today. The National Horse Racing Museum in the High Street is a tribute to the men and the rules that have fashioned this modern 300 year old sport, and most importantly to the horses themselves - without whom none of it would be possible. By arrangement, you can also enjoy guided tours around the training areas, the Jockey Club and the National Stud.

Founded in 1752, the Jockey Club building (erected in 1882) stands in the High Street. The governing body of horse racing in Britain, the Club is next to the museum.

It is likely that Newmarket has the only racecourse in the world which is haunted. A phantom rider has often been spotted joining his colleagues on the turf, occasionally making the other horses shy. Jockeys say that the spirit is obviously taking part in the races, as it tends to keep well up in front with the leaders! Some reckon that it could be the ghost of Fred Archer, who won the Derby on four occasions before his tragic death in 1886 at the age of 29.

James I is thought to have been the first monarch to enjoy the sporting grounds of the heathland surrounding the town; he was so taken by it that he chose to revisit the town on many occasions to watch the hare coursing events. But it was Charles II who firmly established Newmarket as the place for horse racing, taking part in many races himself. His mistress Nell Gwynne used to stay at a house in Palace Street which can still be seen today. Newmarket's largest racecourse is called 'The Rowley Mile', a tribute to Charles whose favourite horse was a stallion called 'Old Rowley' - a name also used by the king himself when he went off on his nocturnal adventures!

Another famous lady associated with Newmarket was the actress

Racing at Newmarket

who dominated the Victorian stage, Lillie Langtry. She owned the house in Gazeley Road which is now the Langtry Hotel. So often it seems that those with the chastest origins attain the dizzy heights, for she was born Emilie le Breton in 1853, daughter of the Dean of Jersey. She would later become the mistress of Edward VII, and Oscar Wilde (despite his personal predilections) declared of her: 'Lillie's beauty has no meaning, her charm, her wit, and her mouth - what a mouth - are far more formidable than weapons!'

AROUND NEWMARKET

EXNING. Stretching across the Heath is a massive, 6 mile long fortification known as the Devil's Dyke. It was probably built sometime during the 7th century, although there may have been an earlier fortification here as the Iceni are known to have had a settlement at nearby Exning. Plague forced them to move their community to what is now Newmarket in the first century. It is interesting to note that the Iceni coinage bore the picture of a horse; an animal that was obviously much loved and revered by this ancient tribe.

The **JOLLY BUTCHERS** public house, in this ancient village, is owned and run by Mick Walker. Mick trained as a chef on the Channel Island of Guernsey and he has now gained a wide following here in Suffolk. The pub, like the village, is old though it probably only dates back as far as the 16th century. At one time the premises housed a butcher's shop thus explaining the unusual name. An attractive cream coloured building, this is very much the village local but many of the customers travel some distance to sample its delights.

A warm and friendly establishment, recently extended to include a spacious restaurant area, there are roaring log fires in the winter and you will be greeted with a smile anytime. As well as excellent food and drink, Mick also organises live music once a month and there are fun nights too.

Jolly Butchers, 18 Oxford Street, Exning

KENTFORD. At a crossroads on the A45 towards the village from

Newmarket is a sad memorial to a young suicide. Known simply as 'The Boy's Grave' it marks the spot where a shepherd boy was buried after hanging himself when he was accused of sheep stealing. No one knows whether he took his own life out of remorse or as an alternative to the horrors of transportation, but his grave is still tended and adorned with fresh flowers to this day. Suicides were traditionally buried at crossroads to prevent their spritis from wandering and strange stories have been told of this particular grave by cyclists who have apparently felt an unseen force preventing them from riding past it.

BURWELL. This pretty fenland village lies just over the border in Cambridgeshire. With a ruined castle, a vast church and an old wharf, there is plenty to see here.

MOULTON. Once on the main thoroughfare between Cambridge and Bury St Edmunds, this pleasant village has two 15th century pack-horse bridges spanning the shallow River Kennett. Today's traffic, however, crosses over a more mundane by-road which fords the river. This peaceful spot has a tendency to flood in winter, although perversely, like many of our English rivers, the Kennett can also run dry in summer.

HANDSELL HOUSE is set back from the road surrounded by an attractive garden in the centre of the village of Moulton. Owned by Jenny Perry, this modern house was designed by a local architect and stands in the grounds of an older residence. Jenny is artistic herself and examples of her work decorate the house. She also opens her house to wonderful bed and breakfast accommodation with a relaxing atmosphere that is hard to beat. The three guest bedrooms are all individually decorated and along with the rest of the house show Jenny's artistic flair to its best advantage. As well as breakfast, Jenny can provide evening meals for those who do not wish to sample the delights of the local pubs. Nestling in a sheltered valley, the charming garden is a picture in the summer and particularly in the evenings when the rich floral aromas come out.

Handsell House, The Street, Moulton

FLINT END HOUSE, in the village, lies just off the Newmarket road. Built in 1820, this late Georgian house is home to Sally and Hugo Bolus. With large rooms, high ceilings and none too straight walls, the couple offer excellent bed and breakfast accommodation, in two comfortable rooms, at their charming, rambling home. Guests have their own sitting room, but such is the warmth of hospitality that you will soon be chatting to your hosts. Sally is also a mine of information about the local area and is happy to suggest sights off the beaten track for you to discover. To set you up for a day's exploring there is a hearty English breakfast, served outside if the weather is warm.

Flint End House, The Street, Moulton Tel: 01638 750966
Mobile: 0421 042350

DALHAM. This pretty village nestles among gentle wooded hills, and the residents of the thatched and white-washed cottages have to cross little footbridges over the Kennett to reach their homes. The Duke of Wellington lived at Dalham Hall for several years, and the estate was later bought by Cecil Rhodes for his retirement. As it transpired, he died in 1902 and never returned to England.

The Affleck Arms, Dalham

THE AFFLECK ARMS at the heart of Dalham is also at the heart of the village's history. This 16th century public house is one of the village's oldest buildings and it takes the name of the family who were Lords of the Manor from 1714 until 1902 when Cecil Rhodes purchased the manor.

Intending to retire to England, Rhodes unfortunately died in South Africa and never saw his manor though his brother erected the village hall in his memory.

Well known throughout the area, the Affleck Arms pub makes a welcome resting place for ramblers where all can find excellent food, an extensive range of spirits and bottled and draught beverages and a warm and friendly atmosphere. The large beer garden to the rear is a picture in the summer months and, well used by the pub's patrons, it also contains a pet's corner for the children. Featured in many of the best pub and eating out guide books, accommodation is also sometimes available.

OUSDEN. **THE FOX** is the only pub in the village of Ousden so it is hard to miss. Built around 300 years ago, The Fox has been a great meeting place for many years and is always busy. Popular with locals, anyone visiting will quickly get chatting, this is a really friendly pub, and the talk is usually of racing and, carrying on the equestrian theme, the local hunt also meets here regularly. The Fox is owned and personally run by Mrs Jacobs and the inn has a great history of long serving landladies; the last one maintained the license for over 60 years! As well as the excellent company and superb beer, the inn is also renowned for its food, served from Tuesdays to Saturdays. With plenty of fresh local produce and not forgetting the local Newmarket sausages, this is a wonderful place for lunch. Charming inside, the French windows at the back open out into the garden which is widely used during the summer months.

The Fox, Front Street, Ousden

JONSYL is a modern single storey house built by its owners, Sylvia and John Pettitt, situated up the hill in the picturesque Suffolk village of Ousden. Standing amid two acres of award winning gardens, the charming and spacious house offers bed and breakfast accommodation in three comfortable bedrooms. This is a super place to stay, handy for the races at nearby Newmarket and in the heart of rural Suffolk. Surrounding the house and garden, Sylvia and John have paddocks with horses and stabling is available as well as space for caravans. A charming couple, you can be sure of a warm welcome and a delicious full English breakfast to follow your comfortable and relaxing nights sleep. A family dinner is available if booked in advance and all guests are made to feel part of the family. As well as the excellent facilities inside that make this a real home from home, there is also a grass tennis court in the garden, a patio where you can sit and relax and dogs are also made welcome.

Jonsyl, Ousden Tel: 01638 500378

KIRTLING. A splendid tower gatehouse here is all that remains of the 15th century mansion that once belonged to Henry VIII's Chancellor, Lord North, who was at one time the jailer of Elizabeth I before she took the throne.

THE RED LION, at Kirtling, is a beautiful old building with an interesting history. Over 400 years old and with a typical Suffolk-style tiled roof, the inn has also been a butcher's shop and slaughter house. There is also a bread oven next to the bar which is probably as old as the building. Owned and personally run by Paul and Lesley Forbes-Lange, the Red Lion has gained an enviable reputation for its cuisine. As well as the delicious food, this is a free house and the Red Lion stocks real ale and features regular guest beers. With wonderful food and drink and a warm and friendly atmosphere this has to be one of the best pubs around.

The Red Lion, The Street, Kirtling Tel: 01638 730162

It was here too, within easy access of Bury St Edmunds, Cambridge and Newmarket, and just five miles from the A45, that you come across a beautiful old farmhouse dating back 400 years. Mrs Ann Bailey, proprietor of **HILL FARM**, is renowned for her hospitality and her ability as a wonderful hostess and chef. Ann has had plenty of practice, having been in the public house and catering business for many years, once holding the position of head chef at the Egon Ronay recommended Queen's Head in Kirtling. With a wide knowledge of the horse racing at nearby Newmarket, Ann is very happy to arrange trips to the town including visits to the Museum of Horse Racing.

A wonderful historic atmosphere is preserved here, yet the bedrooms have en-suite and service tray facilities. Bar billiards and darts can be played in the Hill Farm games room which is equipped with its own little bar, or you can relax and watch television in the superbly decorated lounge.

The luxury of open wood fires, the splendid rural views and the excellent cuisine make staying here a pleasurable experience.

Hill Farm, Kirtling Tel: 01638 730253

Long Melford and the Stour Valley

LONG MELFORD. This small town could not be more aptly named; its tree-lined main street seems to go on and on, covering a distance of 3 miles in all. Guide books tend to refer to Melford as a town, but it has more the feel of a very large, spacious village. A lot of visitors come here specifically to browse around Melford's surprisingly large number of antique shops, most of which lie dotted about the main street with its timber-framed and Georgian houses. Another regular feature of the village, popular with visitors and locals alike, are its book fairs and musical concerts.

The beautiful 15th century Holy Trinity Church stands on a rise above Melford's green. It is renowned far and wide for its striking tower, its magnificent display of flushwork, and the incredible number of windows in the 150 ft nave and chancel which give the interior such a sense of light and space.

On the other side of the green is **Melford Hall**, built during the 1570s and once used by the Abbot of Bury St Edmunds as his country retreat, where he could enjoy venison from the deer park. Now a National Trust property, this mellow red-brick house with its 'pepperpot' towers is full of fine paintings, furniture and porcelain for the public to enjoy; but what interested us especially was the charming collection of water colours by Beatrix Potter. She was related to the Parker family who bought the house in the 18th century, and somehow her pictures seem more quintessentially English than those of our greatest landscape painters!

The **ANTIQUE CAFE** is the only authentic tea room and coffee house in Long Melford and it is conveniently located on Hall Street in the centre of the village. Tricia and John Stanley run the cafe and it is housed in a 300 year old listed building that, at one time, used to be the old foundry. Open seven days a week, the cafe serves a wide variety of home-made cakes and scones as well as a range of light meals and daily specials plus a large selection of vegetarian meals and freshly ground coffees. It is a charming place to stop and take refreshment. Full of atmosphere, with slanting oak beamed ceilings and an open fireplace. It is also licensed for fine wines, beers and ciders. Also in the same building you will find the Hand-Carved Candle Company which makes an interesting diversion from the tasty sandwiches and wicked cream teas. Bring your copy of the 'Hidden Places' with you and you will receive a 10% discount from your bill.

Antique Cafe, 1 Foundry House, Hall Street, Long Melford
Tel: 01787 378535 Fax: 01787 313342

AROUND LONG MELFORD

KENTWELL HALL. Perched on the edge of the moat is the superb 15th century moat house, Kentwell Hall, a remnant from the earlier house which stood on the site. Now fully restored, this magical building has its own great hall and solar. The moat gives Kentwell its unique character and surrounds not only the house, but also a large area of beautiful formal gardens which were laid out in the 17th century. A short distance from the main house, a home farm has been created using relocated and newly built timber-framed buildings. This fascinating working farm contains a wide variety of rare breeds and an interesting collection of farm tools and carts.

Special summer events at Kentwell include their famous 'historical re-creations', days involving over 200 people who dress, speak and behave in Tudor style to create an impression of everyday life at the manor in the 16th century. For details of opening times and special events, telephone (0787) 310207. Delicious home-produced refreshments are available when the house is open.

HARTEST. A pleasant little village sheltered in a valley, with colour-washed houses and chestnut trees on the village green. For a vineyard with a difference visit Gifford's Hall (not to be confused with the house at Wickhambrook). In addition to the free wine tasting on offer, there are a host of other things to see and purchase, including wild flower meadows, rare breeds of sheep and chickens, organic vegetables, cut flowers and a rose garden - all within a 33 acre site. The Hall is open every day from 12.00 am - 6.00 pm from Easter through to the end of October. There is a shop and tea room, and wheelchair access is provided.

DENSTON. The Church of St Nicholas, built in the 15th century, is one of the finest medieval churches in Suffolk. One of 18 churches dedicated to St Nicholas, the patron saint of sailors, and it seemed rather odd to find him so far inland.

There is plenty to admire here, including the medieval glass, the beautiful tracery work throughout, and some particularly fine carvings. The crane clasping a stone in its claw recalls the legend that when a flock of cranes flew down to rest at nightfall, one of them would stand guard just so, and the stone would drop with a loud clunk and wake him if he inadvertently fell asleep on the job! Animal carvings feature everywhere; a fascinating menagerie of mythical as well as more familiar beasts. The unicorn is said to symbolise the Incarnation, while a stag represents the image of a good Christian. There is also a rather odd carving of an elephant that looks more like a pig with a trailing snout!

WICKHAMBROOK. This isolated little village is really a series of hamlets and there are 11 village greens in total! In All Saints' Church there is a fine carved statue of Sir Thomas Heigham. One of his ancestors built nearby Gifford's Hall, a gabled, timber-framed house whose moat-enclosed grounds are open to the public under the National Gardens Scheme.

LITTLE and GREAT THURLOW. The twin villages of Little Thurlow and Great Thurlow have merged to become one large, sprawling community on the west bank of the River Stour. The pretty Hall, its walls festooned with rambling roses in high summer, is open under the National Gardens Scheme, and the views along the grassy riverbanks are quite delightful. Some of the most attractive buildings are in the main street, including a school house founded in 1614 by a former Lord Mayor of London, Sir Stephen Soame.

BROCKLEY GREEN. THE PLOUGH INN is a traditionally-styled country inn located in an elevated rural position between Hundon and Kedington. David and Marion Rowlinson, the owners, have been at the inn for the past 14 years, though it has been in the family a lot longer, and during this time they have carried out much work to provide excellent accommodation as well as improving the dining and functions facilities. The bar has retained all its character and atmosphere of days gone by, with exposed beams, log fires, well-kept traditional ales and home-cooked bar meals. The restaurant's à la carte menu offers an imaginative selection of dishes, all reasonably priced, which includes such delights as Wild Boar with a Morello Cherry and Port sauce and Breast of Pheasant with Plums and Armagnac. With eight luxury en suite bedrooms, it is not surprising that The Plough Inn has been granted Four Crowns from the English Tourist Board.

The Plough Inn, Brockley Green Tel: 01440 786789

CLARE. This small town once commanded an important position on one of the country's old medieval routes, the Icknield Way. Clare's name has rather a charming origin - some believe that the clarity of the waters of the River Stour, which flows through Clare Country Park, gave the town its name. This stretch of the river still seems pretty well looked after, if the swans who inhabit it are anything to go by. As the town was known to have extensive vineyards at the time of the Domesday Book, it has also been suggested that it may have given its name to that popular tipple, Claret.

The ruins of **Clare Castle** with its 13th century keep and 100 ft high motte make an attractive landmark, and further along the footpath by the river are the remains of a Priory that was founded by the Austin Friars in 1249. This was abandoned at the time of the Dissolution, but the order returned some 400 years later in 1953 and still maintain the Priory (converted into a house in 1604) to this day. To the north of the town, the remnants of an Iron Age hill-fort offer further evidence of Clare's ancient heritage.

The wool trade brought great wealth to Clare, and the magnificent Church of St Peter and St Paul stands as a testament to the town's prosperity from the 15th century onwards. The carvings on the Jacobean choirstalls are superb, some of the woodwork being commissioned by Katherine of Aragon. Her symbol was the pomegranate of Aragon, which can be seen in a crest above the rood screen where the letters 'H' and 'K' are linked. Rather a touching sight, as it shows the love that Henry VIII and Katherine must once have felt for one another - before the barren years which were to prove her downfall. It seems particularly ironic that the pomegranate is a traditional symbol of fertility. Henry presented Katherine with a number of estates around the town, and with great generosity she gave 60 acres of her lands to the poor to use for grazing at a peppercorn rent. This land was later purchased by the town and has since been absorbed into the Common.

There are a number of attractive houses in Clare and perhaps the best of them is the **Ancient House** to the south of the churchyard. Built in 1473 as a priest's house, it is now the town museum and its lavish swirls of plasterwork or 'pargetting' irresistibly conjours up the image of royal icing on a wedding cake! Also worth seeing are **Nethergate House** on Nethergate Street, once the working place of weavers, dyers and spinners; and the **Old Maltings** to the north of the church, whose surviving timbered wing once housed the public library.

CAVENDISH. The village offers one of those quintessential portraits of the English rural village: a picturesque group of candy-pink thatched cottages clustered beneath the medieval tower of St Mary's Church on the edge of the broad village green. It comes as no surprise to learn that the village has been the proud winner of the 'best-kept village in Suffolk' award. The name comes from Cafa's Edisc, meaning the enclosure of Caffa's People, and is an indication that there has been a settlement here since Saxon times.

The Sue Ryder Foundation was established here as its Headquarters and Sue Ryder Home in 1952/53 when it moved in to a 16th century timber framed house, previously a farmhouse and then two cottages, with its own beautiful pond in the garden. The Home was established to receive patients blocking hospital beds and gave nursing care to 30 long-term patients, and others who require respite care. The Headquarters links some 80 Sue Ryder Foundation Homes, Domiciliary Teams and Mobile Medical Teams, in different parts of the world.

The Museum, which was created in 1978 and officially opened by Her Majesty, Queen Elizabeth the Queen Mother on 29th April 1979, illustrates the origin of the Foundation and the hard work it does on behalf of the sick and handicapped in many parts of the world. Sue Ryder's formal title is Baroness Ryder of Warsaw: she served from the beginning of World War II until the end with the highly secret Polish Section of the Special Operations Executive. The Museum is open all year round (except Christmas Day) from 10 am to 5.30 pm, and there is a restaurant and gift shop adjoining.

Lady Ryder's late husband was that other great philanthropist and war hero, Leonard Cheshire - who founded the Cheshire Homes for the incurably sick.

In 1381, Sir John Cavendish was in attendance at Wat Tyler's conference with Richard II at Smithfield, when the leader of the Peasants' Revolt was struck down by the Lord Mayor of London and stabbed by Sir John's son. When a number of Tyler's enraged supporters came after Sir John swearing vengeance, he stashed away his valuables in the belfry of St Mary's Church at Cavendish and fled. They later caught up with him near Lakenheath and beheaded him, which ironically enough was the same fate that befell their leader.

If you are seeking quality bed and breakfast accommodation in the area of Sudbury, then make for **THE RED HOUSE** at Cavendish and enjoy this lovely location and the delightful home of Maureen and Brian Theaker. This is a most attractive early 16th century (Grade II Listed) timber-framed house painted red with neat little dormer windows peeping out from the roof over a beautiful, large lawned garden with views of the river and surrounding countryside. Guest accommodation is self-contained with its own entrance. Children are welcome and special facilities can be provided for them. Breakfast is no ordinary affair and the delicious choice offered together with Maureen's home made preserves make this an unforgettable experience. You are sure to want to extend your stay here. No smoking in the bedrooms please. ETB 2 Crown Highly Commended.

The Red House, Stour Street, Cavendish Tel: 01787 280611

CHAPTER TEN

CENTRAL SUFFOLK

Lavenham Guildhall

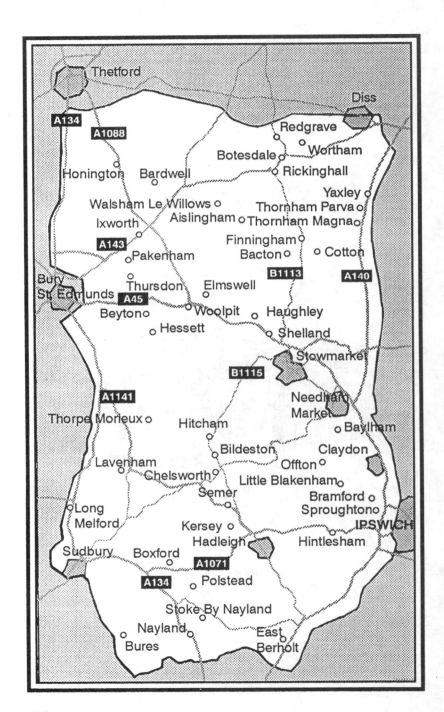

CHAPTER TEN

CENTRAL SUFFOLK

STOWMARKET. This is a lively place with a refreshingly bustling atmosphere, especially on market days. Stowmarket enjoyed a rapid period of growth when the River Gipping was navigable between here and Ipswich, and although that particular trade is now a thing of the past, the town continues to prosper as the main shopping centre for a wide agricultural region.

Far and away the most popular attraction here is the excellent **Museum of East Anglian Life**, which is situated in the centre of town to the west of the market place, in a 70 acre meadow land site on the old Abbot's Hall estate. The displays here cover a wide variety of subjects from domestic and working life to rural crafts, agriculture and the industrial heritage of the region, and there is a continually changing programme of craft demonstrations and special events throughout the year. The annual programme typically includes everything from coopering, candle making, sheep shearing and spinning, to blacksmithing, saddlery, basket making, tractor ploughing, hedge laying and folk dancing - and much, much more!

In addition to all this, part of the open-air section features several historic buildings from around the region which have been carefully re-erected on site. These include an engineering workshop that dates from the 1870s, part of a 14th century farmhouse, and a working watermill and windpump - from Alton and Eastbridge respectively. The Museum also has a collection of steam engines which can be seen at work at various times of the year - as can 'Remus', the Museum's Suffolk Punch horse, just one of various local breeds of farm animal on display. There is a restaurant serving hot and cold meals and snacks, or alternatively, visitors can walk down to the banks of the Rattlesden River and enjoy a picnic in peace and quiet.

AROUND STOWMARKET

THURSTON. This expanding village has three pubs and its village hall is named after William Tyrell Cavendish, who was, unfortunately, on the Titanic when it went down in 1912.

THE GRANGE at Thurston, conveniently located just two miles from the A14, is set in the heart of Suffolk's beautiful countryside and surrounded by villages of great character. This attractive Tudor style country house hotel has been family run for three generations with a chef-proprietor who was trained at some of London's finest hotels, including The Connaught and Claridges. Set in its own extensive, secluded gardens, The Grange offers a warm, friendly and relaxed atmosphere.

The two lounge bars open onto the terrace and garden and offer a diverse menu of excellent food and serve a wide range of fine local and guest beers. For more formal dining the Adam Room has a superb à la carte menu for lunch and dinner as well as a traditional roast lunch on Sundays. All the dishes are freshly prepared from local produce and immaculately presented and served. The 13 bedrooms, with everything you would expect in a high class establishment, are individually decorated and offer the very best in comfort. If you can bear to tear yourself away from this wonderful hotel, The Grange is ideally located for racing at Newmarket and punting on the River Cam in Cambridge.

The Grange, Barton Road, Thurston Tel: 01359 231260

DELL TOURING PARK is a family run camping and caravanning site 5 miles east of Bury St Edmunds. Purpose built facilities for disabled campers and families as well as electric hook-ups, hot showers and a site shop. For the children there is a safe play area that will amuse them for hours.

Dell Touring Park, Beyton Road, Thurston Tel: 01359 270121

PAKENHAM. This village's fine 18th century working watermill is signposted from the village centre. It was built around 1816 on a site which had a considerable and interesting history. Domesday Survey records have proven that there had been a watermill on this site since 1086, thus corn has definitely been ground here for the past 900 years. However, excavations of a nearby Roman site have suggested that there could have been a watermill here as far back as 43-60 AD.

The mill was purchased by the Suffolk Preservation Society in 1981. With the help of a small group of volunteers, they lovingly restored this magnificent watermill to its present condition and rightfully accepted a European Award in 1982 for their sympathetic and talented renovation.

The water which powers the mill comes from Pakenham Fen: about

60-70,000 gallons of treated water are fed into the Fen area each day. A steep drop in the stream of approximately 10 ft is necessary to power a watermill. This drop is made by creating built-up banks and damming the stream to form a millpond. Thus outlets leave the millpond. One is known as the spillway gate, which allows excess water to by-pass the mill; the other is called the shut and its purpose is to direct water onto the waterwheel.

A tour of the mill gives a greater insight into the everyday life of a Miller and also offers an explanation of the mechanisms used in the process.

The 'Tattersall Midget Roller Mill' here is of particular interest. Towards the end of the 19th century, fine white flour was being produced with more efficiency by new roller mills. A few watermills tried to install roller milling machinery, but found it far too expensive. As a compromise, the 'Tattersall Midget Roller Mill' was introduced, which actively combined rollers and separators in one large machine. The Tattersall exhibited at Pakenham is dated around 1913. Unfortunately for the country watermills, even with the aid of this new-found invention they still found it difficult to compete and those that survived only produced animal feed.

Even today, huge overheads comprising of maintenance and insurance quickly absorb profits, and many mills, including Pakenham's, are kept running solely due to the efforts of volunteers, who work hard towards improving, maintaining or staffing the mill.

The Blackbourne stream flowing down to Pakenham Fen with its willows and riverbank recreation park is a beautiful setting for visitors just to walk, rest, have a picnic, or enjoy tea and refreshments at the tea rooms provided adjoining the pump room of the mill.

As a working mill the atmosphere is resonant of the past, and there is so much for all the family to see in such a small area that you will want to spend a good half a day here, savouring this unique Suffolk watermill which is set in surroundings reminiscent of a landscape painting.

Pakenham Watermill & Wildlife Park, Grimestone End, Pakenham
Tel: 01787 247179

What makes Pakenham so unique is that it has two working mills, for to the west of the watermill, near Fulmer Bridge, stands a magnificent five-storey tower windmill; darkly tarred and dramatic enough to have 'starred' in a host of television programmes, including 'Campion'.

Pakenham Fen used to be known as 'fowl mere' (from which the bridge takes its name) and was used extensively for the cultivation of reeds for thatching. There are some splendid buildings in the village, including the 17th century **Nether Hall**, built on the site of an earlier house which belonged to the Pakenham family of which Lord Longford is a descendant.

A circular walk around the village leads close by the house across spectacular parkland, and also en route is **Newe House** from the same period, a handsome Jacobean building with Dutch gables and a two-storey porch. Above the village stands the lovely St Mary's Church, with its striking octagonal crossing tower and beautifully carved Perpendicular font. Walking up The Street, look out for the ancient chalk pit known locally as the Dell, which in spring makes a pretty picture when the snowdrops and aconites are in bloom.

IXWORTH. This ancient village, the Romans and Saxons lived here, is a veritable treasure-trove of beautiful timber-framed buildings standing side-by-side with later houses boasting Georgian facades. Just west of St Mary's Church, a footpath leads to 'The Abbey', and although this Georgian house may seem an unlikely place to bear such a name, the building does indeed incorporate the 12th and 13th century remains of an Augustinian priory that was founded here in 1170. In the church is an effigy to Sir Richard Codington, who was made lord of the manor by Henry VIII in recompense for handing over Codington Manor in Surrey; which was then transformed into the Palace of Nonesuch for Anne Boleyn. Alas, that romantically named showpiece is no more.

WALSHAM LE WILLOWS. On the banks of a willow tree over-hung tributary of the River Bourn, this village's name conjures up thoughts of picnics and boats and lazy summer afternoons. So named a village might not live up to expectations - but not a bit of it. Walsham is simply lovely, with weatherboarded and timber-framed cottages fronting the river which flows through the village. This is English 'riverscape' at its best.

St Mary's Church is no less pleasing to the eye, with its sturdy western tower and handsome windows in the Perpendicular style. Of particular interest inside is the superb tie and hammerbeam roof of the nave, and (unique in Suffolk and very rare elsewhere) a tiny circular medallion which hangs suspended from the nave wall, known as a 'Maiden's Garland' or 'Virgin's Crant'. These marked the pew seats of unmarried girls who had passed away, and the old custom was for the young men of the village to hang garlands of flowers from them on the anniversary of the girl's death. This particular example celebrates the virginity of one Mary Boyce, who died (so the inscription says) of a broken heart in 1685, just 20 years old. There is also see a carving on the rood screen which looks rather like the face of a wolf: this may well be a reference to the benevolent creature that plays such an important role in the legend of St Edmund.

BARDWELL. A fine 19th century tower windmill at the northern end of the village. Unfortunately, the mill lost its sails during the dreadful storms of 1987, so electricity is now the power source used to produce the stoneground flour on offer here. Bread made from this flour is also for sale in the small bakery attached to the mill, and do note that the flour is organic. This enchanting village also boasts a 16th century inn.

HONINGTON. This village, situated in Breckland countryside, was the birthplace of the poet Robert Bloomfield, author of the 'The Farmer's Boy' and 'Rural Tales'. Although he received patronage from the Duke of Grafton, he died half-blind and impoverished in 1823.

There is some beautiful countryside for walkers around here, notably **Knettishall Heath Country Park** to the northeast with its 400 acres of prime Breckland terrain. The Heath has been designated a Site of Special Scientific Interest, and there are circular waymarked walks, picnic areas and facilities for horse riding. This is the official starting place of both the Peddars Way National Trail and the Angles Way Path, the latter stretching for 77 miles from here to Great Yarmouth and taking in the peaceful scenery of the Little Ouse and Waveney valleys.

REDGRAVE. The source of the Little Ouse and Waveney rivers, which form the Suffolk/Norfolk border, can be found here. The ditch to the west of the B1113 is the source of the Little Ouse, while the ditch to the east of the road is that of the Waveney and the rivers flow from here in opposite directions. There is access from the road to the 360 acre valley fen reserve of Redgrave and Lopham Fens, an internationally important wetland site of reed and sedge beds on either side of the Waveney. Among the many small invertebrates that make their home here is the unique Great Raft Spider; in real life, a lot smaller that its name suggests.

BOTESDALE. An attractive village which was once an important thoroughfare in the old coaching days. Its name was derived from St Botolph as there is a chapel dedicated to him here, but other sources cite a local tribal chief called Botwulf.

RICKINGHALL SUPERIOR and INFERIOR. Presumably, the inhabitants of Rickinghall Inferior have now come to terms with the fact that this imaginary line so cruelly distinguishes them from their neighbours at Rickinghall Superior. There was a Roman settlement here and the two villages are separated by the boundary separating East and West Suffolk. The churches of both villages are dedicated to St Mary, and each is rich in fine flushwork and tracery.

WORTHAM. Another church dedicated to St Mary can be found here, this one instantly recognisable by the breadth of its round tower. It is, in fact, the broadest round church tower in England, and may well have been used as a lookout station to warn of invaders. The Waveney was a known route used by Scandinavian marauders on their way to plunder the towns and villages of East Anglia and, appropriately enough, its name means 'troubled water'.

YAXLEY. This large village also has a church dedicated to St Mary! Lovers of unusual church artifacts will find something of particular interest in this beautiful 400 year old church. The item in question is an extremely rare Sexton's Wheel which hangs above the south door and was used in medieval times to select fast days in honour of the Virgin - or Lady Fasts, as they were known. When a pair of iron wheels were spun on their axle, strings attached to the outer wheel would catch on the inner one, stopping the rotation of both and denoting the 'chosen' day. This is one of only two surviving Sexton's Wheels in England, the other being at Long Stratton in Norfolk. Also worth seeing at Yaxley's church is the sumptuously carved 17th century pulpit, which is widely held to be the finest of its kind in the country.

THE BULL AUBERGE lies on the main A140 Norwich to Ipswich road, opposite the B1117 to Eye. Originally a 15th century private house it has been sympathetically converted into a superb inn with its high ceilings and intricately carved beams retained which add an air of style. As well as being a wonderful pub serving excellent beers and wines, the owners, Dee and John Stenhouse, have established an enviable reputation for their high class restaurant here. Well known in the local area, the food here is truly wonderful. The menu changes daily to include only the freshest ingredients and there is always a host of interesting and tasty dishes from which to choose. Fish features heavily, and not just the usual fish but more interesting and exotic species. Well presented in delicious and unusual sauces with crisp vegetables, it is a delight to dine here. Once found, this is just the sort of place you will want to come back to time and time again.

The Bull Auberge, Yaxley Tel: 01379 783604

THORNHAM PARVA. The tiny, thatched church at Thornham Parva stands in the middle of a field and features the most exquisite medieval altar painting (known as a retable); its central panel depicts the Crucifixion, with four saints on each of the side panels. It dates back to around 1300 and is in remarkably good condition. Like so many of these magnificent relics, nothing is known for sure about the artists responsible; although there is some evidence to suggest that it may have originated in the Royal Workshops at Westminster Abbey and that it was made specifically for Thetford Priory.

It is only by chance that this immensely valuable painting rose again to see the light of day, for it was discovered in 1927 amongst a pile of jumble bought at a farm auction in nearby Stradbroke - it still carries the auctioneers tag to this day! Add to this the splendour of the recently restored 15th century wall paintings here. Unfortunately, this simple little church needs to be kept securely locked to guard its main treasure, but a key may be obtained from the house nearest the church.

THORNHAM MAGNA. Just a mile south of its twin, Thornham Magna has a delightful, traditional inn called the Four Horseshoes, which has been offering hospitality to travellers since 1150.

The Thornham Estate has been home to the Henniker family since 1756. **Thornham Hall** burnt down in 1955, but today, visitors can enjoy the 2,500 acres of working farmland, ancient woodland, parkland and wetland that makes up the estate. Thornham Walks have been opened up allowing public access to some 12 miles of footpaths, leading deep into countryside where deer and orchids may be seen, together with a colourful profusion of primroses in the spring. A Field Study Centre has been set up at Red House Yard, helping visitors to appreciate the countryside and rural life by providing a range of courses, activities and guided walks. All types of groups are catered for, and there are excellent facilities for the disabled. There is a charge for any group using the Estate, to cover use of the facilities and insurance.

For further details on all the many facilities here, including accommodation telephone (01379) 838153.

GISLINGHAM.

The Old Guildhall, Mill Street, Gislingham Tel: 01379 783361

THE OLD GUILDHALL in the heart of the old Suffolk village of Gislingham is a charming and comfortable hotel that is a pleasure to visit. Dating back to the 15th century, the hotel exhibits the traditional timber-framed architecture of that era though inside you will find the modern comforts of the 20th century perfectly blended with the traditional and timeless atmosphere. Owned and personally run by Ethel and Ray Tranter, the Old Guildhall offers a quiet and relaxing break in the heart of Constable country. Each of the hotel's charming bedrooms has its own private bathroom as well as a colour television and tea and coffee making facilities. The restaurant serves the best in traditional English cuisine accompanied by a selection of fine wines and excellent service to match. Surrounded by a large and mature typically English garden this is a truly delightful place to take a relaxing and enjoyable holiday.

WICKHAM SKEITH. A treasure trove of coins dating back to the reigns of King Harold and Edward the Confessor was discovered under an oak tree at Wizard Farm in the village. 'Skeith' comes from a Scandinavian word meaning 'race-course' which would be appropriate with Newmarket not so many miles away.

In 1825 the village witnessed the 'trial by swimming' of a local witch; one of the last recorded cases in the county. A poor pedlar, Isaac Stebbing, was accused of driving two local inhabitants mad, presumably by evil curses. As a consequence, his feet and hands were bound together and he was thrown into the village pond three times to see how he fared. Isaac floated like a log on each occasion which meant that he was guilty and it was only the intervention of the parson that saved him from the vengeance of the locals.

COTTON. The village is home to the fascinating **Mechanical Music Museum**. This is a 'must' for those who remember and love the great Wurlitzer Theatre Organ, seen here in a reconstructed cinema setting. Street organs, gramophones, musical boxes and dolls are just some of the items on display in the museum's extensive collection. The museum is open from June to September.

BACTON. This charming, agricultural village was once the scene of a brutal murder. And, on a lighter note, it also has a handsome 14th and 15th century church.

Brickwall Farm, Broad Road, Bacton Tel: 01449 780197

Just outside Stowmarket on the B1113 in the village of Bacton, Margaret and Bill Wright offer highly commended accommodation in their home of **BRICKWALL FARM**. It is an impressive 17th century period farmhouse recently restored to a high standard and is a Grade II listed building. The rooms are well decorated and the original beams and features are shown to great effect. The en-suite bathrooms also have a high standard of decor, and again, have exposed beams and luxury touches. You are sure to enjoy the very good home cooking and Margaret will provide evening meals by arrangement. Very impressive and well worth a visit. ETB 2 - Crown Highly Commended.

MENDLESHAM. Whilst in this area it is almost impossible not to notice the massive mast of the television transmitter that was erected to the south-east of the village in 1959 by the IBA. Standing 1,000 ft high, it now connects these isolated villages to the outside world. Less impressive in stature, but infinitely more agreeable in form, Mendlesham's church boasts some fine carvings and a splendid collection of armour dating back to 1470.

HAUGHLEY. All that now remains of the huge motte and bailey castle, built here by Hugh de Montfort, is a mound behind the church. Nevertheless it is an imposing mound, standing 80 ft high; this was the largest Norman motte and bailey in Suffolk.

To find **Haughley Park**, ignore the signs to the village from the A45 and continue westwards for a mile and a half until you come to the magnificent park and handsome manor house. Andrew Sulyard (who held the presumably enviable title of 'esquire of the body' to Mary Tudor) was granted the manor in 1538, and following the queen's death in 1558, it went to his nephew, Sir John.

This handsome red-brick mansion was built by the third Sir John Sulyard in 1620. In 1961, a major fire destroyed the Jacobean staircase, but this has now been meticulously recreated in oak. The fireplace in the hall was carved in 1964 by the firm of Hallidays of Dorchester, their young carver having taken only two weeks to complete his work.

The 8 acres of gardens and surrounding woodland are lovely, with masses of flowering shrubs and herbaceous plants, and some splendid trees, one magnolia is 40 ft wide, while the oldest oak tree has stood here for 1,000 years. Exploring the many woodland paths will take you past a half-mile stretch of rhododendrons, and bluebells and lilies of the valley create their own special magic in the spring. Haughley Park is now the private residence, but the doors are open to the public from May to September on Tuesday afternoons from 3.00 pm to 6.00 pm.

One of the finest eating places in Suffolk can be found overlooking the green in the historic village of Haughley. The **OLD COUNTING HOUSE RESTAURANT** is a part-medieval timber-framed building which is believed to have been an early bank, or counting house. The interior seats 46 diners in comfort and has a delightful, relaxed atmosphere, with low ceilings and exposed timber beams.

Proprietors Sue and Paul Woods offer first-class service and superb cuisine. During 1996, they organised a highly successful 'gastronomic world tour' on the last Friday of each month which took in such diverse destinations as Mexico, Sweden and the Caribbean.

Old Counting House Restaurant, Haughley Tel: 01449 673617

SHELLAND. **SHELLAND HALL**, the home of Sally Farrington, is well worth the bumpy ride down the drive to this secluded spot off the Woolpit to Stowmarket road. A typical Suffolk timber framed house, built in 1568, it retains many of its original features but also offers plenty of modern comforts. Sally has three guest rooms from which she offers exceptional bed and breakfast accommodation. In such an isolated spot Sally also provides evening meals which rival any to be found in the area. Guests also have their own dining room and a delightful sitting room in which to relax. Also popular, in warm weather, is the swimming pool.

Shelland Hall, Shelland Tel: 01449 786524

ELMSWELL. With an imposing flint-towered church that over-shadows the village, Elmswell's population has grown since the development work of the 1960s.

ELMSWELL HALL is a large Georgian farmhouse situated down a private road leading from the village of Elmswell. Set in some 6 acres of land, Kate Over offers bed and breakfast accommodation in two large, heated rooms on this working farm. An accomplished cook, all guests, after spending a very comfortable night, can be assured of a traditional, hearty English breakfast served in the delightful dining room. There is also a separate guest lounge. In all directions there are wonderful views over the sweeping countryside and, along with the warm, friendly welcome, this is a charming and peaceful place to stay.

Elmswell Hall, Elmswell Tel: 01359 240215

WOOLPIT. Four miles west of Bury St Edmunds lies the village of Woolpit with its glorious church ideally situated to welcome visitors. There is a carpark opposite. The Church of St Mary the Virgin stands proud on the site of a Saxon church. Like many other churches it evolved up to the time of the Reformation with its North and South aisles and the raising of both the chancel and nave roofs. But unlike other churches St Mary is fortunate to have one of the most magnificent 'double hammer beam' roofs in its chapel and also a most noble porch. Up to the time of the Reformation the church came under the control of the Abbot at Bury St Edmunds and the building was held in high respect. A detailed guide is available in the church.

Heading from the church to the village centre you come to the village sign. This depicts not only the church but a wolf and two green children. Folklore recalls that the last wolf in Britain was slain here and that in the 13th century two green children appeared from a cave attracted by the ringing of the church bells.

The name Woolpit does not come from the wool trade and neither is it thought to be derived from the pits used for trapping wolves. Perhaps the word originated from the time of the Danish occupation, when a Danish nobleman died and a pit was dug for his burial which was named after the deceased. In about the 8th century this area of Suffolk had a Danish Earl by the name of Ulfketyle. When he died it is thought that his burial pit was named 'Ulfpit' and early spellings of Woolpit have been shown as 'wulpet' and 'wulpytte'. What we do know is that Woolpit's history goes back over a thousand years. Following the road takes you to the heart of the village, a conservation area, and in the centre is the pump erected to celebrate Queen Victoria's jubilee.

A visit to **ELM TREE GALLERY** is a must. Housed in the 'Old Bakery' it is a building of Tudor origins and an Aladdin's cave of attractive gifts and paintings by local artists. Items for sale include an extensive range of jewellery and probably one of the best selections of greetings cards in the region. Ceramics, toys and many other gift items are also on offer. Tea and coffee, home-made cakes and scones are always available. Open all year. Tel: 01359 240255.

Woolpit is very proud of its **Museum** situated in the Institute opposite the Old Bakery. Run by volunteers it is open Saturdays, Sundays and Bank Holidays from 2.30 pm until 5 pm from Easter until the end of September. The Museum changes its displays annually and aims to tell the story of the evolution of the village of Woolpit. Guided tours of the village are available lasting from 1 to 3 hours, including the Church, Conservation area, Museum, Brickworks and Ladyswell. The Museum can be opened at other times by appointment, groups welcome. Tel: 01359 240822/240764.

The majority of the buildings in the village centre date from the 15th and 16th centuries and are timber framed. Because the village was the site of a brick works almost all the old buildings have been faced with 'Woolpit Whites'. This famous brick, along with the red brick, was made in the village for well over 400 years and has been used in the construction of buildings nationally. One such place to visit is Ladyswell, a moated site at least 1,000 years old, that is now a pocket park. For many years this site has been a place to visit. The waters from the spring were said to cure eye ailments and pilgrims also visited the area on their way to Walsingham. Today the site is maintained by Woolpit volunteers.

The Bull, The Street, Woolpit

Another interesting building is **THE BULL** public house, expertly run by Trevor and Valerie Howling. There is a separate restaurant at the rear of the pub and a conservatory offers an alternative sitting area for the summer evenings. Accommodation is available in en-suite bedrooms where decorations, beds and furnishings are to a high standard. A full English breakfast is cooked to perfection. The garden offers good space and is ideal for children. Well situated for touring in this popular area.

The **SWAN INN**, in the main square of Woolpit, has had a very interesting life. The first authentic record dates from 1625 though it was thought to have been built during the 16th century. With few travellers passing through the village there was little use for an inn at that time as it was probably an ale house.

Swan Inn, Woolpit Tel: 01359 240482

Following extensive building work in 1759, the inn started taking in overnight guests and during the French Wars in the 19th century it was used to billet soldiers and their horses. Further extensions and renovations took place in 1826 and the present brick front was added around this time. Today the Swan Inn, owned by Linda and Nick Day, is still offering hospitality in six bedrooms, all centrally heated with colour TVs and tea and coffee making facilities. Very much the focal point of the village, the pub serves an excellent pint of ale in pleasant and comfortable surroundings. Popular bar meals are available evenings and weekends.

Over the centuries agricultural farming has been the main source of employment in the village; from the days of strip farming until the open field policy of today. **GRANGE FARM** is still a working farm and one time was part of a much larger estate.

Grange Farm Tel: 01359 241143

Today, it is the home of Mr and Mrs Tim Parker and offers good value accommodation. There are three letting rooms, one double and two twin, two of which are en suite. A substantial breakfast is served in the family dining room where you will find many portraits of Parker ancestors. The house is furnished mostly with pieces handed down through the family. About 200 years old, the house is set in a large garden with surrounding ponds and plenty of wildlife. There are caravanning facilities on the farm and a pond for fishing, also a farm shop and butchers providing local produce and soft fruit grown on the farm when in season. There are two bicycles that are available for hire. The Parker's family home is happy and friendly and gives you a feel of country life without costing a fortune.

HESSETT. As befits a church dedicated to the King of East Anglia, St Ethelbert's in Hessett is a splendid flint building which is obviously well-kept up by the parishioners. It has been described as a 'museum church' due to its many notable features, perhaps the best of them being some beautiful 16th century glass and a remarkable set of wall paintings that escaped the desecrations of the iconoclasts in 1643.

LITTLE WELNETHAM. Finding a rake factory in this little village is not as strange as it may first sound, as the local Monkspark and Felshamhall Woods at Bradfield are used to grow coppice. Trees are carefully cut or 'pollarded' to encourage branches to grow straight up like poles, which local woodworkers then transform into brooms, fence posts, scythe handles, and of course - rakes! Apparently, these ancient woodlands have been coppiced in this fashion since 1252, and for those who are interested in finding out more about the process, there is a Visitor Centre here with plenty of useful information.

South Suffolk and the Border with Essex

SUDBURY. This ancient market town is situated in the Stour valley; the river flows around the town in a great loop, and the combination of picturesque watermeadows and gentle, rolling countryside makes for a very pleasant setting.

It is easy to see how such scenes of rural beauty must have inspired Sudbury's most famous son, Thomas Gainsborough. The painter was born here in 1727, and his birthplace and home for many years can be found in Gainsborough Street, just off Market Hill.

Sudbury's origins go right back to Saxon times, and its market was first mentioned in the Domesday Survey of 1086. In those days, the market was held between School Street and Stour Street, whereas today it is held at the bottom of Market Hill, every Thursday and Saturday. This was the largest of Suffolk's wool towns (with silk production coming later) and, unlike Lavenham, it kept its industry because it was a port.

One consequence of this was that it saw far greater changes in its architectural styles than its declining neighbour, and today's visitors can enjoy a wealth of historic buildings from many different periods. Among these are the mid 19th century **Corn Exchange** on Market Hill, now the public library; **Salter's Hall** (a merchant's house) and the **Old Moot Hall** in Stour Street - both 15th century timber-framed houses with ornate carving and oriel windows. The remains of the Dominican Priory in Friars Street, which was founded in 1248, survive in parts as the Priory Gate and the Ship and Star inn.

The 3 miles Valley Walk, passing alongside the river through watermeadows, follows the course of the old Stour Valley railway line. For those that wish to explore the area from the river itself, look out for Sudbury Boathouse at Ballingdon Bridge, where rowing boats can be hired in the summer. Remember to take a sketch pad or, for those less artistically inclined, a camera!

Standing beside the river and overlooking Friars' Meadow, **The Quay** is definitely the place to visit for an excellent evening's entertainment. This 200 year old converted granary is considered to be one of East Anglia's most exciting arts centres, with cabaret, theatre, cinema, musical concerts and arts and crafts classes on offer here throughout the year.

Finally, those who enjoy visiting churches will need to set aside a few hours to indulge in their favourite pastime here, for there is much to see. **All Saints'** Church in Church Street dates back to the 15th century and has a glorious carved tracery pulpit and screens; the 14th century **St Gregory's**, which stands to the north of the town on the Croft, boasts one of the finest medieval font covers in England; and **St Peter's** at the top of Market Hill has some wonderful painted screen panels and a splendid piece of 15th century embroidery on velvet, known as the 'Sudbury Pall'. Now a redundant church, St Peter's is used mainly as a concert hall and outside stands a bronze statue of Sudbury's most famous son.

Gainsborough's House, 46 Gainsborough Street, Sudbury
Tel: 01787 372958

GAINSBOROUGH'S HOUSE is the birthplace of Thomas Gainsborough RA (1727-88) and is a real treasure house full of the work of one of Britain's greatest artists. The Georgian fronted town house, with attractive walled garden, displays more of the artist's work than any other gallery. The collection is shown together with eighteenth-century furniture and memorabilia. The Museum has a commitment to contemporary art which is reflected in a varied programme of exhibitions throughout the year. These include fine art, craft, photography, printmaking, sculpture and highlights the work of East Anglian artists. Telephone for information about opening times. Free entry in December.

The **WAGGON AND HORSES** public house is not that easy to find, down Gaol Lane by the Tourist Information Centre in Acton Square, but well worth it. Owned and run by Nick Irwin, Sudbury's longest serving landlord and a self taught chef, this is a well managed establishment that offers a warm welcome and much more besides. Built around a courtyard, the inn is full of character and charm with many interesting artefacts adorning the walls. The sheltered courtyard also makes an ideal place to sit and drink in the summer. Along with an excellent range of beers, ales and wines, Nick also serves a delicious range of tasty dishes in the small restaurant. The main bar is a long, half-panelled room with a Victorian fireplace. The Waggon and Horses also has an interesting line in pub games. Along the long main bar they hold races using miniature wooden racehorses - a pleasant change from the more usual video games! Accommodation is also available in three bedrooms.

Waggon and Horses, Acton Square, Sudbury Tel: 01787 312147

AROUND SUDBURY

THORPE MORIEUX. St Mary's Church in Thorpe Morieux is situated in as pleasant a setting as anyone could wish to find. With water meadows, ponds, a stream and a fine Tudor farmhouse to set it off, this 14th century church presents a memorable picture of old England. If you have had your fill of church interiors for a while - though St Mary's has much to interest the enthusiast - then at least take the time to wander around the peaceful churchyard here with its glorious profusion of aconites in early springtime, followed by the colourful flowering of limes and chestnuts in the summer.

HITCHAM. This is a charming village of thatched cottages and John Henslow, Charles Darwin's mentor, is buried here. The racehorses of Newmarket may be well beyond the reach of the average purse, but here at the northern end of the village, is Hitcham's Horses. A wonderful shop selling hand-carved rocking horses, they need a lot less upkeep than the real thing!

BILDESTON. The charming **KING'S HEAD** stands opposite the Market Place in the heart of the sleepy Suffolk village of Bildeston. Built in the 1470s, the attractive King's Head was a wool warehouse before becoming an inn in the 16th century. Since then, the inn has been offering excellent hospitality. Today, this family run free house offers a super range of real ales and is renowned for its Beer Festival held every Whitsuntide. In the true traditional of innkeeping, the King's Head also offers excellent food and comfortable overnight accommodation. All the five bedrooms have en-suite bathrooms, televisions and tea and coffee making facilities. The restaurant is open everyday for lunch and dinner and there is a wonderful Sunday lunch menu. Full of character, the King's Head is the perfect place to stay to discover the delights of rural Suffolk.

King's Head, 132 High Street, Bildeston Tel: 01449 741434

CHELSWORTH. Here, a picturesque two-arched bridge crosses the River Brett, which flows close by All Saints Church then makes its way through the parkland of Chelsworth Hall. The centre of the village is a vision of timber-framed, thatched houses, and once a year, almost every property in the village opens its colourful gardens to the public.

MONKS ELEIGH. This is a perfect example of the traditional English village, with colour-washed thatched houses and a 14th century church grouped around the village green and pump. So picturesque is the setting, in fact, that it featured regularly on railway posters at one time to lure visitors to this beautiful corner of England.

LAVENHAM. The jewel in Suffolk's crown Lavenham proudly claims to be the finest surviving medieval town in England. Considerable care has been taken to ensure that the medieval character of this lovely wool-trading town has remained unspoiled by modern developments. As they wander through its twisting streets and marvel at the wealth of magnificent buildings on every corner, visitors to this wonder-

Guildhall, Lavenham

The Crooked House, Lavenham

ful small town find it hard to disagree.

From the 14th to 16th centuries, Lavenham flourished as one of the foremost and wealthiest wool and cloth-making centres in the country, specialising in blue broadcloth. The demise of this industry and the steady decline in the town's fortunes began in the second half of the 16th century and, ironically, it is largely due to the fact that Lavenham never found another industry to reverse its fall from prosperity that it remains such an attractive and fascinating town today. Unlike other places in Suffolk that saw an energetic programme of rebuilding and redevelopment during the 18th century, there is no sweeping evidence of a Georgian 'invasion' as far as Lavenham's architecture is concerned - it was simply not rich enough at that time to make such a thing possible.

And so, centuries later, it stays a delightful medieval and Tudor town which has remained almost untouched by later styles; firmly rooted in its ancient traditions, yet at the same time no mouldering museum piece but a thriving little town with much to offer today's visitors. The residents here have gone to great lengths to maintain the original character of the town: telegraph poles were removed in 1967 and cables buried underground, and even such familiar sights as television aerials have been hidden away in the attics of the houses!

Lavenham's medieval street pattern is still in existence today, complete with the market place and market cross - erected in 1501 and thought to have originally been a preaching cross. This was used as a setting in that wonderful old horror film: 'Witchfinder General'. Although the market place is almost entirely surrounded by timber-framed buildings (Lavenham has more than 300 buildings which are officially listed as being of architectural and historical interest) perhaps the finest of them all is the **Guildhall**. Dating from the early part of the 16th century, this was originally the meeting hall of the Guild of Corpus Christi, an organisation that regulated the production of local wool. It has since served many purposes, and has at various times been a prison, workhouse, almshouse and woolstore. It is now owned by the National Trust and houses a museum of local history, with a fascinating exhibition covering seven centuries of the cloth industry.

Also in the market place is the **Little Hall**, a 15th century former Hall House and now headquarters of the Suffolk Preservation Society. Both the house and its lovely enclosed garden are open to the public during the summer. Dating back originally to the 13th century, **The Priory** in Water Street was first the home of Benedictine monks, and was bought by a wealthy clothier after the Dissolution. The entire building as seen today was completed by 1600. It contains medieval and Jacobean staircases, a Tudor brick fireplace, mullioned windows and the best examples of pargeting to be found anywhere in the town.

Now a private house, the Priory is open to visitors from Easter to the end of October, and you can also explore nearly 4 acres of grounds at the rear of the building, which feature a kitchen garden, a herb garden, a pond and a fascinating derelict building which illustrates the condition the property was in when the present owners took it over. Guided tours for groups can be arranged, and there is also a restaurant serving morning coffee, home-made lunches and afternoon teas, and a gift shop with a most unusual selection of gifts and crafts including woven tapestries and plants from the herb garden.

Across the road, the **Wool Hall** was built in 1464 and was originally the hall of Our Lady's Guild. It now forms part of the splendid Swan Hotel, but was nearly lost altogether in 1911 when the Duchess of Argyll decided to 'up timbers', dismantle the entire building and remove it to Ascot. Local feeling ran so high that the plan was abandoned and the hall was returned to the town and re-erected in its rightful place. Lavenham also has its connections with the Arts: John Constable attended the Old Grammar School in Barn Street and Shilling Grange in Shilling Street was once the home of Jane Taylor. Her name may not ring any bells at first, until you learn that she wrote that immortal nursery rhyme, familiar to us all, 'Twinkle Twinkle Little Star.'

Many of Lavenham's half-timbered houses stand at such crazy angles that you wonder what is actually stopping them from giving in to gravity and sliding down the streets - a good example being the Crooked House in the historic High Street.

The magnificent church of St Peter and St Paul stands on a hill above the town, completely dominating the view. Regarded as the greatest of all the 'wool churches' in East Anglia and declared by the 19th century architect August Pugin to be the finest example of Late Perpendicular in the world, it owes its cathedral-like appearance principally to the generosity of two great families, the Springs and the de Veres, Earls of Oxford. It was built during the late 15th and early 16th centuries to celebrate the end of the Wars of the Roses in 1485. Sadly, its original stained glass fell victim to the Puritan zealot William Dowsing, who was responsible for so much destruction in his role as 'Parliamentary Visitor to the Churches of Suffolk' - so the glass we see today is coloured Victorian. That aside, the interior has much for the visitor to enjoy, and if you are feeling especially fit you can even climb up the massive 140 ft flint tower and take in the glorious views over Lavenham and the surrounding countryside.

THE GREAT HOUSE, overlooking the Market Place in the heart of the medieval town of Lavenham, was built in the 14th and 15th centuries though its imposing Georgian façade was added in the 18th century. Owned and run as a hotel and restaurant by Martine and Regis Crêpy since 1985, the Great House provides an authentic flavour of France in the heart of England.

Traditionally decorated and furnished in a style in keeping with the age of the building, you can be sure of a warm and hearty welcome. The restaurant is well renowned; there is a bistro menu for light lunches and á la carte and table d'hôte menus for gourmet dinners. All the French rural style dishes are freshly prepared using nothing but the best produce. A secluded paved courtyard, bedecked with baskets of flowers, is perfect for al fresco lunches and dinners. The Great House also has four en-suite bedrooms which are charmingly furnished and offer all the comforts demanded by today's traveller.

The Great House, Market Place, Lavenham Tel: 01787 247431

THE RED HOUSE, just a few minutes walk from the centre of Lavenham, occupies a lovely secluded location in a quiet area of the town. This Victorian house was built in 1890 at the cost of £138! Easy to pick out as it is constructed using red bricks, unlike the buildings around, this is the charming home of Diana Schofield. With three comfortable en-suite bedrooms and a delicious home-cooked evening meal by arrangement, Diana offers wonderful bed and breakfast accommodation in the heart of this medieval town. As well as enjoying the comfort of the house, there is a rustic garden that is an absolute treat to sit in and laze away the summer days. As well as being a very accomplished cook, Diana is also a keen archaeologist and there are many interesting artefacts decorating the house. A delightful place to stay with a wonderful hostess.

The Red House, 29 Bolton Street, Lavenham Tel: 01787 248074

BURES. Here, the River Stour turns sharply to the east and heads off towards the coast, creating the natural boundary between Suffolk and North Essex. Straddling the Stour, this little town lies partly in Essex and partly in Suffolk, and on the Suffolk side of the river brick and half-

Stoke-by-Nayland

timbered houses cling to a hillside overlooking the market place and St Mary's Church. Half a mile to the north-east on the road to Boxford, look out for the signpost to St Stephen's Chapel, which was consecrated in 1218 to commemorate the place where St Edmund was crowned King of East Anglia - on Christmas Day, 855 AD. From here it is only a few minutes to the Arger Fen nature reserve, a pleasant stretch of varied woodland renowned for its springtime flowers.

The narrow lane leading east from Bures is a sheer delight. Quickly dispelling any ideas that Suffolk is flat, this twisting road leads you deep into the heart of 'Constable country', high above the River Stour, with green meadows dotted with solitary houses stretching out on either side.

NAYLAND. The narrow winding streets of this pretty village are full of picturesque colour-washed houses with overhanging timbers. Right in the centre of the village are Alston Court, a 15th century house with mullioned windows and a large hooded 17th century door, and the parish church of St James, which dates from 1400. The chief treasure of the church is Constable's 'Christ's blessing of the Bread and Wine', which he painted in 1809. It hangs above the altar and is one of only two paintings by him to have a religious theme.

STOKE-BY-NAYLAND. One of the most memorable views over the Stour valley can be enjoyed by taking the B1087 northeast of Nayland to neighbouring Stoke-by-Nayland.

This delightful village stands on a bluff of land which rises above the meadows of Dedham Vale. The Vale contains many country lanes and footpaths which are ideal for exploring on foot or by bicycle, and the village church with its 120 ft tower appears in several Constable landscapes.

The massive church of St Mary the Virgin seems almost preposterously large for a village of this size. Among the many impressive brasses and memorials inside is a 16th century brass of Lady Howard, an ancestor of two of Henry VIII's wives, Catherine Howard and Anne Boleyn. On a wooded hillside to the south of the church stands a neat little row of timbered almshouses, while just a short stroll from the church in School Street are two extremely fine 16th century half-timbered buildings, the Guildhall and the Maltings, now converted into cottages.

Stoke-by-Nayland stands just a short distance from the River Stour within an Area of Outstanding Natural Beauty,

POLSTEAD. This pretty, tucked away village was the scene of the notorious 'Red Barn Murder'. It was here, in 1827, that a young girl called Maria Marten was brutally murdered by William Corder, her lover and the father of her illegitimate child. It was widely thought that Maria had eloped with Corder to London and married him there, but her stepmother dreamed three times that she had in fact been murdered and buried in the barn. Pressed by his wife, Maria's father dug at the floor of the barn and found her body buried there. Corder was eventually tracked down to Middlesex, where he was married to a woman he had met through a matrimonial advertisement. He was found guilty of Maria's murder and hanged, and his skin was used to bind a copy of the trial proceedings. Together with Corder's scalp, this grisly document can be seen at Moyses Hall in Bury St Edmunds.

Those visitors who want to see the local scenes associated with this dreadful crime will find an excellent guide to the village in the church. The barn itself burned down shortly after the event, and the approximate site of Maria's grave is now marked by a sign - her tombstone having been chipped away over the years by souvenir hunters, eager for fragments to display on their mantle-pieces! The thatched cottage which was Maria's home still stands in what is now called Marten's Lane, as does the farm in the centre of the village where Corder lived - now known as Corder's Farm.

In stark contrast to all this unpleasantness, Polstead is in fact an extremely pretty village, nestling in wooded, hilly countryside and surrounded by cherry orchards - the 'Polstead Black' is regarded very highly by those who know their cherries! Thatched and colour-washed cottages surround the village green at the top of Polstead Hill, and as befits a place whose name means 'place of pools', a broad duck pond fringed with trees dominates the centre of the village at the bottom of the hill. Standing on a rise above the pond are Polstead Hall and the 12th century St Mary's Church, the latter being notable for its unusual brickwork. At this time, brick-making was almost unheard of in England, but the brickwork of the arches and windows suggests that the Norman builders here had perfected the craft which elsewhere was forgotten when the Romans left our shores.

BOXFORD. This is another glorious example of an unspoilt Suffolk village. Surrounded by the peaceful watermeadows of the River Box, Boxford is a traditional weaving village with some of the most highly colourful houses to be found anywhere in the area. St Mary's Church dates back to the 14th century and its wooden north porch is said to be the oldest one of its kind in the county, if not in England.

The White Hart, Broad Street, Boxford Tel: 01787 211071

Considering this is Barry & Marilyn Hayford's first entry into the 'pub' business, they have certainly got it together in fine style at **THE**

WHITE HART. There has been an inn on this site for over four hundred years and in former times was known to have been a Wool Merchant's house. Its more recent claim to fame being - local lad 'Tornado Smith' stayed here; the original wall-of-death being in the pub's car park. Nowadays, the pub has acquired a reputation for a great atmosphere and a very good menu. Try for instance, the house special 'Rocky Mountain' - Granary bread sandwich filled with deep-fried chicken breast, filled with lettuce, mayonnaise and topped with melted cheese; whatever your taste, there's plenty to choose from. Call in on Sunday and join in the quiz or make a point of visiting in August when Barry hosts a Beer Festival with across-the-board live music groups, a selection of thirty ales to sample and a Roast. Anytime is a good time to drop in at the White Hart, you will find a great welcome!

KERSEY. Nestling in the steep-sided valley of a tributary of the Brett, this delightful village seems completely transfixed in time. If approached from the direction of Lavenham, the first sighting of the village will be the massive church of St Mary standing proud on its hilltop, then all of a sudden the village itself comes into view after turning the corner into The Street, with the water-splash at the bottom. This ancient village is a glorious collection of medieval merchants' houses and weavers' cottages their red-tiled roofs weathered with age and covered with lichen.

The sheer size of the church, on Church Hill, points to the prosperity the village once enjoyed through its production of tough Kersey broadcloth. St Mary's suffered greatly at the hands of iconoclasts at the time of the Reformation, and a number of headless angels and mutilated carvings bear witness to the havoc that was wreaked during that dark period in history. Nevertheless, some of its oldest treasures are still intact and, in particular, the ornate flushwork of the 15th century south porch, with its roof of 16 traceried wooden panels inside.

The Bell, Kersey Tel: 01473 823229

One of the most memorable country inns in Suffolk is **THE BELL**, in the centre of Kersey. This timber framed property dates back to 1320 and is surely one of the oldest and most frequently photographed

'Hidden Places' featured in this book. The interior of the inn is very interesting, it features a wealth of exposed oak beams, open fireplaces, stone floors and a unique 'archway' which leads from the main bar into the 'Pink Room'- a private dining area. The Bell is also reputed to be haunted by the ghost of a mysterious man, fear not though, he is friendly - as is the welcome that you can be assured of when you visit! The hosts, Paul and Lorraine are very proud of the good reputation that their pub enjoys, there is an excellent selection of cask ales and fine wines and the home cooked fayre is delicious. So whether dining in the Bar, Restaurant, Pink Room, Covered Patio or Beer Garden, you will surely have a memorable visit, so do not miss this pub at any cost, it is a real treat!

HADLEIGH. A pleasant market town of Hadleigh with a comprehensive variety of architectural styles. Down the mile long High Street, there is a wealth of timber-framed buildings still standing today as a reminder of the prosperity that came from the wool trade in the 14th to 16th centuries. Unlike Lavenham, however, there is also an abundance of plasterwork (some of it pargetted) together with fine houses from the Regency and Victorian periods. The 135 ft broach spire of St Mary's Church soars above the town and providing an interesting contrast alongside is the red-brick Deanery Tower, built by Archdeacon William Pykenham in 1495 and now a Grade I listed building. Opposite St Mary's, in Church Square, is a splendid group of medieval buildings which includes the timber-framed Guildhall with its two overhanging upper storeys, and backing on to this are the 19th century Town Hall and Corn Exchange.

There are two good walks from the town, the first being along the banks of the River Brett with access from the 500 year old red-brick Toppesfield Bridge. This is said to be one of the oldest bridges in England still in use and nearby is Toppesfield Hall, beautifully restored and now the headquarters of the East Anglia Tourist Board. Alternatively, there is a walk along the disused railway line between Hadleigh Old Station and Raydon, a distance of about two and a half miles through peaceful countryside full of wild flowers and birdlife.

Edgehill Hotel, 2 High Street, Hadleigh Tel: 01473 822458

EDGEHILL HOTEL is ideally located on the High Street in Hadleigh near Ipswich. Built in 1590, it is one of the oldest buildings in this part of the town. The Hotel's Georgian facade and the elegant staircase were added during extensive rebuilding work in the early 1700s. Owned and personally run by Angela Rolfe, Edgehill Hotel offers a warm and friendly atmosphere to all their guests. Beautifully restored and tastefully modernised all the nine en suite bedrooms provide the creature comforts of home. The attractive walled garden is a popular place to sit and take afternoon tea or to play a leisurely game of croquet. Great care has gone into serving traditional home cooked English meals, with many of the fresh vegetables coming from the hotel's own kitchen garden. Situated in one of the most picturesque areas of Britain, Edgehill Hotel makes a wonderful and relaxing base from which to explore Suffolk and nearby Essex.

THE PARLOUR coffee shop on the main High Street in Hadleigh is a great place to escape to whilst out shopping. Originally built around 1600, the building has evolved into a dress shop with The Parlour tucked away at the back. This secluded, quiet spot is just the place to take the weight off your feet and enjoy a refreshing cup of coffee and a bite to eat. Always popular at lunchtime, when there is a wide variety of tasty, well prepared dishes available at reasonable prices, this is a cosy and friendly place that offers great service as well. During the summer, there are chairs and tables outside, so that as well as enjoying the delicious food and excellent tea and coffee served here you can also enjoy the sunshine.

Did You Know...

The Hidden Places Series
Covers most of Britain?
For our full list see back of book

The Parlour, 82 High Street, Hadleigh Tel: 01473 822243

ODDS AND ENDS has been called Odds and Ends for the last hundred years and it stands in a prominent position on the main street in Hadleigh. Owned and run as a bed and breakfast establishment by Ann Stevenson, Odds and Ends is an interesting building in itself. Built in the 17th century many alterations have been made over the years and the early Georgian facade makes this a distinctive building in the town. To the rear of the house, the south facing garden is a super place to sit in the summer months. Inside, the pleasant rooms are all traditionally decorated and furnished, giving Odds and Ends a relaxed and friendly feel. All the eight bedrooms are en-suite and they make a real home from home. Ann loves animals and has several cats and dogs herself. Naturally, your pets are welcomed, by arrangement. A super place to stay, with a wonderful atmosphere.

Odds and Ends, 131, High Street, Hadleigh Tel: 01473 822032

WOLVES WOOD. Two miles to the east of Hadleigh on the A1071 is Wolves Wood; and if the name brings to mind a dark and sinister place with wild creatures lurking behind every tree, nothing could be further from the truth. This is actually an RSPB reserve with woodland nature trails, well known for its spring orchids and nightingales in summer. The wood is open all year round at all times, and entry is free.

HINTLESHAM. Hintlesham Hall was originally the Elizabethan home of the Timperley family, but was much altered during the 18th century. More recently, it was owned by that doyen of good taste and good food, Robert Carrier, and although it has since passed into different hands, it still maintains its excellent reputation for fine cuisine. If you wish to admire the exquisite Elizabethan plasterwork ceilings today, you will have to indulge in a meal; although the public footpath that passes through the grounds will afford you a glimpse of the handsome Georgian facade for free!

BIRCH FARM is a beautiful, traditional farm cottage set in a picturesque valley in the village of Hintlesham on the A1071 main road between Ipswich and Hadleigh. This charming cottage, surrounded by some 80 acres of farmland and built in the early 19th century, is owned by Diana and Richard Bryce who offer excellent bed and breakfast accommodation. The two en-suite bedrooms are contained within a superbly converted annexe to the original cottage. The annexe also has a wonderful guest lounge with open fireplace and a fitted kitchen/dining room which has French windows leading onto the annexe's private courtyard.

There is a large playground for the children and many farm animals and pets for them to watch and enjoy. The Farm also has an indoor heated swimming pool and with plenty of gentle country walks straight from the house and quiet country lanes for cycling this is an idyllic location in the heart of the countryside.

Birch Farm, Hintlesham Tel: 01473 652249

BRAMFORD. The pretty little church of St Mary's and a fine collection of 16th and 17th century cottages gives this pleasant village plenty of character. Opposite the church, a 10 acre meadow adjacent to the River Gipping provides a lovely spot for a picnic and fishing platforms have been erected here especially for the disabled. There is also access to the Gipping River Path, a 17 mile walk along the old towpath of the river between Ipswich and Stowmarket. For those who are keen on watersports there is the nearby Suffolk Water Park, where windsurfing and canoeing are available on the lake. Craft may be hired and tuition is also provided.

LITTLE BLAKENHAM. This central Suffolk village is noted for the 5 acre bluebell wood that is thick with camellias, azaleas, rhododendrons, hydrangeas and climbing roses. It is open to the public from April to September on Wednesdays, Thursdays, Sundays and Bank Holidays from 1.00 pm - 5.00 pm.

OFFTON. **MOUNT PLEASANT FARM** lies behind the church in the village of Offton, just 8 miles west of Ipswich.

Mount Pleasant Farm, Offton Tel: 01473 658896

A 16th century Suffolk farmhouse and a Grade II listed building, it has been extended and renovated over the years to provide warmth and modern day comforts but has lost none of its character and charm. Right up until the 1950s, Mount Pleasant Farm was a Glebe Farm belonging to the Church, but today it is owned by Pam and Philip Redman who run its 8 acres with two pedigree flocks of Suffolk and Jacob sheep. The Farm also has a house cow, milking and Angora goats and several pigs are fattened throughout the year.

From this glorious house, Pam and Philip offer excellent bed and breakfast accommodation in three beautifully decorated and furnished rooms; each has either en-suite or private bathrooms. The evening meals are the speciality at Mount Pleasant and consist, in the main, of home-produced meat and vegetables. A traditional farmhouse breakfast is served in the morning.

BAYLHAM. Situated within the scheduled Roman site of Combretovium is **BAYLHAM HOUSE RARE BREEDS FARM**, whose aim is to ensure the survival of rare farm animal breeds which would otherwise be threatened with extinction. Displays and information relating to the Roman remains and the rare breeds, together with gifts and refreshments can be found in the Visitors Centre. Children will be delighted to meet the friendly animals at close quarters in the orchard, there is also a picnic area and a peaceful riverside walk. This is a great day out for all of the family.

Two self-catering units are also available should you decide to base your stay here.

Baylham House Rare Breeds Farm, Mill Lane, Baylham Tel: 01473 830264

NEEDHAM MARKET. The town's crowning glory is the wonderful carvings on the church ceiling. From the outside the church looks unremarkable, but once inside, the strategically placed skylights give the massive hammerbeam roof a glorious infusion of light and allowing visitors to fully appreciate the tremendous skills of those 15th century carpenters. It is so huge, in fact, that if it were to be removed and placed upon the ground, it would be as high as the walls of the church itself. On a less positive note, it is perhaps just as well that the hammerbeam roof catches the eye, for the church is rather sparsely adorned otherwise and has little to commend it apart from its famous roof.

The town's bridge, Chain Bridge, and also Chain House Farm are named after the chains that where laid down during the plague and beyond which the villagers were not allowed to pass.

The River Gipping flows to the east of Needham's High Street, and bordering this is a 25 acre picnic site containing a large lake. Reached either from the town centre or from the junction of the A45/A140, the lake is a glorious wildlife and wetland habitat.

Pakenham Windmill

CHAPTER ELEVEN

NORTH-EAST SUFFOLK

Orford Church

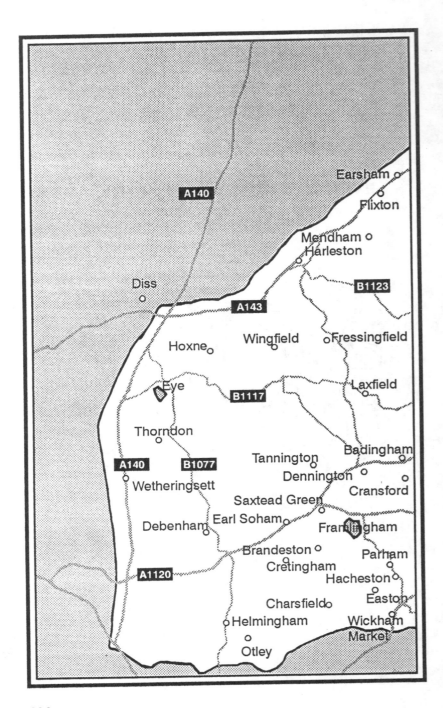

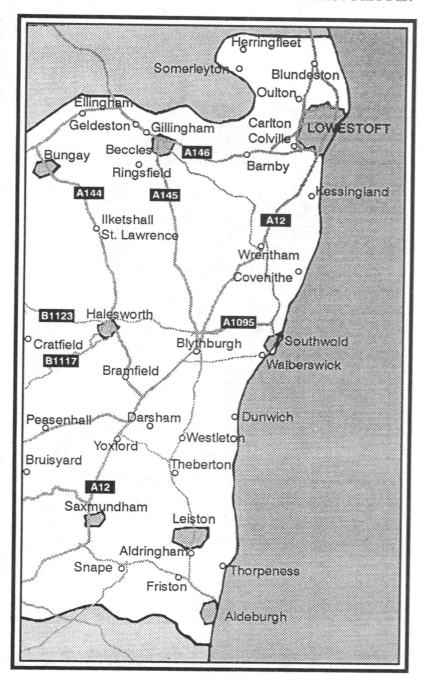

House in the Clouds, Thorpeness

CHAPTER ELEVEN

NORTH-EAST SUFFOLK

Between Eye and Halesworth

EYE. This handsome little market town takes its name from the old Saxon word for island and was, at one time, completely surrounded by water. It was founded in the 11th century by a supporter of William the Conqueror, one William Malet, who built his Norman castle on high ground above the marshes on the eastern side of the town. This was demolished by Cromwell's army in 1655 and now all that remains is the mound itself; serving no other purpose than to provide a superb vantage point over the town and the watermeadows of the River Waveney. The castellated folly that stands on top of the mound was built in 1845, using stones from the ruins of the castle. Alongside, the superb flushwork tower of the 15th century church of St Peter and St Paul soars to a height of 101 ft and inside is a magnificent rood screen, restored in 1925, with exquisite painted panels depicting St Edmund, St Ursula, St Edward the Confessor and Henry VI.

During the mid 19th century, Eye was a flourishing market town but it fell into decline when the railway line by-passed it on the way to Diss. The present Town Hall, built in the mid 1850s, stands on what was the market place in the centre of the town and the former Corn Hall it replaced is now used for a variety of social and charitable functions.

BEARD'S, next to the church in the centre of Eye, is a beautiful 14th century listed building owned by Mr and Mrs Beard. Here you will find a fantastic delicatessen and off license specialising in English and Continental cheeses, local hams, home-made desserts, local wines, beers and ciders; a charming tea room serving delicious light meals, morning coffee and afternoon tea; and, finally, excellent bed and breakfast accommodation. Beard's is a wonderful find in the midst of some beautiful countryside.

Beard's, 39 Church Street, Eye Tel: 01379 870383

AROUND EYE

THORNDON. Standing amid rich cornfield, this peaceful village is home to the famous Dowlands Restaurant; itself a handsome building which is, in parts, Elizabethan.

The charming **BLACK HORSE INN** stands opposite the village

Post Office in Thorndon, just three miles from Eye. Dating back to the 15th century, the building has undergone dramatic changes over the years. There is also a large fireplace that is ideal for toasting you toes in front of during the winter and, unusually, there is an old well next to the kitchen, now topped by glass. Today, the Black Horse is owned and personally run by Julia and Rod Waldron and they serve an excellent pint of real ale, including Greene King Abbott, as well as Guinness and Addlestones cider and there is a superb, popular restaurant here and bar meals are also available. This is a wonderful inn to drop into and enjoy some real English hospitality.

The Black Horse Inn, The Street, Thorndon Tel: 01379 678523

WETHERINGSETT. This rural village is best known for two of its rectors, the 17th century geographer Richard Haklyt and GW Ellis (who was not a priest at all!).

Wetheringsett Hall, Hall Lane, Wetheringsett Tel: 01449 766120

WETHERINGSETT HALL, in the village, lies just off the main A140 road between Norwich and Ipswich. Terri and Stephen Webb, the owners, have sympathetically converted an ancient Suffolk barn on their property into three self catering cottages which provide an idyllic, tranquil base for the perfect family holiday. Used for the stabling of horses until shortly after the Second World War, the barn cottages now each feature a large living room, gallery bedroom together with a fully fitted kitchen and bathroom. Beautifully decorated and furnished, the cottages are designed to accommodate two adults and two children in comfort and well behaved pets are also welcome. Horseriding and a swimming pool are available by arrangement and the surrounding countryside is perfect for walking or cycling.

DEBENHAM. The art of rush weaving still flourishes in Debenham, an attractive village where little streams trickle merrily along the back streets then meet to form the River Deben. The river flows beside and under the main street and, in a building beside the bridge in Water Lane, the weavers practise their craft and visitors can purchase samples of their work, including baskets, mats and carpets.

On a ridge above the village stands St Mary's Church, which is known to date back in parts to Saxon times and boasts a splendid roof of alternating hammerbeams and crested tie beams on arched bases. A number of the older village houses were destroyed by fire in 1744, but there are still many interesting buildings left to see. The best of these include the fine row of Tudor houses opposite the church; the 16th century Red Lion Hotel with its original decorated plaster ceiling; the old market hall with its overhanging upper storey, which dates back to 1666 and was later used as Hitchams School; and opposite this, the 15th century timber-framed Guildhall which now houses the Debenham Gallery. One former village resident went on to found a large chain of stores, called 'Debenhams'.

CRETINGHAM. A delightful village with a fine Tudor pub; it was here that a vicar of the parish was murdered by his curate.

BRANDESTON. In 1645 the villagers of Brandeston took the unusual step of declaring the local vicar, John Lowes, to be guilty of witchcraft. This was during the height of the Civil War, and it is likely that their actions were prompted by Lowes' well known Royalist sympathies. He was interrogated by the infamous 'Witchfinder General', Matthew Hopkins, who put such intense pressure on the 80 year old clergyman that he eventually broke down and admitted his 'guilt'. One of the trumped-up charges that poor Lowes had to answer to was the sinking of a ship off the coast at Harwich, despite the fact that there was no evidence to suggest that any such vessel had gone missing at that time. He was hauled off to Bury St Edmunds to be executed and, as no priest was allowed to conduct the burial service of a condemned witch, he was forced to read it to himself before his sentence was carried out.

A failed lawyer from Manningtree in Essex, Matthew Hopkins preyed upon the superstitions of those unsettled times to carve himself a new career at which he truly excelled. Between the years 1645 to 1646, his new-found profession as 'Witchfinder General' enabled him to fully utilise his talent for bullying old women into confessing to the most ludicrous of crimes. A profitable business it proved to be too: Stowmarket, for example, paid him the then handsome sum of £23 for his services.

Although the precise number is unknown, it is thought that Hopkins was responsible for the sentencing and execution of around 400 unfortunate souls. His methods of detecting witches ranged from identifying household pets as 'familiars' to seizing upon physical blemishes such as warts or moles and declaring them to be the marks of the Devil. One of his favourite tricks was to stab at these areas of his victim's body with a retractable blade, and when astonished witnesses saw that no blood flowed from the 'wound', they could do little but agree with the witchfinder's prognosis! Obtaining the desired confession was then a simple matter of endlessly walking his victims up and down their cells for days and nights on end, starving them half to death, or employing any number of other equally dreadful tortures that fell within the bounds of the law at that time. Needless to say, any lonely old woman living on her own with a pet moggy as her sole companion was an easy target for this evil man.

Eventually, Hopkins' methods proved too much for even the hardened sensibilities of those harsh times, and his reign of terror came to an end in the summer of 1646. It is known that he retired to Manningtree in relative affluence and that he died the following year, but reports differ as to how he met his end. Some say that he died of tuberculosis, but those with a keen sense of poetic justice may prefer to believe the other story. This states that he was accused of being a witch himself and, after failing one of his own favourite tests by floating in the water into which he was thrown, he was found guilty and hanged.

HELMINGHAM. **Helmingham Hall** is a lovely moated Tudor Hall with a working drawbridge that is still drawn up every night. It stands within a 400 acre park where there is also a safari ride and herds of 600 red and fallow deer, Highland cattle and wild Soay sheep. Although the Hall itself is not open to the public, the park and gardens can be seen every Sunday between 2.00 pm and 6.00 pm from 28th April to 15th September. There is a superb walled kitchen garden and wild flower garden, and a more recent attraction is the traditional Knot garden with its glorious collection of old-fashioned roses - the combination of scents here can only be described as heavenly!

Traditional cream teas are served in the Old Coach House, and the Stable Shop and farm shop stock a varied range of gifts and produce from the gardens. Helmingham Hall has been the family seat of the Tollemache family since the late 15th century, and they have been in almost unbroken occupation ever since. In 1886, one of the family established a local brewery, which later merged with another to become the famous Tolly Cobbold of Ipswich - a name which every visitor to this part of England will quickly become acquainted with.

OTLEY. Far smaller than Helmingham's moated house, but dating from the same period, the fine timber and brick **Otley Hall** is open to visitors at weekends throughout the summer months. During the 16th century it was the home of Bartholomew Gosnold, the founder of

Jamestown in Virginia and the discoverer of Cape Cod.

CHARSFIELD. The cottage garden at Charsfield claims neither the heritage nor the grandeur of the gardens at Helmingham Hall, but is a wonderful display of colourful flowers and vegetables. The quarter of an acre garden of a semi-detached house in Park Lane known as 'Akenfield', it was named after Ronald Blythe's thought-provoking book of the same name. Blythe partly based his book on the village of Charsfield, which he describes as 'a little arable kingdom where flints are the jewels and where existence is sharp-edged'. This description is probably just as apt today as in 1967 when the book was first published, offering a unique insight into the harsher realities of living and working in these idyllic rural areas. The garden is open daily between 24th May to 28th September, from 10.30 am till dusk.

EASTON. The lovely village of Easton can be found near the River Deben and it is without doubt one of the most colourful places in this part of Suffolk. To say that the locals enjoy a spot of gardening would be an obvious understatement, for during the summer months the entire village seemed bedecked with flowers of every conceivable colour. **Easton Park** lies to the west of the village, protected by a 2 mile long crinkle-crankle wall that completely surrounds it.

EASTON FARM PARK is a delight to visit, and will give you and your family a wonderful day out. It was opened to the public in April 1974, and has given enjoyment to thousands of people ever since.

Cattle at Easton Farm Park

Set in one of the most picturesque parts of the Deben valley, the farm buildings were built by the Duke of Hamilton as a model farm in 1870. Buildings on the site were either cleared or refaced to fit in with the new design. No farmhouse existed on the site. The Duke lived at Easton Park, which was demolished in 1929, but surrounded by the serpentine wall still visible in the village today. However, there are two cottages, one for the farm foreman and the other for the laundry and dairymaids. At that time there were also two small cowsheds for the milking of the Red Poll dairy herd, stables for the Suffolk Punches which worked on the farm, poultry units, a laundry, an unusual octagonal dairy, as well as the usual barns and cart sheds.

The estate was split up and sold in 1919, following the death of the Duke, who had no male successor. Since then the estate has been sold on more than one occasion, and improved farming methods and changes of lifestyle have rendered most of the buildings unsuitable for modern agriculture. However as listed buildings they lend themselves very well to be used as the centre for the Farm Park.

On the low-lying water meadows you can see the farm animals. Some are commercial, and some have become quite rare due to their unsuitability for modern requirements. The same meadows, along with the wooded areas, some natural and some cultivated, make up the Nature Trail which, along with the rest of the Farm Park, won the Farming and Wildlife Advisory Group - Bayer Farm Trails Award.

It is interesting to note some of the facts about Easton Park because, as well as providing a pleasant day out for all the family, it is capable of producing 1.5 million litres of milk, 5000 tonnes of wheat, 2000 tonnes of barley, 1300 tonnes of sugar, 135 tonnes of oilseed rape, 400 tonnes of freezing peas, 150 tonnes of green beans and 5500 tonnes of potatoes. Impressive isn't it?

The Dairy Centre was built specifically for the use of the public, with walkways over the top of the cow cubicles and a viewing gallery over the milking parlour. It gives the public a better insight into where their daily pint of milk really comes from; not a bottle as some people think!

The Victorian Dairy

In total contrast to the very modern Dairy Centre is the Victorian Dairy, an ornate building with marble shelves and painted doors, with a fountain in the middle which was used to keep the air moist for the butter and cheese etc. It is a unique building, and is especially interesting because of its octagonal shape.

Do not miss seeing the 'Suffolk Trinity', the three breeds of Suffolk in their home county: Red Poll cattle, Suffolk Punch horses and Suffolk sheep; it is a rare combination. Today Red Poll cattle are a rare breed, and in today's world the Suffolk Punch horse is becoming almost as rare. It is the Suffolk sheep that are still used commercially in modern agriculture.

The farm also has a working blacksmith's forge, and a resident blacksmith. You could be forgiven for thinking of a forge being a building solely for the shoeing of horses, which primarily it is, but with the mechanisation of farming it became the forerunner of the modern workshop, and the blacksmith was a mechanic, mending and making machinery by hand.

Old steam engines are always good to see. At Easton there is a splendid steam engine called 'Little Ben', which was built in 1878 by Ransome Sims and Jefferies. He can often be seen at work about the Farm Park.

In between seeing all these things, do find time to enjoy the tearoom which has a wide range of refreshments, including dairy cream teas and home-made cakes. There is also a gift shop, which is full of nice things, most of them at affordable prices.

There is something very special about Easton Farm Park; the ambience is right. You do not feel overpowered by commercialism, as so often happens. Visitors are free to wander about at their leisure and take in the beautiful countryside with walks down the farm trails and along the banks of the Deben.

The children will enjoy themselves, because they can really get close to the animals. Even toddlers can get friendly with the smaller animals, such as rabbits and chickens etc. Grandparents will enjoy the sense of the past; the beautiful Victorian buildings and the vintage machinery will remind them of the 'Good Old Days'. A place wholeheartedly recommended for all the family, no matter what the age.

Easton Farm Park, Easton Tel: 01728 746475

Back in the little village of Easton is the delightful pink- washed 16th century **WHITE HORSE INN**, with its pretty exterior and white rail fencing looking more like a cottage, and a little open garden leading to the entrance. Here you can truly relax and enjoy a friendly atmosphere and the magnificent rural setting. Order your glass of refreshment and consider the imaginative menu of dishes specially prepared from fresh

Framlington Castle

Herringfleet Drainage Windmill

foods and at very realistic prices. Try the Chicken breast cooked in leek and stilton sauce. The selection changes daily and on Sunday there is a fixed price menu. Snacks are available at the bar, bookings are taken for the restaurant and private dinner parties are catered for. There is a sunny garden with kiddies play area. Quite delightful.

The White Horse, The Street, Easton Tel: 01728 746456

PARHAM, whose moated grange is now a farmhouse, is well worth a visit for those interested in the role played by Allied fighter pilots during the Second World War. The **Air Museum** here is devoted to the history of East Anglian aviation during that particular time. A detailed exhibition of engines, photographs and other memorabilia from the RAF, the US 8th Air Force, and indeed the German Air Force too, is housed at the Museum in the control tower of the former base of the USAAF 390th Bomber Group. In addition to the excellent collection of material in the Museum itself, a library and archives centre has also been established in one of the base's old Nissen huts. The Museum is open every Sunday from 12.00 am - 6.00 pm, March to October, and admission is free.

FRAMLINGHAM. Sitting atop its hill, brooding over the little town below, **Framlingham Castle**'s 13 towers and linking walls are so well-preserved that you can readily imagine the bustling scenes of medieval life they would have witnessed at the time of its construction in the 12th century. The reed-fringed mere which lies alongside adds its own special charm to the picture. One amusing aspect of the castle is that the battlements of many of the towers and parts of the walls are surmounted by somewhat incongruous looking red-brick twisted chimneys, added during the 16th century. These additions do not even serve a practical purpose as most of them are, in fact, false!

The second Earl of Norfolk, Roger Bigod, built the structure seen today on the site of his grandfather's original wooden dwelling, which was surrounded by a ditch and palisade. After the Bigods, the castle changed hands many times. The Howards, Dukes of Norfolk, were here until 1635 when they sold the estate to the Hitchams, and perhaps its most famous occupant was Mary Tudor, who was given the castle by her brother, Edward VI. It was here that she organised her campaign against

Lady Jane Grey, and here that she proclaimed herself Queen.

The castle's near immaculate condition is attributable to the fact that in all its history, it was only once under siege - by King John in 1215. Apart from its defensive role, it was also used as a prison for priests who dared to defy Elizabeth I, and in the 17th century, after Sir Robert Hitcham bequeathed the castle to Pembroke College, Cambridge, it became a home and school for local paupers. The 18th century poor house was built against the inside of the west wall in place of the castle living quarters, and is now the home of the castle's custodian. It is quite a climb up the spiral staircase, but worthwhile to walk right around the top of the walls as far as the ninth tower and enjoy the glorious views over mere, town and surrounding countryside. Framlingham Castle is now maintained by English Heritage, and in the north wing is the **Lanman Museum** with its collection of farm and craft tools and domestic bygones.

Framlingham itself is a thriving little market town with narrow streets containing many buildings of character, some excellent antique shops and a number of fine inns. St Michael's Church contains the tombs of Sir Robert Hitcham and several of the Howards, together with a beautiful and very rare Carolean organ presented by Pembroke College in 1708.

WHEEL WRIGHTS family restaurant lies opposite the church in Wellclose Square in the heart of Framlingham. The charming building used to be stabling for horses from the nearby mill and it has a wonderful high, vaulted ceiling. Serving everything from a light snack to a full dinner, there is no minimum charge and bookings are advisable for large parties. Closed on Wednesdays and Sundays, Wheel Wrights serves the very best in home-cooked food.

Wheel Wrights, Wellclose Square, Framlington Tel: 01728 724132

Boundary Farm, Framlingham Tel: 01728 723401

BOUNDARY FARM, the home of Katherine and Gerry Cook, lies just out of Framlingham off the Saxmundham road and next door to Boundary Gallery which is signposted. The farm house, set in a large and charming garden, has been built in two parts; the original house is over 300 years old and is Grade II listed. From every window there are magnificent panoramic views across rolling fields. Offering bed and breakfast accommodation in three rooms, Katherine and Gerry, not forgetting Holly the friendly dog, extend a warm welcome to all their guests. This is a wonderful, quiet place to stay, with comfortable rooms where you will be treated as one of the family. There is a great breakfast, served in the guests' dining room, to set you up for a day's touring and, when you get back, the garden is the perfect place to laze away the rest of the day.

SAXTEAD GREEN. The main attraction in this village is undoubtedly the charming 18th century mill that stands on the marshy green from which the village takes its name. This is a wonderful example of a traditional Suffolk post mill, so-called because it was built on a single pivot post around which the entire body of the mill rotates when the wind changes direction. This particular mill is known to date back to at least 1796, although there has been a mill on the site since 1309. Its working life came to an end in 1947 and, although it no longer grinds corn professionally, it is still maintained in perfect working order today by English Heritage. Visitors can climb the steep wooden ladder into the body (or 'buck') of the mill, which is built of elegant white weatherboarding and stands upon a brick roundhouse. Once inside, the various floors can be explored and the intricate mill machinery studied. The mill is open from the beginning of April to the end of September, every day except Sundays.

EARL SOHAM. The long winding main street of this delightful old village was once part of a Roman road. The large mere here was only drained in 1970 and it caused the Romans to diverge from their usual straight roads.

The Falcon Inn, Earl Soham Tel: 01728 685263

THE FALCON INN in the village is a delightful place on the main A1120 Stowmarket to Yoxford road. Owned and personally run by Lavinia and Paul Algar, the pub dates back to the 16th century and still retains much of its country inn feel. Named after one of the Earls of

Soham, who was a great falconer, the inn has plenty of tables outside, to front and rear, where you can soak up the sun as well as enjoy your drink. Well known locally for its excellent pub food, their steak and kidney pies are a dream and well worth coming out of your way to try. As well as offering wonderful food and drink, the Falcon also has three comfortable letting rooms. A super inn in a central location within easy reach of Woodbridge and the coast.

DENNINGTON. A rather unusual creature can be found carved on one of the bench-ends in the centre aisle at St Mary's Church in Dennington. One of many glorious carvings in the church that escaped the depredations of Dowsing, this is the only carving in England of the sciapod; a mythical creature of the African desert, humanoid in appearance but sporting an enormous boat-shaped foot which he appears to be using as a sunshade. Either that, or he is indulging in some sort of esoteric meditation.

GRANGE FARM lies in the village of Dennington, off the main A1120 road, approximately two and a half miles down the B1116 and past the Bell pub. The house, home to Libby Hickson, dates from the 15th century though there has been a farmhouse on this spot since the 1200s. A long, sweeping driveway takes you up to this charming farmhouse built of warm, now mellowed bricks and covered with creepers of pyracantha and wysteria. The building has a superb all-weather tennis court and is surrounded on three sides by a large moat: feeding the fish is a popular pastime for guests in the summer. The farmhouse offers bed and breakfast in three charming rooms and breakfast is a feast which includes Libby's home-made marmalade and bread and other local produce. It is a real treat to stay here and there is the lovely, large garden to relax in after a day out in the countryside.

Grange Farm, Dennington Tel: 01986 798388 or 0374 182835

CRANSFORD. BOUNDARY GALLERY is signposted on the B1119 Saxmundham road, off the A12 and one mile from Framlingham. Established in 1990 by Nicole Harris, herself an artist, the gallery offers a peaceful and tranquil location for viewing a wide range of quality work all by Suffolk painters and craftsmen and women. Attractively housed in a converted Victorian stable block, the gallery has constantly changing exhibitions of landscapes, seascapes and still lifes by well known local artists of, often international, renown. With a range of paintings in all media and fine craftsware also on display there is bound to be something to catch your eye. The Gallery is open from 10.30 to 4.30 Thursdays to Sundays throughout the year, and Bank Holidays and Wednesdays from July to August.

Boundary Gallery, Cransford Tel: 01728 723862

BRUISYARD. This village is famed for its church dedicated to St Peter. A short distance to the west, is the **Bruisyard Vineyard and Herb Centre**, a splendid winery producing award-winning Bruisyard St Peter English wine. In 1974/75, 10 acres were planted with over 13,000 Müller Thurgau grapevines and in late October each year, bunches of ripe grapes are harvested and transported to the winery for pressing, fermentation and bottling. Visitors can see this process in action before trying the final product in the winery courtyard. In the grounds, there is also a large ornamental herb garden, a wooded picnic area, water gardens and a delightful restaurant and tea shop.

Bruisyard Vineyard and Herb Centre, Church Road, Bruisyard Tel: 01728 75281

BADINGHAM. **Badingham House** is now the home of the Academy of Transcendental Meditation. During the summer months, it is possible to visit the grounds to enjoy the woodland walks and contemplate the walled garden and tranquil lake - but those who wish to contemplate further should make their own enquiries.

COLSTON HALL is easy to find, near Badingham village, it lies just off the A1120 Stowmarket to Yoxford road, in the heart of rural Suffolk. The Hall, an Elizabethan farmhouse, is home to Liz and John Bellefontaine who offer excellent accommodation, either bed and breakfast or self-catering, from their heavily beamed home. When you stay at the farm, mentioned in the Domesday Book, you will be offered wonderful fresh eggs and home-made marmalade for your hearty breakfast. The spacious farmhouse has three beautifully decorated and comfortably furnished en-suite bedrooms, while a converted seventeenth century stable has another three charming rooms for bed and breakfast guests. The farm's granary was converted, over a hundred years ago, into a pretty cottage which has recently been modernised to provide self-catering accommodation for six people. Lambing at Easter, coarse fishing, indoor carpet bowls and leisurely country walks, will tempt you to include Colston Hall in your visit to Suffolk, whenever you stay here you will certainly have a memorable holiday.

Colston Hall, Badingham Tel: 01728 638375 Mobile: 0850 896 744

PEASENHALL. At St Michael's Church a most peculiar creature can be seen climbing up one side of the arch of the porch, all set to encounter the dragon ascending the other side. This is the 'woodwose' or wildman of the woods, covered in hair from head to toe and holding what looks like a shield, or possibly a lyre of some kind, in his left hand.

LAXFIELD. All Saints' Church is distinguished by the most glorious flushwork to its Perpendicular tower, roof and nave. The village is widely held to be the birthplace of that notorious iconoclast, William Dowsing. He was chosen by Cromwell to wreak havoc in Suffolk's churches and to destroy just about everything that was glorious in them. Stained glass, crucifixes, screens; in fact, anything of beauty that was deemed to be 'superstitious', carved or painted, was smashed or burned. It is said that at the height of his campaign of licensed desecration, Dowsing was destroying as many as 1,000 church ornaments in a single day!

Thankfully, plenty of interesting relics remain to be viewed at the **Laxfield and District Museum**, which can be found opposite the church in the timber-framed, brick-nogged Tudor Guildhall. In addition to the various displays of local natural history and geology, the other exhibits include a costume room, a mock-up of a Victorian kitchen and village shop, and a beehive which gives the viewer an insight into the industrious lifestyle of these busy creatures and their fascinating hexagonal abodes.

HOXNE. Somewhat confusingly pronounced 'Hoxen' as opposed to 'Hoxney', its curious name is thought to mean a 'hock-shaped spur of land'. This is a lovely little village, full of charm and character, with thatched cottages around the green and houses of timber, brick and plaster on the outskirts. It was here in 870 AD that King Edmund was defeated by the Danes and captured, according to a local legend, after attempting to hide under nearby Goldbrook Bridge. Apparently a newly married couple spotted the glint of his spurs reflecting in the River Dove and, hoping for a reward, they denounced him to his enemies. Not surprisingly, Edmund uttered a dreadful curse on all newly-weds who might cross the bridge from that day on!

A Benedictine priory was founded here to commemorate Edmund's martyrdom and his body lay buried in the chapel for many years before it was transferred to Bury St Edmunds. Nothing remains of the priory today, but the 16th century timber-framed Abbey Farmhouse now stands on the site. In the church of St Peter and St Paul is an oak screen depicting scenes from the life of the saint, which was carved from the wood of a tree that collapsed in 1848; said, in fact, to be the self-same oak to which the king was tied and shot full of arrows by the Danes centuries before. Legend has it that when the tree fell down, an arrowhead was discovered embedded in the trunk.

WINGFIELD. In this little hamlet is one of the most historic seats of education in this country, **Wingfield College**. It was founded in 1362 as a college of priests, following a generous bequest from Sir John Wingfield, Chief of Council to the Black Prince. Surrendered to Henry VIII at the time of the Dissolution, it then became a farmhouse in the 18th century and is now a private house; but behind the Georgian façade lies the original medieval building with its splendid Gothic timber-framed great hall. The College is open to the public at weekends during the summer and is also used as a venue for a superb range of music concerts and arts events throughout the year.

On a hill to the north-west of the village are the remains of a castle built in 1382 by the first Earl of Suffolk, Michael de la Pole.

FRESSINGFIELD. In the church of St Peter and St Paul the bench where Alice de la Pole, wife of William, the first Duke of Suffolk, carved her initials can still be seen. Perhaps the sermon failed to hold her attention that day, or maybe she was contemplating the possibilities of carrying on the literary traditions of her family: her grand-father was the great English poet, Geoffrey Chaucer.

Another high-born lady associated with Fressingfield is 'Fair Margaret' of Willingham Hall, whose great beauty is said to have captured the heart of the future Edward I, here on a hunting expedition. Answering a summons from his father, Henry III, Edward left his new-found love in the care of the Earl of Lincoln; an unwise move as it transpired, for the Earl then married her himself!

MENDHAM. **WESTON HOUSE FARM** lies in the village of Mendham, just off the main A143. Surrounded by miles and miles of unbroken countryside and standing in its own large garden, the house, which dates back in parts to 1698, is the home of June Holden and her family.

With a long verandah running right across the front, this house is a real picture and there a splendid views across the Waveney Valley. For the past 15 years or so, June and her husband have been offering excellent bed and breakfast accommodation from their delightful home in three en-suite bedrooms. Fortified by a large and delicious traditional English breakfast, Weston House is ideally situated for many of the attractions of coastal Suffolk.

Weston House Farm, Mendham Tel: 01986 782206

MENDHAM MILL stands in over six acres of secluded gardens and grounds down a private road in the village of Mendham, in the heart of the beautiful Waveney Valley. Originally a flax mill, it became a flour mill in the 16th century and continued to grind flour up until the 1920s. Historically important, the buildings are of typical East Anglian clap board construction and, of equal interest, the Mill was the birthplace of the artist Sir Alfred Munnings whose father was the Miller.

Mendham Watermill, Mendham Mill Lane, Mendham Tel: 01379 853248

In 1938 the Grade II listed Mill was converted into outstanding accommodation. Owned today by Gillian and Harry Hibbert, they offer the choice of two different sized apartments that make the perfect holiday home. The larger, the Millers House, is on three levels and can sleep up to eight in comfort and style whilst the Millers Nest a spacious ground floor flat, is ideal for two, three or four people. Taken on either self-catering or bed and breakfast terms this is first class accommodation, in a wonderful position, that provides every comfort in relaxed and peaceful surroundings.

CRATFIELD. Many of the houses in this peaceful Suffolk village date from the 1700s to the 1900s. With carefully tended trees and hedgerows, this village is a haven for wildflowers. **THE CRATFIELD POACHER** in the village of Cratfield is no ordinary public house. It has, at various times, been attacked by a giant, inflatable octopus; been the venue for Christmas *in July*, and has had a *beach* specially imported, complete with belly dancers and palm trees! Graham Barker and his wife, Elaine are no ordinary hosts and the bizarre stunts that they have dreamt up have entertained everyone and, at the same time, raised thousands of pounds for charity.

The building which now houses the pub was originally a butcher's and later became a draper's, post office and small shop with a licence to sell beer - the first post office in Britain to offer this worthwhile service! Graham and Elaine took it over in 1982 and since then they have built up its reputation and character, transforming what was once a small taproom into what is probably the best pub in the area, attracting visitors from all over the country.

The Cratfield Poacher, Bell Green, Cratfield Tel: 01986 798206

Certainly this is now a public house of exceptional quality. The real ales which are carefully kept include a selection of the very best from all over the country, the atmosphere is typically warm, as you would expect of this part of Suffolk and the food which is served is delicious (and very good value for money too!). The interior of the Cratfield Poacher is very special indeed and contains a vast and fascinating collection of miniatures hanging from the oak beams, stuffed birds of prey, foreign currency and other bric-a-brac. In particular, look out for the original Suffolk pargetting featuring poaching scenes.

Children are made very welcome, and they will enjoy the play area in the garden. This wonderful pub is a quite remarkable place and you should go out of your way to pay it a visit. Once you do you will quite likely want to return again and again. The Cratfield Poacher is open all day including Saturdays and Sundays.

BRAMFIELD. The massive Norman round tower of St Andrew's Church is separate from the main building and was built originally as a defensive structure with walls over 3 ft thick. This, however, did not deter William Dowsing from making his way here in April 1643 and destroying '24 superstitious pictures: one crucifix and picture of Christ: and twelve angels on the roof'. The church itself dates back to the 14th century and is thatched, and has two particularly interesting features inside.

The first is the magnificent monument to Sir Arthur Coke and his wife, with Arthur kneeling, resplendent in full armour, and Elizabeth lying on her bed with a baby in her arms. On a more light-hearted note is the long-winded and highly amusing epitaph to Bridget Applethwaite, who succumbed when: 'the Fatigues of a Married Life, Borne by Her with Incredible Patience', finally did for her! After enjoying the 'Glorious Freedom Of an Early and Unblemisht Widowhood' for several years, 'She Resolved to run the Risk of a Second Marriage-Bed, But DEATH forbad the Banns'. It appears that she was unwilling to give in gracefully to 'that Grand Enemy of Life', for she suffered 'terrible Convulsions, Plaintive Groans or Stupefying Sleep, Without recovery of Speech, or Senses', before finally throwing in the towel on 12th September 1737.

YOXFORD. This is a former 18th century coaching town set in the valley of the River Yox. The Three Tuns Hotel was then the destination of coaches that would turn off the London to Yarmouth road for rest and refreshment before the last stretch of their journey into Yarmouth; but sadly the hotel is no more, having burnt down in 1926. However, there is a wealth of interesting shops displaying all manner of arts and crafts and antiques.

A reminder of the village's glorious past is the 1830 cast-iron signpost outside St Peter's Church, which is reputed to be one of only two of a kind in the country. Its hands, pointing to London, Yarmouth and Framlingham, are set unusually high so as to be on the level of the driver's seat on a stagecoach.

Among the varied styles of architecture to be found in Yoxford's long High Street are a number of traditional colour-washed cottages, some of them in the distinctive 'Suffolk Pink'. Visitors who have come to know and love this pretty colour in their travels around the county may be somewhat put off to learn that at one time it was achieved by mixing copious dollops of pig's blood into the plaster. However, the same effect was also arrived at with sloe juice.

THE OLD MILL HOUSE lies back from the A12 London road on the outskirts of the village of Yoxford. As its name suggests, the house was built, in 1814, for the local mill owner where it presided over the workers and their cottages. Those days are long since passed and now the house stands in its own quiet and secluded grounds up a private driveway. Owned by Rosemary and Ted Draper, the couple offer excellent bed and breakfast accommodation in two charming and well furnished bedrooms. This really is a beautiful house and guests can also make use of the wonderful garden. Sitting by the pond, surrounded by hanging baskets and patio tubs brimming over with flowers is a delightful way to end a busy day exploring the surrounding countryside.

The Old Mill House, Yoxford Tel: 01728 668536

HALESWORTH. Although there is nothing of outstanding architectural interest in this little market town, the Market Place has a fine (if rather shabby) example of an Elizabethan timber-framed house, and the picturesque group of buildings round a courtyard known as The Maltings are worth seeing too. The **Halesworth and District Museum** in Steeple End, which has been converted from a row of 17th century almshouses, contains a good collection of fossils, prehistoric flints and medieval finds from local excavations. Above this is **Halesworth Art Gallery** with its various exhibitions of paintings and sculptures, and entrance to both the museum and the gallery is free.

Sir William Jackson Hooker and his son Joseph lived at Brewery House to the north of the town, not far from The Maltings. Both were renowned botanists, and were, respectively, the first and second directors of the Royal Botanic Gardens at Kew.

South of the Broadlands

BECCLES. Just outside this market town is **Roos Hall**, a distinguished 16th century red-brick manor built by Sir John Suckling, an ancestor of Lord Nelson. It is still owned by his descendants today, and is open to the public by appointment. This is said to be one of England's most haunted houses: one ghost haunts a guest room, another loiters in the garden, and on Christmas Eve, a coach pulled by phantom horses and driven by a headless coachman turns into the drive and pulls up at the

Roo's Hall, Beccles

Beccles Marsh Trails

front door. To top it all, one of Old Nick's footprints (or should that be hoofprints?) can be seen on one of the walls!

The most scenic approach into Beccles is by water, for here the River Waveney is at its very best. This was once a busy port with wherries transporting their goods from the sea ports to the inland towns, but today it is the pleasure boats that dominate the scene, and many readers will be familiar with Beccles as the starting point of their holiday on the Broads.

The 97 ft high stone-faced bell tower of St Michael's rises above the town, detached from the 14th century church. It was here in 1749 that Catherine Suckling married the Reverend Edward Nelson, to give birth, nine years later, to one of the greatest seamen England has ever known. A series of fires that raged through Beccles in the 16th and 17th centuries did much damage to the church and completely destroyed most of the town's buildings; but the church was sympathetically restored by the Victorians, and Beccles itself was virtually reborn from the ashes as a handsome red-brick Georgian town.

Some of the town's buildings worth seeing include the flint-faced Waveney House Hotel, the 18th century octagonal Town Hall, and that marvellous old 17th century coaching inn, the King's Head; there are also two worthwhile museums in Newgate. The first is the **Beccles and District Museum**, whose exhibits on local history include 19th century costume, farm implements and memorabilia from the old sailing wherries; and the second is the **William Clowes Print Museum**. This is very informative on the history of printing since the 1800s, with woodcuts, books and printing machinery showing just how far the industry has progressed since that time. All this seems a far cry from the desk top publishing systems and laser printing available to us all today. The museum is open from June to August, Monday to Friday from 2.00 pm to 4.00 pm, and admission free. Guided tours around the factory can be arranged.

AROUND BECCLES

EARSHAM. The **Otter Trust**, on the banks of the River Waveney at Earsham, is a mile to the west of Bungay and just over the border into Norfolk. The Trust has one of the largest colonies of otters in the world and, during the summer, visitors can watch these fascinating mammals going about their daily business in their natural habitat.

PARK FARM is easy to find down a private road off the main A143 Diss to Great Yarmouth road between the towns of Harleston and Bungay. Standing on a hill and surrounded by its own glorious garden, this large Victorian farmhouse is the home of Bobbie Watchorn. Once part of an estate owned by the Duke of Norfolk, Bobbie offers wonderful bed and breakfast accommodation from the house that is second to none. On arrival you will be greeted with a cup of tea and welcoming smile, as well as being given the once over by the friendly family dog.

There are three splendid en-suite bedrooms, all light and airy and decorated and furnished to the same high standard as the rest of the house. Breakfast is taken in the lovely dining room, which overlooks the garden, and includes home-made muesli, the farm's own free-range eggs and locally produced Norfolk bacon. There is a cosy lounge ideal for relaxing in after a delicious home-cooked evening meal; you'll also find board games and jigsaws to enjoy. This is still a working farm and, as well as having use of the beautiful garden, guests can also visit the collection of rare breeds and unusual farm animals.

Park Farm, Harleston Road, Earsham Tel: 01986 892180

FLIXTON. Home of the 'Bungay Buckeroos' during the Second World War, the village is also the home of the **Norfolk and Suffolk Aviation Museum.** The museum can be found south-west of Bungay on the B1062 between Flixton and Homersfield, and includes material on the USAAF Liberator base which was located here during the Second World War.

BUNGAY. The ancient fortress town of Bungay lies halfway between Diss and Lowestoft, at the point where the A143 and several other important roads meet to bridge the River Waveney. The river skirts the town on three sides and forms the natural border between Suffolk and Norfolk. It played a vital part in Bungay's fortunes for hundreds of years, with coal, corn, malt and timber being the principal cargoes of the lighters and sailing wherries that plied between here and the coast until well into the 18th century. Although it is now no longer navigable above Geldeston, the Waveney continues to be a favourite haunt of anglers and the boating fraternity.

Bungay has a great deal going for it as far as sight-seeing is concerned. To the west of the Market Place with its fine lead-covered 17th century **Butter Cross** are the impressive remains of **Bungay Castle,** built by the last Earl Bigod in 1165. To the north are Bungay's two surviving churches (the Domesday Book recorded five), the oldest and smallest being Holy Trinity; its north wall dating back to around 1000 and its Saxon round tower being added some 40 years later. St Mary's Church had to be rebuilt after it was largely gutted by a fire that swept

through the town in 1688 - even the bells were melted by the flames. This no doubt accounts for the rather sparse state of the church interior today, although thankfully its magnificent 90 ft Perpendicular tower survived.

Most of the town's buildings were not so lucky: above a modern supermarket, opposite the west end of the church, the carved sills in the upper windows of a 16th century merchant's house can still be made out; one of the very few original properties to escape the conflagration. As a consequence, Bungay is now mainly 18th century in character, and the fine Georgian buildings with their red-brick façades still lend an air of prosperity to the town. It has also benefited immeasurably since being by-passed, making it a very pleasant place to wander around on foot, with many narrow streets leading out from the Market Place to explore.

There is a rather unusual weather-vane atop a lamp-post near the Butter Cross, which, rather than the familiar friendly cockerel, is surmounted by a particularly savage looking dog straddling a bolt of lightning. This is a reference to Black Shuck (sometimes called Old Shuck), a demon dog who crops up all over East Anglia in many different guises and with varying degrees of temperament!

It is generally agreed that he takes the form of a calf-sized, shaggy hell-hound with either one or two huge eyes of fiery red or green. Around the coast, his terrifying howls are said to warn of impending disaster at sea; in Norfolk he is particularly sinister, and locals say that no one who sets eyes on him will live to tell the tale. In Cambridgeshire his appearance also presages imminent death; but, by contrast, in Essex he has often been known to protect those who are travelling off the beaten track.

In Suffolk, if treated with respect he is relatively harmless - but woe betide those who do anything to upset him! Black Shuck's demeanour was far from benevolent at Bungay in 1577, when he is said to have made an unexpected and dramatic appearance at St Mary's Church during a terrible storm. According to a contemporary record, he created even more havoc than William Dowsing was to accomplish in Suffolk churches just 66 years later, by flying down the aisle in a ball of fire and tearing out the throats of at least two startled parishioners.

GELDESTON. Situated at the head of navigation at the River Waveney, **THE LOCK INN** was once frequented by smugglers and is reputed to be haunted! This remote, candlelit Inn has been owned and run by Graham Merveyn for the last 12 years and was built back in 1572, it is accessible only by boat or the local causeway over the marshes. Records indicate that this stretch of river was in frequent commercial use well before 1670 and the lock itself was last used in 1934. Norfolk's most remote pub is positioned in One and a half acres of land, you can sit and watch the passing wildlife on the many benches, or if you prefer something more sporty then fishing on the river could be just up your street. The bar serves real ales in cosy surroundings, with real oak beams, huge open fires and genuine antiques being very much the order of the day. The atmosphere is warm and inviting, offering plenty of local colour and character within this traditional Inn. Every Friday and Saturday, sometimes even in the week, local live bands fill the bar with music, bringing the Locks Inn to life and taking you back to the early days in its history, when many a night it would be filled with raucous smugglers.

The Locks Inn, Station Road, Geldeston Tel: 01506 518414

Placed just 2 minutes walk from the River Waveney you will find the **WHERRY INN**. This property first became a pub in 1690, with its first ever landlord being called John Gilling. These days Wherry Inn is run and owned by Colin and Vicki Harber and offers the traveller a safe haven steeped in the traditional trappings of a village pub. The bar areas are filled with original oak beams and the rooms are warmed by large log fires that prove to be very popular on those cold, winter evenings. Real ales are served throughout the day and in the summer months the patio and beer garden are the perfect place to cool off and enjoy a drink or two. The food is home-cooked and plentiful with fresh fish being a speciality and daily specials are changed regularly and include many foreign dishes for you to savour. All these meals are served in the non-smoking dining room and in the summer there is a children's room so that families can have somewhere to entertain their kids. The Wherry Inn offers a friendly and comfortable atmosphere for locals and tourists alike.

Wherry Inn, 7 The High Street, Geldeston Tel: 01508 518371

ELLINGHAM. The **BIRD IN HAND** is a typical village inn in the centre of Ellingham. A place where the locals meet, the Bird in Hand, owned and personally run by Jackie and her son David, also extends a warm and friendly welcome to all visitors. Serving a range of real ales, with guest beers, this cosy inn also has a 16 cover, intimate restaurant that offers a range of home-made game and steak and ale pies that use only the best fresh local produce. With a small garden to the side that also contains a brick barbecue, the pub offers a unique cook your own barbecue where diners can buy a pack of raw food from the bar and help themselves. A popular and interesting way to enjoy excellent food, without the washing up, in the open air. And super beer is on tap!

Bird in Hand, Yarmouth Road, Ellingham Tel: 01508 518200

GILLINGHAM. This village, on the Norfolk/Suffolk border, has three churches, one of which is now in ruins. A former rector, who was a very keen horseman, had a saddle fitted into his pulpit so that he could 'ride' while preaching!

The Swan Motel, Loddon Road, Gillingham
Tel: 01502 712055 Fax: 01502 711786

THE SWAN MOTEL stands in its extensive grounds, set back from road just off the main A146 in the village and near to Beccles, Lowestoft,

Norwich and Great Yarmouth and in the heart of rural East Anglia. A privately owned and run, high quality motel, the Swan Motel is ideally located for the tourist and businessman alike. The main building is an old road house and this holds the excellent restaurant and bar whilst, behind the pub, lies the attractive, modern accommodation. The restaurant is open seven days a week and offers extensive à la carte and table d'hôte menus. During the summer there are barbecues outside in the delightful gardens and tasty bar snacks are available. When ever you venture here, the warm and friendly atmosphere will ensure that you have a great time.

The accommodation comprises fourteen luxury en-suite bedrooms and includes a honeymoon suite with four poster and spa bath and a room specially adapted for disabled guests. A popular establishment that people return to time and time again.

RINGSFIELD. **THE HORSESHOES** inn lies in the heart of the village of Ringsfield. Deep in the centre of rural Suffolk, Ringsfield and its neighbouring village Weston have become very intertwined over the last few hundred years. Ringsfield was originally situated in the valley but during the Black Death it was wiped out and was later rebuilt on the hill next to Weston. The villages have grown since then and now the road acts as their boundary. This explains why the pub is in Ringsfield but its carpark, in Weston, is only a few yards away!

The Horseshoes is a warm and friendly pub, very much the village local. Owned and personally run by Philip Murray, you can be sure of a good pint of ale, excellent pub grub and interesting conversation.

The Horseshoes, Cromwell Road, Ringsfield Tel: 01502 713114

Lowestoft and the Coast

LOWESTOFT, which has the distinction of being the most easterly town in Britain, saw its heyday as a major fishing port during the late 19th and early 20th centuries, when the rivalry between its herring fishermen and those of its sister port of Great Yarmouth was legendary. After the

First World War, the herring grounds suffered from overfishing and the numbers of the fleet declined dramatically, but the fishing industry continues to be an important part of life in Lowestoft today. It is well worth wandering down, in the early morning, to the harbour to watch the trawlers chugging in with their catch after a long night spent far out at sea. Guided tours of the fishmarket and of the fishing harbour in a trawler are also available during the summer.

The town is divided into two by Lake Lothing, dug originally for peat extraction, and the old harbour that was built at the mouth of the lake in 1827-31 is now the home of the Royal Lowestoft Yacht Club and the lifeboat station. The commercial part of the port, with its dry dock and shipyard, can be found further upriver and is used mainly by ships carrying grain and timber. The main holiday resort lies south of the harbour, and was developed in the mid- 19th century by the building company of Sir Samuel Morton Peto, which was also responsible for Nelson's Column and the Houses of Parliament. Here, also, is **South Beach**, with its golden sands, safe swimming, two piers, and all the ubiquitous seaside amusements.

To the north of the harbour, over the bascule bridge that links the two halves of Lowestoft, the main shopping area leads uphill to the old part of town. In the High Street are some elegant Georgian houses and, leading off to the east, are the steep cobbled alleyways known as **The Scores**. In the old days, these were lined with fishermen's cottages and curing houses and led down the cliffs to the original village on the beach; but the bombing raids of the Luftwaffe destroyed most of the older buildings, and the village site is now a sprawling industrial estate, dominated by the immense Birds Eye factory.

Things get distinctly better further north, with **North Beach** below Gunton Cliffs and the northern esplanade. Built at the turn of the century, this never really had much hope of seriously rivalling the southern resort, but its failure to do so makes it a pleasant alternative for those visitors who prefer things a bit quieter.

The northern part of town is also home to the **Maritime Museum** in Whapload Road, which offers one of the finest exhibitions of maritime history in the country. This includes models and displays of fishing and commercial boats, lifeboats, fishing gear, shipwrights' tools and paintings, and is open daily during the summer from 10.00 am - 5.00 pm. Another similarly appropriate museum that is well worth a visit is the **Royal Navy Patrol Service Museum** at the peculiarly named Sparrow's Nest park. There are displays of naval uniforms, documents, photographs and models, and entry here is free.

The history of the town is not exclusively concerned with the fishing industry, however, for in 1664 a witchcraft trial took place at Bury St Edmunds involving two Lowestoft women; one that was to become so notorious that it actually set a precedent for the famous Salem trials in Massachusetts in 1692. Rose Cullender and Amy Duny were charged with the crime of practising sorcery and bewitching several local children over a number of years.

Following a series of ludicrous testimonies from 'reliable' witnesses and the children themselves, 'evidence' to rival that of Matthew Hopkins' fertile imagination 20 years earlier, the presiding judge pronounced both women guilty, and they were hanged on 16th March that year.

America may have had its troubles with witches, but at the **Pleasurewood Hills American Theme Park** in Corton Road, nothing unearthly (apart from some of the fun rides, perhaps) to trouble anyone! There are over 50 rides in all, together with shows and attractions to please all members of the family.

Lowestoft also has interesting artistic and musical connections. Benjamin Britten was born here in 1913 and several of his compositions were premiered in the village of Aldeburgh to the south. Another son of Lowestoft was the Elizabethan playwright and poet, Thomas Nashe, born here in 1567. One of his plays, 'The Isle of Dogs', was so strong in its condemnation of the abuses of state power that Nashe was able to test the phrase 'suffering for one's art' by being thrown into the Fleet prison! His final work, written in 1599 in praise of the red herring trade at Yarmouth, was 'Lenten Stuffe'. Finally, Lowestoft was the first place in England visited by Joseph Conrad, not as a writer, but as a deckhand on a Lowestoft trawler. His experiences as such were to greatly influence his later works.

Lowestoft Museum, Broad House, Oulton Broad, Lowestoft
Tel: 01502 511457

LOWESTOFT MUSEUM, housed in Broad House, is situated in Nicholas Everitt Park, on the edge of Oulton Broad. It was opened in 1985 by Her Majesty Queen Elizabeth and HRH The Duke of Edinburgh; their signatures can be seen in the commemorative visitor's book in the foyer. The museum houses a wide range of collections including those on local history, geology of the area, domestic 'bygones', local works of art and, perhaps most importantly, the town's collection of Lowestoft Porcelain, the third largest in the world after the Victoria and Albert Museum and Norwich Castle. Run by the Lowestoft Archaeological and Local History Society, the museum has many displays of the archaeological finds from several local sites now lost to the sea or by road improvements. There is a costume case which contains Victoriana and also the Mayoral Regalia. The domestic history room has many items dating from the 18th to the early 20th century including early radios and there are also toys, children's clothes and samplers on display. Displays of topical local interest in the foyer are changed at regular intervals.

The museum building, Broad House, is itself of historic interest. The original building was put up in 1685 and it has seen many alterations over the years; the central part is octagonal and dates from the Regency period. The house was occupied by the Everitt family and, when the last of the line, Nicholas Everitt, died in the 1920s, the whole estate was bought by Howard Hollingsworth and given to the town as a park.

The museum is run purely by volunteers and there is no charge for admission though donations are greatly appreciated.

Fed by the River Waveney and connected to Lowestoft by Lake Lothing and its lock, **Oulton Broad** is one of the most attractive stretches of inland water in England. It is linked to the Norfolk Broads by the Waveney, and you can explore the river by taking a boat trip from the Boulevard, just to the south of the Broad. In summer this vast lake becomes a hugely popular holiday resort, with sailing regattas, motorboat races, coarse angling, an August water carnival, and all types of boat for hire.

It is also the setting for a tangled web of ghostly intrigue, all centred on a 16th century house in the locality called Oulton High House. The spirits said to haunt the house are a phantom horseman accompanied by a pack of hounds, and a lady in white carrying a goblet of poison. The simplest version of their story is that they were a married couple, and the husband poisoned the wife after discovering that she was having an affair. The more complicated (if not totally incomprehensible) version is that the wife's lover murdered the husband, then fled with her abroad, taking the family jewels with them. Years later, the daughter of the original couple was kidnapped from the house on the eve of her own wedding - her intended husband being killed when he tried to intervene - and was taken to her mother, who for reasons best known to herself, ended up poisoning her!

FAIRWAYS GUEST HOUSE is situated in a quiet, residential area of Lowestoft yet it is just two minutes walk from the seafront through the attractive and colourful Kensington Gardens. Owned and personally run by Gillian and Armando Montali, Fairways is the ideal place to stay, whether on business or holidaying in Lowestoft.

A warm and friendly guest house with a relaxed atmosphere, Fairways has spacious and comfortable rooms that make this the place for a really carefree holiday. All the seven (four en-suite) bedrooms are decorated and furnished to a high standard and equipped with all the comforts of home including colour television and tea and coffee making facilities. The popular ground floor lounge, with colour television, is a super place in which to enjoy a pre-dinner drink and convivial company after your meal. Fairways prides itself on the excellent, home-cooked cuisine that is served in the light and sunny dining room. A mix of traditional English and speciality dishes are served, all of which make use of the wonderful local fish and fresh meat and vegetables. All in all, Fairways is an excellent guest house that many larger establishments would do well to match.

Fairways Guest House, 398 London Road South, Lowestoft
Tel: 01502 572659

ALONG THE COAST

HERRINGFLEET. The charming parish church of St Margaret stands above the River Waveney with its Saxon round tower, thatched roof and beautiful glass. Here too is Herringfleet Drainage Windmill, a 19th century smock mill in full working order. Access to the mill is on foot only and visitors can watch the mill at work.

SOMERLEYTON. This is an attractive estate village of Neo-Tudor, thatched red-brick cottages grouped around the green, together with the present Hall to the east of the village. The Hall and cottages were all the work of Sir Samuel Morton Peto, the Victorian civil engineer and later Member of Parliament for Norwich who was responsible for the development of Lowestoft.

Somerleyton Hall and gardens, with its famous maze, is a beautiful family home, and one in the true sense of the word, for Lord and Lady Somerleyton living here. They have five children. They are very proud of their heritage, and their ambition is to conserve it, not just for themselves and their children, but also for the many visitors who come each year to enjoy the house and particularly the garden, which is ever changing.

The story of the house and family is recorded in an excellent guide, available when you visit the house. Each room has its own particular attraction. For example, the Oak Room is representative of the 17th century, here the panelling is from the original Jacobean house, and was made from oaks grown within Somerleyton's extensive parklands. The carvings on the chimney breasts are partly by the hand of Grinling Gibbons.

Between the windows of the northern wall of the Oak Parlour hangs an exquisite silver and gilt moulded mirror, which was originally made for the private apartments of the Doge's palace in Venice, and was once owned by Queen Anne. That is a brief description of just one room! Each room has paintings, silver Meissen and superb antiques. It is a delightful way to spend an afternoon, and that is simply talking about the house!

The gardens and grounds have long been considered of first rate importance. Twelve acres of garden surround the Hall. One of the most popular features has always been the Maze, one of the finest in Britain. There is a profusion of colour from the plants and shrubs and as you wander through the gardens you constantly come to arches and statues and a very special pergola which is 300 ft long. A miniature railway was opened in 1972, and gives hours of pleasure to children and adults alike. Those taking a ride are able to have a different view of the house and park, also various breeds of cattle, and horses.

Three miles from Somerleyton is Fritton Lake and Country Park. It is another part of the Estate activity which is open to the public. The two mile long lake is one of the most beautiful expanses of water in East Anglia, and attracts many visitors each year, who enjoy fishing, boating, playing pitch and putt, windsurfing, viewing wildfowl, or simply relaxing in this beautiful setting. Children spend much of their time in the adventure play area. Somerleyton Hall is open to the public from Easter to the end of September. Please telephone (01502) 730224 for details.

Somerleyton Hall, Somerleyton Tel: 01502 730224

BLUNDESTON. Passing by on a walk from Yarmouth to Lowestoft, Charles Dickens misread the signpost to this village, and 'Blunderstone' was later immortalised as the birthplace of David Copperfield. The morning light shining on the sundial of the church porch was the first thing to meet the gaze of young Copperfield each day, as he looked out of his bedroom window in the nearby 'Rookery'. As for the churchyard: 'There is nothing half so green that I know anywhere, as the grass of that churchyard; nothing half so shady as its trees; nothing half so quiet as its tombstones.'

OULTON. This is a lively village with a whole host of shop, restaurants and pubs. Oulton Broad, which separates the village from Lowestoft, is one of the finest yachting lakes in the country and it is also the only place on the Broads where there are power-boat race meetings.

PARKHILL HOTEL is a delightful place, standing in six acres of lawns and parkland at Parkhill, on the A1117 Great Yarmouth to Oulton Broad road. A beautiful 18th century private house, it was bought by the present owners, Ruth and David Truman, in 1980 and converted into a splendid hotel. A quiet and secluded spot, the hotel has 18 comfortable en-suite bedrooms and this is an ideal place to spend a relaxing time close to Suffolk's famous coast.

The hotel's popular Victorian-style restaurant, which is open to non-residents, offers an excellent à la carte menu full of tempting dishes. The extensive wine list compliments the menu perfectly. Parkhill Hotel also has a range of rooms that offer very versatile conference facilities.

Parkhill Hotel, Parkhill, Oulton Tel: 01502 730322

CARLTON COLVILLE. A pleasant village; in Chapel Road is the **East Anglia Transport Museum**, where trams and trolley buses, all in full working order, are shown to good advantage in an authentically re-constructed 1930s street setting. Together with other interesting modes of transport such as motor cars, a narrow gauge railway, steam rollers and various battery powered vehicles, there is plenty to see and do. The admission fee is reasonable (with all rides included in the price) and opening times should be checked by picking up a leaflet from any local Tourist Information Centre.

BARNBY. **THE SWAN INN**, in the village of Barnby, lies just off the main A146 between Beccles and Lowestoft. A popular pub, the Swan is owned and run by Donny Cole, a friendly and jovial host. As well as being a focal point for the village, the pub also has an excellent restaurant, the Fisherman's Cove, that is well known throughout the area. Like the pub, the restaurant has a nautical theme, with many authentic fishing artefacts decorating the room. With a warm and intimate atmosphere, the restaurant specialises in delicious fish dishes, personally selected daily from the local fish market by Donny. To avoid disappointment it is advisable to book a table for dining at the restaurant at the weekends.

The Swan Inn, Barnby Tel: 01502 476646

KESSINGLAND. This is a small resort with a wide beach of sand and shingle that extends for some two and a half miles, and it is a popular place for swimmers and sailors.

This was once the richest village in England and although not in possession of this title today, it still contains some impressive examples of architecture.

It was on the outskirts of Kessingland that we discovered the **Suffolk Wildlife and Rare Breeds Park**, which has an extensive collection of all our favourite zoo animals, such as lions and bears, wolves and beavers, and reptiles and birds. Many rare breeds of cattle, pigs, sheep and poultry are accommodated here too; and among the most unusual of these are the miniature South American horses, the tail-less Manx Rumpie chickens, and the miniature Dexter cattle - standing less than three feet high!

Situated in 100 acres of idyllic Suffolk countryside, the Park provides an interesting and educational attraction for all members of the family. There is a large cafeteria and a children's play area too, so you can quite easily make a day of it here. The Park is open daily from 10.00 am, from Easter to October.

WRENTHAM. This ancient village has changed little over the years and its church, dedicated to St Nicholas, dates from the 15th century.

QUIGGINS RESTAURANT, in the heart of Wrentham, is a distinctive 250 year old listed building. Tastefully converted from a shop some twenty years ago, the building still retains many of its original features such as the old beams as well as a beautiful, ornate cash register from its days as a shop. Today, this superb restaurant is owned and personally run by Jill and Dudley McNally, who have decorated it with family photographs, pictures and ornaments to create a warm, homely atmosphere.

With a comfortable lounge area diners can enjoy a pre-dinner drink in a relaxed and friendly atmosphere whilst making their choice from the extensive à la carte and fixed price menus. There is also a wide ranging wine list that specialises in New World wines. The elegant, candlelit dining room it the perfect place to enjoy the absolutely delicious food. Dishes vary from traditional English to adventurous international, but all are prepared from the freshest of local ingredients. Fish, you are in East Anglia, is always an excellent choice and comes fresh from nearby Lowestoft. A member of 'Les Routiers', and holder of their coveted Casserole and Corps d'Elite Awards, and recommended by the 'Best Hotels and Restaurants in the Eastern Counties' guide, Quiggins Restaurant is a superb evening, or lunchtime, experience.

Qiggins Restaurant, 2 High Street, Wrentham Tel: 01502 75397

COVEHITHE. A tiny coastal village, Covehithe has the most remarkable church. Not especially remarkable in itself, though attractive enough, but eminently memorable beacuse of its dramatic setting. The original 15th century church of St Andrew's was really always too large for the size of the community it served and, after it was ruined during the Civil War, it became a victim of economics. The dwindling parish was simply unable to justify rebuilding the church to its former size and glory, and in 1672 a tiny thatched church was built within the confines of the former nave, using materials from the ruins of the original church. Above this 'church-within-a church' looms the massive tower of the old St Andrew's; one of the most effective navigational aids along this stretch of the coast, and left standing by Cromwell's men for that very purpose.

Much of this part of the Suffolk coastline is under attack from the remorseless pounding of the waves and, in the past, entire villages have been completely lost to the encroaching sea. From the top of the crumbling cliffs there are wonderful views of the beautiful, seemingly endless, sandy beach, backed by grey shingle and low, windswept hillocks. It is said that this sparsely inhabited part of Suffolk boasts one of England's remotest and loveliest coastlines and, given favourable weather conditions, most would readily concur. Beware the east wind, however, for when it blows even the sight and sound of wild seabirds loses its charm.

SOUTHWOLD. This impressive seaside town certainly has a lot to offer the visitor. There is an excellent sandy beach, sailing, bird watching, plenty of good walks and an attractive little theatre.

Much of the town's charm is due to the variety of its old buildings which come in many shapes, sizes and styles of architecture. One of the most elegant of these is **Buckenham House** in the High Street. With its redbrick façade and small-paned sash windows, this house looks like a classic Georgian town house, but in fact its roots go back much further. The house is named after Richard Buckenham, a prosperous Tudor merchant with business interests in brewing and fishing who owned a number of other properties in Southwold. It is likely that he had it built in the mid 1500s, and that he and his wife, Christian, were the original occupants. At that period the house would have been timber-framed and the scale of this original building can be judged by the dimensions of the present cellar. Then, as now, this spacious basement room was approached by steps from the street. In Tudor times, the cellar would have been used in connection with the family's brewing activities.

In the first half of the 18th century, Buckenham House was given its Georgian façade, then in 1752 it became the vicarage of Southwold. One of the last of the vicars to reside there was a keen photographer who took a wonderful series of photographs of the building's interior.

However, what makes Southwold so special is that it simply does not conform to most people's idea of a typical seaside town. Some how Southwold has somehow managed to remain virtually unchanged for the past hundred years and is now one of the most popular resorts on the east coast; with none of the trappings of rampant commercialism. The town is practically an island, bounded by creeks and marshes, the River Blyth and the North Sea, and its attractive mixture of period houses and colour-washed cottages are built around a series of delightful greens. These mark the sites of many of the buildings that were lost in a great fire in 1659, never to be rebuilt.

There are two particularly memorable buildings in the town, the first being the splendid Perpendicular church of St Edmund King and Martyr, home of a well-known character called 'Southwold Jack'. This is a 15th century mechanical figure made of painted oak and dressed in the regalia of an armoured foot soldier, who strikes the bell of the church clock with his battle-axe. The other great landmark, and one that can be seen from practically every part of the town, is the 100 ft high, gleaming white inshore lighthouse, built in 1890 with a beam that can be seen some 17 miles out at sea. In the shadow of this, and much photographed as a result, is the little Victorian pub called the Sole Bay Inn; this is named after the Battle of Sole Bay in 1672 when the combined French and British fleets beat off the Dutch in a bitter sea battle off the coast here.

Fishermen still land their catches in the harbour at the mouth of the River Blyth. The Sailors' Reading Room in East Street is a favourite haunt of the old 'salts', who no doubt yearn for the days when fish brought in a profit and boats and skills could be safely handed down from father to son. Today's fishermen face an uphill task as EC regulations make a farce of the old traditions, with quotas and regulations being the final nail in the coffin of what currently looks to be a doomed national industry.

Further round the seafront, there is an excellent view of both sea and town from Gun Hill, so called from the six 18 pounder guns that stand there. It is said that they were presented to the town by the Duke of Cumberland in 1745, who landed here on his way to Scotland to take on Bonnie Prince Charlie. The guns had to be hidden away during both world wars, after the Germans used their presence to claim that the town was fortified and bombarded it from the sea.

BLYTHBURGH. In the 15th century this was an extremely prosperous port, with a busy quayside full of ships engaged in the wool trade. Unfortunately, ships got bigger and the river silted up, and when a bad fire compounded the problems of declining trade, Blythburgh dwindled in size to become the little village it is today.

A legacy of those affluent times is the beautiful church of the Holy Trinity, whose sheer size and splendour has earned it the inevitable nickname of the 'Cathedral of the Marshes'. Visible for miles as it rises up above the surrounding reed beds, the church is a surprising and spectacular sight at any time - but especially so at night, when it is floodlit.

During a terrible storm in 1577, lightning struck the church while a service was in progress and the steeple crashed down into the nave, shattering the font and killing two members of the congregation. The scorch marks that can still be seen today on the north door were said to be clawmarks left by the Devil in the guise of Black Shuck, as he sped from the church towards Bungay - for this was the same day that he paid his equally unwelcome visit to St Mary's there. Further trouble came in 1644, when William Dowsing and his colleagues arrived to indulge in an orgy of desecration. Windows, ornaments and statues were smashed, the wooden angels in the roof were blasted with hundreds of bullets, and the church was turned into a stable for the Roundhead's horses, with tethering rings screwed into the pillars of the nave.

Thankfully, not being classified by Dowsing as 'superstitious' or 'idolatrous', the marvellous bench-ends at Holy Trinity have survived intact. They depict the Labours of the Months and the Seven Deadly Sins, and two favourites are Gluttony and Slander. South of the altar is a kinsman of 'Southwold Jack' (they are known collectively as 'Jacks-o'-the Clock'), a charming little fellow who strikes the bell with his hammer and nods his head if his cord is pulled. Another unusual feature here is the priest's chamber over the south porch; an ancient little room which has been carefully restored, complete with an altar made of wood from HMS Victory.

Toby's Walk Picnic Site, to the south of the village, is a 25 acre former gravel quarry which has been given a new lease of life thanks to the extensive planting of trees and the reintroduction of natural gorse.

WALBERSWICK. A busy port until around the 16th century, Walberswick is now a quiet and graceful residential community with large, neat houses and well-tended gardens. At the end of the village, the little riverside harbour is packed with fishing boats and small sailing craft in the summer, and from here the unmade road leads down to the sandy beach.

The first thing to catch the eye, on entering this village, is the tall medieval church of St Andrew. Dwindling parish finances forced it to be partly dismantled at the end of the 17th century, and the present church was built within the ruins of its predecessor in much the same way as its namesake at Covehithe. Nevertheless, the fine tower and south aisle remain, and the interior is full of character.

MARYS OF WALBERSWICK, in the village, is a charming and unusual restaurant with covers for forty five people. It was originally tearooms, and still has a flourishing trade for morning coffee and afternoon tea. We are told that people travel for miles to sit in the garden and enjoy cream teas or jam and cream doughnuts.

It was for dinner that we came to Marys of Walberswick. The interior is lovely and so informal. There are many nautical pictures on the walls, of local scenes and old fishing smacks. There are some splendid portraits of local fisherfolk, with their weatherbeaten faces. Here and there fishing nets are draped, and overall it gives a theme that is totally right for a restaurant in Walberswick, where fishing has been a part of local life for generations.

Marys of Walberswick, Manor House, Walberswick
Tel: 01502 723243

The menu is a mixture of English and French, specialising in local produce, particularly fish and game. Fish is caught locally, and the game comes from the excellent shooting to be found in Norfolk and Suffolk.

The lunchtime à la carte menu, which also has vegetarian dishes, is supplemented with the day's specials. There are always dishes like home-smoked cod roes or the very unusual baked banana with stilton and cream, mouth-watering! The restaurant is licensed, and has a small but very well-chosen wine list, something appealing to everyone's palate and pocket.

In Winter and Spring every Friday lunchtime the menu changes to one featuring the best in Old English Cookery. Excellent value it is also an interesting experience. On New Year's morning they had a Victorian breakfast, which was a sell out! There is also a self-catering one-bedroom flat above the restaurant that is very well equipped.

DUNWICH was once East Anglia's capital city and one of the most important ports on the east coast of England. It was founded by the missionary St Felix, who sailed here from Burgundy in 632 AD to bring his message of Christianity to the natives. Experts believe that the main part of Dunwich once extended for some 7 miles beyond its present boundaries, but in a great storm in January 1326 the town was engulfed by the sea. Some 400 houses and three of its nine churches were swept out to sea, and this was just the beginning of the town's inevitable decline. The huge bank of sand and shingle that the storm threw up across the mouth of the harbour diverted the course of the River Blyth and cut it off from the sea, virtually killing the town's trade overnight.

For the next 700 years, the relentless erosion of wind and tide continued to take its toll, and all that remains of the village today are a few Victorian terraced cottages and a church. The only reminders of old Dunwich itself are the ruins of a Norman leper's chapel next to the church, the archways of a medieval friary that was built on the spot where St Felix was supposed to have landed, and a solitary tombstone from the graveyard of the medieval All Saints Church, which fell into the sea around 1920. One of the cottages houses the **Dunwich Museum**, which chronicles the history of this fascinating place from Roman times to the present day.

The locals say that when a storm is threatening, the sound of submerged church bells can still be heard tolling deep under the waves as they shift in the current. The more fanciful among them may speak of strange lights appearing in the ruined Greyfriars Priory, and of the eerie sound of long-dead monks chanting over the sound of the wind. Add to these stories the fact that bones from ancient graveyards are still sometimes washed up on the beach and you have an atmosphere of undeniable drama and mystery.

Dunwich Heath (or Common) and **Westleton Heath** combine to form a large area of sandy heathland once grazed by sheep, but now taken over by gorse and heather and their respective nature reserves. Dunwich Common, which will be familiar to all readers of the ghost stories of MR James, provides stunning views over Dunwich Forest, the marshes and the sea. Strangest of all is the view to the south beyond the wetlands of Minsmere, where the endless vista is suddenly broken by the futuristic vision of the mighty nuclear power station of Sizewell.

WESTLETON. This delightful village is far enough away from the crumbling cliffs to be secure in the knowledge that it has nothing to fear from the cruel sea. In contrast to its neighbour, Dunwich, its history is not one of diminished prosperity and a dwindling population. Westleton today is presumably much as it has always been; an archetypal English village with a village green and pond, some pleasant houses and an unpretentious thatched church.

THE CROWN, in the village of Westleton just off the A12, has a been offering hospitality to weary travellers for many, many years. Back in the 12th century, when the building was owned by Sibton Abbey, the bishop lived here and would take in guests. Years later, the Crown became a busy coaching inn, lying as it then did on the road between London and the port of Lowestoft. Today, the tradition of warm hospitality is continued by the inn's proprietors Rosemary and Richard Price.

A first class establishment, the Crown has 19 en-suite bedrooms that offer excellent, comfortable accommodation with a touch of luxury. The oldest part of the building is the lounge and this is where the beer was once brewed, but today, you might prefer to relax here and enjoy a glass or two before your meal. With an excellent menu, table d'hôte in the restaurant or a lighter, but equally delicious, menu in the bar area, the Crown is also a super place to come and enjoy a lovely meal. Set in landscaped gardens and close to Suffolk's Heritage Coast, the Crown makes a wonderful base from which to explore the county.

The Crown, Westleton Tel: 01728 648777

Minsmere Reserve is centred around the mouth of the River Minsmere, and covers more than 1,500 acres of reedbeds, heath and woodland, together with a series of man-made islands and lagoons. It is without doubt one of the best bird reserves in Britain, and this mixed habitat supports an astonishingly varied number of species that come here to breed. The seemingly endless list includes everything from nightjars, nightingales and marsh harriers, to bitterns and the rare avocet with its curious 'letter-opener' bill. Even those who profess to not being expert birdwatchers by any means agree a few hours spent in the hides observing native and migratory birds in their natural habitat is enough to make even those with a casual interest eager for more. A permit is needed to gain access to the main reserve, but anyone can use the large public hide to be found along the shore from the car park on Dunwich

Common. Further details, opening times and permits can be obtained from the reserve's reception centre.

THEBERTON. The village, which has an exceptionally pretty church that displays a scrap of German zeppelin that was shot down nearby in 1917, was the home of the 19th century travel writer Charles Montagu Doughty.

THE LION INN, in the heart of Theberton, is a charming, red brick pub owned and personally run by Jill and John McGee. Though the couple have not been here long they have used their considerable experience in the licensing trade to establish an enviable reputation for warm, friendly hospitality and also for excellent food and drink. A cosy pub inside, there is an unusual wood burning stove to take the chill off winter evenings whilst you enjoy a pint or two of well kept ale and a tasty meal. Obviously an old building, the Lion Inn has seen many things over the years. Being so close to the marshes, this was a great smuggling area but, more recently, locals will happily tell of the German Zeppelin incident of 1917. The exploits of the village's Victoria Cross holder, Charlie Doughty White, are chronicled in a framed article on the pub's wall. In fact, if there is anything you would like to know about this interesting area, the Lion is the place to come and ask.

As well as providing the village with its popular meeting place, Jill and John also have a small camp site behind the pub - an ideal place to pitch your tent.

The Lion Inn, Theberton Tel: 01728 830185

THE ALDERS, near Theberton, offers excellent farmhouse bed and breakfast accommodation within easy reach of the Minsmere bird reserve, Suffolk Heritage Coast and Snare Maltings its concerts and arts festivals. This former working farm is set within five acres of picturesque grounds and is situated approximately half-a-mile from the B1122 Leiston to Yoxford road. (It may be advisable to telephone the owner, Mrs Janet Baxter for directions.) Formerly two farm cottages, the Alders retains much of its original character and charm, with many of the rooms having superb views over the surrounding countryside. The three spacious letting rooms are all comfortable and well-appointed, and Mrs Baxter's renowned English breakfasts include home-made marmalade and free range eggs.

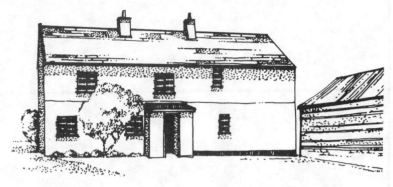

The Alders, Potters Street, Theberton Tel: 01728 831790

SAXMUNDHAM. There is something hauntingly beautiful about its name, and indeed this is an ancient market town which was once an important stopping place on the London to Yarmouth road. The reality, however, does not live up to expectations: the coming of the railway to the town in the 19th century brought with it both industry and the less inspiring side of Victorian architecture, and there is little here today to encourage the visitor to linger.

LEISTON. The award-winning **Long Shop Museum**, in Main Street, is well worth a visit to get an feel for the character of this interesting town. The museum is housed in the restored Grade II listed factory of the engineering works that was originally founded here in 1778 by Richard Garrett. In the early days, the firm specialised in manufacturing ploughs, threshers, seed drills and other types of agricultural machinery, and then progressed to steam powered units for use in factories, farms and mills. The museum now displays many of the original Garrett products, including traction engines, a trolley bus and an 1846 fire engine. Open daily from the end of March to the end of October, this really is a fascinating place to visit.

To the north of the town is the well-known **Summerhill**, the experimental school founded here in 1927 by the radical Scottish educationalist and author, Alexander Sutherland Neill. This is the school which 'began as an experiment and became a demonstration', and the philosophy by which it was run influenced many teachers both here and abroad. Further north are the impressive remains of **Leiston Abbey**, founded in 1182. The Premonstratensian order settled here in the 14th century after abandoning their increasingly uncomfortable site in the Minsmere marshes, and those parts of the Abbey where the fabric is still intact are now used as a summer school for budding young musicians who are unusually gifted.

It is ironic that Leiston, whose former major employer once benefited so much from the coming of the steam age, has now had little

Moot Hall, Snape

alternative than to embrace the nuclear age, firmly represented by Sizewell, just 2 miles to the east of the town. Its presence certainly solved a potentially disastrous local employment problem when the Richard Garrett works finally closed down in 1980. Whatever your thoughts may be on this emotive subject, it is definitely worth visiting the station to get a first-hand look at this awesome monument to modern technology. There is an excellent exhibition here which aims to answer all the questions on energy, nuclear power and its relationship with the environment. Admission is free, and for details of opening times and guided tours you should telephone the Sizewell Visitor Centre on (01728) 642139.

ALDRINGHAM. The little church of St Mary in this quiet village has a quite exceptional 15th century font and the delightfully named Parrot and Punchbowl Inn was a well-known centre for smuggling activities in the 17th century. Opposite this, now popular, pub is the renowned Aldringham Craft Market. Founded in 1958, the Craft Market is open daily all year round, and its three galleries contain an extensive range of craft work, fine art, imaginative gifts and ladies' clothes.

THORPENESS. This unique holiday village was planned at the beginning of the century by the playwright, barrister and architect, Glencairn Stuart Ogilvie. Its half-timbered, mock-Tudor style houses stand between the sea and there is also a 65 acre boating lake known as The Meare.

The two most unusual buildings in this decidedly eccentric village can be found facing each other on a ridge to the north of The Meare, along a track called Uplands Road. People who wander around wool-gathering were usually referred to as having their 'head in the clouds', so what did the inhabitants of the famous 'House in the Clouds' spend their time doing? This memorable structure, an 85 ft high five-storeyed affair with a clapboard cottage perched on top, is not quite what it seems. In was, in fact, originally a water tower and the 'cottage', complete with fake windows, pitched roof and chimney, housed the tank. Water was pumped into this by the early 19th century postmill standing opposite, which was itself moved from Aldringham for this purpose, and this provided the domestic water for the village.

The five-storied house below the tank is, however, quite genuine; and its early tenants presumably had no qualms about the 30,000 gallons of water just above their ceiling. Such fears are quite groundless today, as the water tower ceased to function as such in 1929, when Thorpeness had become so popular that a larger tank was required to cope with demand. Its replacement, incidentally, was disguised by the imaginative Mr Ogilvie as a sort of medieval keep, and became redundant itself when mains water came to the village.

FRISTON. The village, with a Norman church, occupies an exposed position some 350 ft up on the downs overlooking the sea.

SNAPE. The village (whose name means 'boggy place') has an interesting 12th century church of flint and brick, and just to the east of this, excavations in 1862 unearthed a 48 ft ship dating back to around 625 AD. Relics from that excavation and other interesting finds can be seen at **Moot Hall**, a handsome manor on the seafront built with imposing chimneys.

SNAPE MALTINGS is a remarkable collection of red brick granaries and malthouses on the banks of the River Alde, situated just off the A1094 to Aldeburgh. Once one of the largest maltings in East Anglia, the unspoilt rural charm of the area is retained here and there is plenty for the visitor to see and do. Trips on the river, which run between Easter and October, are an ideal way to see this peaceful estuary. A haven for wildlife, it is renowned for its colonies of avocet and shelduck.

From June to November a varied programme of arts and crafts courses are run at Snape Maltings. Ranging from watercolour painting to embroidery, the courses make an ideal break where you can learn new skills as well as enjoy the tranquillity of the site. Finally, there is a whole host of craft and interest shops here, along with a tea shop, pub and restaurant, that go a long way to make this an excellent day out for all the family.

Snape Maltings, Snape Tel: 01728 688303/688305

ALDEBURGH. A delightful old town which has one of the many strange Martello Towers erected as a defence against the French invaders led by Napoleon. Today it is possible to hire the Tower as a holiday let through the Landmark Trust and, interestingly enough, it is said to contain a million bricks. Details of the let can be had from The Landmark Trust, Shottebrooke, Maidenhead, Berkshire, SL6 3SW.

The town has resisted commercial ventures and benefited from this as it presents a gentle and timeless air that must have convinced Britten to live here.

UPLANDS HOTEL stands opposite the parish church in the quiet seaside resort of Aldeburgh, just minutes from the sea front. Originally built as a private residence for the Garrett family in 1841, this Regency country house first became a guest house in 1904. With lovely views over the charming town and the sea, the hotel has a secluded, walled garden with plenty of chairs in which guests can relax and enjoy a really restful

Southwold

break. Uplands is well known for its excellent cuisine and the Dining Room, overlooking the garden, offers a choice of table d'hôte, à la carte and vegetarian menus, and fresh fish, bought locally, features heavily. All the twenty guest bedrooms are comfortably furnished and equipped with television, tea and coffee making facilities and telephones. Uplands Hotel prides itself on the high standards of personal service and friendly hospitality all guests receive and you could not wish for a more charming place.

Uplands Hotel, Victoria Road, Aldeburgh Tel: 01728 452420

CHAPTER TWELVE

IPSWICH AND SOUTH-EAST SUFFOLK

Otley Hall

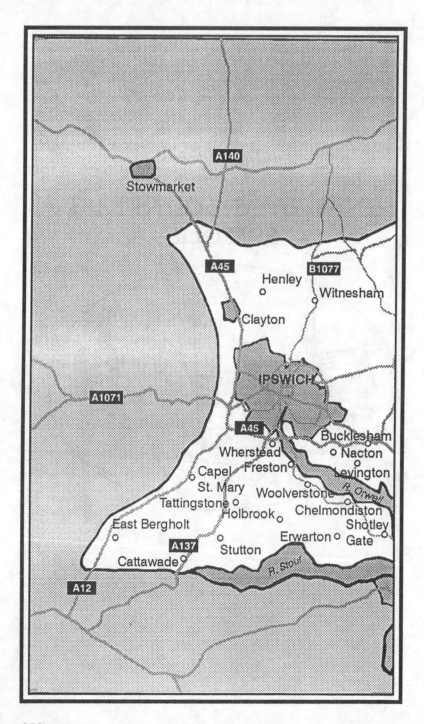

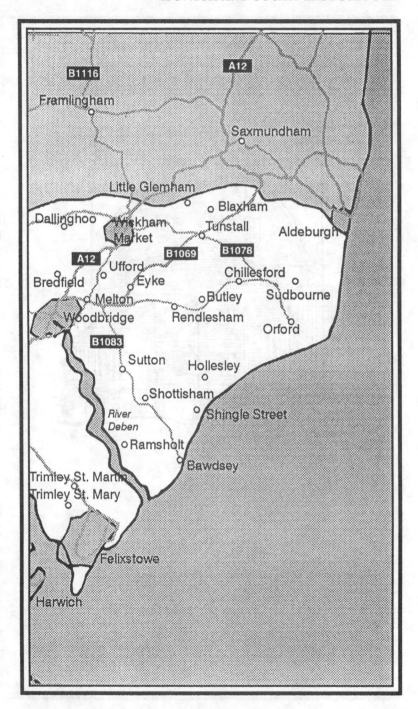

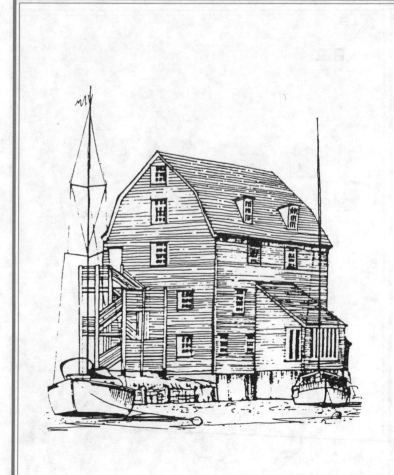

Woodbridge Tidal Mill

CHAPTER TWELVE

IPSWICH & SOUTH-EAST SUFFOLK

Woodbridge and North of the River Deben

WOODBRIDGE. Some say that the name of this historic town means simply 'wooden bridge', or perhaps 'bridge by the wood'; while others claim that it is derived from an Anglo-Saxon phrase meaning 'Woden's Town' which would indicate that this has been an important community since earliest times. Whatever the truth may be, this splendid old market town, which stands at the head of the tidal Deben estuary, has a distinctive charm of its own and offers visitors the chance to admire a wealth of old buildings, ranging from the merely interesting to the authentically historic.

This opportunity is greatly enhanced by the fact that traffic is restricted here during the day; the result of this excellent piece of town planning being that the humble pedestrian can enjoy the town to the full, with none of the usual problems of noise and fumes and the fear of being mown down as you cross the street. Woodbridge is a renowned centre of the antiques trade, and inveterate browsers can spent several happy hours here searching for bargains, lapping up the atmosphere and exploring the narrow cobbled alleyways.

The town's greatest benefactor was Thomas Seckford, a prosperous 16th century merchant, MP and barrister, who was also Master of the Rolls during the reign of Elizabeth I. There is a perhaps apocryphal story concerning him which claims that the Queen allowed him to attain great power and wealth, despite the fact that she objected strongly to the stench which arose from his boots! Be that as it may all seekers of hidden places owe him a great personal debt, as he was the patron of Christopher Saxton, 'the father of English cartography', whose atlas of England and Wales (published in 1579) was the first national atlas of any country in the world and provided us with England's first ever accurately surveyed road maps. What Seckford and Saxton would make of the vast network of roads and computer generated Ordnance Survey maps today is anybody's guess.

Seckford founded the original Seckford Almshouses in Seckford Street (the present buildings are a Victorian replacement) and in 1575 built the great **Shire Hall** which dominates Market Hill, a jewel among the many timber-framed buildings that lend the town such an air of distinction. Its Dutch gables and inner staircase were added in the 18th century, when the open ground floor, originally used as a corn exchange, was also enclosed. Opposite the Shire Hall is **Woodbridge Museum**, a treasure trove of information on the history of the town and its more notable residents, and from here it is a short stroll down the cobbled alleyway to the magnificent parish church of St Mary, where Seckford was buried in 1587. Also commemorated here with a splendid three-tiered monument is Jeffrey Pitman, a local tanner and haberdasher who exceeded his humble beginnings by becoming High Sheriff of Suffolk.

Lord Alfred Tennyson was a past contented patron of the Bull and stayed here when visiting the town. His friend and fellow poet, the eccentric Edward FitzGerald (born in nearby Bredfield), had lodgings over a gunsmith's shop on Market Hill and is best remembered as the translator of that famous lyrical epic, 'The Rubaiyat of Omar Khayyam'; disrespectfully referred to by schoolboys as 'The Rubber Boat of Hymie Cohen'.

A country gentleman by birth, 'Old Fitz' (as he was known to his friends) was a man of many contradictions, for although he led a generally reclusive life ('Every year and every day I am creeping out of the world in my own way') he was also known to dress flamboyantly and had a knack of surrounding himself with renowned eccentrics. In his quieter moments, there was nothing he enjoyed more than sailing his small yacht on the River Deben. FitzGerald died in 1883 and was buried in the churchyard at Boulge (his family lived at Boulge Hall, demolished in 1956), two and a half miles north-west of the town. It is believed that the rose bush which marks his last resting place is a descendant of the one on Omar Khayyam's grave in Iran.

Church Street leads into Woodbridge's main street, **The Thoroughfare**, with its handsome red-brick and half-timbered houses and numerous original shop fronts; and to the east of this lies the Quayside and the River Deben. The Deben is a most impressive waterway, very popular with the sailing fraternity, and the Quayside seems a different world altogether to the rest of the town. Boatbuilding, sailmaking and associated industries have been a part of life in Woodbridge since at least the 14th century, and work in these skilled professions still goes on today, albeit now with pleasure craft as opposed to sea-going vessels and warships.

It is perhaps appropriate therefore that the Woodbridge **Tide Mill**, an 18th century clapboard mill which dominates the waterfront, should have a roof shaped like the hull of a boat. As its name suggests, it draws its power from the tidal waters of the Deben, and, amazingly enough, a tide mill has stood on this site since 1170. The present mill has been carefully restored to full working order and is open to the public from May to the end of September every day except Mondays, and on Saturdays and Sundays in October. Its grinding machinery operates at specific times subject to tides. Woodbridge also has a more conventional four-sailed windmill, which again is fully operational. This is **Buttrum's Mill**, a 19th century tower mill which can be found to the west of the town, open at weekends during the summer.

Given its close associations with shipbuilding and maritime pursuits, it seems appropriate that just a mile to the east of Woodbridge on the opposite bank of the river, one of this country's most famous ships was discovered at the **Sutton Hoo burial site**. A dozen barrows stand on this elevated site in a windswept area of sandy heath and, when the fourth of them was excavated in 1939, a 90 ft long clinker-built Saxon ship was found beneath the mound. Even more exciting, it contained one of the greatest hoards of treasure to be discovered in this country, which is now housed in the British Museum. Although it is not known whether the burial was intended as a cenotaph or a tomb (for no human remains were found) it is widely believed that the treasure belonged to King Raedwald of the Uffinga (or Wuffinga) dynasty, who was King of East Anglia from around 610 to 625 AD.

The hoard itself is priceless, and includes a purse containing 40 gold coins, a bronze and iron helmet, a gilded shield and a magnificent sword decorated with gold and jewels. Further excavations and surveys were begun in the 1980s to provide a better understanding of the Anglo-Saxon period and for more information regarding recent excavation news and discoveries, write to: The Sutton Hoo Society, c/o National Westminster Bank, Cumberland Street, Woodbridge, Suffolk.

The Sutton Hoo site can be reached from Woodbridge by ferry, or by taking the A1152 from Woodbridge then turning south onto the B1083, from which the site is signposted. There is also an exhibition concerning this exciting discovery at the Woodbridge Museum.

One mile south-west of the town lies the beautiful Elizabethan **Seckford Hall**, ancestral home of the Seckfords for 520 years and said, by some, to be haunted by the ghost of the most distinguished member of the family, Thomas Seckford. When Sir Ralph Harwood purchased the Hall in 1940, it was derelict; after the war he restored it and transformed it into a hotel, and 10 years later it came into the hands of the Bunn family who it has been with ever since. Today, it is a superbly run hotel and restaurant with an international reputation, and although the atmosphere is eminently friendly and hospitable, the Hall is every bit as regal as when Elizabeth I is said to have held a Court here.

One fascinating aspect of its history is that the Hall is said to contain a secret tunnel which once ran from the hotel kitchen to the cellars of **Woodbridge Abbey**. The Abbey, located just below St Mary's Church in Woodbridge, was the town house of Thomas Seckford, and its earliest parts (now the preparatory department of Woodbridge School) were built on the site of an old Augustinian priory. If the tunnel does indeed exist, it has now been blocked at both ends and it is likely that it would have been used in the days of 'the Master' for smuggling activities.

AROUND WOODBRIDGE - NORTH OF THE RIVER DEBEN

BLAXHALL. Stone Farm in the village takes its name from a 5 ton slab of rock in the yard, known somewhat unimaginatively as 'The Blaxhall Stone'. When this innocent-looking boulder first came to public attention about 100 years ago, it was reported to be about the size of a loaf of bread. Since then, the locals claim that it has grown over the years to reach its present dimensions! Apparently, it was once a widely held belief that pebbles could grow to immense size in the potent East Anglian soil. The Blaxhall Stone it may be, but there is more than a touch of the 'Blarney Stone' about it.

LITTLE GLEMHAM. The Elizabethan mansion Little Glemham Hall stands in its own parkland with delightful gardens to the south of this attractive village. It was the 18th century home of Dudley North, son-in-law of the founder of Yale University, and is sometimes open to the public during the summer.

WICKHAM MARKET. A market no longer, as it happens, for that went to nearby Woodbridge many years ago, Wickham does, however, have a picturesque watermill beside the River Deben.

BREDFIELD. The character of this sleepy village is summed up perfectly by an eccentric plaque on the wall of the lovely old thatched village pub, The Crown. It states: 'On this spot 1742 absolutely nothing happened'. Nothing is still happening in Bredfield today and long may it continue not to happen: one of the joys of exploring the back roads of England in search of hidden places is to unexpectedly stumble across a quiet little village where nothing has really changed for the past hundred years or so.

Actually, something did happen in Bredfield, just 67 years after the 'nothing' that happened in 1742; for in 1809 the poet Edward FitzGerald was born here. The vicar of Bredfield in the mid 1800s, incidentally, was one of FitzGerald's 'set', George Crabbe, son of the Aldeburgh poet.

UFFORD. This village of charming thatched cottages and farm-houses takes its name from Uffa, the founder of the Uffinga dynasty of East Anglian kings.

Beside the gate of St Mary's Church are the ancient village stocks, a relic of the past not often found in this county. In addition to its beautiful Victorian stained glass, the pride of the church is its superb 15th century telescopic font cover, a great towering spire of sumptuously carved woodwork whose pinnacles soar towards the ceiling to a height of 18 ft, crowned by a pelican.

MELTON. On the outskirts of Woodbridge, the village's new church has an ancient and particularly interesting sacrament font.

THE HORSE AND GROOM in Melton was originally a coaching inn, which was built in the 16th century. This charming building is situated in the middle of the village, and today is at the heart of village life. John and Glenda, the owners, are very proud of the popularity which their pub enjoys, both with visitors and locals alike. The atmosphere of the pub is enhanced by its original oak beams, cosy 'snugs' and open fires. The pub is listed by CAMRA in its 'Real Ale Guide' and serves a fine selection of cask condition real ales, all worthy of sampling.

The pub also has a superb family dining area called STABLES RESTAURANT, where all the family, including children are made welcome. The food is excellent and represents very good value for money. Be sure to pay this lovely pub a visit.

The Horse and Groom, Yarmouth Road, Melton Tel: 01394 383566

RENDLESHAM. **Rendlesham Forest** is the oldest and largest of the several areas of woodland that make up the Forest of Aldewood, which covers around 14 square miles between Woodbridge and Southwold. This part of the forest is close-set with lofty pines, and its dark interior has a rather foreboding atmosphere.

Rendlesham itself is said to have been the site of a royal village of the Wuffinga dynasty, although there is not much to support this apart from the close proximity of the Sutton Hoo burial site.

BUTLEY. At the north-eastern edge of Rendlesham Forest, the village has a splendid 14th century gatehouse of ruined Butley Priory, an Augustinian priory founded by Ranulf de Glanville in 1171.

CHILLESFORD. The name of this lovely old village means 'gravel ford'. Chillesford is known to geologists for the *Coralline Crag* in which more than 400 species of mollusc have been preserved, over a quarter of them now extinct. Also, the backbone of a 30 ft prehistoric whale was discovered here in the village brickworks. There is an interesting walk across open fields from Chillesford to Orford known as **Friars Walk** (old maps show this as *Froize* Walk, as in the name of the village pub).

To the north is **Tunstall Forest**, another part of Aldewood. It extends up to the River Alde, and is airier by far than neighbouring Rendlesham. Its larches and Corsican and Scots pines are spaced well apart, with fern and bracken underneath, making it an altogether more comfortable place to boldly go! The rare red squirrel makes its home here and as do the shy red and fallow deer.

THE FROIZE INN is built on the site of Chillesford Friary, being mid-way between Orford Friary and Butley Priory. Historically, the Friars are known to have supplied refreshment to weary travellers in the form of a Savoury Pancake called a Froize. The building of the Froize Inn dates back to approximately 1490 and is built of distinctive Chillesford Red Brick. In May 1995, there was a change of ownership when Alistair and Joy Shaw (formerly of the Kings Head Inn, Orford) took over the running of the Froize. As one of the few Free-Houses in the area the aim has been to offer a good selection of Real Ales from the local breweries and a comprehensive and interesting wine list to compliment Alistair's cooking. Early in 1996 there was a competition to name the pub's own beer, the name of 'Nun Chaser' being finally selected. As the inn is situated at the head of the river, the menu leans heavily to fresh local seafood including such treats as halibut in a sorrell and shrimp sauce, and whole bass with ginger and spring onion sauce, but also features local game and produce, finished off by a choice of real home-made puddings. The Froize has plenty of potential with large bedroom accommodation, two acres of garden, play area, camping and caravanning area, paddock and delightful thatched barn. With so much room to let off steam, families with children are definitely welcome. Closed Mondays for a rest!

The Froize, The Street, Chillesford Tel: 01394 450282

SUDBOURNE.

Anyone looking for a very quiet location with no noise other than the local animals, Mrs Wood has the perfect spot for your bed and breakfast at **LONG MEADOWS**. There is ideal walking from the doorstep and a lovely garden to sit in and admire which Ann is justly proud of. Children over 12 can be catered for and pets are welcome by arrangement. Lovely spot.

Long Meadow B&B, Gorse Lane, Sudbourne Tel: 01394 450269

ORFORD. This coastal village is protected from the ravages of the North Sea by the 6 mile long shingle bank, Orford Ness. The village actually stands on the sheltered banks of the River Alde, with the River Ore to the south.

Boasting a market place and a castle, Orford might be mistaken for a town, but the sheer peacefulness of the place, and the fact that it is somewhat off the beaten track, leads one to feel it is really a village. The truth of the matter is that Orford was certainly an important town at one time; the massive castle keep and the obvious former splendour of the partly ruined church of St Bartholomew are ample evidence of that. It was also a thriving port, but the steadily encroaching Orford Ness (said to grow at the rate of some 15 yards each year) put paid to that as it gradually cut the town off from the sea.

Today, Orford has dwindled to the size of a small brick and timber village, surrounded by a vast area of lonely marshland to the north and south. A quiet and peaceful place for most of the year, it becomes much livelier during the summer when colourful pleasure craft make their way up the River Ore to the south of the village to moor alongside the quay.

From the quay boat trips can be taken to the 300 acre **Havergate Island**, now an RSPB reserve, which boasts Britain's oldest and largest breeding colony of avocets. Tours of the reserve are escorted by the warden, and permits and visiting times must be obtained in advance by writing to: The Warden (Havergate Island), 30 Mundays Lane, Orford, IP12 2LX.

On the way up Market Hill to the broad market place in the heart of the village is the famous Butley-Orford Oysterage fish restaurant. The sign outside this establishment commemorates Orford's very own twisted interpretation of 'The Little Mermaid'; this one decidedly less cute and lovable than the Disney version! The 'Wild Man of Orford' was apparently caught in the nets of local fishermen sometime in the 13th century. Ralph of Coggleshall chronicled the event, and relates how this naked and hairy 'merman' was taken to the castle where he lived for several months on a diet of raw fish, refusing to utter a word even under torture, before making his escape back to the sea.

Orford Castle stands to the west of the market square, and is now maintained by English Heritage. It was built as part of Henry II's coastal defences in 1165, using the then revolutionary polygonal design which was said to give the defense greater stability and to confuse its attackers. The design has certainly stood the test of time, for the superbly restored 90 ft keep with its three huge rectangular turrets looks as if it could stand for at least another 800 years. From the top of the tower there are splendid views over the village and the coast. Seawards, the most prominent landmark is the red and white striped lighthouse on Orford Ness, and it was on the Ness, incidentally, that pre-war radar research was carried out under the supervision of Sir Robert Watson-Watt.

The Dunwich Underwater Exploration Exhibition held in The Craft Shop, Front Street, provides an interesting insight into the history of the disappearing village of Dunwich. It is open daily all year round from 11.00 am - 5.00 pm. As well as telling the story of the devastating effects of coastal erosion, the exhibition shows exactly what has been found so far during the exploration of submerged Dunwich.

SHINGLE STREET. At this aptly named small village, a row of white cottages stands above a vast stretch of shingle which has been thrown up by storms into a high bank, and runs up the coast to the mouth of the River Ore and Orford Ness. Parts of it were used for target practice during the war, but it has now been designated a Site of Special Scientific

Interest due to its rare coastal plants.

To the south of the hamlet, against this backdrop of shingle beach and rolling seas, a series of five Martello towers rears up along the coast between here and Felixstowe; not the most attractive of buildings, but a memorable part of our heritage and a reminder that once we were obsessed by the fear of invasion from France.

BAWDSEY. The late-Victorian Bawdsey Manor lies to the south of the village, towards the mouth of the River Deben. Radar research was transferred here from Orford Ness in 1936 when the manor was converted into a coastal warning station; its equipment ever vigilant for German bombers. Bearing in mind that radar was still pretty much in its infancy at the beginning of the war, there must have been some fascinating blips on the screen with all those migratory birds coming in to land on Havergate Island.

PUFFIN FERRIES is the oldest ferry in Britain and it runs from Bawdsey across the River Deben to Felixstowe Ferry. There has been a service here since 1200 and today this pedestrian and cyclist ferry is owned and run by Peter Weir. Part of the Heritage Coastal walk and recognised cycle routes it is an interesting form of transport that adds something special to a day out on the coast.

Puffin Ferries, Bawdsey Tel: 01394 450637

RAMSHOLT. The village is a popular stop with those who have sailed down the River Deben from Woodbridge or up the river from Bawdsey. From here it is also possible to take a foot passenger ferry across to Felixstowe Ferry and hence on to Felixstowe itself.

In this lovely setting, and reached by a half-mile walk along a footpath from Ramsholt's disused ferry quay, stands the solitary Church of All Saints with its Norman round tower.

SHOTTISHAM. While in the area, it may be of interest to some to learn that there are a number of historians who claim that King Edmund was not captured and martyred at Hoxne at all, but met his end somewhere to the east of Shottisham and Sutton. Those in the 'anti-Hoxne' camp suggest that he found himself here after fleeing from a final battle with the Danes either at Orford, or possibly in Staverton Forest to the west of Butley. This, incidentally, is one of the oldest forests in England, and is known to date back to pre-Druidic times. The ferry that once took passengers from Ramsholt to the opposite bank of the Deben has long since gone.

Ipswich and Constable Country

IPSWICH, the county town of Suffolk, is one of the oldest towns in England. It has been a port since the time of the Roman occupation and the Anglo-Saxons developed it into the largest port in the country in the

7th century. In 1200, Ipswich was granted a charter by King John and it prospered throughout the Middle Ages, both as a centre of shipbuilding and as an important merchant community; its wealth based mainly on the Suffolk cloth trade. Periods of uncertainty were to come, however, particularly when the market for Suffolk cloth fell into decline in the mid 17th century. This particular problem was alleviated in the following century, when the town enjoyed a revival as a food distribution port during the Napoleonic Wars.

A potentially more serious problem which Ipswich has always had to live with is the fact that it is an inland port, 12 miles from the open sea and the risk from silting is ever present. This came to a head at the beginning of the 19th century, when a vigorous programme of dredging and dockbuilding had to be introduced to stop the harbour from becoming completely choked. Trade recovered and a period of industrial growth was to follow; the **Wet Dock** was constructed in 1842, the handsome red and yellow brick **Custom House** (now the headquarters of the Ipswich Port Authority) was built three years later, and, with the construction of important new rail links, the future of Ipswich was assured.

The town's most famous son was undoubtedly Cardinal Wolsey, born here sometime around 1475. The son of a prosperous butcher and grazier, he attended Magdalen College, Oxford, and through skilful manoeuvring went on to become Archbishop of York and then a Cardinal and Lord Chancellor under Henry VIII. His plan to make himself indispensable to the monarch had succeeded beyond all bounds, for he found himself deep in Henry's confidence, with full control of England's foreign policy and with more power than any minister of the Crown had enjoyed since Becket. His estates and personal wealth were considerable and he established both a grammar school at Ipswich and what would later become Christ Church College at Oxford.

Wolsey's catastrophic fall from grace was, of course, precipitated by his dithering over Henry's longed-for divorce from Catherine of Aragon. This prevarication, coupled with his inherent arrogance, not only angered the King, but made him many enemies both at home and abroad. Eventually he was forced to give up the Great Seal, his lands were seized by the Crown and, when arrested for high treason, he died en route to London from York.

Notables from the world of the arts with Ipswich connections include Thomas Gainsborough, who settled here for many years as a portrait painter before moving to Bath; David Garrick, the renowned actor and manager, who made his debut here in 1741 as Aboan in Thomas Southerne's 'Oroonoko'; and Charles Dickens, who stayed at the Great White Horse in Tavern Street while still a young reporter from the Morning Chronicle, hot on the local election trail. Soon after, he was to immortalise the inn in 'The Pickwick Papers' as the place where Mr Pickwick wanders inadvertently into a lady's bedroom, and his none too flattering description of the establishment brought threats of a libel action from the landlord.

If there is one slight pall over the town, it is that many of its oldest buildings were effectively destroyed by the Victorians in their haste to bring 'modernity' to Ipswich. Of those that survived, perhaps the best loved is the **Ancient House** or Sparrowe's House in the Butter Market, home for 200 years to the Sparrowes who were merchants by trade. The house itself dates back to the 15th century, but its most outstanding feature was added later, sometime around 1670. This is the exquisite pargeting that embellishes the building above the ground floor, including the coat of arms of Charles II and symbolic representations of the known continents at that time. The building is now a very good bookshop.

Historic architecture of the ecclesiastical kind has proved more resilient, for Ipswich has no less than 12 medieval churches still standing. St Margaret's with its ornate flushwork and splendid double hammerbeam roof is undoubtedly the finest, while tucked away behind St Mary at the Elms is one of the town's oldest cottages, dating from 1467.

The dock area to the south of the town is a fascinating place. It stretches for over a mile along both banks of the River Orwell and, in addition to the great cargo vessels laden with everything from timber and grain to raw materials, graceful yachts and sailing barges can be seen moored in the harbour basin.

The people of Ipswich are lucky to have a beautiful green space to the north of the town, just a few minutes walk from the main shopping area. This is **Christchurch Park**, 65 acres of wooded parkland, graced by the distinguished Tudor country house called Christchurch Mansion where Elizabeth I once stayed in 1561. The house contains a splendid domestic museum with furnishings from Tudor to Victorian times, as well as the **Wolsey Art Gallery** and the newly-opened **Suffolk Artists' Gallery**, with a wonderful collection of paintings by Constable and Gainsborough and that ever-popular equestrian painter, Sir Alfred Munnings. The other museum in town is the **Ipswich Museum** in the High Street, whose galleries cover a wide range of subjects including British birds, ethnography, geology and archaeology. Replicas of both the Mildenhall and Sutton Hoo Treasures can be seen here, as can an excellent reconstruction of a Roman villa and potter's workshop. The Museum is open all year round, Tuesday to Saturday from 10.00 am - 5.00 pm, but closed on Bank Holidays.

There is a good choice of guided walks and tours on offer in the town, ranging from visits to the docks and merchants' houses, a tour of Christchurch Mansion, and a 'travel through history in the footsteps of Henry VIII and Catherine of Aragon'. For dates and times of these and more, call into the Tourist Information Centre at the Town Hall in Princes Street.

THE CHOCOLATE HOUSE is a charming tea rooms and chocolate shop in the centre of Ipswich's pedestrian shopping area, just up the road from the Tourist Information Centre. The elegant tea rooms serve a whole range of snacks and light meals including filled jacket potatoes and home-made quiches. The cakes and patisseries, all made in the shop, are mouth-watering and well worth trying as is the delicious selection of teas and coffees, whose aroma fills the tea room.

The Chocolate House, 1A St Stephen's Lane, Ipswich Tel: 01473 210146

During the summer months, the Chocolate House takes on a continental air, when tables and chairs are placed outside and customers can enjoy the sunshine as well as the delicious food and drink. As well as offering the perfect place to rest and take refreshment when out and about in the town, the chocolate shop is a must for all chocoholics. With well over a hundred varieties of Belgian delicacies to choose from there is something for everyone. The divine Cappuccino is a dream. For that special present, individual selections of chocolates can be beautifully gifted wrapped or there are a whole host of ready filled boxes.

Mount Pleasant, 103 Anglesea Road, Ipswich Tel: 01473 251601

MOUNT PLEASANT enjoys a superb elevated position in a quiet conservation area yet it is only ten minutes walk from the centre of Ipswich. A large Victorian house, set in a small town garden with secluded courtyard, Mount Pleasant is owned by Geraldine and David Harrison who, as well as running a language school, offer excellent bed and breakfast accommodation. There are three well appointed bed-rooms all elegantly decorated, as is the rest of the house. The comfortable guest's lounge is a popular meeting place in the evening and office facilities are available if required. The substantial breakfast served to all guests includes delicious fresh croissants still warm from the oven and aromatic freshly made coffee. Whether touring the area or in Ipswich on business, Mount Pleasant is a great place to stay.

Stelvio Guest House, Crane Hill, London Road, Ipswich
Tel: 01473 690342/601802 Fax: 01473 690342

STELVIO GUEST HOUSE is a large Edwardian house in a quiet residential area of Ipswich, close to the main A12 and A14 roads. Owned by Jayne Malin and Neil Holford, this charming guest house offers friendly accommodation at very reasonable prices. There are five comfortable bedrooms all of which have their own en-suite with shower, basin and w/c or private w/c and basin. Jayne is an accomplished cook and serves a range of continental and traditional dishes in the evening with a substantial breakfast to set you up for the day. The house stands in fantastic gardens which the guests are free to enjoy. Beautiful Chantry Park is very close by.

Redholme, 52 Ivry Street, Ipswich Tel: 01473 250018

REDHOLME lies in a quiet residential area of Ipswich, close to Christchurch Park, yet it is just ten minutes walk to the town centre. This large, red brick Victorian house was built in 1884 for a local wool dyer and it stands in its own large, well-kept and secluded garden.

Owned by Pat and John McNeil, the couple offer first class bed and breakfast accommodation, with an optional evening meal by arrangement, from their delightful home. There are four, en-suite bedrooms, one of which is suitable for a family, and Pat and John serve up a wonderful, large breakfast that will keep you going all day. The quiet and peaceful garden is a delight and also has an outdoor swimming pool which is the ideal place to relax in after a day out exploring Ipswich and the surrounding area.

AROUND IPSWICH - CONSTABLE COUNTRY

HENLEY. **THE CROSS KEYS** pub has a perfect location on the Henley Road and is a family run business by Adrian, Mary and their daughter Anita; "A family pub with a family welcome". You will find a great atmosphere here and it is rumoured there's an 'old sea dog' ghost who puts in an appearance from time to time. The pub has three principal rooms which include a games room with all the traditional games such as Snakes & Ladders, Scrabble, Chess etc. and is dedicated to sea stories with a definite Naval theme. There's a Pool Table room and a third room has a totally home from home feel for relaxing and recounting the day's events. A small restaurant provides good food and deserves its growing good reputation.

The Cross Keys, Main Road, Henley Tel: 01449 760229

WHERSTEAD. This small village lies the west bank of the River Orwell to the south of Ipswich. Edward FitzGerald's family made their home at Wherstead Lodge, in the village, before moving to Boulge.

In a county that is generally thought of as being flat, it is interesting to note that Wherstead's main attraction is a dry ski slope! For those who prefer more gentle pursuits, there is a charming woodland walk just off the road through **Spring Wood**, renowned for its profusion of beautiful flowers throughout that particular season. The village also offers fine views of the mile-long Orwell Bridge, which carries the A45 over the

Orwell estuary and speeds heavy lorries on their way to the harbour at Felixstowe.

TATTINGSTONE. **Tattingstone Wonder**, on the road between this pleasant village and Sutton, is a marvellous 18th century folly built by local landowner Thomas White in 1790. Faced with the knotty problem of having to provide accommodation for his estate workers, but not wanting to spoil the view from his newly built mansion, Tattingstone Place, he hit upon the novel idea of building their cottages in the guise of a church. Very convincing it is too, with its mock medieval tower and high 'nave' - though the brick chimney does tend to give it away!

Tattingstone lies on the western edge of Alton Water, a large reservoir neatly 'sandwiched' between the A137 and the B1080. There is a pleasant country walk around the perimeter and a wide variety of waterfowl and wildlife to observe. Alternatively, the reservoir is home to a whole host of watersports and leisure activities, including fishing, sailing, windsurfing and even sub-aqua diving.

CATTAWADE. Where the main railway line crosses over Cattawade Creek is this strangely named village. The somewhat mystifying definition of its name is 'a ford frequented by wild-cats', conjuring up a bizarre vision of ferocious moggies attempting the crossing.

EAST BERGHOLT. John Constable was born in this pretty, scattered village in 1776, and if it has now geared itself ever so slightly to cater for Constable-mania, who can blame it? The actual house in which the painter was born no longer stands, but its site is marked by a plaque on the fence of its successor, now a private house called 'Constables'. A little further along Church Street is the tiny Moss Cottage, which Constable once used as a studio.

It was at the Old Rectory that he first met his future wife, Maria Bicknell. There is a memorial to her at St Mary's Church, together with a somewhat garish stained-glass memorial window to Constable himself, and his parents and his old friend Willy Lott are buried in the churchyard. The unusual timber-framed structure in the churchyard is a bell-cage, built in 1531 and a 'memorial' of sorts to Cardinal Wolsey. He had apparently pledged money to the church for a bell tower and the cage was intended as a temporary resting place for the bells until its completion. When Wolsey fell from grace and the funds were not forthcoming, the tower was left unfinished and the bells have been in their cage ever since. They hang upside-down and are rung by hand by pulling on the wooden shoulder stocks; no mean feat, as these five bells are said to be the heaviest in England.

A leafy lane leads south of the village to the River Stour, where two of Constable's best known subjects still stand today, looking just as they did when he first painted them. The first is **Flatford Mill**, the brick watermill owned by Constable's father, built in 1733 and now owned by the National Trust and run as a residential field study centre. A little way downstream is the charming **Willy Lott's Cottage**, subject of Constable's most famous work, 'The Haywain', and also maintained by the National

Trust. Neither is open to the casual visitor, but there is a way-marked trail laid out by the Trust along the banks of the river for memorable views of cottage, mill, lock and weir. Under Flatford Bridge, a replacement for the bridge that Constable painted many times, is Bridge Cottage, with a National Trust shop, a tea garden and a permanent exhibition of the painter's life and works. There are also facilities for boating and fishing.

Exploring this delightful area around the banks of the willow-lined river, it is with the knowledge that here, too, Constable walked, sketchbook in hand, drawing constant inspiration from the idyllic riverside scenery. He would return here many times after heading for London to become a student at the Royal Academy, and much of his greatest work was done within a 10 mile radius of his beloved home.

Also at East Bergholt are **Stour Gardens**, where sweeping lawns, colourful flower beds and small ponds are laid out neatly below Stour House, former home of the journalist and author Randolph Churchill, son of Sir Winston. The gardens are open daily.

STUTTON. The village lies on the southern edge of Alton Water. At the **Alton Water Sports Centre** on Holbrook Road, windsurfers and sailing dinghies can be hired. Day membership is available, and the Centre also provides training courses in the summer.

South-east of the village, St Peter's Church stands in quiet isolation overlooking Holbrook Bay, and a footpath from the church leads down to the water's edge, around the eastern side of the bay, and all the way along the northern bank of the Stour estuary to Shotley Gate.

HOLBROOK. The massive neo-Georgian **Royal Hospital School** is the descendant of the school for the sons of officers and men in the Royal Navy and Royal Marines which was founded in 1712, originally attached to Greenwich Hospital in London, but transferred to Holbrook in 1933. Its central tower, topped by a white stone pinnacle, is a landmark for miles around and can be seen from both sides of the Stour estuary.

Half a mile further north, standing by a tributary of the Stour at the entrance to Holbrook itself, is **Alton Mill**. This weather-boarded mill has stood here for more than 200 years, on a site occupied by a succession of watermills since before the Domesday Survey of 1086.

The lane heading south-east from the mill leads into the heart of the **Shotley Peninsula**, the marshy promontory set between the estuaries of the Orwell and the Stour. This attractive area is rich in birdlife, and is especially renowned for its breeding waders, redstart, lapwing and snipe.

HIGHFIELD is a delightful 'home from home' on the outskirts of Holbrook which offers luxurious accommodation ideal for visitors to this fascinating area. The house is the home of Bryan and Sally Morris who offer a warm welcome into a relaxed, happy atmosphere where you will be sure to enjoy your stay.

Three beautifully presented double rooms are available, all of which are well equipped with tea and coffee making facilities, television, radio and central heating. One of the rooms even has a balcony which overlooks the large well kept gardens which surround this lovely house. All of the rooms offer beautiful views across the lawns to the rolling fields and the River Stour. Two of the rooms have en-suite facilities.

The prices are very reasonable and include a hearty English breakfast, or continental if you prefer. There are many excellent pubs and restaurants in the immediate area, including the Compasses Inn which is just a five minute walk away. Sorry no smoking, no pets and no children.

Highfield, Harkstead Road, Holbrook Tel: 01473 328250

ERWARTON. Just beyond this village is the impressive red-brick Jacobean gatehouse with a rounded arch, buttresses and pinnacles. This belongs to **Erwarton Hall**, the family home of the Calthorpes. Anne Boleyn was the niece of Philip Calthorpe and visited the house on numerous occasions, and legend has it that her heart was buried in the family vault at St Mary's Church. Credibility was lent to the story when a heart-shaped casket was discovered there in 1836.

SHOTLEY GATE. Situated right at the end of the peninsula, the village overlooks the Stour estuary marshes. This was once the home of HMS Ganges, the Royal Navy's training base, but now there is a busy marina where an entirely different breed of seafarer holds sway.

PIN MILL. The tiny riverside community of Pin Mill lies on the west bank of the Orwell estuary. This is a favourite haunt of sailing and watersports enthusiasts, who flock to the idyllically situated 17th century fisherman's pub, the Butt and Oyster, with its strong associations with smuggling and the books of Arthur Ransome. The graceful, red-sailed Thames sailing barges, a familiar sight further down the coast as far as Kent, can still be seen on the water. They were once built here at Pin Mill and, in July, you can watch these beautifully restored vessels take part in the annual barge race which takes place from Buttermans Bay.

The origin of Pin Mill's name is unsure; some say it is a reference to the wooden 'pins' or pegs once made here that were so vital to the boat-building trade, while a more charming explanation is the story of the local landowner who gave his daughter the profits from windmills on his land as 'pin' money. To the east of the quay is Cliff Plantation, an ancient 17 acre coppice of alder and oak owned by the National Trust.

WOOLVERSTONE. The large marine here, along the banks of the Orwell, is used by the Royal Harwich Yacht Club. Overlooking the Orwell here is Cat House, where it is said that a stuffed white cat placed in the window of this dwelling would once have given local smugglers the 'all clear'.

FRESTON. Here, is an odd six-storey tower built of red-diapered brickwork sometime around 1550. Some say that **Freston Tower** is a pure folly, and the oldest one in England, if so, while others of a more practical persuasion claim that it was used as a look-out tower to warn of enemies approaching up the river. A favourite explanation, however, is that it served as a 'day-school' for Lord Freston's daughter. A day school quite literally, for on Mondays it is said that she started off on the ground floor learning charitable works, then progressed floor by floor up the spiral staircase to tapestry on Tuesdays, musical studies on Wednesdays, classics on Thursdays, English on Fridays and painting on Saturdays, then, having reached the top floor, she was given a day off for thoughtful contemplation and worship on Sundays. Who knows if the story is true or whether she benefited or not from these dizzy 'heights' of learning, but it certainly makes a great tall story!

NACTON. Here, close to the medieval church at the southern end of Nacton village, is **Orwell Park**, now a school but in the 18th century the home of Admiral Sir Edward Vernon. The Admiral was known to his men as 'Old Grog' because of his fond attachment to a cloak of coarse grogram cloth. This nickname was then transferred to his none too welcome gift to naval life - a daily ration of rum diluted with water, to replace the tot of neat rum to which sailors had previously been accustomed.

LEVINGTON. The village is perhaps best known for lending its name to a brand of potting compost, developed here at the Fisons plant. To the south of all this activity is a picturesque farming community overlooking the River Orwell.

On the foreshore below the village is an extensive marina with all the normal bustle associated with boating activities. The coastal footpath, along the banks of the Orwell, leads across the Trimley Marshes and on to Felixstowe.

TRIMLEY ST MARY. Trimley Marshes, created from former farmland, is a wonderful area of grazing marsh, reedbeds and wetlands. A strangely haunting place, it is renowned among nature lovers for its abundance of interesting plant life and the many different species of wildfowl, waders and migrant birds to be found here.

FELIXSTOWE. The town presents two distinctly different faces to the world, neither one intruding upon the other. To the west of the town is the busy cargo and container port, which has steadily developed to become one of the largest in Europe; while to the east is the attractive Edwardian seaside town, developed into a full-blown holiday resort by the Victorians.

In striking contrast to Lowestoft, 50 miles from here at the other end of the Suffolk Coast Path, seaside Felixstowe is unashamedly commercialised. The resort is strung out round a wide, gently curving bay, where the 2 mile long seafront road is separated from the promenade by beautiful seafront gardens of well-kept flower beds and trim lawns.

Jutting out into the North Sea is the pier, once long enough to carry an electric tramway, but foreshortened during the Second World War for security reasons. The **Spa Pavilion** offers every entertainment from cabaret and brass bands to symphony concerts and amateur dramatics, while facilities at the Leisure Centre include swimming pools, sauna and sunbeds, indoor bowls, an entertainment hall, a restaurant and bars. There is safe swimming from the sand and shingle beach, but be warned - although Felixstowe enjoys a sheltered position and has an enviable sunshine quota, the sea breezes can be fairly bracing!

Other facilities and entertainments to be found here include everything from putting greens and crazy golf to tennis, roller skating, regattas and raft races. The emphasis is very much on all-round family entertainment, and the town is also served with a good variety of shops, restaurants and pubs.

The original fishing hamlet from which the Victorian resort of Old Felixstowe developed can be found beyond the golf course at the northeastern side of the town. This is **Felixstowe Ferry**, a collection of holiday bungalows, boatyards and ramshackle fishermen's sheds where freshly caught fish or a tub of local cockles can be bought. From here, the little ferry carries passengers across the mouth of the River Deben to Bawdsey Quay, under the expert guidance of the Brinkley family who have operated the ferry for generations. Looming overhead are two Martello towers on the shingle.

Bounded on one side by the River Orwell and on the other by the River Deben, the Felixstowe Peninsula is one of the prettiest areas in Suffolk; its winding lanes leading through a delightful collection of quiet rural villages and lively riverside communities. At the southernmost tip of the Felixstowe Peninsula is **Landguard Point**, where a nature reserve of shingle beach and grassland supports a variety of coastal plants and migratory birds. Just to the north of the Point is **Landguard Fort**, built here to guard the entrance to Harwich Harbour in 1718, predating the Martello towers by nearly 100 years. It replaces a previous fort built in the 1540s, and today houses a collection of documents, maps, photographs and artifacts relating to its proud history. It is open on Wednesday and Sunday afternoons during the summer, and guided tours are available.

Beyond the fort is an excellent vantage point from which to look out across the harbour to see the ships departing from Felixstowe docks, passing perilously close to the small public viewing area.

OAKS TEA ROOM, in the heart of this interesting town, enjoys a popularity which is undoubtedly due to its traditional approach. A high standard of courteous service, an excellent selection of mouth watering snacks, delightful teas and rich aromatic coffees, starched coloured tablecloths and fine white china crockery all combine to make this one of the most elegant tea rooms that you are likely to visit.

All of the food is freshly prepared on the premises by the owners, Ken and Anita Friend. Simply put, it is delicious and offers excellent value for money. Be sure to sample one of the fine array of flavoured butters which are available. The flavours include, amongst others, Cinnamon, Lemon and Honey. This is the ideal place to visit for a light lunch or snack whilst you are shopping or sightseeing, for it is situated very near to the busy High Street with parking nearby. Open seven days a week from 9.00 am to 5.00 pm. Closed at 2.00 pm Sundays. No smoking.

Oaks Tearoom, 1 Crescent Road, Felixstowe Tel: 01394 273444

Flatford Mill

The Gatehouse at Erwarton Hall

CHAPTER THIRTEEN

NORTHERN ESSEX

Colchester Castle

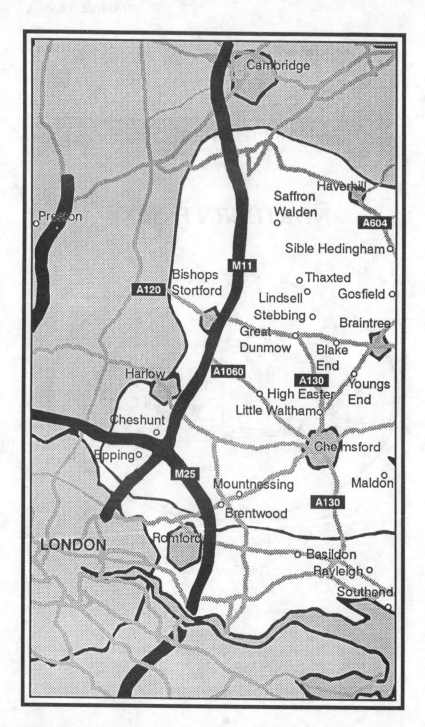

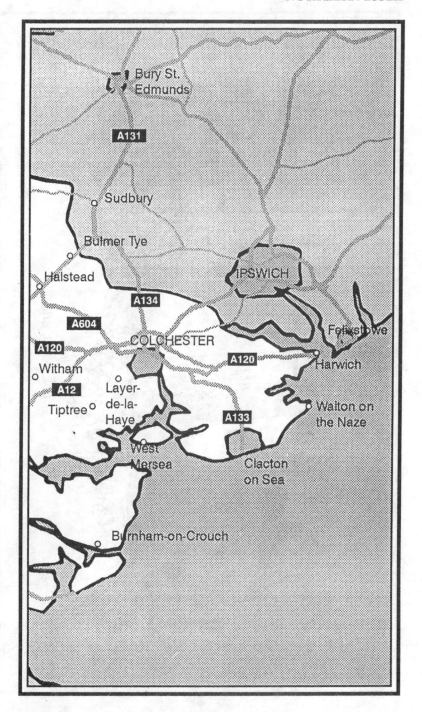

Colchester Castle

CHAPTER THIRTEEN

NORTHERN ESSEX

Colchester and North-East Essex

COLCHESTER. The ancient garrison and market town stands in the midst of rolling East Anglian countryside. Colchester is England's oldest recorded town, a settlement being established here as far back as the 7th century BC. To the west of the town are the remains of the massive earthworks which protected pre-Roman Colchester. During the 1st century the town was the capital of the south-east and an obvious target for the invading Romans. In AD 60 Queen Bodicea carved her name in the annals of history by sacking the town and destroying its glorious temple before her uprising was crushed; an attack that led to the building of the town walls. The oldest part of the town is still surrounded by those Roman walls, which include the huge **Balkerne Gate**, the west gate of the Roman town, magnificent to this day.

When the Normans arrived, Colchester (a name coined by the Saxons) was a important borough and they built their tremendous castle on the foundations of the Roman temple of Claudius.

Later occupations are marked by the houses of the Flemish weavers in the Dutch Quarter to the west of the castle and the Civil War scars visible on the walls of Siege House on East Street. Today the town is presided over by its lofty town hall and an enormous Victorian water tower nicknamed 'Jumbo'. Jumbo was the name of London Zoo's first African elephant controversially sold to Phineas Barnum in 1882. The tower, its four massive pillars made of one and a quarter million bricks, 369 tons of stone and 142 tons of iron supporting a 230,000 gallon tank, was named in his honour.

Colchester was once famed for its oysters and roses. There is still an annual Oyster Feast, a civic banquet worthy of Royal patronage, and the annual Colchester Rose Show. The famous Colchester Oysters are still cultivated on beds in the lower reaches of the River Colne, which skirts the northern edge of the town

There is plenty to see and explore in the town and there can be no better place to start than the **Castle** and its museum. The Normans built the castle on the site of the temple of the Emperor Claudius using many Roman bricks in its construction. The keep, the largest ever built in Europe, is the only part still standing and now houses the **Castle Museum**, which contains an interesting collection of Iron Age, Roman and medieval relics. The castle is open all year round from Monday to Saturday, except Christmas and Good Friday, and open Sundays from

King's Quay Street, Harwich

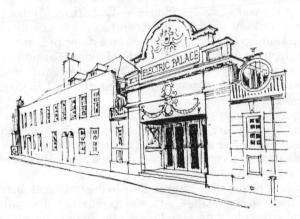

Electric Palace Cinema, Harwich

April to September.

Behind the High Street, to the west of the castle, is the **Dutch Quarter**, a charming and quiet corner of this bustling town. Dutch Protestants arrived here in the 16th century, forced to flee the Spanish rule in the Netherlands, and revitalised the local cloth industry and creating their own prosperous corner of the town.

Close to the castle, on East Hill, is **Hollytrees Museum**, which is a fine Georgian House that houses a wonderful collection of costumes and antiquities. It opened as a museum after it was purchased for the town by Viscount Cowdray in 1920. Hollytrees is open all year; Mondays to Saturdays, except Christmas and Good Friday. Almost across the road from Hollytrees is the **Natural History Museum**, whose exhibits illustrate the natural history of Essex and which is situated in the former All Saints' Church. Housing the museum here saved the church, with its fine flint tower, from demolition in 1958.

Another former church houses the **Museum of Social History**. This interesting museum contains historical displays of rural crafts and country life. Its home the historic church of Holy Trinity in Trinity Street is the only Saxon building left in the town. An arch opposite the church leads to **Tymperleys**, once the home of William Gilberd, who entertained Elizabeth I with experiments in electricity, and today houses a magnificent collection of antique clocks; nearby in West Stockwell Street lived the Taylor sisters, writers of 'Twinkle, Twinkle, Little Star'.

Close to Colchester Town railway station are the ruins of **St Botolph's Priory**. The priory was a victim of the long siege of Colchester during the Civil War, when the Royalist, who held out for eleven weeks, were finally starved into submission. On Bourne Road to the south of the town centre is **Bourne Mill**. This rather striking stepped and curved gabled building is constructed of stone taken from the nearby St John's Abbeygate and was built in 1591. Originally a fishing lodge, it was converted into a mill in the 19th century and is still in working order.

There is so much to take in that it might be best to join one of the guided town walks or even hop aboard one of the open-topped bus tours. Details from the Tourist Information Office on Queen Street.

Those with a hankering for the arts there is plenty to see; the **Charter Hall** features a regular programme of concerts and dance and there is live theatre at the Mercury Theatre.

Colchester Zoo, just off the A12 outside the town, stands in the 40 acre park of Stanway Hall, with its 16th century mansion and church dating from the 14th century. Founded in 1963, it has a wide and exciting variety of attractions including an aquarium, birdland, all the breeds of big cat and a model railway, as well as the opportunity to meet the penguins and, for the brave, the chance to wear a snake!

ROMAN HILL FARM, a typical, 17th century, Essex white weatherboard house that was originally part of a farm, lies just south of Colchester in the village of Blackheath. The surrounding arable land is now owned by the Ministry of Defence. Owned and personally run by

Ann Mallows, Roman Hill Farm offers excellent accommodation in three guest bedrooms that are comfortable and tastefully decorated. You can be sure of some wonderful food whilst staying here as the owner is a Cordon Bleu cook. The home-made marmalade at breakfast is a real treat. A friendly, relaxing home, Roman Hill Farm has a charming guest sitting room that is a super place to relax in with feature Inglenook fireplace, complete with a large woodburning fire. The delightful garden is surrounded by woodland.

Roman Hill Farm, Mersea Road, Blackheath, Colchester Tel: 01206 767157

AROUND COLCHESTER

WIVENHOE. This riverside town, on the banks of the River Colne, was once renowned as a smugglers' haunt and there is a very pretty quayside that is steeped in history. There are still strong connections with the sea with boat building replacing fishing as the main industry.

The Victorianised church, which was damaged during an earthquake in 1884, contains some impressive 16th century brasses. Nearby Wivenhoe Park became the campus for the University of Essex in 1962.

BRIGHTLINGSEA. The town, the only arm of the Cinque Ports outside Kent and Sussex, is a haven for the yachting fraternity and is the home of national and international sailing championships. Brightlingsea can also lay claim to have one of the oldest occupied buildings in Essex, the 13th century **Jacobes Hall** which is, today, a restaurant.

All Saints' Church stands on a hill about a mile out of the town, its 97 ft tower visible over 17 miles out to sea. A light was once placed in the tower to guide the town's fishermen home. There are plenty of superb walks along Brightlingsea Creek and the River Colne, which offer a chance to watch the bird-life and the plethora of boats on the water.

ST OSYTH. This pretty little village has a fascinating history and centres around its Norman church and the ancient ruins of St Osyth Priory. The priory was founded in the 12th century by Augustinian Canons, who named their new priory after the martyred daughter of Frithenwald, first Christian King of the East Angles. Little of the original building remains, but an impressive late 15th century flint gatehouse, complete with battlements, can still be seen. The Priory ruins stand in extensive and beautiful grounds, deer roam free in the deer park and peacocks patrol the shady lawns. In the gatehouse building is an interesting collection of ceramics and jade.

CLACTON-ON-SEA is in itself a great family holiday destination, with a 7 mile long stretch of golden sand and a pier that offers a wide variety of traditional holiday amusements. It is also a major leisure centre with plenty of indoor and outdoor sporting facilities, as well as many familiar high street names for those who enjoy shopping as a sport.

The town started life as an unobstrusive little village, Great Clacton, about a mile inland. The successful seaside resort was developed for profit from the 1860s onwards by a railway promoter in conjunction with a steamship company to attract Londoners looking for a week by the seaside.

The small pier, later greatly enlarged, and the town's first hotel, the Royal, were both built in the 1870s and, with the coming of the railway ten years later, the town's success was sealed.

LITTLE CLACTON. Though it shares its name with the nearby brash seaside resort, Little Clacton couldn't be more different. A quiet village, it has won Best Kept Village Awards, Little Clacton features a lovely Jubilee Oak, planted to celebrate Queen Victoria's Jubilee.

FRINTON-ON-SEA. Once a quiet fishing village, the town developed in the 1880s into the gentile, family resort it is today. The area south of **Frinton Gates** has a unique local character, being laid out with detached houses set along broad tree lined avenues. The Church of Old St Mary in the town contains some panels of William Morris stained glass, well worth seeking out by admirers of his work.

WALTON ON THE NAZE. The town's seafront was developed in the 1800s and provides a fine illustration of the character of an early Victorian seaside resort. The shape of the Naze is constantly changing, eroded by wind, water and tide. 1796 saw the demise of the medieval church and somewhere beyond the 800 ft pier lies medieval Walton and much of the naze or headland. Inhabitants have been enjoying the bracing sea air at Walton since before Neolithic times, flint-shaping instruments have been found here, and fossil teeth and ears of sharks and whales have been discovered in the red crag cliffs.

During the 19th century Walton was a source of seaholly for making love potions, but today offers donkeys, deckchairs and amusements on the pier. The large, windowless and rather grim looking edifice on the highest point of the Naze is Trinity House Tower, built in 1720 to warn shipping of the treacherous off-shore West Rocks.

TENDRING HUNDRED. The 'hundred' in the village name comes from the county divisions of Saxon times of which Tendring was a centre. To this day it is still called the Tendring District, although the centre has moved to the Town Hall at Clacton.

In 1582 thirteen local women accused of being witches were sent for

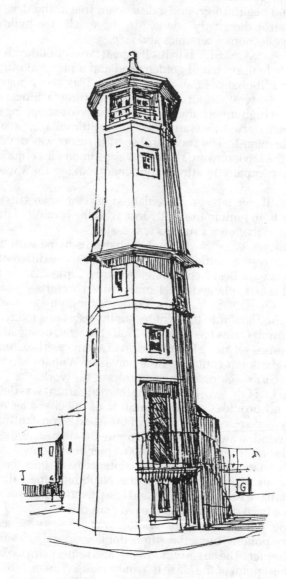

The High Lighthouse, Harwich

trial at Chelmsford. One, Ursula Kemp, faced hearing her illegitimate 8 year old son stand witness against her before she was hanged. The Witchfinder General arrived here in 1645 and more local 'witches' were executed on his evidence. Tendring's church, with its magnificent hammerbeam roof, provides an ideal place to ponder such unjust cruelty.

HARWICH. The town's name probably originates from the time of King Alfred, when 'Here' meant army and 'Wic' a camp. This attractive old town was built in the 13th century by the Earls of Norfolk to exploit its strategic position on the Stour and Orwell estuary and the town has an important seafaring history which continues today. During the 14th and 15th century French campaigns it was an important naval base.

The ship which carried the Pilgrim Fathers to America in 1620, The Mayflower, was a frequent visitor and its Captain Christopher Jones lived in Kings Head Street. The famous diarist Samuel Pepys was MP for the town in the 1660s.

With all this rich history it's perhaps no surprise that the town has a fascinating maritime heritage trail which takes visitors around the old town. Highlights of the trail include the High and Low lighthouses dating from 1818; when in line they indicated the safe shipping channel into the harbour. They replaced wooden structures and, in 1862, were themselves replaced when the shifting sandbanks altered the channel. Both are rather unusual designs; the Low lighthouse is now the towns **Maritime Museum**, and the 90 ft and nine sided High lighthouse is now a private residence. These two were replaced by iron structures, one of which still stands on the front at Dovercourt just along the coast. Shipping now relies on light buoys to find its way.

Today the Treadwheel Crane stands on Harwich Green, but for over 250 years it was sited in the Naval Shipyard. It is worked by two men walking in two 16 ft diameter wheels and is the only known example. Amazingly it only fell into disuse in the 1920s. Another fascinating piece of the town's history is the Electric Palace Cinema, built in 1911, and now the oldest unaltered purpose built cinema in Britain. It was restored by a trust and re-opened in 1981.

The importance of the port during the 19th century is confirmed by **The Redoubt**, a huge grey fort that was built between 1808 and 1810. Its design is an enlarged version of the Martello towers which dotted the English coast awaiting a Napoleonic invasion which never came. Today the Harwich Society has largely restored it and it is open as a museum.

The old town also contains many ancient buildings, including the **Guildhall** which was rebuilt in 1769 and has graffiti, probably carved by prisoners when it was used as a gaol, and is well worth putting an afternoon aside to explore.

MISTLEY. In the 18th century local landowner and MP Richard Rigby had grand designs to develop Mistley into a fashionable spa to rival Harrogate and Bath, adopting the swan as its symbol. All that remains of Rigby's ambitions is the Swan Fountain, a small number of attractive Georgian houses and **Mistley Towers**, the remains of a church, otherwise demolished in 1870, which had been designed by the flamboyant architect Robert Adams.

MANNINGTREE. The Walls, on the approach to Manningtree along the B1352, offers unrivalled views of the Stour estuary and the Suffolk coast, and the swans for which the area is famous. Back in Tudor times Manningtree itself was the centre of the cloth trade and later a port full of barges, carrying their various cargos along the coast to London. Water still dominates today and the town is a centre of leisure sailing.

The town's most notorious inhabitant though stayed firmly on dry land. Matthew Hopkins, the reviled and self-styled Witchfinder General, lived here in the 17th century. Witchcraft was supposedly rife across East Anglia and many innocents were put to death in any number of barbaric ways as a result of the Witchfinders trails.

LAYER-DE-LA-HAYE. Close to the Abberton Reservoir and Nature Reserve, this is now a much sought after commuter and retirement village.

SECRET CHARTERS, based at Titchmarsh Marina on the secluded Walton Backwaters, offers an unusual day out for all the family. Terry Secretan, the owner and an experienced skipper, offers an enjoyable a day out on his safe, stable and spacious Catalac 27 cruising catamaran in the sheltered waters made famous by Arthur Ransome in his book 'Secret Waters', the sequel to 'Swallows and Amazons'. No sailing experience is required as you will be taken by an expert, though there is ample opportunity to learn if you would like. On the other hand, you can let the skipper take the strain and enjoy the multitude of seabirds and wildfowl, the occasional seal and a picnic on a secluded beach. Children are particularly welcome and the day out is yours; with plenty of space for lounging in the comfortable cockpit or in the light and airy saloon. Sit back and take advantage of luxury sailing.

Secret Charters, 'Pippins', Abberton Road, Layer-de-la-Haye
Tel: 01206 734727

LAYER MARNEY. This quiet hamlet has the colossal gatehouse of a mansion that was going to rival Hampton Court but was never completed. The magnificent four red brick towers, covered in 16th

390

century Italianate designs, known as the **Layer Marney Towers**, were built by Lord Marney in the 1520s. As well as spectacular views from the top of the towers, there are formal gardens and a rare breeds farm to enjoy.

EASTHORPE. This village is home to the oddly named **House Without a Name**, a building with a very chequered history dating back to the early 15th century. These former farmworkers cottages have also served time as a shop and a gentlemen's drinking club before becoming licensed premises. The then owners attended court for a licence and had not chosen a name for the pub. The building was therefore listed as The House Without a Name and the name has stayed with the pub to this day.

MARKS TEY. Normans from Marck, near Calais, gave the village its name when they came over in the 11th century. The church is certainly distinctive with its oakboarded tower, but its chief treasure is its 15th century font. Also made of oak it has eight intricately carved panelled sides which are a delight to behold.

ALDHAM. The village was, for a time, home to the famous Essex historian Philip Morant, who held the post of vicar here. He was buried in the local churchyard.

CHAPPEL. Here, on a 4 acre site beside Chappel and Wakes Colne Station is the **East Anglian Railway Museum**. For every train fan young or old this is the place to try your hand at being a signalman and get a whiff of steam, as well as admire the beautiful restored locos and items of rolling stock. As the British Rail line runs north it crosses the dramatic 32 arch viaduct across the Colne Valley, built 1849 and quite a sight.

EARLS COLNE. The de Veres, Earls of Oxford, and the River Colne bestowed the village with its name. Aubery de Vere founded a Benedictine priory here in the 12th century and both he and his wife, William the Conqueror's sister, were buried there. Today the site is marked by a redbrick Gothic mansion. Though the commuter culture has spread modern housing around the village a cluster of timbered cottages helps to preserve a village atmosphere.

Central Essex

BRAINTREE. This small town, along with its close neighbour **Bocking**, are sited at the crossing of two Roman roads and were brought together by the cloth industry in the 16th century. Flemish weavers settled here, followed by many Huguenots. One, Samuel Courtauld, set up a silk mill in 1816 and by 1886 employed over three thousand Essex folk. Samuel Courtauld's mill still survives in Braintree, whose rather magnificent former Town Hall is one of the many Courtauld legacies. It was built in 1928 with oak-panelled walls, murals by Grieffenhagen showing stirring scenes in local history, and a grand central tower with a five-belled striking clock. A smaller but none the less fascinating reminder of Courtauld's generosity is the 1930s bronze fountain, with bay, shell and fish, at the centre of Braintree.

In Bocking there is an impressive parish church and a walk down Church Street repays the curious with the sight of a fine postmill. Famous naturalist John Ray was born in nearby Black Notley and there is a statue of him in Bank Street, unveiled by botanist David Bellamy in 1985.

Huguenot names such as Courtaulds are connected with international enterprises to this day and their reason for coming to Britain is a fascinating, if poignant, tale. The Huguenots formed in France in 1559 as an organised Protestant group taking direction from Calvin and the Calvinistic Reformation in Geneva. To begin with they were able to live and worship freely, but as political and religious rivalries grew the Catholic majority started persecuting them; a century of war, massacres and bloodshed followed. Finally in 1685 all their rights were taken away. In the ensuing chaos many died and thousands fled. It was to turn out France's loss, for the Huguenots were amongst the most industrious and economically advanced elements in French society. Others gained at France's expense; Huguenots poured into England, and especially East Anglia, where their skills soon made them welcome and valued members of the community.

AROUND BRAINTREE

SIBLE HEDINGHAM. The village was the birthplace of Sir John Hawkwood, one of the 14th centuries most famous soldiers of fortune. He led a band of mercenaries to Italy where he was paid to defend Florence and where he also died. There is a monument to him in the village church, decorated with hawks and various other beasts.

Hedingham Antiques and B&B, 100 Swan Street, Sible Hedingham
Tel: 01787 460360

In the centre of the village of Sible Hedingham on the A604, Patricia Patterson runs a most unusual (if not unique) business combining **HEDINGHAM ANTIQUES** and **BED AND BREAKFAST** accommodation in her lovely Victorian house. The antique shop specialises in Mahogany, Oak and Walnut furniture, silver & plate, china & glass, and

Art Deco. Furniture restoration is carried out on the premises. To the rear of the shop is a 'Second Hand Warehouse' which is an absolute Aladdin's cave. The accommodation is very comfortable with lots of stripped pine; the bedrooms have en-suite facilities, television and hospitality trays. A full English breakfast will set you up for a good start to the day. ETB 1 Crown.

CASTLE HEDINGHAM takes its name form the Norman castle that stands over village. It was one of England's strongest fortresses in the 11th century and even now visitors can still get a feel for its power and strength. The impressive stone keep rises over 100 ft and has 12 ft thick walls. It was owned by the Earls of Oxford, the powerful de Veres family, one of whom was among the barons who forced King John to accept the Magna Carta. Amongst those entertained at the castle were Henry VII and Elizabeth I.

The village itself is a maze of narrow streets radiating from Falcon Square, named after the half-timbered Falcon Inn. Georgian and 15th century houses comfortably jostle for space and the Church of St Nicholas, built by the de Veres, avoided Victorian 'restoration' and is virtually completely Norman.

At the **Colne Valley Railway**, a mile of the Colne Valley and Halstead line between Castle Hedingham and Great Yeldham has been restored and now runs steam trains operated by enthusiasts.

BULMER TYE. **BULMER TYE HOUSE** is a wonderful family house down a treelined drive, just off the A131 in Bulmer Tye.

Bulmer Tye House, Bulmer Tye Tel: 01787 269315

Owned by Noël and Peter Owen, the timber framed farmhouse, dating back to the 1600s, has evolved over the years, the front is Georgian and there are Victorian additions. Set in 3 acres of mature gardens, this rambling house is an ideal place to stay and Noël and Peter offer excellent bed and breakfast accommodation in a choice of four bedrooms. The breakfasts are delicious with home-made bread and free range eggs. Noël is a specialist writer and lecturer on antiques and Peter is an accomplished cabinet maker, specialising in clavichords. Hidden deep

Clock Tower, Halstead

in the garden is his workshop - a real treat to visit.

BORLEY. This unassuming little village, close to the Suffolk border, has the rather sinister reputation of having once had the most haunted house in Britain. **Borley Rectory** was destroyed in a fire in 1939, but, before then, both the house and grounds were supposedly the scene for frantic psychic activity with mysterious lights and noises and hand-written messages appearing on the rectory walls. The church, not to be outdone, has also been the scene of several visitations and footsteps, chanting and organ music have been heard behind its locked doors!

LITTLE MAPLESTEAD. Here is one of the very few round churches in the country. Built more than 600 years ago by the military order of the Knights Hospitallers, their 'Preceptory' at Little Maplestead was suppressed more than 400 years ago by Henry VIII.

HALSTEAD. Rather unimaginably Halstead's most famous product was mechanical elephants. Life-sized and weighing half a ton they were built by W Hunwicks. Each one consisted of 9000 parts and could carry a load of eight adults and four children at up to 12 mph. Rather less unusual but certainly better remembered are the products Tortoise Foundry Company famous for their warm but somewhat smelly 'tortoise stoves'.

Certainly the most picturesque reminder of Halstead's industrial heritage is George Courtauld's white, weatherboarded, three-storey mill across the River Colne at the Causeway. Built in the 1700s it is still the most handsome building in town.

GOSFIELD. Gosfield Lake Leisure Resort, the county's largest freshwater lake, lies in the grounds of Gosfield Hall. This Tudor mansion was remodelled in the 19th century by its owner, Samuel Courtauld. He also built the attractive mock Tudor houses in the village.

The Green Man, The Street, Gosfield Tel: 01787 472746

THE GREEN MAN pub and restaurant, in the village of Gosfield, is owned and run along traditional lines, with a public and saloon bar, by John Arnold and Janet Harrington. Dating back to the 1800s, the building has probably always been an ale house and many of the original features, including a fine inglenook fireplace near the bar, remain. With a warm and cosy interior, The Green Man is popular with those who enjoy a good glass of real ale and traditional English food. Janet looks after the restaurant side of the business and it is entirely due to her expertise that The Green Man has its excellent reputation for cuisine. The menu changes daily, with the most popular dishes being steak and kidney pudding, pheasant in red wine and not forgetting the treacle pudding. All produce is locally supplied and freshly cooked on the premises.

COGGESHALL. This is a pleasant, old cloth and lace town that has some very fine timbered building. **Paycockes**, owned by The National Trust, is a merchant's house of about 1500 and has some unusually rich panelling and wood carving. The National Trust also own the recently restored **Grange Barn**, which dates from around 1140 and is a magnificent example of an estate store barn built for the monks of the nearby Cistercian Abbey.

YOUNGS END. **THE GREEN DRAGON** pub and restaurant, just north of the Essex Showground, is a series of Grade II listed buildings dating from the 1700s. Owned and run by Mandy and Bob Greybrook, the small holding consists of an ale house and barn. The restaurant, housed in the now connected barn, is warm and inviting with its original timber beams, high roof and, at the far end, a wooden horse feeder that would once have been filled with hay. Renowned for its seafood, the restaurant uses local produce which is all freshly prepared on the premises. The traditional bar, aptly located in the old ale house, features real ales, IPA and seasonal guest beers. There is a beer garden that, during the summer, has a children's tuck shop next to the small aviary that is alive with finches, budgies and quails.

The Green Dragon, Youngs End

BLAKE END. Midway between Braintree and Great Dunmow on the A120 look out for **BLAKE HOUSE CRAFT CENTRE**, (by the Saling Oak Pub). The Centre specialises in Arts, Crafts and Antiques and is housed in Grade II listed and restored barns and stables with a wealth of old exposed timbers; it was originally the farm courtyard. Sharon

Potter runs the 'Cottage Craft shop and Tea Room' where you can enjoy light lunches, home-made cakes and cream teas in the Old Cart Lodge. The Centre has 15 shops and workshops offering an amazing variety of goods for sale from bird tables, jewellery, hockey specialities, craft kits, toys, collectables; there's a dried flower workshop, a 'Trade In' shop and many more diverse interests and services. Especially noteworthy are the Special Events; in July the Country Memories Day featuring Birds of Prey, Bee Keeping, Vintage Tractors, Lace Making etc, and in September the Viking Battle Weekend should not be missed. Ring for further information.

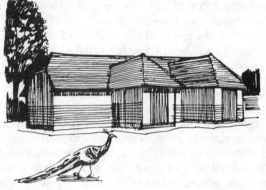

Blake House Craft Centre, Blake End Tel: 01376 320662

STEBBING. This is a delightful village with charming old cottages and farmhouses and a graceful 14th century church which has a notable rood screen.

The White Hart, High Street, Stebbing Tel: 01371 6383

THE WHITE HART, situated on the High Street in Stebbing, is a 'hidden place' not to be missed. Built in the 15th century, this traditional English pub has all that you would expect. Oak beamed ceilings, a roaring open fire and a fine selection of well kept ales all contribute to its warm, welcoming atmosphere. A good selection of reasonably priced bar snacks are also available.

The North-West Corner of Essex

SAFFRON WALDEN. The town was named after the Saffron crocus, which was grown in the area to make dyestuffs in the Middle Ages. A great deal of the street plan of the town from those times survives as do hundreds of fine buildings, many timbered with overhanging upper floors and decorative plastering (pargeting). Gog and Magog (or perhaps folk hero Tom Hickathrift and the Wisbech Giant) battle in plaster forever on the gable of the **Old Sun Inn**, where, legend has it, Oliver Cromwell and General Fairfax both lodged during the Civil War.

On the local Common, once Castle Green, is the largest surviving turf maze in England. Only eight ancient turf mazes survive in England: though there were many more in the Middle Ages, but if they are not looked after they soon become overgrown and lost.

Though many miles from the sea Henry Winstanley, born here in 1644, is said to have held trials with a wooden lantern in the lavishly decorated 15th-16th century church, before building the first Eddystone Lighthouse; which was lost with him in a fierce storm in 1703. At the **Town Museum**, as well as the gloves worn by Mary Queen of Scots on the day she died, is piece of human skin which once coated the church door at Hadstock.

The town was also famous for its resident Cockatrice, which was hatched from a cock's egg by a toad or serpent and could kill its victims with a glance. The Cockatrice was blamed for any inexplicable disasters in the town. Like Perseus and Medusa the Gorgon, a Cockatrice could be destroyed by making it see its own reflection thereby turning it to stone. The Saffron Walden Cockatrice's slayer was said to be a knight in a coat of 'cristal glass'.

To the north of the town is **Bridge End Gardens**, a wonderfully preserved example of an early Victorian garden, complete a hedge maze, which is open only by appointment. (Appointments can be made at the Tourist Information Centre.) Next to the gardens is the **Fry Art Gallery** which exhibits work by many notable 20th century artists who lived and worked in the area before and after the Second World War, as well as contemporary artists working in Essex today. Close to Bridge End is the Anglo-American War Memorial dedicated by Field Marshal the Viscount Montgomery of Alamein in 1953 to the memory of all the American flyers of the 65th Fighter Wing who lost their lives in the Second World War.

Audley End House was, at one time, home of the first Earl of Suffolk and the original house, with its two large courtyards, had a magnificence claimed to match Hampton Court. Unfortunately the subsequent earls lacked his financial acumen and much of the house was demolished as it fell into disrepair. Today it still remains one of England's most impressive Jacobean mansions; its distinguished stone

Stebbing Church

façade set off perfectly by Capability Brown's lake. The remaining state rooms still retain their palatial magnificence and the exquisite state bed in the Neville Room is still hung with the original embroidered drapes.

In the rolling parkland grounds are several elegant outbuildings, some of which were designed by Robert Adam. Amongst these are an icehouse, a circular temple and a Springwood Column. A popular miniature steam railway runs in the grounds and certainly anyone visiting this corner of Essex should make time to stop and take in this wonderful house which reflects the rise and fall of the aristocratic country mansion perfectly.

THE OLD HOOPS restaurant, in the centre of Saffron Walden, has a long and interesting history. The building is at least 400 years old and was frequented by Samuel Pepys in 1660 when it was then known as the White Hart. It was also the site of 'The Fenman's Wager' - a bet of 5 shillings was made that the inn keeper's daughter, carrying 2 glasses of ale at a time upstairs, would be worn out before the 20 drinkers were drunk. The girl won and the bet was lost. Owned by Sue and Ray Morrison the building now has a wide spread reputation as an excellent restaurant. Amid relaxed and friendly surroundings Ray, a classically French trained chef, serves up a delicious array of mouth-watering modern English dishes. The menu changes weekly and popular favourites include Lamb Dijonnaise and Musselcress Soup. Open for lunch 12.00-2.15 pm, and from 7.00 pm for dinner Tuesday to Saturday.

The Old Hoops, 15 King Street, Saffron Walden Tel: 01799 522813

BRIDGE END ORCHARD, owned by Nesta Beynon, lies on the northside of Saffron Walden and offers bed and breakfast accommodation to the discerning customer. Built in the 1950s the house, an interesting 'Y' shape, has been added to over the years and takes its unusual name from being built in the orchard of Bridge End Cottage, one of the oldest buildings in the town. The three guest bedrooms are charming, individually decorated and all have either en suite or private bathrooms. Breakfast is fruit juice, fresh fruit with special home-made yoghurt and full English breakfast. Guests also have their own sitting room and full use of the garden and patios. Secluded with a high brick and flint wall, this is very much a cottage garden, quiet and peaceful with many trees giving a woodland feel.

Bridge End Orchard, 35 Bridge Street, Saffron Walden
Tel: 01799 522001

AROUND SAFFRON WALDEN

HADSTOCK. As well as claiming to have the oldest church door in England, this village also has a macabre tale to tell. The church's north door was once covered with a piece of human skin, now to be seen in Saffron Walden Museum. Local legend says it is a 'Daneskin', from a Viking flayed alive.

Lining doors with animal leather was common in the Middle Ages and many so called 'Daneskins' are just that. However, the skins at Hadstock and at Copford also in Essex are almost certainly human, the poor wretch at Hadstock undoubtedly having his hide nailed there as a warning to others. The door itself is Saxon, as are the 11th century carvings, windows and arches, rare survivors that pre-date the Norman Conquest.

STEEPLE BUMPSTEAD. The village, which grew up around a ford, lies on the Suffolk border. Edith Cavell, the Great War heroine, worked as a governess here and worshipped at the church. At the crossroads stands the lovely old **Moots Hall**, with oversailing upper storey and arched and timbered ground floor. Moots were originally Saxon meetings to settle disputes, though by 1592 this one was being used as a school, and was most probably used as a guildhall or market house at sometime.

Folkmoots were more often held in the open-air; usually at conspicuous landmarks, especially as much of Britain was then heavily wooded. These were frequently ancient barrows such as at Mobberley in Cheshire. Particular trees or stones were also chosen as at Appletree, Derbyshire, Staine in Cambridgeshire and Maidstone in Kent, and at Stone in Somerset the meeting stone still stands.

Thaxted Town

HEMPSTEAD. The highwayman, Dick Turpin, was born here in 1705. His parent kept the Bell Inn, later renamed the Rose and Crown and more recently 'sub-titled' Turpin's Tavern. Gilt letters announce 'It is the Landlord's great desire that no-one stands before the fire' over the wide hearth where logs still burn, and pictures all around celebrate the infamy of the innkeeper's son.

Inside the village church, an impressively and life-like bust on his tomb recalls the town's rather worthier son, William Harvey (1578-1657), chief physician to Charles I and the discoverer of the circulation of the blood, as recorded in his 'De Motu Cordis' of 1628.

Like many others Hempstead once boasted a village cockpit and its faint outline can still be traced, though the steep banks are now crowned with trees.

GREAT SAMPFORD. This pretty village has attractive gabled houses and, opposite the Bull Inn, is an Elizabethan manor house. A large pond and three cornered green complete the picture.

FINCHINGFIELD. A showpiece commuter and retirement village holds the dubious distinction of probably being the most photographed village in Essex. Finchingfield certainly has everything to complete the perfect picture postcard, a fine guildhall, a church on a hill, a post mill, quaint cottages, a river, a charming green enlivened by the noisy occupants of the duckpond and a 'causeway' giving open views of the whole village.

The gardens of the nearby Elizabethan mansion, **Spain's Hall**, are open on Sunday afternoons in the summer.

GREAT BARDFIELD. The old market town's pleasant mixture of old cottages and shops is nicely complemented by the 14th century church and is surveyed by a timber-framed 16th and 17th century hall from its hill above the River Pant. Perhaps the Great Bardfield's most notable feature is, however, a restored windmill that goes by the strange name of 'Gibraltar'.

THAXTED. This small country town has a recorded history which dates back to before the Domesday book. Originally a Saxon settlement, it developed around a Roman road. Yet, though the town is full of beautiful old buildings, is has a special character all its own. To its credit Thaxted has no need of artificial tourist attractions and is today what it has been for the last ten centuries, a thriving town.

Thaxted has numerous attractively pargeted and timber-framed houses, and a magnificent **Guildhall**, built as a meeting place for cutlers around 1390. The demise of the cutlery industry in 1500s led it to becoming the administrative centre of the town. Restored in Georgian times it became the town's Grammar School, as well as remaining a centre of administration. Once more restored in 1975 today the Parish council still meet here.

The town's famous windmill was built in 1804 by John Webb and last ground wheat in 1907 though it has now been returned to full working order. Close to the windmill are the town's Almshouses, which still provided homes for the elderly over 250 years after they were built for that very purpose.

Thaxted Church stands on a hill and soars cathedral-like over the town's streets. It has been described as the finest Parish church in the country and, though many towns may protest long and loud at this, it certainly is magnificent. It was also the somewhat unlikely setting for a pitched battle in 1921. The rather colourful vicar and secretary of the Church Socialist League, Conrad Noel, hoisted the red flag of communism and the Sinn Fein flag in the church. Incensed Cambridge students tore them down and put up the Union Jack; Noel in turn ripping that down and, with his friends, slashing the tyres of the students' cars and motorcycles. A fine bronze in the church celebrates this adventurous man of the cloth.

Planet Suite composer Gustav Holst lived in the village from 1914-25 and often played the church organ. To celebrate his connection with the town there is a month long festival in late June/early July which attracts performers of international repute.

Conrad Noel's wife is remembered for encouraging Morris dancing in the town and, today, the famous Morris Ring is held on the Spring Bank Holiday attracting over 300 dancers from all over the country who dance through the streets. Dancing can also be seen around the town on most Bank Holiday Mondays, usually in the vicinity of a pub!

LINDSELL. The **LINDSELL ART GALLERY**, in this tiny village, is well worth making the effort to visit. John and Judy Garrett will be there to welcome you to the gallery which has a permanent display of work by local artists including Eleanor Tanner who provided the lovely illustration of Thaxted for the front cover of this book, and Judy herself whose paintings of flowers we noticed in one of the tea rooms in Thaxted.

Lindsell Art Gallery, Lindsell Tel: 01371 870777

Throughout the year, there are exhibitions at the gallery, and this enterprising and talented couple also run a picture framing business which stocks a wide range of mouldings and mount boards. The gallery is on one level and there is easy wheelchair access. In addition to the prints and paintings which are very reasonably priced there is also a selection of greetings cards and small gift items. The gallery is becoming increasingly popular, and if you have enjoyed touring this lovely part of the world, what better memento to take home with you than a picture to remind you of your stay in the area.

LITTLE EASTON. The charming 12th century church in this small village is rich in historic features. Its Maynard Chapel features some outstanding marble monuments of the family as well as some famous brasses. The church's oldest treasures are, however, a well-preserved and priceless 12th century wall painting and several 15th century frescoes. The most recent additions, two stained glass windows, were unveiled in 1990. The Window of the Crusaders and the Window of Friendship and Peace are a lasting memorial to the American 386th Bomb Group. Known as 'The Crusaders', they were stationed nearby for 13 months and lost over 200 of their number in that short time.

GREAT DUNMOW. The town is famous for the 'Flitch of Bacon', an ancient ceremony which dates back as far as the 11th century. A prize of a flitch or side of bacon was awarded to a local couple who had been married harmoniously for a year. Amidst great ceremony the couple would be seated and presented with their prize! This old custom is still carried on every leap year, and The Flitch has the key to the Priory where the original chair is kept.

Homelye Farm, Braintree Road, Great Dunmow Tel: 01371 872127

Tracy Pickford welcomes many Dutch, American and Australian guests to **HOMELYE FARM**, such is the popularity of this working farm and the really neat accommodation in the converted stable block dating back, along with the earlier parts of the farmhouse, to the 14th century. The three well-appointed, bright and airy rooms are at ground floor level and each has private facilities. Breakfasts are flexible to suit guests who on warm days can choose to eat alfresco at the picnic tables in the meadow next to the stables. The farm is a mixed working farm with cattle and arable and Tracy's husband Neil will take guests on a tour of the farm if requested and many of the original features and furniture can be seen inside the house. Very relaxed and welcoming. Registered with the ETB. Advisable to book ahead.

TAKELEY. The village is built on the line of the old Roman Stane Street. There are plenty of pretty 17th century timbered houses and barns to be seen in the village and the church still has many of its original Norman features along with some Roman masonry. Rather unusually it has a modern font that is surmounted by a 6 ft high medieval cover.

HATFIELD BROAD OAK. This very pretty village has many notable buildings for the visitor to enjoy including a church dating from Norman times, some delightful 18th century almshouses and several distinctive Georgian houses.

Nearby **Hatfield Forest**, which leant its name to the village, was once part of the ancient Royal Forests of Essex. The remaining 1049 acres are now protected by the National Trust and offer splendid woodland walks along its chases and rides.

SAWBRIDGEWORTH. Quite a number of fine old buildings survive in this small town, many of which are Georgian. To the south is **Pishiobury**, a fine house built by James Wyatt in 1782 and now a school. In St Mary's Church are 15 wonderful ancient and beautifully preserved brasses.

ROYDON. Around a mile south-west of this village are the ruins of Tudor **Nether Hall**, a manor house that belonged to the Coates family. Here Thomas More came to woo and win the elder daughter of John Coates. Preserved in the village itself are the old parish cage, stocks and a whipping post.

STANSTED MOUNTFITCHET. Though rather close to London's third airport, Stansted, there are plenty of reasons to visit this village. Certainly pilots approaching the airport may be surprised at the sight of a **Norman Village**, complete with domestic animals and reconstructed motte and bailey castle, standing just two miles from the end of the runway. The original castle was built after 1066 by the Duke of Boulogne, a cousin of the Conqueror.

Next door to the castle is **The House on the Hill Toy Museum** where children of every age are treated to a unique and nostalgic trip back to their childhood. There is every toy imaginable here, many of them now highly prized collector's items. There is a shop selling new toys and a collectors' shop with many old toys and books to chose from.

BUNTINGFORD. This small town grew upon Ermine Street, at a crossing of the River Rib. The High Street has a wealth of architecture from 17th century gables, overhangs and archways, Tudor buildings and a handful of elegant Georigan houses.

St Peter's Church, at the south end of the village, was probably constructed on the site of an earlier chapel. Originally built as a 'chapel of ease', St Peter's was completed in 1626. It is notable that the material used was red brick (only one other church of that period was built in brick), and it is laid out in the form of a Greek cross with the altar at the south end.

The town also still retains its rare one-handed turret clock. Dating back to the early 1600s, clocks of that period were always single handed;

the clock has been renovated and an electric winder added.

PRESTON. THE RED LION, a 200 year old Grade II listed pub on the village green in the village of Preston, was the first public house in Britain to be owned by the village in which it sits. The previous owners, Whitbread, wanted to modernise it and convert it into a steak house in 1982. When the local villagers objected, the brewery threatened to close it down. The resourceful and determined locals were left with no option but to group together and purchase it. Three years ago they appointed Phil and Sue to manage it and since then they have established the Red Lion as being one of the very best pubs in the area. The pub has become a focus for village life, visitors are made very welcome and the atmosphere is happy and lively, as you would expect of such a close-knit community. Take your choice from one of the five real ales that are served here or enjoy a delicious meal selected from a wide and varied menu. You will not be disappointed, for the care which is taken over the condition of the ale and preparation of the food is second to none. The reputation of this remarkable pub has spread far and wide, indeed HM Queen Elizabeth, The Queen Mother wrote a letter to the villagers congratulating them on their enterprise in buying and running the pub and her letter now hangs proudly in the bar. Be sure to call in, for pubs of this calibre are few and far between.

The Red Lion, The Green, Preston Tel: 01462 459585

The Centre of Essex

CHELMSFORD. Roman workmen cutting their great road linking London with Colchester built a fort at what is today called Chelmsford. Then called Caesaromagus, it stands at the confluence of the Rivers Chelmer and Can. The town has always been an important market centre and is now the bustling county town of Essex. It is also directly descended from a new town planned by the Bishop of London in 1199. At its centre are the principal inn, the Royal Saracen's Head, and

Layer Marney Tower

the elegant Shire Hall of 1792.

It was John Johnson, the distinguised local architect who designed both the Shire Hall and the bridge over the River Can, who also rebuilt the Parish Church of St Mary when most of its 15th century tower fell down. The church became a cathedral when the new diocese of Chelmsford was created in 1913. Since then it has been enlarged and reorganised inside.

The Marconi Company, pioneers in the manufacture of wireless equipment, set up the first radio company in the world here in 1899. Exhibits of those pioneering days of wireless can be seen in the **Chelmsford and Essex Museum** in Oaklands Park, as can interesting displays of Roman remains and local history.

AROUND CHELMSFORD

LITTLE WALTHAM. LITTLE BELSTEADS lies just south-east of the village of Little Waltham and opposite a pay and play golf course. A part Victorian, part Edwardian farmhouse, Little Belsteads is owned, and run as a bed and breakfast establishment, by Felicity and Jon Tredwell. The acre of garden, which guests are free to use, backs onto the meadows of the original farm. The house has always been in the family, except for a brief 10 year period, having been built for Felicity's great grandfather. There is one large family bedroom, with en suite shower room, colour television and tea and coffee making facilities. The full English breakfast includes a 'special' and home-made bread, preserves and biscuits are usually available.

Little Belsteads, Back Lane, Little Waltham Tel: 01245 360249

GOOD EASTER. A quiet farming village, now in the commuter belt for London, whose claim to fame is the making of a world-record daisy chain (6,980 ft 7 inches) in 1985. The village's interesting name is probably derived from 'Easter' the Old English for 'sheepfolds' and 'Good' from a Saxon lady named Godiva.

HIGH EASTER. Close to Good Easter and thus named as it stands on higher ground than its neighbour.

THE PUNCH BOWL is an outstanding Restaurant at High Easter, 15 minutes from Chelmsford and Dunmow. Personally run by David and Penny Kelsey, their team create an wonderful ambience and delicious food for a memorable evening. Famous for its home-made desserts, fresh fish and local produce, you will need to book.

Complimentary celebration cakes. Restaurant open Tuesday to Saturday evenings, Sunday for lunch.

The Punch Bowl, High Easter Tel: 01245 231222/231264

BEAUCHAMP RODING. One of eight Rodings, it was at Beauchamp Roding that a local farm labourer, Isaac Mead, worked and saved enough to become a farmer himself in 1882. To show his gratitude to the land that made his fortune, he had a corner of a field consecrated as an eternal resting place for himself and family. Their graves can still be seen in the undergrowth, besides the present drive to Rochets house.

Beauchamp's Church, St Botolph's, stands alone in the fields, marked by tall 15th century tower and reached by a track off the B184. Inside the raised pews at west end have clever space-saving wooden steps, pulled out of slots by means of iron rings.

CHIPPING ONGAR. Today firmly gripped in the commuter belt of London, Chipping Ongar began as a market town protected beneath the walls of a Norman castle. Indeed, the town's name comes from 'cheaping' meaning market.

Only the mound and moat of the castle remain, but the contemporary Church of St Martin of Tours still stands. Explorer David Livingstone was a pupil pastor of the town's 19th century Congregational Church.

GREENSTED. St Andrew's is famous as the only surviving example of a Saxon log church extant in the world. Over 1,100 years old, it is built from split oak logs held together with dowells. Over the centuries, the church has been enlarged and restored; additions include the simple weatherboarded tower, the tiled roof and the stained glass windows. The body of King Edmund is known to have been rested here in 1013.

MOUNTNESSING. This village has a beautifully restored early 19th century windmill as its main landmark, though the isolated church also has a massive-beamed belfry.

THE PRINCE OF WALES stands on a military road built by the Romans in the 3rd century AD. As a building, it is mentioned in the Domesday Book, and for several centuries was a bakery which drew its supplies of flour from the windmill opposite. Today the pub enjoys an old-world atmosphere with original oak beams and an open log fire. Serving a range of 'Traditional Ales' including award winning bottled Old Bob and Bishops Ale, it has been voted Pub of the Year for three consecutive years by CAMRA and is currently Pub of the Year for 1996. Its Ridleys IPA Bitter has also been voted Best Bitter at the Great British Beer Festival and its Mild Ale was voted Champion Mild at the same festival. Additionally the pub serves a full menu of home prepared food including beef & Guiness pie and locally cured ham off the bone.

The Prince of Wales, 199 Roman Road, Mountnessing
Tel: 01277 353445

BRENTWOOD. A pleasant shopping and entertainment centre, the town was on the old pilgrim and coaching routes to and from London. Mainly post war in character, the town is the headquarters of Ford Motors. Thorndon Country Park and Weald Country Park, both former stately deer parks, lie outside the town.

Mrs Joan Colley, 2 Kensington Road, Pilgrims Hatch, Brentwood
Tel: 01277 229668

Located in a quiet residential area of Brentwood, **Joan Colley** and her husband welcome guests for bed and breakfast in their extended family home. Breakfast is served in a room at the side of the kitchen where you can see your three course English breakfast being cooked. Joan collects porcelain figures and has gifts from overseas guests, many of which have a story attached. Bedrooms are nicely decorated and have television and tea making facilities. The garden with pond is available for all to use. This is a relaxed family home where even the family pets make you welcome. Registered with the Tourist Board.

BILLERICAY. There was a settlement here as far back as the

Bronze Age though there is no conclusive explanation of Billericay's name. There is no question about the attraction of the High Street though, with its timber weather-boarding and Georgian brick. The Chantry House, built in 1510, was the home of Christopher Martin, treasurer to the Pilgrim Fathers.

The Peasants Revolt of 1381 saw the massacre of hundreds of rebels just north-east of the town at **Norsey Wood**; today this area of ancient woodland is a country park, managed by coppicing (the traditional way of ensuring the timber supply) which encourages plant and bird life.

STOCK. A fine old tower windmill and a delightful church with a traditional Essex style wooden belfry and spire lend character to this pleasant village of well-kept houses.

The placid waters of nearby **Hanningfield Reservoir** were created by damming Sandford Brook and transformed the scattered rural settlement of Hanningfield into a lakeside village. Now on the shores of the lake, the 12th century village church's belfry has been a local landmark in the flat Essex countryside for centuries. Some of the timbers in the belfry are said to have come from Spanish galleons, wrecked in the aftermath of Sir Francis Drake's defeat of the Armada.

WRITTLE. From a tucked-away corner of St John's Green, in this village, came Britain's first regular broadcasting service; an experimental 15 minute programme beamed out nightly by Marconi's engineers. Opposite the Green, the Cock and Bell is reputed to be haunted by a young woman who committed suicide on the railway and along the street is the Wheatsheaf, one of the smallest pubs in the country.

The church features a cross of charred timbers, a reminder of the fire which gutted the chancel in 1974. Ducks swim on the pond of the larger and quite idyllic main village green, which is surrounded by lovely Tudor and Georgian houses.

SANDON. The village green has produced a notable oak tree, remarkable not so much for its height as for the tremendous horizontal spread of its branches. Around the green are a fine church and a number of attractive old houses, some dating back to the 16th century when Henry VIII's Lord Chancellor, Cardinal Wolsey, was Lord of the Manor of Sandon.

DANBURY. The village is said to take its name from the Danes who invaded this part of this country in the Dark Ages. In the fine church, under a rare 13th century carved oak effigy, a crusader knight was found perfectly preserved in the pickle which filled his coffin when the tomb was opened in 1779. Fine carving is also a feature of the bench ends and the oldest have inspired modern craftsmen to continue the same style of carving on all the pews. In 1402, 'the devil appeared in the likeness of Friar Minor, who entered the church, raged insolently to the great terror of the parishoners... the top of the steeple was broken down and half the chancel scattered abroad'. And, in 1941, another devil, a 500 lb German bomb, reduced the east end to ruin.

To the south is **Danbury Common**, where acres of gorse flower in

St Giles the Leper Hospital, Maldon

a blaze golden colour for much of the year, and, to the west, **Danbury Country Park** offers another pleasant stretch of open country.

MALDON. At the top of this waterside town, a narrow staircase in a church tower leads to the wonderful **Plume Library** (open mid-week afternoons and Saturday mornings), which is still much as it was when the founder, Dr Plume, died in 1704. He built it as a home for the 6000 books he had collected and then gave it to the town. The Public Library is below.

The steep winding streets of Maldon are full of intriguing shops and welcoming inns. The town's High Street, of which the Moot Hall is a distinctive feature, runs right down to the River Blackwater estuary. Filled with craft of all shapes and sizes, the quayside is overlooked by the Queen's Head pub, which organises an annual mud-race across the river at low tide.

Above the town stand the ruins of **St Giles the Leper Hospital**, founded by King Henry II in the 12th century. As with all monastic buildings, it fell into disuse after Henry the VIII's dissolution of the monasteries, though it retained its roof and was used as a barn until the turn of the century.

Just outside the town lies the site of one of the great decisive battles of England's early history. At the Battle of Maldon in 991 the English leader, Byrthnoth, was killed by the invading Danes after a fierce three day battle. As a result of this defeat the English King, Ethelred the Unready, was obliged to pay an annual tribute to his conquerors; though the Danes soon tired of this arrangement and overthrew Ethelred putting Cnut on the throne. Maldon is also famous for its sea salt, produced for generations by evaporating sea water.

SOUTH WOODHAM FERRERS. The empty marshland of the Crouch estuary, a yachtsman's paradise, was chosen by Essex County Council as the site for one of its most attractive new towns schemes. At the centre this successful 20th century new town, is a traditional market square surrounded by pleasant arcades and terraces built in the old Essex style with brick, tile and weatherboard. Though no hidden place Woodham certainly make a pleasant change from most new town developments.

ALTHORNE. The church of St Andrew's, over 500 years old, has a fine flint and stone tower, built in the Perpendicular style. Inside the church is an octagonal font of about 1400 which still has its carving of saints and angels intact. Purists have found them rough, but the less critical will enjoy the sheer vigour the capture. A brass plate dated 1508 records that William Hyklott 'Paide for the werkemanship of the wall'; an inscription over the west door remembers John Wilson and John Hill, who probably paid for the tower.

To the south, where Station Road meets Burnham Road, stands the villagers' own War Memorial, the solid structure of beams and tiles affording shelter for the sad list of names. To the north, is the golden-thatched, white-walled Huntsman and Hounds, which dates partly from the 14th century. A wicket gate leads through the garden to the saloon and a dark and timbered interior, with deal tables, high backed benches and the tiniest of bar counters.

STEEPLE. This small community of thatched and weather-board cottages stands on the south bank of the Blackwater estuary, where the dazzling white yachts with multi-coloured sails and the occasional stately sailing barge can be see. The countryside around the village is a rich green land of fertile meadows, patterned by lanes bordered with banks of trees.

BRADWELL-ON-SEA. The first regular inhabitants of this little community at the head of the Dengie Peninsula were the Romans, who built a huge fort here. Little remains of the fort today as, in around AD 650, the Saxons used its bricks, stones and tiles to build the tiny chapel of St Peter-at-the-Wall. In the 14th century the chapel was abandoned and forgotten for 600 years, except by farmers who used it as a barn. Now restored and re-consecrated it is well worth the half mile walk from the car park to reach it.

In the village itself Erskine Childers, who fought for the Irish Republican Army and was shot by the Irish Free State in the 1920s, wrote the wartime thriller 'The Riddle of the Sands' at Bradwell Lodge, an attractive and part-Tudor former rectory. To the north, Bradwell's vast nuclear power station looms over a nature reserve.

To the south lies the vast and remote marshes of the **Dengie Peninsula**. The salty tang of sea air here, brought inland by the east-coast winds, gives an exhilarating flavour to the marshlands. Like the Cambridge and Lincolnshire fens, this once waterlogged corner of Essex was reclaimed from the sea by 17th century Dutch engineers. The views across the marshes take in great sweeps of countryside, inhabited only by wildfowl, seabirds and cattle grazing on the saltings. The old market town of Southminster and the marshland villages of Asheldham and Tillingham dramatically rise from this flat and often desolate expanse of the landscape.

BURNHAM-ON-CROUCH. From the gaily coloured cottages along the quay, the town climbs away from the seashore, its streets lined with an delightful assortment of old cottages, Georgian and Victorian houses and shops. This is the yachting centre of Essex. In Tudor times sailing barges thronged the estuary where now yachts tack to and fro. Seafarers still come ashore to buy provisions, following a tradition that goes right back to the medieval times when Burnham was the market centre for the isolated inhabitants of Wallasea and Foulness Islands, out in the estuary, who travelled in by ferry. The whole area was, and still is, famous for its oyster beds.

THE CROOKED COTTAGE tea rooms, on the banks of the River Crouch at Burnham-on-Crouch, overlooks the fishing harbour. Previously owned by the Burnham River Company, the 350 year old building was originally a row of four fisherman's cottages. Today, the converted cottages have lost none of their old charm and the original beams and timbers add warmth and atmosphere to these delightful tea rooms. Owned and personally run by Anne Woolfson, the interesting double sided, centrally situated fireplace and the comforting ticking of a grandfather clock enhance the friendly welcome all customers receive. Open every day except Monday but only at weekends in the winter, this is a pleasant place to come and enjoy a cup of tea, one can choose from 18 types, and home-made cake or a light meal. Every Sunday traditional lunch is served. The walls are decorated with paintings by a local Japanese artist and everywhere you look there are cats - of the ceramic variety - that Anne has been collecting for years. Anne's other claim to fame is the Burnham Mustard Company which she started. The business has outgrown its site and been taken over by a local company but the mustards are still available to buy.

The Crooked Cottage, The Quay, Burnham-on-Crouch
Tel: 01621 783868

Tourist Information Centres

ALDEBURGH, The Cinema, High Street 01728 453637
BECCLES, The Quay, Fen Lane 01502 713196
BRAINTREE, Town Hall Centre, Market Square 01376 550066
BRENTWOOD, 14 Ongar Road 01277 200300
BURY ST EDMUNDS, 6 Angel Hill 01284 764667
CAMBRIDGE, Wheeler Street 01223 322640
CHELMSFORD, E Block, County Hall, Market Road 01245 283400
CLACTON-ON-SEA, 23 Pier Avenue 01255 423400
COLCHESTER, 1 Queen Street 01206 282920
CROMER, Bus Station, Prince of Wales Road 01263 512497
DISS, Meres Mouth, Mere Street 01379 650523
ELY, Oliver Cromwells House, 29 St Mary's Street 01353 662062
FAKENHAM, Red Lion House, Market Place 01328 851981
FELIXSTOWE, Leisure Centre, Undercliff Road West 01394 276770
GREAT YARMOUTH, Marine Parade 01493 842195/846345
HADLEIGH, Toppesfield Hall 01473 823824
HARWICH, Essex County Council, Parkeston Quay 01255 506139
HOVETON, Station Road 01603 782281
HUNSTANTON, The Green 01485 523610
HUNTINGDON, The Library, Princes Street 01480 388588
IPSWICH, St Stephen's Church, St Stephen's Lane 01473 258070
KING'S LYNN, The Old Gaol House, Saturday Market Place 01553 763044
LAVENHAM, Lady Street 01787 248207
LOWESTOFT, East Point Pavilion, Royal Plain 01502 523000
MALDON, Coach Lane 01621 856503
MUNDERSLEY, 2a Station Road 01263 721070
NEWMARKET, 63 The Rookery 01638 667200
NORWICH, The Guildhall, Gaol Hill 01603 666071
SAFFRON WALDEN, 1 Market Place, Market Square 01799 510444
SHERINGHAM, Station Approach 01263 824329
SOUTHEND-ON-SEA, 19 High Street 01702 215120
SOUTHWOLD, Town Hall, Market Place 01502 724729
STOWMARKET, Wilkes Way 01449 676800
SUDBURY, Town Hall,Market Hill 01787 881320
WISBECH, District Library, Ely Place 01945 583263

Index

THE HIDDEN PLACES

If you would like to have any of the titles currently available in this series, please complete this coupon and sendto:
M & M Publishing Ltd
118 Ashley Road,
Hale, Altrincham, Cheshire, WA14 2UN

	Each	
Scotland		
Ireland	£ 5.90	......
Northumberland & Durham	£ 5.90	......
The Lake District & Cumbria	£ 5.90	......
Yorkshire and Humberside	£ 5.90	......
Lancashire & Cheshire	£ 5.90	......
North Wales	£ 5.90	......
South Wales	£ 5.90	......
The Welsh Borders	£ 5.90	......
Somerset Avon Gloucestershire & Wiltshire	£ 5.90	......
Thames and Chilterns	£ 5.90	......
East Anglia (Norfolk & Suffolk)	£ 5.90	......
The South East (Surrey, Sussex and Kent)	£ 5.90	......
Dorset, Hampshire and the Isle of Wight	£ 5.90	......
Heart of England	£ 5.90	......
Devon and Cornwall	£ 5.90	......
Set of any Five	£20.00	
Total £		

Price includes Postage and Packing

NAME..

ADDRESS...

....

..................................POST CODE....................................

Please make cheques payable to: M & M Publishing Ltd